Combe Florey House · Nr Taunton

6ᵗʰ October 1960

Darling Stitch

Trumpets arrived from the steep 'with the author's compliments'. Thanks no end for the comps. Same to you with notes on. This morning a letter from you, for which more thanks.

Trumpets is absolutely ripping. Dismiss all doubts. I agree with you that the title is not very apt but that won't matter at all

more

Ria

Cra

Vol

the

of

cu

was

po

Eu

cur

the

you

so

vi

exp

a

FROM MR. EVELYN WAUGH
ETHIOPIA.

Darling Pug

Do you remember this writing paper on which I used to write to you when you stitched me up as a war-correspondent in 1936.

What has become of you? What is going to become of you? What is the future of my two daughters?

I came to London for the day for my son's wedding. The heat was stupefying. I met panpa Kinross who told me you had moved into your mansion. Next day there was a photograph of me taken at that wedding, which was a ghastly shock. Since then I have eaten & drunk nothing and look like Dr Maugham. I should like you to see me before I put it all on again. Any chance of beguiling you here? If not, do write a long letter to faithful old

Bo

Evelyn to Diana, 6 October 1960 (page 281).
Evelyn to Diana, early July 1961 (page 289). Most of the letters to Diana from Abyssinia are written on this paper.

The Letters
of
Evelyn Waugh
and
Diana Cooper

The Letters
of
Evelyn Waugh
and
Diana Cooper

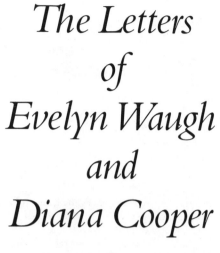

EDITED BY
ARTEMIS COOPER

Ticknor & Fields
New York
1992

For information about permission to reproduce selections from this
book, write to Permissions, Ticknor & Fields, 215 Park Avenue South,
New York, New York 10003.

Library of Congress Cataloging-in-Publication Data
Waugh, Evelyn, 1903–1966
The letters of Evelyn Waugh and Diana Cooper / edited
by Artemis Cooper
p.   cm.
ISBN 0-395-56265-1
1. Waugh, Evelyn, 1903–1966—Correspondence.   2. Cooper, Diana,
Lady, 1892–   —Correspondence.   3. Authors, English—20th century—
Correspondence.   4. Actors—Great Britain—Correspondence   I. Cooper.
Diana, Lady, 1892–   . II. Cooper, Artemis, 1953–   .   III. Title.
PR6045.A97Z484   1991   91–300271
823'.912—dc20   CIP
[B]

First published in Great Britain in 1991 by Hodder and Stoughton as
Mr Wu and Mrs Stitch: The Letters of Evelyn Waugh and Diana Cooper.

Printed in the United States of America

MP 10 9 8 7 6 5 4 3 2 1

Contents

Illustrations   vi

Acknowledgements   vii

Introduction   1

Part I   1932–39   11

Part II 1940–49   73

Part III 1950–59   107

Part IV 1960–66   275

Bibliography   328

Index   329

Illustrations

The photographs which appear between pages 120 and 121, and pages 216 and 217, are drawn from family photograph albums, except where acknowledged.

Acknowledgements

Work on these letters has been a delight from the start – I found myself laughing aloud when typing them out – so my first thanks go to Auberon Waugh and my father, John Julius Norwich, who gave me the opportunity to do this book.

Mark Amory, Alan Bell, Selina Hastings and my father all went over the text, and I am extremely grateful for the many corrections and suggestions they made. Any remaining mistakes are entirely my own. The final draft was copy-edited by Jane Birkett with great skill and tact, and Diana LeCore compiled the index.

Sally Brown, of the Department of Manuscripts, was particularly kind and helpful during my days at the British Library. Mark Amory's *Letters of Evelyn Waugh* and Michael Davie's *Diaries of Evelyn Waugh* were my most constant books of reference, and their excellent work made mine immeasurably easier. With the aid of his enormous library and the patience of a loyal friend, Hugo Vickers unravelled many knotty problems; and the help of Mrs Wendy Trewin was invaluable on the theatrical references in the letters. I am also much obliged to Lady Berkeley, Fleur Cowles, the Duchess of Devonshire, Xan Fielding, Richard Garnett, the Hon. Desmond Guinness, Sir Rupert Hart-Davis, Sir Ian Gilmour, Louis Jebb, Patrick Leigh Fermor, Susanna Johnston, Charlotte Mosley, John G. Murray, the Earl of Oxford and Asquith, Lady Sibell Rowley, Michael and the Lady Anne Tree, Tony Wakefield, and Harriet Waugh.

I would like to thank, too, Anthony Rota and John Byrne of Bertram Rota Ltd, and Lord Goodman and Robin Perrot of Goodman Derrick & Co., for all their efforts in the recovery of Evelyn Waugh's letters to Diana Cooper.

One of the great pleasures of editing these letters has been the active involvement of my editor, Ion Trewin. He would arrive for the afternoon with a leather bag full of books and papers, and his boundless energy and enthusiasm gave the task of footnoting all the excitement of a treasure hunt.

Lastly I would like to thank my husband, Antony Beevor. Despite the pressure he was under from his own deadlines, he made the time to help me reach mine. I am, as always, profoundly grateful for all his support and encouragement.

Introduction

Diana Cooper kept almost every letter she had received during the course of her long life. Her collection was kept in the basement of her London house, and filled a metal filing cabinet, a chest of drawers, several trunks, and some brass-bound boxes. The letters were filed alphabetically, and in her last years, she often thought about the huge gap under 'W': for the bulk of her letters from Evelyn Waugh had been missing for ten years. When she died, in June 1986, she believed they were lost for ever.

During the last week of September 1987, my father, John Julius Norwich, was invited to lunch by Anthony Rota, a prominent London dealer in antiquarian books and manuscripts. Was he aware, Rota asked, that someone was discreetly offering for sale a collection of letters from Evelyn Waugh to Lady Diana Cooper? John Julius was delighted to hear they had been found – and determined to get them back.

In 1976, Mark Amory, who was then assembling Evelyn Waugh's letters for the Collected Edition, visited my grandmother to ask if he could see her letters from Evelyn Waugh. Diana was propped up in her white lace bed surrounded by books, newspapers, the morning mail, an elusive engagement book, some even more elusive pencils, and a telephone. Like Mrs Algernon Stitch – her fictional alter ego in Waugh's novels – her bed was office and drawing room combined; but now in her eighties, she spent more time there than before.

She directed Mark downstairs to the basement, where he expected to find a sizeable correspondence – for Christopher Sykes, in his biography of Evelyn Waugh (which appeared in 1975), had named Diana as one of four people with the largest collections of Waugh letters. (Curiously, although Sykes gratefully acknowledged the loan of Diana's letters, he seems to have made no use of them in his book.) Waugh had, in fact, written about three hundred letters and postcards to Diana, spanning thirty years: but Mark came back upstairs with only twenty.

'I thought that was all you would find,' sighed Diana. 'The last person to borrow the letters was Christopher Sykes, and when I asked him where the rest were he said he had sent them all back, when he finished the book.' Together they telephoned Christopher Sykes, and asked again if he was sure he had returned all the letters. Sykes was adamant that he had.

Neither Diana nor Mark Amory had the slightest doubt about Christopher Sykes's honesty. If Sykes was convinced he had returned them, then the famously disordered state of his papers prevented their rediscovery. Diana could hardly contradict an old friend and call in the police; and in his edition of *The Letters of Evelyn Waugh*, Mark Amory was obliged to write that 'the great majority of those to Lady Diana Cooper are lost'. Diana resigned herself to the possibility that they had been burnt or thrown out by mistake.

Christopher Sykes suffered from Parkinson's disease; and following the death of his wife in 1983, he sold his library, his papers and his house and moved to a nursing home in Tunbridge Wells. There he died in December 1986, only a few months after Diana. The following year, the letters quietly appeared on the market.

Since Anthony Rota knew only the name of the dealer who had passed on the offer for sale, but not the current holder of the letters, John Julius felt that legal advice had to be sought, and that no better advice could be had than from Diana's old friend, Lord Goodman.

The following day, John Julius and I sat in Lord Goodman's office while he telephoned John Wilson, the Oxford autograph dealer who had contacted Anthony Rota. Mr Wilson explained that he did not wish to be obstructive but, as the letters had been offered to him in confidence, he had to seek the permission of the dealer before revealing his name. This provoked a memorable reassurance from Lord Goodman: 'Oh *no*, Mr Wilson. I am sure that *nobody* who lives in *Oxford* could ever be *obstructive*.' The chain was traced back to two dealers who lived in Wiltshire. The next link proved to be a dealer in Marlborough called Christopher Gange.

Gange said that he had bought the letters for £3,000 from the man who had acquired them from Christopher Sykes: Rupert Collens, another Marlborough book dealer, who was once better known by his real name, Sir Rupert Mackeson. (Sir Rupert's dramatic and, it was ruled, illegal deportation from Rhodesia had kept his name in the papers for some time in 1979.)

Their shops were only a couple of hundred yards apart, and very different. Christopher Gange sold books and antiques. The books were smartly aligned on their shelves, and a selection of gleaming china and furniture was displayed in a large, airy room. Sir Rupert's premises were smaller, very battered about the edges, and filled to bursting with books and sporting prints.

Lord Goodman's firm, Goodman Derrick, requested an immediate

2

undertaking that no attempt should be made to sell the collection until the question of ownership had been settled. This was refused by the solicitors acting on behalf of Christopher Gange, so an injunction was sought and obtained, and the letters were frozen.

I remember the afternoon of the injunction well. It was pouring with rain. Learned Counsel held the umbrella as we ran from the Temple to the Law Courts, in a desperate rush to find a judge who might grant the injunction by the end of that working day. 'I do hope you don't mind me saying so, Miss Cooper,' said Learned Counsel excitedly, 'but I *am* enjoying this case!'

Sir Rupert's position was that he had bought a trunk full of papers from Christopher Sykes, which included a number of letters, plus a blue folder of letters from Evelyn Waugh to Diana Cooper. According to Sir Rupert, Christopher Sykes had indicated that everything in the trunk was his property.

Sir Rupert went on to claim that he had sold the letters to Christopher Gange in 1984: not in Marlborough, but in the Portobello Road, where he had a stall at the time. Portobello Market is one of the relatively few places where a transaction can be made 'in market overt': in other words, where full title to an item sold passes to the buyer, regardless of whether the seller had good title to it or not. Yet although the letters were supposed to be in Christopher Gange's possession, Sir Rupert Mackeson took full control of the negotiations shortly after the injunction was granted.

Our case rested on the fact that Diana had done all she could, in the circumstances, to retrieve her letters; and that they remained the property of her Estate.

Over the next few weeks, rumour and counter-rumour flew back and forth within the small world of manuscripts. Fascinating but largely irrelevant details were divulged by an anonymous informer, whom we rather predictably dubbed 'Deep Throat'. The most curious coincidence, although it had absolutely nothing to do with the case, was that James Waugh, one of Evelyn's sons, sometimes worked for Sir Rupert Mackeson.

Friends rang us to pass on nuggets of information, others offered to act as mediators – among them Christopher Sykes's son Mark, who is a friend of Sir Rupert's. On our side, the issue was clear from the beginning. We wanted the letters back, but we did not want to go to court, which would be ruinously expensive for both parties. In order to avoid a court case, we were willing to make an ex gratia payment of £5,000 if Christopher Gange dropped his claim to the letters. This offer had been made very early on; and although Gange and Sir Rupert turned it down, it was never withdrawn.

The comings and goings continued for a year. Sudden flurries of activity and speculation were followed by long pauses. Then, towards the end of October 1988, our case was immeasurably strengthened. John Byrne, a colleague of Anthony Rota's who had begun to catalogue the rest of Diana's letters, found a packet of fifty more letters from Evelyn Waugh. They had been filed under 'S' for Sykes, and with them was a note in Diana's hand: 'Dear Christopher, please send these letters back as soon as possible because I am so attached to them.' Sykes had returned this batch, including her original note, evidently in the belief that he was returning all of her Waugh letters.

Over the next few weeks a number of bizarre deals and proposals arrived from Sir Rupert, via a tall, nervous man who took snuff and described himself as 'Sir Rupert's account executive'. Most intriguing was the suggestion that if we did not drop our claim, Sir Rupert would write a book which would uncover the whole Establishment conspiracy and reveal who had killed Lord Lucan. My father rejected these suggestions, while repeating his offer of £5,000 for the letters. After a lot of huffing and puffing by correspondence, Christopher Gange finally accepted the offer, and Diana's collection of letters from Evelyn Waugh was, once again, complete.

In 1989, the letters of Evelyn Waugh to Diana Cooper were sold to the British Library. Until recently, Diana's letters to Waugh formed part of the collection of Waugh Papers temporarily housed at the Rhodes House Library, Oxford. Within the past year, however, this collection has also been sold to the British Library – so both sides of the correspondence are now under one roof.

Evelyn Waugh and Diana Cooper met one evening in the early summer of 1932, when Waugh was twenty-eight, and Diana nearly forty. According to Waugh, the meeting took place at a supper party given by Hazel Lavery, the second wife of the painter Sir John Lavery. Christopher Sykes says the party was given by Emerald Cunard. Diana, on the other hand, wrote that they met after a performance of *The Miracle*. But wherever the evening began, it ended at the Café de Paris in Bray, by the River Thames, which was the final goal of a treasure hunt. Diana drove there with Evelyn, and they shared a table with Christopher Sykes. 'What I remember most vividly of the evening,' wrote Sykes in his biography of Waugh, 'is Evelyn's imitations of Lady Cunard which made us laugh till it hurt and we wanted him to stop.'

Waugh's brilliant comic talent had already produced *Decline and Fall* (1928) and *Vile Bodies* (1930), and their success had liberated him from the world of schoolteachers and publishers (his father was Chairman of Chapman & Hall) in which he had grown up. He was now living beyond his means among the *jeunesse dorée*, dining with society hostesses and cultivating the role of young literary lion and bachelor about town.

The last few years had been turbulent. In 1929, his world was shattered by the desertion of his first wife, Evelyn Gardner. They had been married barely a year. To Harold Acton, Waugh wrote: 'I did not know it was possible to be so miserable and live.'

When he emerged from his despair, his friends were not surprised to notice a new hardness and bitterness in Waugh; but the disaster of his first marriage did not sour his relationships with women for long. He indulged in brief encounters with the girls of the '43', a well-known nightclub-cum-brothel in Gerrard Street, and the occasional casual affair; but he also enjoyed the company of women for its own sake, particularly if they were witty, intelligent, and good listeners. Diana Guinness (later Lady Mosley) and her husband Bryan (later the second Lord Moyne) were among Waugh's closest and most loyal friends at the time of his divorce. He was, for a while, quite infatuated with the beautiful, nineteen-year-old Mrs Guinness; but after the birth of her son Jonathan in 1930 they drifted apart.

Soon afterwards Waugh fell in love with Teresa 'Baby' Jungman, daughter of the painter Nico Jungman. She and her sister, Zita, started the craze for fancy-dress balls and treasure hunts, and were among the brightest of the Bright Young Things. Yet for all her high spirits, Baby Jungman was a devout Catholic. She was prepared to offer friendship, but firmly rejected Waugh's sexual advances; and since he was, in Catholic eyes, still married, there was nothing he could do to alter this frustrating situation.

He had come to the conclusion that 'the world was unintelligible and unendurable without God', and that the Church of Rome professed the only true religion: and in September 1930, he was received into the Catholic Church – fully believing that, by embracing it, he would have to abandon all hope of another marriage.

The following month, Waugh went to Ethiopia to attend the coronation of the Emperor Haile Selassie. It was a gamble, for apart from three articles for *The Graphic*, there were no further commissions to finance the trip. From Ethiopia he travelled to Aden, went back to Africa via Zanzibar, and from there to Kenya, the Belgian Congo and South Africa. He returned in March 1931, five hundred pounds poorer; but the journey was worth the investment, for it produced two books. The first, *Remote People*, was published in November and established Waugh's name as a travel writer. The second was the novel *Black Mischief*.

Much of *Black Mischief* was written at the Easton Court Hotel, Chagford, Devon. The Easton Court Hotel was owned by Norman Webb and an American, Mrs Postlethwaite Cobb. Their favourite guests were young writers, and the place was run like a comfortable country house for friends.

Waugh also worked on the novel at Madresfield, near Malvern in

Worcestershire, which was his spiritual home at the time. In this red-brick Victorian house lived the Lygon brothers: William (Lord Elmley), Hugh and Richard; and their sisters, the Ladies Lettice, Sibell, Mary and Dorothy. They were the children of the 7th Earl Beauchamp and his wife Lettice. The Earl was a highly distinguished man: a former Governor of New South Wales, Chancellor of London University, and a Knight of the Garter. All this, plus the fact that he had three sons, earned him the poisonous envy of his brother-in-law Bendor, the 2nd Duke of Westminster, who hounded him from public life by denouncing him as a homosexual. The Duke then invited Beauchamp's four daughters to testify against their father – a suggestion they treated with the contempt it deserved.

Lord Beauchamp went into exile in Italy, and the shattered Lady Beauchamp left Madresfield with her youngest son. The rest of her children continued to live in the family house, which they were now at liberty to fill with their friends. Waugh was a frequent visitor. He had shared rooms with Hugh Lygon at Oxford, and his relationship with the youngest sisters, Mary and Dorothy, was that of a mischievous uncle.

Waugh's hopeless passion for Teresa Jungman, who was also a close friend of the Lygons, continued unabated; but the empty place that Diana Guinness had once occupied in his affections was not filled until he met Lady Diana Cooper.

In 1932, most people still found Diana Cooper astonishingly beautiful; but she was likely to describe herself as 'faded – but not, thank God, overblown'. She was the youngest child of the Duchess of Rutland; and Diana shared the widely held belief that her father was not the Duke, but Henry John Cust, Member of Parliament, poet, and sometime editor of the *Pall Mall Gazette*. Harry Cust's career had fallen short of the brilliant future predicted for him at Cambridge. He was extremely good-look-ing, and his name had been linked with those of several beautiful and aristocratic women.

Nevertheless, Diana was the acknowledged daughter of the Duke of Rutland; and this, plus the fact that her husband was an outstanding junior minister, meant that she moved by right in the circles Waugh aspired to. Yet she was also irrepressibly adventurous. She had withstood her mother's opposition to the penniless, untitled Duff Cooper, and married him in June 1919. Soon after that, she had shocked society by embarking on a career as a film actress. (Her mother was horrified; only when she heard how much Diana was to be paid did her scruples shrink to manageable proportions.) Diana's reasons were simple: she wanted to build up some capital so that Duff could leave the Foreign Office and embark on a political career.

This aim was achieved in 1924, when Duff became the Conservative

Member for Oldham. In 1931 he won the St George's Division of Westminster as Baldwin's champion, in a much publicised contest. He had been given his first appointment as a junior minister in 1928; and by the time he resigned over Chamberlain's handling of the Munich crisis ten years later he had risen to be First Lord of the Admiralty.

Diana's acting career, which lasted until 1933, had made her well-known on both sides of the Atlantic. Her repertoire was highly successful, but hardly broad-ranging. A wartime morale-boosting movie for D. W. Griffith was followed by two costume dramas for J. Stuart Blackton. Then, in 1923, Max Reinhardt gave her the part in which she made her name and fortune: the Madonna in what was basically a medieval morality play, acted in mime, set to music and called *The Miracle*.

From 1924 to 1928, Diana spent six months of every year in the United States, touring with this lavish production which inspired deep emotion all over the country. The letters that she and Duff wrote to each other, every day they were apart, give an insight into their extraordinary marriage.

Duff Cooper was brave, honourable, highly civilised, and excellent company. He was prone to notorious outbursts of anger – though these were never directed at Diana, whom he loved profoundly. Conjugal fidelity was not among his qualities; yet Diana came to accept that Duff's need for romantic affairs was as deep as his need for wine and books: without them, life was not worth living. Their different tastes in social life meant that they were often apart. They had many friends in common, but Duff was a club-man who liked excellent food and wine, comfortable surroundings, political cronies and bridge for high stakes. Diana's tastes were for treasure hunts, impromptu theatricals and high Bohemia. She sometimes tried to make Duff jealous about one or other of her 'lovers', with singular lack of success. Diana relished the company of men; but Duff knew that she kept them at arm's length, craving no more than a devoted admiration.

Their only son was born in 1929. To the Manners family name of John was added Julius, for he was born by Caesarian section. He was an easy, engaging child, adored by his parents – and Diana, John Julius feels, played a more active part in his life than most mothers of her age and class. He learned multiplication tables on her bed, and together they went shopping, saw films and chased fire engines – the last being one of Diana's favourite pastimes.

In 1932 the producer C. B. Cochran, who had been responsible for *The Miracle*'s first production in 1911, brought the play back for a British revival. Tilly Losch played the Nun, and once again Diana was the Madonna. *The Miracle* had been pronounced safe for Catholic consumption by the Jesuit Fathers of Farm Street, yet when Evelyn Waugh saw the play with Teresa Jungman in April 1932, he took great exception to it. In a letter to Dorothy Lygon, he wrote:

'So I went to see a disgusting thing called *The Miracle* . . . And I sat next to the Duke of Norfolk. He didn't know me but I knew him and I thought here is the man I respect as the natural leader of English Catholics and why is he at this blasphemous play because it is full of blasphemy as an egg is full of meat.'

His views were probably just as vehement when he sat with Diana at the Café de Paris in Bray on the evening of their first meeting. Yet by the end of 1932 he was so passionately devoted to her that he accompanied her and her mother the Duchess on *The Miracle*'s tour of Manchester, Glasgow and Edinburgh. Even the 'blasphemous play' seems to have found a place in his heart:

'Goodness how I want to see you again', he wrote from British Guiana in March 1933. 'I think of this week with tears in my eyes as being the last week of *The Miracle* – but perhaps it will be given another few months. What fun if it was still on when I got back.' (In fact, *The Miracle* was already over: the curtain closed on the last performance at the Golders Green Hippodrome at the end of January 1933.)

In her photographs, Diana's blond beauty looks distant and classical. She refused to smile for the camera, thinking that photographs of beautiful women should look like Pre-Raphaelite portraits. And yet, in Cecil Beaton's words, she behaved as if she were a brunette. She had a quick mind, a zest for life, an ability to seize the moment and turn an expedition into an adventure; and she would not be bullied, even by a character as strong as Waugh's. His friendship and admiration for her lasted for life – though in later years he wished for more tranquillity and less excitement. 'Your idea of friendship is to do things together', he wrote to her; 'mine simply is to be together'.

As with any correspondence that spanned thirty years, sometimes the letters follow each other closely, sometimes months pass between one letter and the next. During the early 1940s, the correspondence on both sides dwindles to a trickle; but it starts to swell again once the war is over, and the bulk of their letters dates from the 1950s. The flow is still strong in the 1960s, but Waugh comes to London less and less, and one can see him begin to tire of life. He died in 1966.

As Waugh grows older, the razor edge of his impatience is blunted, he mellows and becomes more resigned. Diana hated old age, and after Duff's death her habitual restlessness became an escape from despair. But despite the changes in their lives, these letters rarely lose their intimacy: for Diana and Waugh demanded the best from each other, were never satisfied with anything less. Frances Donaldson wrote: 'No one, I think, would ever have said to him, as one might to almost anyone else . . . what is it that has gone wrong between us? There was the hideous risk he might tell you.' Diana dared, and Waugh's answers are forceful. They were neither of them afraid to write what they felt. The letters are confiding, astringent, furious, funny, apologetic – sometimes all at once. Waugh's letters were often accompanied by newspaper clippings, photographs of himself, his family, or a painting he had just bought. To my delight I discovered that Diana had pasted some of these into her scrapbooks, and several appear in this volume among the illustrations.

Almost every morning of Diana's life was spent in bed, writing to her friends; and when she died, she left a vast collection of letters: from Conrad Russell, Martha Gellhorn, Patrick Leigh Fermor, Iris Tree, Maurice Baring, Hilaire Belloc and Enid Bagnold – to mention a few of her more prolific correspondents. She was as prone to losing things as most people, but comparatively few of her letters from Evelyn Waugh have gone astray; for every letter, postcard and telegram from a friend was treasured as a token of love.

Of hers to Waugh, however, only about a third remain (if one assumes that the correspondence was approximately equal, as the surviving letters imply). Although he was writing to Diana a great deal in the 1930s, the majority of her letters from this period are lost: probably because Waugh had no permanent home until 1937, when he and his second wife Laura settled at Piers Court, Stinchcombe, in Gloucestershire.

I have included as many letters as I can, and those that do not appear are mostly concerned with possible dates or places for their next meeting. Much planning and arranging has also been cut from the text, as well as libellous passages, and some hurtful ones. Since the originals of these letters are now accessible to scholars, they have been edited for the general reader. My first aim has been to make the correspondence easy to read: italics are used for the titles of books, plays and paintings, punctuation has been added where necessary to clarify a sentence, and ampersands have usually been changed to 'and'. Both Waugh and Diana were poor spellers, and this has largely been corrected – though the more inspired mistakes have been left in. They were also not very good at dating: I have rectified this where possible, putting the dates – and any inclusions of my own – in square brackets. A bibliography at the end of the book lists the main published sources I have used for the footnotes.

At the same time, not all the idiosyncrasies and inconsistencies in these letters have been ironed out. When referring to the 'Dutch girl' (Teresa Jungman), Waugh sometimes writes Dutch, sometimes dutch. Similarly, Diana's Jewels (her son, John Julius, and daughter-in-law, Anne) are sometimes jewels, or even jewells. Also, their very different styles demanded different ways of editing. For example, I have corrected Waugh's lack of apostrophes in words such as 'didn't' and 'haven't'; but Diana's use of 'thro'' and 'tho'' seems to add to the Shakespearean flavour of her eccentric idiolect, and these have been left in their abbreviated form. From the early 1950s, Waugh occasionally writes to Diana in capital letters. This was because Diana complained that her failing eyesight was not up to his small handwriting. Yet the tone of these letters is modified by the use of capitals, and they have been retained in the text.

Waugh and Diana had a number of names for each other. Waugh's nickname 'Bo' was short for Boaz, a name coined with the Lygons at Madresfield and implying initiation into some arcane Masonic ritual. He called Diana 'Baby', which was how she saw herself. 'The youngest of a family remains a baby until she dies. I still . . . accepted inferiority as normal, loved chocolates, found many books "too grown up" . . . ' To others, particularly the Mitford sisters, she was 'Honks', probably a reference to her rasping voice. 'You know I call Honks "Baby"?' Waugh wrote to Nancy Mitford. 'Embarrassing but true.'

He also refers to Diana as 'Pug' and 'Hoopers' – yet his most memorable name for her, in some of these letters as well as in his novels, was Mrs Stitch. Diana sometimes called him 'Mr Wu': the title of a song by George Formby, and the name of a Pekingese dog who had rather a truculent expression. 'Mr Wu' and 'Mrs Stitch' are not the names most frequently used, but they best characterise their curious intimacy – like that of an old couple, who had never needed to be lovers.

PART I

1932–39

IN THE SUMMER OF *1932*, VENICE WAS THRONGED WITH those the gossip columnists called 'Society People'. Lavish parties and dinners were given by Lady Cunard, Mona Harrison Williams and Laura Corrigan; and among their guests were Chips Channon, Diana Cooper, Cecil Beaton, Evelyn Waugh, Oliver Messel, Randolph Churchill, Sir Richard Sykes and the 'Lucky Strike' heiress, Doris Duke.

These last were at the centre of what later became known as the 'Murano incident', which began when Sir Richard made a pass at Miss Duke in her car. Miss Duke was furious. She told the chauffeur to stop, and Sir Richard was unceremoniously thrown out. On 29 August, a large party gathered on the island of Murano to celebrate Diana's fortieth birthday. Sir Richard Sykes, still smarting from his humiliation, deliberately burnt the back of Miss Duke's hand with a 'Lucky Strike'. Randolph Churchill sprang to her defence, and a dreadful fight ensued. Diana recalled the occasion to Cecil Beaton's biographer, Hugo Vickers:

'Everyone had been drinking like fishes for an hour before. Now all the wives were clinging to their men to stop them joining in . . . Oliver Messel and Cecil Beaton were fighting like bears and, as I thought, doing splendidly! . . . The next day I was covered with tuberoses, which were sent when you'd behaved outrageously.'

In his biography of Ronald Knox, Waugh wrote that 'the accumulation of common experiences, private jokes and private language . . . lies at the foundation of English friendship'. To the pool of words and in-jokes he shared with his friends, the Murano incident added the word 'sykesed' – which meant anyone who had been roughed up or anything broken. In the same way, to be chucked or stood up was to be 'laycocked' – a particular fault of Waugh's friend Robert Laycock (who was to become his commanding officer during the war). Baby Jungman, who would not yield to his sexual advances, was part Dutch – so anything difficult or refractory was 'Dutch'; while Highclere, the house of the Earls of Carnarvon, was used to mean all that was most comfortable and luxurious.

Two intriguing words which appear in these early letters are 'Boulby' and 'Bartleet'. Robert Bartleet was the son of the vicar of Madresfield, and Mr Boulby seems to have been a member of the production staff of The Miracle; but one can only guess at the wealth of associations that their names would have conjured up to Diana, as she read these letters.

Evelyn to Diana

Buck's Club   *[mid-September 1932]*
18 Clifford Street
New Bond Street, W1

Dearest Diana

Well, so I am back in London and that is pretty sad after all the fun in Venice. How I loved it and thank you v. much.

After you left I got in an aeroplane and went to Salzburg. I won't tell you much about that because you know it pretty well I expect but I met the Miss Tree[1] you told me of v. Bohemian and she had a little boy who goes to a school where they wear no clothes and are taught by a master named Oscar but there are little girls there so it is all right and Miss Tree's boy is in love with one called Anne and the headmaster is called Mr Curry and he teaches them oeconomics and it made Miss Tree's son write an article in the *Daily Herald* about Pacificism but when X-examined he seemed to have an incomplete grasp of the subject.

So I bought an aeroplane (model) and flew it in a square with a fountain and some stone horses and I went to a public castle where a stag had water coming out of his antlers. Mr Churchill MP came to luncheon he had diarhoea well I can't spell that but it is what we all had in Venice off and on. He was 6 times better than Randy.[2]

So I went to see my parents who were pretty gloomy on account of being v. old and poor. Then I had lunch at Ritz Hotel with Dr Kommer[3] and an American Princess and Mr C. B. Cochran[4] and an Austrian gigolot and at the next table were S. Lygon[5] and D. A. Cooper[6] and T. Macdougal[7] so I said to S. Lygon you come and have a cocktail at 6 and she thought what fun but when she came I gave her hell about her vulgar article in *D. Express* and she cried and said Lord Beaverbrook wrote it. Then I came to this club and there was Perry so I had chickens with him

---

[1] Iris Tree (1897–1968), youngest daughter of Sir Herbert Beerbohm Tree. Poet, writer, and romantic vagabond, she and Diana were friends from childhood. Married first the American painter and photographer Curtis Moffat; their son, Ivan (b. 1918) worked in films.

[2] Winston Churchill (1874–1965) was then a back-bench Conservative MP, and completing his life of the 1st Duke of Marlborough (published the following year). His only son Randolph (1911–1968) met Waugh in 1930. Waugh claimed that they broke off relations for ever approximately once a year, and always made it up.

[3] Dr Rudolf Kommer (d. 1943), 'Kaetchen' to his friends. Came from Czernowitz in the Bukovina. As assistant to Max Reinhardt, he had known Diana throughout her career in *The Miracle*.

[4] The producer C. B. Cochran (1872–1951).

[5] Lady Sibell Lygon (b. 1907). Lord Beaverbrook had inserted a reference to Diana's 'raucous voice' into one of her occasional pieces for the *Daily Express*. From 1939–52, Lady Sibell was married to Flight-Lieutenant Michael Rowley.

[6] Lady Dorothy Ashley-Cooper, daughter of the 9th Earl of Shafterbury. In 1935 she married Antony (later 1st Viscount) Head.

[7] Tommy MacDougal, a swashbuckling Master of Fox Hounds who had a reputation as a great lover (sometimes known as Captain MacDougal-de-doo). Waugh liked to pretend he was illiterate.

13

and today I had more with him and with J. Norton and Lady Brownlow too.[1]

So I saw F. Pakenham's[2] baby and gave it a book, but it can't read yet.

So I saw Diana Guinness[3] and Randy again and who do you think, why, SYKES[4] and Lady Lavery[5] and Mrs Greville[6] and Bogey Harris[7] and E. Tatham and Diana Churchill.[8] Now I am off to Emerald Isle, not Lady Cunard's.[9] Bad joke.

By the way they gave me a huge bill here for Goodwood so I refused to pay most of it because I was only there one day and they charged me for 3 but I say this because I don't want Duff to think I'm making him pay for my lunch and drinks because I've paid for that.

S. Lygon says that R. de T.[10] lost £700 last week and has run away but I expect that's all a lie don't you?

The version of the Murano incident current in London is that Michael[11] was thrown into the canal by 20 gondoliers.

Met a chap you nursed in a hospital. Goodness how he loved you.

---

[1] Jean Norton (d. 1945) and Katherine Brownlow (d. 1952) were daughters of Sir David Kinloch, Bt. Jean's husband, Richard, was later 6th Baron Grantley (1892–1954). Katherine's husband Peregrine (also 'Perry' or 'Periwinkle'), 6th Baron Brownlow (1899–1978), was Personal Lord-in-Waiting to Edward VIII at the time of the abdication.

[2] Frank Pakenham (b. 1905). Labour politician and author, whose idealistic temperament has involved him in great causes and philanthropic works. Succeeded as Earl of Longford 1961. He married Elizabeth Harman in November 1931, and their first child, Antonia, was born 27 August 1932.

[3] Diana Mitford (b. 1910). Married 1929–34 to Bryan Guinness, later 2nd Baron Moyne. She wanted to be friends with Waugh, but found his devotion claustrophobic. In 1936 she married Sir Oswald Mosley, founder of the British Union of Fascists.

[4] Sir Richard Sykes (1905–70), who succeeded his father as 7th Bt. in 1919. He enjoyed breeding horses and playing the organ, and in 1942 he married Virginia Gilliat.

[5] Hazel Lavery, née Martyn (d. 1935), an American who became the second wife of the painter Sir John Lavery in 1910. She was the model for the Irish colleen, with harp and shawl, on the old Irish pound note.

[6] The Hon. Mrs Ronald Greville (d. 1942), heiress to the McEwan brewery fortune. In 1891 she married the Hon. Ronald Greville (1864–1908). King George VI and Queen Elizabeth spent the first part of their honeymoon at Polesden Lacey, her luxurious house in Surrey.

[7] Henry 'Bogey' Harris (d. 1950), expert on furniture and painting. In her Diaries 1915–1918 Lady Cynthia Asquith describes him as a mystery – 'I believe no one knows his income, occupation or love affairs.'

[8] Diana Churchill (1909–63), eldest daughter of Sir Winston Churchill. From 1932–5 she was married to John Miller Bailey; and in the same year as their divorce, she married the Rt. Hon. Duncan Sandys (created Lord Duncan-Sandys in 1974). They were divorced in 1962.

[9] Maud Cunard (1872–1948), née Burke, American heiress and great hostess. In 1895 she married Sir Bache Cunard; they separated in 1911. She changed her name to Emerald in 1926.

[10] Raymond de Trafford (1900–71), irrepressible gambler and youngest son of Sir Humphrey de Trafford, 3rd Bt.

[11] Michael Parsons (1906–79). Succeeded his father as 6th Earl of Rosse in 1918. That summer in Venice, he had boxed the ears of Anne Armstrong-Jones, in a jealous rage provoked by her stepping out on to a balcony with another man. She sent back the tuberoses he offered in apology, but married him three years later. (Anne's maiden name was Messel: her son Antony Armstrong-Jones later married Princess Margaret.)

Lord Donegall[1] thinks we were all hired by Miss Duke to bash Sykes. Let's forget all about Murano.

David[2] proposed to Rachel when affected by heat-wave and both of them fainted. But that may not be true either.

All love
Bo

Evelyn to Diana

Buck's Club   *[October 1932]*

Dearest Diana

I sent you a copy of *Black Mischief*[3] today. The third – but I wanted you to see the pictures one of which – the frontispiece, is funny.

When I say the book is good all I mean is that I have done what I wanted to (with the exception of six or seven minor gaucheries) and that I think people may enjoy it without any grave sacrifices of intelligence or taste. I don't begin to credit it with any real value. It is good in just the same sense that Capt. Hance's horsemanship is good.

I loved my visit to Manchester and it is a joy to know you and more of you.

I hope to come next week but there's a great deal of work I've got to get through. I will telegraph.

You won't ever talk to me, will you, in the way you address Dr Kommer fr. Cz[ernowitz].

The sleeper [sleeping car] I had was not at all as you described yours.

E. or Bo

Evelyn to Diana

Savile Club   *[25 October 1932]*
69 Brook Street, W1

Dearest Diana,

Obsessed by homesickness for Manchester. Ashamed about yesterday's bandits. Tired because I was run away with by a horse this morning

---

[1] Edward Chichester (1903–75), 6th Marquess of Donegall.

[2] Lord David Cecil (1902–86). Younger son of 4th Marquess of Salisbury. Writer, critic, and Professor of English Literature at Oxford 1948–70. In 1932 he married Rachel, eldest daughter of the critic Desmond (later Sir Desmond) MacCarthy.

[3] Published by Chapman & Hall on 1 October.

and then had a long train journey. Lonely without you. Depressed by visit to my father and by finding none of the letters waiting for me that had hoped.

Well I won't go on about myself.

Tea was a little forbidding wasn't it and dark but I hope you enjoyed Watley[?] and Bartleet a bit. Bartleet has been in a sexual stupor ever since and has made his mother promise to take him to *Miracle*. I said he could drink all 2nd act but he seemed to have forgotten drink in sumble stumble.[1]

Here are photographs of Jackie G.B.H. and top of Captain's[2] head, also Poll[3] and back of Capt's head.

Here is Henry Yorke's[4] letter re Blackers might interest you. Agate[5] trouble about being stay at home.

If lunch possible Thur, wire.

Bo

Evelyn to Diana

[telegram]   *25 October 1932*

To Lady Diana Cooper, Theatre Royal, Birmingham

INTERNAL DISSENT ONLY LOVE AND HEROINE WORSHIP STILL SKY HIGH BOAZ LIKE BRUTUS WITH HIMSELF AT WAR GBY

Evelyn to Diana

Easton Court Hotel   *[late October 1932]*
Chagford
Devon

Darling Diana

Well I came here on Saturday and what was decent was to find that dutch girl was going to a house called Bartleet [Madresfield?] in the same

---

[1] Sexual stupor: a good example of the '-umble' slang, much in fashion at the time.

[2] Captain J. H. Hance. In the words of Frances Donaldson, 'Hance . . . taught riding to the *jeunesse dorée* and owed his success with them to the fact that he cursed them like a sergeant-major'. The Captain's name was rarely mentioned without the suffix 'God bless him', or G.B.H. for short. Jackie G.B.H. is his daughter.

[3] Lady Dorothy Lygon (b. 1912), youngest of the Lygon sisters: known as 'Coote', and to Waugh as 'Poll' or 'Pollen'.

[4] Henry Yorke (1905–75). Better known as the novelist Henry Green.

[5] James Agate (1877–1946), critic and diarist. This was possibly a Waugh word for unfavourable criticism, for Agate was not impressed by *Black Mischief*.

train. But she got off at Westbury and since then everything has been bad as I must write 6 articles and 2 short stories. There are a great many Americans in this hotel. 1 honeymoon couple of blond man and a negress and 1 pr Lesbians who share a single bed and came to mass yesterday morning.

I shall be back on 3rd and would like you to take me to the League of Percy exhibition say in the late afternoon. After that I said I would go to a ball of a despicable woman named S. Maugham[1] – will you be there? if so please let us be together. After that will you lunch and dine on 4th 5th 6th 7th and 8th?

When did I see you last. Thursday? Well that night I went to a fine fight between Norman the Butcher and the Black Eagle (all in) and in the end after great ill feeling B.E. stunned N. the B. by butting him on the top of the head.

Friday. That fast Lady Ancaster[2] lacocked[3] me for lunch so usual ritz usual dutch girl. Hangover was hell – Emerald, Mitford[4] and music and I sat next to a Nicaraguan nympho. Sat. I went to communion with dutch girl to ratify treaty (morbid) and to see a man about a ship. He was husband to your Miss Tree [Curtis Moffat] and lived in a very modern flat but he didn't make much sense and it doesn't seem I shall go round the world with him. Then lunch ritz dutch and to train and then I am back where I began letter.

All things bright and beautiful to you

Bo

Evelyn to Diana

Easton Court Hotel   *[?1 November 1932]*
Chagford

If not lunching Ritz Monday will call for you there soon after 3. Your mother is giving a cocktail party.

Hope I win prize at Percy.

Slept 9½ hours with window open.

Bo

[1] Syrie Barnardo (1879–1955), daughter of the founder of the orphanages. She married the novelist William Somerset Maugham in 1917, two years after the birth of their only daughter Liza. They were divorced in 1927. Syrie was a fashionable decorator, who became known for her 'off-white' and 'white on white' interiors.

[2] Eloise, daughter of W. L. Breese of New York, wife of 2nd Earl of Ancaster (d. 1953).

[3] Chucked: Robert Laycock (1907–68), later Major General Sir Robert, known as 'the Chucker'. Waugh was to serve under him in Egypt and Crete in 1941.

[4] Nancy Mitford (1904–73), eldest of the six daughters of the 2nd Baron Redesdale. She had been a lodger with Waugh and his first wife, Evelyn Gardner, in Canonbury Square.

17

[P.S.]
I don't hold it against you that you haven't written because clearly people in London can't write and those in the country can – but I do think it shows great oblivion that you should send your note to Savile.

Evelyn to Diana

[telegram]   *[Thursday] 3 November 1932*

To Lady Diana Cooper, Central Hotel, Glasgow

WEDNESDAYS CHILD IS A CHILD OF WOE THURSDAYS CHILD HAS FAR TO GO

Evelyn to Diana

[telegram]   *3 November 1932*

To Lady Diana Cooper, Central Hotel, Glasgow

PLEASE DONT GIVE BIRD TO EARLY WORM TOMORROW[1]

Evelyn to Diana

Easton Court Hotel   *[8 November 1932]*
Chagford

Dearest Diana

I wonder if you saw in this morning's *Times* the death of a man called Bartleet at Bovey House near Beer. I cut it out and sent it to Duff.

Well I am just as far from Glasgow as if I was already in Guiana. I wish I could have come that evening but there it was and I had nowhere to stay in London to wait and had to work at once and all that so I came here.

I am glad you liked the letter about *Miracle*. I haven't seen it yet but no doubt shall. You said be offensive to the minister so I tried to be though I thought his article fairly harmless really. What did Duff think. Mr Boulby sent me three posters this morning and another Glasgow paper wants to reprint it so I hope it is proving good publicity. Well what have I done? I had a very hard drinking week after I left you, plastered by

---

[1] *The Miracle* was then on tour; and Waugh would take a few days off every now and then to join Diana, and keep her company.

18

luncheon most days. Not proud of this, just telling you. Then I went to Sachie and Georgia[1] for week-end. It rained all the time and we had mulled claret and very girlish gossip. Then I went to a very low class party given by a Mrs McGrath and had a very pious few days going to church with that Dutch girl. I was 29 years old and dined with the Dutch girl's sister [Zita]. Had one night out with Hubert[2] and then came here. Have written 2 short stories and a broadcast talk. I have only my Glasgow luggage – stiff collars etc. which is difficult and so I can't ride or hunt but that makes me do more work.

I thought it was a very unseemly picture of Jackie [Hance]. Made her look 50. Will you be alone Edinburgh next week? Might come only should have to work 4 hours a day and not drink much champagne as am saving for Guiana. Want if possible to go to Venezuela too which sounds heavenly.

Wish I could persuade you to be Catholic. You see you have the real mens catholica (Latin for Catholic mind) and all that isn't happy in your nature would be made straight. But I won't go on – at least I will, but not in writing but when I see you.

Saw Ld. Dudley[3] at luncheon party and he spoke of Bartleet.

Pauper Balfour is here. Very amusing and industrious writing a social history of the 20s.[4]

All love
Bo

Evelyn to Diana

Chagford   [*pstmk 10 November 1932*]
[*postcard*]

O.K. Glasgow Monday. Will try to make same train as you but more likely sleeper and breakfast Tues. Which train Mon by way? Went to a

---

[1] Sacheverell Sitwell (1897–1988), brother of Osbert and Edith Sitwell, and later 6th Bt. He married Georgia Doble in 1925. They lived at Weston Hall, a Gothicised 17th-century manor in Northamptonshire.

[2] Hubert Duggan (1904–43). Brother of Waugh's great friend Alfred Duggan, and stepson of Lord Curzon. Conservative MP 1941–43.

[3] Eric Ward (1894–1969), who succeeded his father as 3rd Earl of Dudley in 1932. His first wife, Lady Rosemary Leveson-Gower, died in 1930. In 1943 he married Laura, née Charteris: formerly Viscountess Long of Wraxall, and later Duchess of Marlborough.

[4] Patrick Balfour (1904–76). Nicknamed 'Pauper', he became 3rd Baron Kinross in 1939. For some time 'Mr Gossip' in the *Daily Sketch*. The book referred to here is *Society Racket: A Critical Survey of Modern Life* (1933). Waugh had read the first draft, and commented elsewhere to Diana: 'Pauper Balfour wrote a book saying all rich people live in blocks of flats which doesn't seem to me to be true.' Balfour, who went on to write several books, including a biography of Kemal Atatürk, appears as Lord Kilbannock in Waugh's *Sword of Honour* trilogy.

Narkover[1] yesterday kept by a female millionaire and who should I find making a model aeroplane but Ivan Tree [Moffat]. Will tell you more of this Narkover heckler Tues or supper Mon. Sailing tropics Dec. 2nd.

Waugh was about to embark on a journey that was to take him through the heart of British Guiana. He gave no specific reason for choosing South America; but it was a very remote part of the world in 1930, much of it uncharted, and promised ample opportunities for an up-and-coming travel writer. Waugh obtained a number of commissions from magazines and newspapers before he left.

He felt in need of a change. Baby Jungman was being very 'Dutch', and he felt oppressed by the devotion of Audrey Lucas, with whom he had been having an affair off and on since 1930. He also felt ready for an arduous journey. In an article written on board SS Ingoma, *on his way to South America, Waugh says: 'Some measure of physical risk is as necessary to human well-being as physical exercise . . . everyone instinctively needs an element of danger and uncertainty in his life.'*

Evelyn to Diana

SS Ingoma   *[2 December 1932]*

Dearest Diana

Going slow down the Thames.

I can send this when we drop the pilot. Not much of a ship. No heating or hot water or lights over the beds etc. 30 passengers but only about 12 adult whites. Crew all black. Frightfully cold and probability of bad weather ahead. I felt very low indeed at going. The Dutch girl saw me off and gave me a St Christopher on a chain to put round my neck – gold, Cartier, very expensive saved out of her pocket money. Deeply moved.

The bar is locked until we are at sea.

Then it will be better.

No smoking in the lounge only in a little bar with 2 bridge tables.

It will be very uncomfortable until it gets hot enough for the decks.

I think of you and *The Miracle* constantly – and long for news which I shan't get until May I suppose.

All love
Bo

---

[1] An imaginary boys' preparatory school – much on the lines of Dickens's Dotheboys Hall – featured in the humorous columns of J. B. Morton ('Beachcomber') in the *Daily Express*. The school mentioned here is Dartington Hall, Devon.

Evelyn to Diana

[*At sea on SS* Ingoma]   [*3–8 December 1932*]

Dearest Diana

It's no good I can't write clearly because it is so rough and this ship rolls so much that it isn't possible to sleep at night. However I am being very ostentatious with a big cigar and large appetite. Perhaps when it gets calm and warm after the Azores the passengers will be more fun. At present they stay in their cabins all day except a few very old men who sit sullenly in the lounge. The ship isn't at all like Highclere. What is more no Boulbies or Bartleets so far. Fog horns and electric bell ringing incessantly but no band thank goodness but a sinister panatrope. Crew all lascars. Some livestock. 2 prize bulls, 1 horse, couple of fox hounds and six hens. I sit at captain's table next to a Trinidad negress dumb with Glenlike[1] refinement. (She not me.) So your party will be over by the time you get this. I know it was a success. It was nice of you to send me a wireless message. I felt low when it came and was cheered up. If I'm not careful I shall be like Little and [?] Lea writing from loneliness which is all wrong. So I will stop and start again when there is something dramatic to say.

So yesterday night I was bitten by a bed bug caught it. Took up with young man of Portuguese origin on his way to prospect gold. Also red haired widow.

Dec 7th Consistently rough. Very little sleep at nights. Tempers becoming uncertain. Nothing to do all day except read. As usual I brought all the wrong books. 1,800 miles away from you. Too far.

8th. Everyone has been confident that it would be calm the moment we passed the Azores. Well need I say it, it is just as rough. Waves all over the decks.

Write Poste Restante, Georgetown, Demerara, British Guiana any time for a week after receiving this and it will reach me. Tell me about *Miracle* and Xmas party and scandals and how you are and if your delusions are better.

Well now I am 3700 miles away and nothing exciting has happened so I will stop.

Bo

---

[1] Possibly a reference to Christopher Tennant, 2nd Baron Glenconner (1899–1983). Glen is the name of the family's house near Innerleithen, Scotland. When head of Special Operations Executive (SOE) Cairo during the war Lord Glenconner was so rarely seen, and worked in such high administrative circles, that his subordinates called him 'God'.

Evelyn to Diana

Hotel Tower   *[26 December 1932]*
Lots 74 & 75, Main Street
Georgetown
British Guiana

Darling Diana

Well you will say I don't know this handwriting but that is on account of my having bought a stylo pen.

So we reached Georgetown 2 days late what with bad weather and bad seamanship. It is not at all a nice town – large, laid out in rectangular blocks, very broad untidy streets, shabby two storied wood buildings – tropical veg, ford cars, chickens and donkeys. Not hotter than Venice less hot I think, but steaming damp and rather depressing. I shan't mind leaving as soon as I can fix it O.K.

The voyage got better as it got calmer and two perfectly good Boulbies appeared. I also took up with a Belgo-Indian engineer whose mother is a lumber merchant in the forest and offers to lend me a 'bush negro' for a guide if I go to Surinam [Dutch Guiana]. Perhaps you don't know what a bush negro is. Well it is v. interesting. A ship load of slaves got away in the eighteenth century and started an African life on their own in the forest and kill everyone who comes to see them and never go to the coast except this one bush negro who works in my chum's mother's forest so it is exciting.

Well this hotel is kept by an Irish-Portuguese gentleman named Hermandez and it is most up to date with a shower bath and a panatrope which plays Harry Lauder records from nine in the morning. Mr Hermandez is very cheerful this morning because there is a rival hotel called Park and a Dutchman from Surinam shot himself at the Park last night on account of being lonely on Christmas Day. I was not lonely because I went to a great dinner party at Government House and we ate turkey and plum pudding and mince pies and there were all manner of jokes such as india rubber rolls that squeaked and a spoon that fell in two. And we drank to the King and to Absent Friends.

I have gone over big with the Governor[1] on account of my not approving of the teaching of Kiswahili to the Baganda. You might not think that that was the grounds on which a great friendship would be built but it is. I was just airing my general knowledge during my first luncheon and the Governor heard me say that it was wrong to teach the Baganda Kiswahili and he leaped in his chair with joy because that is one of his chief subjects and no one yet has ever agreed with him. So that was lucky as he

---

[1] Sir Edward Denham (1876–1938), Governor of British Guiana 1930–4, and author of *Rubber in the East*.

now thinks me a young man of marked ability and is taking me for a trip in his launch for two or three days to the Mazaruni.

I sent you cable to wish you a happy Hoggmany – I hope it arrived all right. I long to see all *The Miracle* racket again and I suppose never shall. Phyllis would love it here with all the blacks but they seem to me an inferior lot – oafish and hobbledehoy and the girls make themselves hideous with sun-bonnets and shapeless European frocks but their diction delights me. I changed my hotel the first day and the chambermaid said very gravely 'I shall miss your beauty'. Today I sent back some cold coffee to be heated and the waiter said, 'What a blunder they have made.'

Plans are still vague but there is a slightly cracked gentleman going to Rupununi on the 3rd and I think I may join him.

All love
Bo

Evelyn to Diana

Georgetown Club   *[2 January 1933]*
British Guiana

Dearest Diana

Unless anything odd happens you won't hear of me for some time now but you mustn't think that I've stopped thinking for a moment about you and all *The Miracle*. I never see a blackman (at the rate of about 60 a minute) but I think of Miss Stanley and never go into this club except in the company of Mr Boulby. Alas there is not much here to remind me of Wade[1] or Glen.

Please tell Duff that his dictum that you can always tell when you have trodden on a snake because you can hear it hiss, is not altogether accurate. I saw it done on Tuesday – and there was no sound.

Well I was explaining why I wouldn't write to you. It is because I am going up into the bush and there aren't any post offices there. I don't quite know where I am going. First to a place called Kurupukari on the Essequibo. One can't very well get up there by boat this weather so I am riding from the Berbice river with Mr Haynes.[2] I expect you have heard of him. He told me he was very well known in England on account of being a member of the Royal Geographical Society. Anyway in case you haven't I will tell you he is commissioner for the Rupununi district. As no one at all lives there it is very easy work. He is not quite like a magistrate in England or even Africa where they have brisk young men from Cambridge. Here they use local talent. Mr Haynes is half black and more than half crazy. He wrote in one of his official reports to the Governor

---

[1] Diana's maid, Miss Kate Wade, who was with her for the best part of forty years.
[2] Mr Haynes appears as Mr Bain in *Ninety-Two Days*.

23

that he obtained a great deal of advice from the parrots who flew into his kitchen and talked to the cook. Also that he had a submarine horse which swam all the rivers under water.

He is impotent, he told me, on account of a surfeit of quinine but he likes now and then to have parties of girls over from the Brazilian border and play the banjo to them and kiss them. 'But,' he said, 'even before I was impotent the girls never liked me because I am so thin and dark. Now you – you are white and fat and will have the pick of the bunch.'

After Kurupukari I shall have to go on alone to a place called Takutu [?] where a Jesuit is thought to be still living. After that I don't know where I'll go but it ought to be interesting anyway and I'll be back on All Fools' Day or thereabouts and tell you what happened. I expect Mr Haynes will have provided some pretty tall stories by then.

The trip with the Governor was very pansy. Here is a photograph I took in the impenetrable of a chap, not His Excellency, crossing a bridge.

So last night was what they call Hogmany but Christians call Circumcision. And there was a Portuguese ball and a Black Ball and 3 white balls, one for the upper class and 2 for the lower. I went to one upper and one lower white ball. Everyone very tipsy. There is an excellent form of chicken here called Green Swizzle.

Mr Haynes will not let me take my stores except a case of rum, a tin of sardines and some gunpowder.

If you were to write to me Poste Restante Georgetown I might get it but then again I mightn't.

All love
Bo

Evelyn to Diana

Mom-Mom Creek   *28 January [1933]*
Takutu River
Rupununi

Darling Diana

Well this is the end of British Guiana and tomorrow or the day after as soon as I can find a guide I go off to Brazil to a place appropriately called Boa Vista. There are 2 schools about what happens after that because some say there won't be any water in the Rio Branco till May while others say I can get down to Manoas [Manaos] in 5 days. If the latter are right I shall probably be in London before this letter which I am sending back by a very doubtful service to Georgetown. The trail through the bush was not too good – tedious and intensely uncomfortable. I got sick with boredom at Mr Haynes and left him after a week and went on alone. After

24

that things were more interesting as we had a series of mild disasters – pack horses lying down and refusing to move etc. After another week I got out of the forest into open grass land and everything was bliss. Little ranches scattered about, populated with people of any nationality – black, Indian, Brazilian, Spanish – even a Syrian and a Chinese – and all wildly eccentric. Just my tipple. Only one Englishman and he is usually in jug not for the distressing and almost universal[1] but on account of sykesing the police every time he draws his pension. I have stayed – among others – with a black man who in a vision saw the Love of God and pronounced it to be spherical in shape and slightly larger than a football, and a lady who had a son by her brother. Now I am with a priest who has never had a visitor before and couldn't sleep for the first 3 nights of my visit on account of excitement. The only newspaper he gets is *Punch* so I have been able to tell him a lot of news. He studies *Punch* very diligently though and has two partially tame toucans which are highly coloured birds with immense beaks. The Indians are no good – timid and drab – but I am hoping for some rough stuff on the way back in Dutch Guiana where there are some interesting sykeses called Bush Negroes.

I think about *The Miracle* constantly and hope you are having fun but not so much fun as we had at Loose [Cooze?] and Thompson Towers. There is a good site for a Camera Obscura here. Give my love to everyone to whom it would be acceptable. In case I do get held up at Boa Vista and don't reach England till June (unlikely) please include me in holiday plans – preferably among grand architecture. I have seen all I want of nature for the time being.

I met a Brazilian who told me that there was a war going on in Europe I hope that isn't true. The last English paper I saw was Dec 8th.

All love
Bo

Evelyn to Diana

Boa Vista   *10 February [1933]*
Brazil

Darling Diana

Goodness the boredom of Boa Vista. I have been here for a week and there is no prospect of getting away for at least another six days – probably it will be much more. I am already nearly crazy. No one here speaks a word of English. The Benedictine priest (Swiss) knows a few sentences of French but for the last four days he has been down with

---

[1] '. . . that distressing and almost universal complaint, The Piles' (from the old label on boxes of Bromo lavatory paper). In this case, Waugh means homosexuality.

fever. There are no books except an ant eaten edition of Bossuet's sermons and some back numbers of a German pious periodical for children. One cannot get drunk as the only liquor in the village is some very mild, very warm beer, which I can drink at a table in the store in a cloud of flies stared at by Brazilians in pyjama suits and boaters. There are of course no cars or boats for hire and nowhere to go in them if there were. No roads outside the village at all – bush on one side, pampas on the other – vast, shallow river full of sand banks on other sides. No hotel or café or life of any kind. Everyone asleep most of the day. At least it is comfortable. The only house with a floor or doors was built as a Benedictine mission. There were six in the community but they have all had to go down to Manoas with shattered health except the Swiss who looks like dying any moment. However I have a very decent cell in the house and the services of a mental defective (a fat Indian boy with filed teeth) who giggles all day and has never remembered to bring me anything yet. But there are 4 German nuns in another house and they send me across delicious food in aluminium saucepans. So that is something. Meanwhile I read Bossuet and try to write articles and look down the river in hopes of seeing a boat.

Frankly no amount of fun compensates for this sort of misery and I shan't ever again undertake a journey of this kind alone. I am getting homesick and shall return direct as soon as I get to Manoas. I don't think there will be a book in my experiences up to date. However I have been able to brood a bit in solitude and discern solutions to some of my immediate problems.

What a dull letter. I'm sorry but what else can I write?

Longing to see you again and drink wine and smoke cigars and eat European food. Listen how about Portugal for a holly [holiday]? Not far from England. Not americanized. Odd architecture.

I haven't of course had a letter since I left London or seen a paper later than Dec 8th so anything may be happening to you all. The priest said he heard everyone in London was dying of 'flu'. How glad I am you are in the provinces. I will post this in Manoas so you'll see by the post mark how long I had to wait.

All love
Bo

Evelyn to Diana

[no address]   *2 March [1933]*

Darling Diana

No luck at Boa Vista so I have come back to Guiana and am turning towards Gower Street,[1] but I expect this letter will precede me because a

[1] 90 Gower Street, where Duff and Diana lived 1920–38.

gentleman called Mr Melville has promised to take it to Kurupukari, while I am going by a very unpansy route over the Pakaraima Mountain and down to Potaro which may take a long time. I got lost coming from Brazil and was saved by a number of coincidences which I call supernatural.

Goodness how I want to see you again. I think of this week with tears in my eyes as being the last week of *The Miracle* – but perhaps it will be given another few months. What fun if it was still on when I got back.

I am going to get a motor-car when I reach England and learn to drive it. And I shall learn Portuguese and photography. That ought to get me through the year.

I will send you a telegram when I return.

I haven't found any present for you yet unless you would like a walking stick of rare and very heavy wood. If I find any diamonds in the Potaro I will bring them back for you.

I had my hair cut by a priest.

I was 60 hours with only one meal except some milk.

I have got very thin but not very brown.

Love to Duff and J.J. and any chums who remember me.

Bo

Evelyn to Diana

Hotel Tower   *[?late March 1933]*
Georgetown

Dearest Diana

Out of the wild wood at last and everything is Highclere. Longing to see you and everyone and to eat a lot and to see architecture and art and things like that. Since I last wrote I walked over some mountains and then I was lame for a bit owing to a poisoned jigger and I stayed at a dismal camp and lots of Indian villages and I saw Kaietewn which is a famous water-fall. I have brought back a stuffed alligator for John Julius. I shall be back in England first week in May. Shall visit parents for a day or two and arrange luggage and dentist and barber and bank and editors and publisher and so on and then come to London and have some orgies and I think I shall try to be intellectual for a bit. I have got some beryls for you, quite valueless but I found them myself so that makes them interesting. I got 3 letters and all said what a delight your Xmas party was and another one from my mama who saw *Miracle* at Golders Green and was full of heroine worship. Did you read about the lady in the Catholic Church at

Oxford who put her baby in the crib. She had obviously been seeing *Miracle* too.

Goodness how famous I am in this town since you cabled.[1]

All love
Bo

Evelyn to Diana

Grand Pump Room Hotel   *[May 1933]*
Bath

Darling Diana

So I have come back and now I am in Bath because after all that forest it is better to be in good architecture. A perfect Glen hotel with Club servants. Since my association with you I can't stay anywhere without a suite and look back with horror to those days of bed and bath and writing in a lounge so I have some nice rooms looking out on an arcade. I can get to the place where they drink water without going out of doors. I have drunk a lot of vintage port and finished five months' mail mostly Xmas cards and a Colefax suit – four to Ace of meeting you on 15th which I have said yes to so that will be decent and then I hope to see you constantly. Don't be too much disappointed with me.

Imagine the horror of finding an article you wrote rechristened by the *Daily Mail* 'MY ESCAPE FROM MAYFAIR'.[2]

I am also involved in heavy Catholic trouble and am printing a vastly pompous open letter to the Cardinal Archbishop.[3]

So a paper said you had begun a flower shop.[4] Please book my button-hole order – a dark carnation no wire or leaves before 9.30 daily to the Savile from 15th May to end of July. Hope for special and advantageous terms. If more than 2/6 a week I go elsewhere.

I have a crocodile, dead, for J. Julius.

[1] Diana, who tended to treat officials of the British Colonial Service like Thomas Cook representatives, had presumably left a long message for Waugh at Government House.

[2] The article, about the Rupununi District, was posted to Waugh's agent, A. D. Peters, from Boa Vista.

[3] Ernest Oldmeadow, editor of *The Tablet*, and twelve prominent English Catholics who signed a letter of protest printed in that organ, condemned *Black Mischief* for being 'obscene and blasphemous'.

[4] In her autobiography, Gertrude Lawrence wrote: 'I went into business with two friends, Lady Diana [Cooper] and Felicity Tree (Mrs Cory Wright), and we opened a flower shop in Berkeley Square . . . Our flower shop was lovely with flower frescoes on the walls by Oliver Messel . . . I don't think it made any money, though it was fun while it lasted. We called it "Fresh Flowers, Limited," and our friends called it "Faded Flowers, Incorporated."'

Evelyn to Diana

Savile Club [?1933]

Darling Diana

There isn't one particle of Bognor that I don't know and remember and want again. It is so inextricably woven into the pattern of my history that I cannot think of it without a strange pride and tenderness. What fools we were to end it all what utter utter fools.[1]

London is worse than can be imagined. 2 telegrams from Colefax. The Shy Bride of Amsterdam whining indecision. Kommer asking me to luncheon to meet Lady Dashwood and Randolph Churchill, a tearful dinner with little Blondie[2] when she talked about Duggan, very drunk, with such shining generosity that I could only say don't say any more you are making me cry so terribly.[3] So tonight that American princess is taking me to a play. Beatrice Mrs Guinness[4] had a tooth knocked out in Berlin so I sent her sweet Williams from your shop.

I have to go to a banquet in my honour at Oxford on Wed so will probably go to Pakenhams with Oop van Zoom on Tues. Could combine with you Oxford Thursday. Free for luncheon Mon or dinner Mon or dinner Thurs or dinner Fri and longing for Bog[nor] Sat. We think Capt. Bullock will propose marriage to Maimie tonight.[5] Laycock will propose dishonour luncheon tomorrow.

I am spending weekend in London closetted or closeted? which? with work. Got severe beating from my agent for idleness.

Hate everyone except you and Maimie. Health vastly improved by Boy.[6] Slept 9 hours undrugged with 2 windows open.

All love
Bo

Evelyn to Diana

[postcard, no address] [?August 1933]

Venice address is S.S. Kraljica Marija. Cruise 36 c/o Pardo & Bassari P.O. Box 350 Venice.

[1] A parody of Act I of Noël Coward's *Private Lives*.
[2] Waugh's name for Lady Mary Lygon, who was more often known as Maimie.
[3] See note 1.
[4] The mother of Baby and Zita Jungman, known as 'Gloomy'. She was married to Nico Jungman 1900–18, after which she became Mrs Richard Guinness. She died in 1942.
[5] Captain Malcolm Bullock MBE (1890–1966), barrister and MP for the Waterloo Division of Lancashire. His wife, Lady Victoria (née Stanley), had died as the result of a hunting accident in 1927. If he did propose to Mary ('Maimie') Lygon, she must have refused him, for in June 1939 she married HH Prince Vsevolode Ioannovitch of Russia. Captain Bullock never married again.
[6] 'A bottle of the Boy' – champagne. 'The Man' was brandy.

Lovely time Bognor. Special mention Goodwood-staying, Butlin's Zoo (advertised Dover Street Station I noticed) Mr Belloc,[1] Lord Moyne's[2] anti-Highclere, Jermyn Street pub crawl.

Bought new Revelation luggage also lots of semi tropical clothes so what with umbrella shall be pretty slap up for new papists and old Hazel [Lavery].

Love and gratitude. Till 12th

Bo

In August 1933 Waugh accompanied his rich friend Alfred Duggan on an Arnold Lunn Hellenic cruise, in one of his many attempts to take him in hand. He had known Duggan, who was a Catholic, since Oxford; since then Duggan had become an alcoholic and abandoned his religion. Waugh believed that if only his friend could liberate himself from the bottle and return to the faith, his talent and fine qualities would re-emerge, and he spent many years trying to effect the transformation. (His efforts were eventually rewarded, for in his forties Duggan became a successful writer of historical novels. They were set in the Dark Ages, and Waugh commented that Duggan wrote 'as though he were describing personal experiences and observations').

There were other friends of Evelyn's and Alfred Duggan's aboard the Kraljica Marija: *their Oxford contemporary Christopher Hollis, and Father Martin d'Arcy SJ, who had instructed Waugh and received him into the Catholic faith.*

Also among the passengers were Viscount Cranborne, later 5th Marquess of Salisbury ('Bobbity'), his wife Elizabeth ('Betty'), and their sons. Also Laura, Lady Lovat, who was accompanied by her children Hugh and Magdalen. Waugh is particularly scathing about Lady Lovat in these letters, despite the fact that she was recently widowed, and a Catholic. He revised his opinion of her a few years later, however, for she cared devotedly for Maurice Baring in the last few years of his life.

It was a pleasant, if not very memorable cruise; but was significant for Evelyn in that it introduced him to Katharine Asquith and Laura Herbert.

Katharine Asquith, who was one of Diana's dearest friends, was

---

[1] Hilaire Belloc (1870–1953), poet and critic. Evelyn asked Duff if he would introduce him to Belloc and Duff did so, inviting Evelyn to join them at one of their regular lunches. Evelyn said little, and was on his best behaviour throughout the lunch; but after he left, Belloc remarked: 'He is possessed'.

[2] Walter Guinness, 1st Baron Moyne (1880–1944). A close friend of Churchill's, his career in politics ended in Cairo, where he had been appointed Resident Minister. He was shot by Zionist terrorists in November 1944.

then in her late forties. In 1907 she had married Raymond Asquith, eldest son of the Prime Minister, and the most brilliant of that doomed generation that was to die in the First World War. From her father, Sir John Horner, she inherited the Manor House of Mells, Somerset; and it was here that she brought up her three children, Julian, Perdita and Helen. She converted to Catholicism after Raymond's death; and when Monsignor Ronald Knox came to live at Mells in 1949, it became the centre of a group of Catholic friends which included Waugh and Christopher Hollis.

In September, towards the end of the cruise, Duggan and Waugh were asked by fellow-passenger Gabriel Herbert to come and stay at the Villa Altachiara, Portofino, a house belonging to her mother, Mary Herbert. Waugh and Duggan found themselves part of a large house party which included Gabriel's siblings: Auberon, Bridget and Laura. But the second Mrs Evelyn Waugh did not make much of an impression on him at the time. In a letter to Katharine Asquith sent from Portofino, Laura is described as a 'white mouse'.

Evelyn to Diana

SS Kraljica Marija   *[September 1933]*

Darling Diana

Well I wrote a story about you only you mustn't think it is you because I have made you have a Belleville[1] and quite a different character and I made the pansy into a chorus girl so it is not really about you or *The Miracle* except that you told me the story[2] and I have made Boulby into a pouncer.

Then I came to Venice and in the train was Mr and Mrs Bobbity[3] and a son and the bastard so I said where are you going and they said for a cruise and here they are and the bastard makes a pretty sight playing backgammon all day with Lord d'Abernon.[4]

Passed Brandolin[5] with tears and reached ship. Very old and

[1] Rupert Belleville was the lover of Diana's friend Venetia Montagu.

[2] On 2 September 1933, Waugh wrote from the ship to W. N. Roughead (the partner of A. D. Peters, Waugh's agent since 1927): 'I want to make an alteration to the *Bystander* story . . . I think the name Lady Priscilla looks too much like Diana Cooper so please have it altered throughout to Elsa Branch, no title . . . and omit the reference to peers' daughters on stage.'

[3] The Viscount Cranborne (1893–1972), who succeeded as 5th Marquess of Salisbury in 1947. He married Elizabeth Vere, daughter of Lord Richard Cavendish, in 1915. They were accompanied by two of their three sons.

[4] Edgar Vincent (1857–1941), created 1st Viscount d'Abernon in 1926. He was Ambassador to Berlin 1920–26, a Trustee of the Tate and National Galleries and Chairman of the Lawn Tennis Association. Among his publications are *A Grammar of Modern Greek* and *Alcohol: Its Action on the Human Organism*.

[5] Palazzo Brandolin, San Barnabà. It was here that Duff and Diana had stayed in the summer of 1932, as the guests of the American hostess Mrs Laura Corrigan.

inconceivably badly run. None of the servants speak any language except Serbian so there is no food or drink or bath towels.

Now I have remembered that it spoils letters to be badly written so I will try to do it clearer only it is a Serbian pen too.

I may say that on the Calais boat were Mr Taglioni, Mr Quaglino and Mr Quaglino's head waiter all looking like gangsters in pearl grey suits and jaunty hats.

Well the cruise so far has been very jolly. Mr Duggan has behaved irreproachably except for farting at an invalid giantess name Lovat.[1] She gets into such odd postures at mass that no one can look anywhere else.

There is a decent matronly lady named Mrs Asquith whom you told me about and her daughter [Lady Helen Asquith] is quite on a small scale compared with Lady Lovat's, but she has many more warts. She spends her day reading Euripides with her little brother[2] who wants to pass an examination.

I eat with a highly intelligent princess called Infanta Beatrix[3] who tells me about the hereditary diseases of the royal families. There is another princess called Marie Louise who is the centre of the rowdy set and can be seen any evening standing rounds of champagne cocktails to rows of tarts in highly-coloured cache-sexes and brassieres.[4]

A poor young lady named Legge[5] had her brains knocked out in the swimming pool.

I am terribly pursued by a dreadful young man called Colon who thinks I am a celebrated novelist.

Mrs Asquith says will I stay at Mells when you are doing *The Miracle* at Frome or when it is in Somerset so that is all right.

We drink very nasty Serbian wine.

Well this is not the diary I promised to write but I will tell you more at Venice.

All love
Bo

[1] Laura Lister (d. 1965). Daughter of the 4th Baron Ribblesdale, she married Simon Fraser, 14th Lord Lovat (1871–1933) in 1910. Lord Lovat had died in February.

[2] Julian Asquith (b. 1916), known to his friends as 'Trim'. Born in the year in which his father Raymond died in action. Succeeded his grandfather as the 2nd Earl of Oxford and Asquith in 1928.

[3] The Infanta Beatrix (b. 1909), daughter of Alfonso XIII of Spain. In 1935 she married Italian Prince Alessandro Torlonia.

[4] A joke. Princess Marie Louise (1872–1956) was the youngest child of Queen Victoria's third daughter Princess Helena, and her husband Prince Christian of Schleswig-Holstein. In 1891 she married Prince Aribert of Anhalt; but when no children followed, her husband's father annulled the marriage, exercising his medieval right as a sovereign prince. The Princess never married again, since she piously believed her marriage vows still binding. She devoted the rest of her life to charitable works.

[5] The Hon. Diana Legge (b. 1910). In 1937 she married Major the Hon. John Hamilton Russell, who was killed in 1943. In 1946 she married Brigadier Adrian Lewis Matthews.

Evelyn to Diana

SS Kraljica Marija   [September 1933]

Darling Diana

I am dazed and incredulous at Mrs Asquith's telegram that you won't be in Venice so I am going to Ravenna instead.

I had a very beautiful photograph for you of the Infanta Beatrice but Mrs A. pinched it.

Everybody is very ill on this ship except me.

A very silly lord I expect you know named Cocky[1] has joined the ship.

Lady Lovat hasn't been the same since Alfred's fart. I think she is trying to act *The Miracle* all the time. It is terrible how I despise her and her daughter and her son.

Rhodes was decent and I shall go there for my honeymoon next time I get married.

Not so Sparta.

Mistra v. good.

Saw foreign chaps making raisins out of grapes.

Went to Troy.

It is touching to see how the Bobbities are enjoying themselves. Tomorrow I have to take the Infanta to Delphi. Yesterday it was the labyrinth of Minos. She dotes on me. Not so Marie Louise or Mrs Bobbity. Mrs A[squith] and Lady Helen and Lord O[xford] and A[squith] are very well behaved and a great lesson to those Frasers.[2] Why only yesterday Hugh Fraser turned a hose into the second officer's cabin and that is no way to behave.

Poor Father d'Arcy is very ill and worried but he has a good argument now and then with Chris [Hollis] and me and that cheers him up.

There was a don named Shepherd who gave a lecture and danced like a Dervish and opinion was divided on whether it was a Good Thing. Most of the party said NO and Miss Magdalen giggled, but there was a Cambridge clacque is it spelled clacque. The test case was Dame Georgiana Butler who is of high intellect. That evening and after breakfast she was pro Shepherd but had ratted by luncheon. Then there is bitter ill feeling between the Hellenes and the Bizantinists and Shepherd leads the Hellenes and a Mr Wilson the Bs. Asquiths are Hellenes Duggan Hollis and me Bizantines. Then there is another grave controversy about the Turks. Poor Lady Lovat is pro-Turk.

---

[1] Thomas, Lord Cochrane (1886–1958). He succeeded his father as 13th Earl of Dundonald in 1935.

[2] Hugh (1918–84) and Magdalen (1913–69) Fraser, children of the 14th Lord Lovat. In 1945 Hugh became a Conservative MP, and later Secretary of State for Air. In 1956 he married Lady Antonia Pakenham. Magdalen married the 4th Earl of Eldon in 1934.

Father d'Arcy is very jealous of a canon called Wigram.

Well it is sad about Venice so give my love to Honor and Chipps.[1]

XXXX E

Evelyn to Diana

[Portofino]   [September? October? 1933]

Darling Diana

I am so sorry that I disappointed you by not saying enough about my fellow passengers. I hasten to make good the omissions.

Sir Percival Marling V.C.[2] and Lady Marling

A faithful and affectionate couple seldom seen out of each other's company. Tireless walkers. Sir Percival tended to become peevish when kept waiting. Lady Marling dressed in a royal manner. Sir Percival wore cricket club ties. Their only appearance in cruise society was at a party given by the Croatian ship owner at Ragusa when Sir P. became a little pop eyed at the collection of Mestrovik's.[3]

Mr and Mrs Raines

Mrs Raines held the purse strings and was paying for the cruise. She only missed Mass once Mr Raines never. They carried a cine-kodak. They complained that Mr Hollis did not speak to them every day. Thought I was charming in bus. Had come on cruise on Father d'Arcy's assurance that there would be no scenes of licence. They had been on a cruise to Norway where they had been greatly disedified.

Miss Marjorie Glasgow

A very rich young lady whom I had met before on account of her mother giving parties I used to go to before I became fastidious. She was the leader of the left wing nudists. She was attended by three naked Counts, one Polish, one Belgian and one Italian, one carried her gramophone, another her backgammon board and the third her sunbathing mattress.

Lady Jean Mackintosh

Leader of the right wing nudists. Dived off side of ship into sewage and

---

[1] Sir Henry 'Chips' Channon (1897–1958), Conservative MP, best known for his posthumously published diaries. In 1933 he married Lady Honor Guinness, eldest daughter of the second Earl of Iveagh. They were divorced in 1945.

[2] Colonel Sir Percival Marling (1861–1936). He won the VC while serving with the Mounted Infantry in the Suakin campaign of 1884.

[3] Ivan Mestrovic (1883–1962), Yugoslav sculptor.

swam great distances. Champagne cocktails. Polite to Lady d'Abernon. Face like hairless monkey. Despised me.

Mrs Violet Blundell
Was poisoned with ptomaine on first day and made rare appearance. Was kissed every morning by Princess Marie Louise. When well, mad about me. Numerous Cartier charms on bracelet. Smelt of powder.

Mr Duggan
Broke up badly during last days of voyage on account of switching from beer to Jugo-Slavian brandy. Last seen sauntering jauntily away from outgoing Paris train.

Mrs Peveril
Very common lady. Lady Jean (see above) was overheard to refer to her as 'red haired Jewess'. Mr Lunn told her and bitter controvy. resulted. No apologies offered or accepted. Did the Infanta's packing for her. Bought Croatian jewelry.

Father Sir John O'Connell[1]
Knee high to a duck. Took 38 minutes to say mass as against d'Arcy's 25. Was overheard deriding St Joan of Arc to Canon Wigram. Controversy resulted.

Mr Coglan, pronounced ':' [colon]
Out to cut social ice and failed all round.

The Hon. Peter Acton[2]
Remained on ship in port. Was sick at night through overindulgence in Jugo-Slavian mineral water. Generous, amiable, usually sound asleep.

The Hon. Diana Legge
Was struck on head by diving gentleman. Giggled with Cecil children and Frasers.

The Hon. Magdalen Fraser
Giggled with Legge, Cecils, her brother and by herself. No deportment. Untidy.

Earl of Oxford and Asquith
Big winner on good sense and good manners. Studious, holy and respectful.

---

[1] The Revd Sir John O'Connell (1868–1943). Formerly a solicitor, he was married in 1901, knighted in 1914, widowed in 1925 and ordained in 1929.

[2] Peter Acton (1909–46). The brother of the 3rd Baron Acton, he and his wife were killed in a plane crash over Africa.

Dame Georgiana Butler.

Lost marks as blue stocking through admiring Mr Sheppard's lecture on the *Odyssey* before she had consulted rival highbrows. Ratted on this before luncheon next day but never recovered lost prestige. Thought highly of me.

Lady Dunsany

Wore two hats simultaneously. Tired at Troy.

Lord Newton

Uncommunicative. Fine P. G. Wodehouse figure.

Canon Potts

Went for donkey tour from Athens to Gytheion with 2 other Canons and a spinster.

Miss Kitty Matthew

Tried to make nudist set but failed left and right wings and centre. Reduced to dancing with Coglan. Her father scrubbed her face to remove paints.

Mr Justice Dumas and Miss Dumas

A very unimportant couple.

CANON WIGRAM[1]

A man of unexampled excellence. Roused wild jealousy in Father d'Arcy. Slept with a neurotic giantess named Lovat. Admirable range of jokes on all subjects from buggery in the bar to ecclesiology in the dining saloon. Had been outraged by Turkish commandant in internment camp during war. Very false teeth and continual fly button trouble. Beard. Father d'Arcy suspected him of leading Protestant landslide among Catholic converts but was discovered to have no religious beliefs. Have arranged for him to conduct *Miracle* tour when we go to Somerset.

Dr Glover

Was given hell by [Arnold] Lunn on account of his being a Baptist.

Lord Cochrane

Suffered terribly all the time. Beat Mrs Hollis by short head in detestation of whole cruise.

[1] Canon William Ainger Wigram (1912–1953). Canon of Malta (Collegiate Church of St Paul) since 1928. He had previously been head of the Archbishop of Canterbury's mission to the Assyrian Christians.

Miss Sanderson
  There were six Misses Sanderson on board.

Mrs Asquith and Lady Helen Asquith
  O.K.

Miss Herbert[1]
  Showed tendency to go off alone and climb rocks. Appreciated Duggan, Hollis, etc. Moody.

Lady Cranborne and family
  Hadn't heard of Greek art before and was knocked flat by it. Big mixer. Distributed visiting cards to all foreigners encountered ashore and asked them to stay if they ever came to England. She will regret this. Her husband fell in love with a fine looking lady named Lund. She did some quick stuff with Mr Mackintosh (see Lady Jean above). Cranbornes led sex life of ship. Dreary oaf named Robert Cecil[2] balanced things on Miss Legge's head. (One way and another Miss Legge's head came in for a good deal of misuse.) Gnome bastard named Michael prematurely aged. Predict future for gnome bastard.[3]

Well there were about 200 other passengers and I will tell you about them from time to time during the coming year.
  After the cruise was over I went to Ravenna with Katharine and Trim and then to Bologna. Then I came to stay in a very dangerous house where all the young people are covered in festering sores. It is full of wasps, horseflies and mosquitoes and my bedroom is named Lord Surrey. There is a little boy[4] who throws stones at his elders. There is a giantess[5] who plays the oboe and the accordion. Music all the time and philosophic discussion with a nit-wit mural decorator.[6] Mr Acton is staying here too I believe but he hasn't woken up since his arrival. There is a decent hostess[7] who makes barking noises when the orchestra is not playing.

All love
Bo

[1] Gabriel Herbert (b. 1911). In 1943 she married Alexander 'Alick' Dru.
[2] Robert Cecil (b. 1916), who succeeded his father as 6th Marquess of Salisbury in 1972. In 1945 he married Marjorie Wyndham-Quin.
[3] Robert's younger brother Michael Cecil died the following year.
[4] Auberon Herbert (1922–74).
[5] Eve Myers, daughter of the writer Leopold Myers.
[6] John Spencer-Churchill (b. 1909). He describes himself as 'Mural and portrait, townscape, landscape painter, sculptor, lecturer and author since 1932'.
[7] Mary Herbert (1889–1970). Shortly to become Waugh's mother-in-law. She was born the Hon. Mary Vesey, and married Aubrey Herbert MP (1880–1923) in 1910. Aubrey Herbert, who was twice offered the throne of Albania, was a half-brother of the 5th Earl of Carnarvon (the patron of Howard Carter who discovered the tomb of Tutankhamun).

Diana had a house near Bognor, in West Sussex. A gift from her mother, West House was a large cottage with Gothic windows, separated from the shingle beach by a walled garden. In October 1933 she lent it to Waugh, who needed a period of isolation in which to start a book about his travels in South America.

It was uphill work, because his weeks in Guiana had not been a great success. He had met some remarkable characters – some of whom found their way into his novel A Handful of Dust; *but much time had been spent waiting around in a mood of enervated exasperation, and the journeys into the interior had been more monotonous than exciting. Another cross to bear was the success of* Brazilian Adventure *by Peter Fleming, a brilliantly funny book about an ill-starred expedition to the Matto Grosso. Waugh gave it a generous review in the* Spectator, *but it cannot have raised his spirits.*

At the same time, he was much preoccupied with Baby Jungman, for he had heard that the Catholic Church might grant an annulment of his first marriage. On the day the civil divorce came through, he went up to London and proposed – and Baby Jungman refused. 'So that is that, eh,' he wrote to Mary Lygon. 'Stiff upper lip and dropped cock.'

He returned to West House, more hurt and disappointed than his words imply. The book on British Guiana was finished in a month. It was called Ninety-Two Days, *and dedicated to Diana.*

Evelyn to Diana

[West House   [October 1933]
Aldwick
Nr Bognor]

Darling Diana

Well I came here and was a little drunk when I got into train so felt low on arrival. Mrs Brougham[1] very welcoming and kind but still low. However I've made a start with the book and found a goat and kid and walked to Bog and back. Trouble is I think of dutch girl all day – not sweet voluptuous dream, no sir, just fretful and it sykeses the work but I'll soon stop that. Do write to me and tell me the doings.

I am much under compliment about this decent house.

Bo

---

[1] Mrs Broome, the gardener's wife and caretaker. Waugh spells her name like the one-horse closed carriage, which is pronounced the same way.

Evelyn to Diana

[West House   *[October 1933]*
Aldwick]

Darling Diana

Well things are a little better. That is to say the book has begun. 500 words the first day, 1,500 yesterday and a little over 2,000 today. Time was I could write 3,000 a day and think nothing of it. Still it is getting longer and if I go on even like this it will be done some time. What is more I am getting a little interested in it. Not much, but when I am not writing I think of it sometimes instead of never. As soon as a chapter is typed may I send it to you and will you read it and tell me what is worst. You see I want to dedicate it to you if you'll let me, so I don't want it to be very bad.

I hadn't seen the surroundings of your house before, dashing past them in motor-cars, and you know they are pretty hellish. But I've found a fairly empty place called Pagham with some mud that stinks and I walk there every day.

Mrs Brougham is very decent and wants to be chatty so soon I'll let her rip.

I sykesed a green vase today – no great value I should say but I daresay you have some particular reason for preferring it to anything else in the world. Sorry. Otherwise haven't abused hospitality so far as I know.

I have to come to London for the day on Wed for divorcing and would pop in on you at six if asked to do so.

It's too much to expect you to write and I don't expect it.

Mice come out and stare me out of countenance.

I read *Young Men in Love* by M. Arlen. Who marked your copy? V. interesting.

Love and x x x x x x x x

Bo

Evelyn to Diana

[West House   *[October 1933]*
Aldwick]

Darling Diana

Well I got back tired from London. It was delightful seeing you and that decent goat though for too short a time. Read that chapter please and say all you think of it. It wouldn't do at all to have your name on a book in which there was anything to make you ashamed. I'll send another chapter in a day or so and then another and so on as I get them from the typist. After seeing you I met my Dutch girl and had some dinner with her and she saw me off. She became a little light-headed through taking a glass of Guinness and asked questions all the evening, mostly 'Why?' and 'What?' So it was not a great treat for me.

If you come and visit me I will get you some fireworks but anyway write long and often because that would help me.

What devil prompted you to advise Chichester for cinemas? I tramped there and arrived at dusk very cold (this was Friday) and the cinemas didn't open till 6.30 and there was no bus till 5.35 so I wandered about dodging bicycles and I thought I'd have muffins for tea and there must be about 20 tea shops in Chichester all kept by Ladies but there were no muffins so I had pretty soggy toast.

I saw a letter from Little on your hall table but with great show of decency didn't open it or take it away.

I am getting fairly humble apologies by every post from people connected with the Hearst press. Did you read the mangled story?[1] It is not absolutely bad even as it stands.

Love
Bo

Evelyn to Diana

[West House   *4 November [1933]*
Aldwick]

Darling Diana

I hope you enjoyed Thursday a little. It was the greatest possible delight to me. If you had any pleasure from my visiting you in Glasgow, double that and you will know a little of what I feel about it.

So stimulated that I broke all records with a 4,000 word day yesterday.

You left behind you a veil, a powder box and some cigarettes. Shall I sleep with them under my pillow or send them back to you?

I believe the book will be finished next week so try and keep some dates for the week after. Shall we make a date for the evening of the Dunn–Lynn party and have fun first? I'd even go so far as to dress up if required.

What do you think of the idea of my going to a University – which – and studying anthropology?

Master Brougham [Teddy Broome, the gardener's son] has some fireworks today.

Looking forward eagerly to the two minutes' silence on 11th. Wish they'd make it two days.

---

[1] In September 1933, *Hearst's International* and *Cosmopolitan* had published 'The Man Who Liked Dickens', a short story used as the basis for chapter VI of *A Handful of Dust*.

That book you lent me is mostly about buggers.

Trying out the exercises but can't rotate the arse very easily.

My homage to Lord Beaverbrook, Mrs Maugham, S.B. [?], Major the Honble. Maurice Baring, Lady Lavery, [Cecil] Beaton, [Oliver] Messel, [Peter] Watson, [David] Herbert, [Rex] Whistler, [Jack] Wilson and all your set.[1]

X X X X X
Bo

The novel A Handful of Dust *was now beginning to take shape in Waugh's mind, and he decided to escape the English winter and the distractions of his social life by a visit to Morocco.*

Evelyn to Diana

Hotel Bellevue   *Thursday 4 January 1934*
Fez

Darling Diana

So now I am at Fez.

Journey out in Kaiser-etc. very dull. The only pretty people were seasick all the time.

Had all my cigars confiscated at Tangier.

Took night train here.

Bright sun, intense cold, hotel entirely without heating. Wish you were here to share things. City of astonishing beauty all gardens and streams. Moors pretty bughouse at the moment on account of Ramadan which means nothing to eat drink or smoke all day.

French hotel much patronised by military.

Went round the quartier reservé last night. Very bright and cheerful. Little fifteen-year-old Arab girls for fifteen–twenty francs each. Bought one but didn't enjoy her much.

Very smart English lady in evening clothes and a thing in her hair going round brothels too with four Jews. I wonder who.

[1] William Maxwell Aitken, 1st Baron Beaverbrook (1879–1964). Owner of the *Daily Express*, he held a number of Cabinet posts in Churchill's wartime government. Maurice Baring (1874–1945), poet, journalist and author; served in RFC during the First World War. Cecil Beaton (1904–80), photographer, stage designer and diarist, knighted 1972. Oliver Messel (1904–78), stage designer. Peter Watson (1908–56), connoisseur, financer of *Horizon*, and (with Greta Garbo) one of the great loves of Cecil Beaton's life. The Hon. David Herbert (b. 1908), brother of the 17th Earl of Pembroke, who in 1950 moved to Tangier. Rex Whistler (1905–44), painter, designer and illustrator. John C. Wilson (1899–1961), American theatre manager and Noël Coward's business partner.

Tell Sexy[1] to stay at hotel called Palais Jamai then I shan't see him.
Now I will write to my mama and then a novel.
Please come here soon. It will make it fun like Edinburgh.

No love to anyone.

Bo

Evelyn to Diana

c/o British Consulate   *[January 1934]*
Fez
Morocco

Darling Diana

I am not really surprised at getting no letters from you because I know
what your life is with babies and husbands and all those chums. I hope
you are having fun with them all. But though I don't expect a letter I do
expect you. When are you coming? I am keeping all sight seeing until
your arrival.

As for me, well I am sober and fairly industrious, sleeping well. Novel
is ⅓ done – rather more. I think it is excellent. I reread *Vile Bodies* and
Decline and Fall last week and was very much cheered up to find how I
have improved at writing.

I see no one ever except the British Consul once a week or so but when I
dine there it is always for French officials and I speak French so badly and
so little that I don't enjoy it much.

Do you know of anyone called Jock Menzies? I have called a character
that in the book and now am haunted by the feeling that it is the name of a
real person.

I have formed an attachment for a young lady named Fatima. She has a
round brown face entirely covered by a network of blue tattooing – very
becoming. She is very unlike the Dutch girl in all particulars. I see her a lot
but as we neither speak a word of the other's language our association is
rather limited. I am thinking of taking her out of the quartier reservé and
setting her up for my exclusive use but the legalities are formidable – also I
think she'd be lonely away from the other girls. She has a gold tooth she is
very proud of. She is about 15 years old she thinks. She ran away from
Meknes because a Russian gentleman in the Foreign Legion cut her
stomach open with a razor, leaving a nasty scar.

There is a lot of fun goes on in the hotel among the soldiers but I am out
of all that. In fact very lonely. Do come soon.

---

[1] Waugh's name for Cecil Beaton.

Don't tell Mrs Asquith about Fatima. Has that decent earl [of Oxford and Asquith] got his scholarship?

There was a newspaper with a huge photograph of Lady Sibell [Lygon] on the front on account of Uncle Bendor's action and the consul's wife said 'Let me see, Lady Sibell Lygon is the Duke of Westminster's *fourth* wife, isn't she?'

Bo

Has Maimie married the pauper prince?[1]

Evelyn to Diana

Fez   *[January 1934]*

God it was decent getting a letter from you. Do you think Bobbity's lady is named Mrs Lund – if so she is a corker. I suppose that this will be the final end of the Church of England. Well there is nothing here to tell you about except Fatima and my book. Fatima is very well and was lately given a green celluloid comb with glass diamonds in it and she's as pleased as punch bless her so I gave her a lalique glass ring[2] I happened to find in an overcoat pocket and she rightly thought very little of that. As for the book, well it is at a crisis at the moment. I have finished the first section which was to have been 20,000 words and it is nearly 50,000 so there is the alternative of making it 150,000 words long (*Black Mischief* is about 70,000) or else finding a new ending and finishing it off in 2 weeks and coming back to disturb those silent days you are taking twice a month. So I am going south to Marrakesh for a bit not to think about it and I hope when I get back it will come right. Of course from prestige etc. it would be good to make it long but I am that lazy and anyway one has to think about the book and not the reviewers. What I have done is excellent. I don't think it could be better. Very gruesome. Rather like Webster in modern idiom. Very fine scene where bereaved and heartbroken father plays animal snap with unknown American woman all afternoon while his little boy lies dead upstairs. Although he is called John Andrew this little boy is not John Julius so you must not think so, nor are the married couple Perry and Kitty [Brownlow] though you might think that but there is someone called Polly Cookpurse who is my idea of Doris.[3] There

---

[1] Waugh's name for Prince George (1902–42), the fourth son of King George V. In October 1934 he was created Duke of Kent, and the following month he married Princess Marina, youngest daughter of Prince Nicholas of Greece.

[2] A gift from Mary Lygon (see *The Letters of Evelyn Waugh*, ed. Mark Amory, p. 84).

[3] Doris Delavigne (1900–42), who in 1928 married Viscount Castlerosse, social columnist and leader writer for the *Sunday Express*. Rosa Lewis said of her: 'Young Doris may go far on those legs of hers, but mark my words, she doesn't know how to make a man comfortable.'

is also a brilliant scene at the '43' and a divorce expedition to Brighton with a tart – all excellent. And there is a woman called Mrs Beaver who runs a decorating shop, not so good, and a groom who ought to be better. But the general architecture is <u>masterly</u>.

My last act was to leave the proofs of Guiana with you and I note that you don't mention these but I don't take any account of that (1) because I think it's most likely you forgot (2) if you found it unreadable I should be in complete agreement with you. I get constant letters from Lygons but no one else. A letter from Katharine announcing Trim's scholarship and attributing it all to prayer instead of the poor boy's own gifts and industry.

I think it quite likely I shall be back in March, sweetened by solitude.

I am particularly glad that a copy of that pamphlet[1] turned up as there are only 2 or 3 in existence and I may want to reprint it one day. You might show it to Mrs Asquith who is constitutionally pro Oldmeadow.

Will Duff lecture in French or Flemish to those Belgians. Walloon.

Packets of love to all
X X X X X X X X X X X X X X X X X X Bo

Evelyn to Diana

Savile Club   *[late May/early June 1934]*

Darling Diana

I think it was wrong of me to get drunk as I did in your house last week. It did not in any way diminish the delight I always have in staying at Bognor but I think it may have added to the distress of having me as a guest. Talk it over with Beaton and I am sure he will sympathize fully.

I hope your party at the Ritz Hotel was a wow. I'm sure it was.

After I left you I went to play dominoes with the poor. Then I saw my parents and their poodle. I told them all about Noël.[2]

Please let me know what time you will be leaving for Wilton next week.

I go to stay with my rich brother[3] for the weekend and after that I don't know where.

---

[1] The pamphlet was the only appearance in print of 'Waugh's Open Letter to the Cardinal Archbishop of Westminster' (*Letters*, pp. 72–8), in which he refutes the attack on *Black Mischief* made by Ernest Oldmeadow of *The Tablet*.

[2] The Coopers' cocker spaniel.

[3] Alec Waugh (1898–1981), novelist and travel writer. Evelyn's elder brother. His first novel, *The Loom of Youth* (1917), was a scandal and a great success – being the first book to suggest homosexual goings-on in British public schools. He went on to write many more novels, the best remembered being *Island in the Sun* (1956). From 1919–21 he was married to Barbara Jacobs; from 1932–69 to Joan Chirnside; and in 1969 he married the American writer Virginia Sorensen.

I go to T. S. Eliot protestant play[1] tonight and if I like it I will advise you to go.

All love
Bo

Evelyn to Diana

DET NORDENFJELDSKE DAMPSKIBSSELSKAB   [13 July 1934]
[Aboard the Prinsesse Ragnhild]

Dearest Diana
We land today at Tromso – appropriately enough on Friday 13th. So far trip agreeable and dull. I don't like Norwegians at all. The sun never sets, the bar never opens, and the whole country smells of kippers. Tomorrow we sail for Spitzbergen.[2] I expect to be in England at the beginning of September (with beard). Do leave a note at the Savile before then saying what your plans are. My love to Duff and John Julius.

Bo

Diana to Evelyn

Kildonan   [September 1934]
Barrhill
Ayrshire

Dearest Bo. I've read Handfulers[3] aloud to Barbie Wallace,[4] Joan Guinness,[5] and Sheila Loughborough[6] and the success has been dynamic. The book has, and is now being fought for by the men. As for myself I can not tell you, because I am not educated, and inarticulate and uncoordinated in thought how beautiful I think it. You were so very hostile when you left for the Pole that you froze the voicing of my praise.

---

[1] *The Rock*, which is about building a church. It opened at Sadlers Wells on 28 May and ran till 9 June.
[2] A reconnaissance expedition organised by Alexander Glen, then a 22-year-old undergraduate at Oxford. He was accompanied by Henry Lygon, and (at the last minute) Waugh, who had no idea how strenuous it was going to be. Glen's university expeditions are described in his book *Young Men in the Arctic* (1935). Knighted in 1967, he was Chairman of the British Tourist Authority 1969–77.
[3] *A Handful of Dust*, published by Chapman & Hall on 4 September 1934.
[4] Barbara Wallace (1898–1981). Daughter of Sir Edwin Lutyens, she married the Rt. Hon. Euan Wallace in 1920.
[5] Joan Yarde-Buller (b. 1908). Married Loel Guinness, 1927–36, Prince Aly Khan 1936–49. In 1986 she married the Viscount Camrose.
[6] The Australian wife of Francis St Clair Erskine, Lord Loughborough, whom she married in 1915.

I read the whole of the 2nd ½ with a lump in my throat, produced by the chapter, and the verse, if you follow me.

Back Mon or Tues.

Love
Diana

Evelyn to Diana

Easton Court Hotel   *[early November 1934]*
Chagford

Dearest Diana

Alas, the pony fair is over and the unsold animals turned loose on the moor again. I daresay John Julius would have found the present an embarrassment, though it would have played very prettily with the goats at Bognor.

I have been here since I left London except for a Saturday to Monday visit with a midget[1] in Cornwall and another to Mells where Katharine took me sharply to task on most subjects. I lunched with your farmer,[2] who, like most of us, is very much more agreeable outside of London. He gave me a partridge to eat – a Frenchman with red legs. It was altogether delightful at Mells except for a lady called Violet B-Carter.[3] We visited a house of portentous ugliness where the dutch girl used to stay. Tomorrow I go back to the midget. But I haven't been to London. Had I done so I would have let you know, in order to fan the flame you speak of, though not in hope of getting very much warmth or light. But I should hate the embers to become quite extinguished because there may always come a time when you will be more at rest again, and then we could grill a bone or two. ~~The trouble is that I find the pleasures of friendship need much more leisure than you can possibly give to it at the present. Also that I am jealous and resentful and impatient though you are none of these things. It is no interest to me to see you in a crowd or for odd snatches of ten minutes at a time. Perhaps in thirty years time when some of your adherents have died off or fallen away . . .~~

I have thought twice about crossing out the last paragraph from 'bone or two' onwards, but I'll let it stand, and anyway I expect you will find the handwriting indecypherable indicipherable indecypherible I don't know.

---

[1] Lady Diana Abdy, wife of Sir Robert Abdy, Bt., and daughter of the 5th Earl of Bradford. Lived at a house called Newton Ferrers in Cornwall.

[2] Conrad Russell (1878–1947), 4th son of Lord Arthur Russell. His life was spent farming his land, cultivating his mind and writing long and entertaining letters to his friends. He adored Diana and named one of his cows after her – 'I always know Diana by her white rump'.

[3] Lady Violet Asquith (1887–1969) married Sir Maurice Bonham-Carter in 1915. Created Baroness Asquith 1964.

I hunt a little on the moor. They call it cubbing but as often as not we kill old foxes and there have been some good runs. I wrote two very poor short stories and read up stuff about Campion.[1]

My great friend Patrick Balfour comes for a few days next week, also Cristina Hastings.[2]

The Times this morning has some exciting photographs of rock churches in Cappadocea. I would like to go there after Christmas. I think, too, I shall have to go to Prague for a night or two on the Campion trail. If either of these expeditions interest you, let me know.

I hear that Duff is to be Viceroy of India.[3] Would he think of taking me as a secretary?

Love
Bo

On third thoughts, I did cross out the paragraph. It now reads rather ungrateful

Evelyn to Diana

Easton Court Hotel   *[Autumn 1934]*
Chagford

Darling Diana

Back again at Chagford and Campion.

I hope you are getting the teeth to work again, though it was full of sex appeal when you writhed on the bed in hunger. I have thought about that a lot.

After I saw you I went to stay with P. Chetwode.[4] She has a white pony rather like the one you sold for £30 only more skittish but P. Chetwode made me ride him in a red flannel martingale and that was embarrassing. She is being a very brave girl with Mr Betjeman and has a German cook and grooms the pony herself and there was a bath and soap and bromo and all manner of unexpected comforts in her house.

Then I went to Oxford and had luncheon with M. Bowra.[5] Julian [the Earl of Oxford and Asquith] was there but did not say anything. Also

---

[1] The Blessed Edmund Campion (1540–81), Catholic martyr who was hung, drawn and quartered in the reign of Elizabeth I. Waugh was about to embark on his biography.

[2] Daughter of Marchese Casati of Milan. Her first husband was John, Viscount Hastings (later 15th Earl of Huntingdon). Her second, Wogan Philipps, later Lord Milford.

[3] This was a job for a distinguished elder statesman, not (as Duff then was) a junior minister.

[4] Penelope, daughter of Field Marshal Lord Chetwode. She had married the poet John Betjeman (1906–84) the year before.

[5] Maurice Bowra (1898–1971). Oxford don, and Warden of Wadham College from 1938. Knighted in 1951.

Maud Yorke[1] who said a lot. Then I came to London again and went twice more to *Young England*.[2] I proved E. Stanley (of A.)[3] a liar about an island named Jan Mayen. Then I had dinner with Katharine. There was a wop duchess there who had written a poem to me. I took Katharine and Helen with the Elweses[4] to *Young England*. I have put K in very embarrassing position by giving her an obscene book – not Horn Book – to sell in aid of nuns.

Having great fun with St James's Club and Phylys'[?] client who thinks me a bugger.

Then I went to stay with Juliet[5] and did not enjoy it <u>at all</u> in spite of great quantities of food and wine. The wop duchess turned up again.

I have your life of Queen Elizabeth[6] safe and will send it back. It is not very good.

X X X X X

Bo

Evelyn to Diana

Easton Court Hotel   *[?Autumn 1934]*
Chagford

Darling Diana

I think I owe you a collins[7] for my visit to Juliet which was very nice and I met some foreigners and nancies. Now I am at Chag for some time so come and do some cubbing on Dartmoor with me.

---

[1] Maud Wyndham, Henry Yorke's mother. Daughter of the 2nd Lord Leconfield, she married Vincent Wodehouse Yorke in 1899.

[2] A ridiculously *Boy's Own Paper* patriotic play which became a cult success. Waugh and his friends went night after night, and yelled out the fruitiest lines before the actors could.

[3] Edward Stanley (1907–71), 6th Lord Stanley of Alderley. He was much married: 1932–6, Lady Victoria Chetwynd-Talbot; 1944–8, Sylvia, widow of Douglas Fairbanks (who became Mrs Clark Gable the following year); 1951–7, Thérèse Husson; and in 1961, he married Lady Crane.

[4] Simon Elwes (1902–75), fashionable portrait painter. He married Gloria Rodd in 1926. Waugh called him 'the Pouncer'. Elwes thought this unfair – but he was also fond of saying that he could not paint a good portrait of a woman unless he had slept with her.

[5] Lady Juliet Duff (1881–1965), daughter of the Earl of Lonsdale. She was married to Sir Robin Duff between 1903 and his death in action in 1914; and to Major Keith Trevor, 1919–26. In the introduction to *Dear Animated Bust*, a collection of Maurice Baring's letters to Juliet Duff, Waugh's daughter Margaret FitzHerbert states that she was not very clever or beautiful 'though both Baring and Belloc thought her lovely. Her gift was that of sympathy. She was a good listener.'

[6] By J. E. Neale (1934).

[7] A thank-you letter, alluding to the insufferable Mr Collins in Jane Austen's *Pride and Prejudice*. After a long stay with the Bennets, he leaves with the words 'Depend upon it, you will speedily receive from me a letter of thanks for this, as for every mark of your regard during my stay in Hertfordshire.' (ch. XXI)

48

I took Lady Helen [Asquith] out but she has a head for liqueur like steel.
I met a foreign lady who said that Duff had a genius for doing imitations so she must be thinking of Sutro.[1]
I lectured to 350 women at Harrods stores goodness it was dull.
Love to all good farmers and buggers

Bo

Evelyn to Diana

St James's Club   [late July/early August 1935]
Piccadilly, W1

So it is all O.K. about Abyssinia and unless those mischiefous peace makers bugger it up I sail on 12th. God it is decent. The D. Mail is the one so it is all your doing.
My great friend P Balfour will be there too.[2]
Now I can go to Gerald's[3] to finish some work. Shall be in London 8th–12th. Any good bye?

Bo

The absorption of Ethiopia, or Abyssinia as it was more usually known in the 1930s, into the Italian Empire in Africa had been on Mussolini's agenda since 1925. It would link the two existing Italian colonies of Eritrea and Somalia; and Abyssinia's exploitation by over a million Italian emigrants would, it was hoped, solve Italy's economic problems. In 1932, Mussolini approved a plan to start the invasion of Abyssinia at the beginning of the 1935 rainy season; and in preparation, arms and men were poured into Somalia and Eritrea.
    By the summer of 1935 Mussolini's intentions were abundantly clear, both in Whitehall and Fleet Street. Waugh, who had been to Abyssinia to cover the coronation of Haile Selassie five years before, now wanted to return as a war correspondent – and thought himself amply qualified for the job. In his own words, 'anyone who had

---

[1] John Sutro (1903–85), British film producer, and a rich friend of Waugh's at Oxford: it was there that Sutro founded the Railway Club, whose annual dinner took place on a specially hired train. He was associated with Alexander Korda in London Film Productions, and produced 49th Parallel (with Laurence Olivier), The Seventh Veil and A Woman of No Importance.

[2] Patrick Balfour was sent to Abyssinia as special correspondent for the Evening Standard.

[3] Gerald Tyrwhitt Wilson (1883–1950), 14th Baron Berners. Author, painter, composer and eccentric, he had a travelling piano installed in his Rolls-Royce. He lived at Faringdon, Oxfordshire.

actually spent a few weeks in Abyssinia itself, and had read the dozen or so books which constitute the entire English bibliography of the subject, might claim to be an expert, and in this unfamiliar but not uncongenial disguise I secured employment with the only London newspaper which seemed to be taking a sane view of the subject.'

At this time, Waugh's opinions were succinctly expressed in the title of an article he wrote for the Evening Standard *in February 1935: 'Abyssinian Realities: We can Applaud Italy'. These feelings set him defiantly against most of his contemporaries (including Diana and Duff), as well as most of the national newspapers. The* Daily Mail, *however, was sympathetic to fascism and was taking what Waugh called 'a sane view'.*

In their biographies of Waugh, Christopher Sykes and Martin Stannard state that he owed his appointment as war correspondent for the Daily Mail *to his agent, A. D. Peters; and that Peters had a number of rejections from various newspaper editors before he could place his client. Yet Diana always believed that her words to Rothermere on Waugh's behalf had a lot to do with it, and this is indeed what Julia Stitch does for William Boot, the hero* malgré lui *of* Scoop. *Further confirmation comes in a letter of Waugh's to Diana in 1961, in which he asks, 'Do you remember this writing paper on which I used to write to you when you stitched me up as war correspondent'.*

During the first half of the year, Waugh had been seeing more and more of Laura Herbert. They had met again at Pixton, the Herbert family house in Somerset which lay within a few miles of Mells and Katharine Asquith. In early 1935, Waugh wrote to Mary Lygon: 'I have taken a great fancy to a young lady named Laura. What is she like? Well fair, very pretty, plays peggoty beautifully . . . She has rather a long thin nose and skin as thin as Bromo and she is very thin and might be dying of consumption to look at her . . . she is only 18 years old, virgin, Catholic, quiet and astute.' He was much in love with her by the time he left for Abyssinia, on 7 August.

Evelyn to Diana
[On board ship, heading for Djibouti; typed]   *[August 1935]*

Darling Diana Perhaps you will think this is a bill on account of the typewriting and not read it Sad but you see thr Daily mail have given me one and said I must learn to use it and soon it will be too hot in Red Sae. So must practice now. It is decent to be going . When I last wrote I was to go later but it was changed. Now I am near Crete and it is i warm and v few passengers all v dull no one pretty except a half caste gil no girl in the second class and I havent been able to find her since we sailed. One other English chap gouing to Abyssinia for thr Chronicle[1] He has had in-noculatins and injections and vaccinations &a gas mask and helmet £ medicine chest well he is a married man and I have told him so often that we are going to certain death that i have come to believe it toto . There is also a v common Frog photographer.

It is all sir garnet[2] at Pixton[3] on account of this lucky war.
as I see it three things may happre (a)Brilliant wop victory with death by gas of bo balfour and the poor News Chronicle chap. Then it is the soup for Eden & duff is the next prime MINISTER[4] (b)Wops run away triumphant blacks massacre bo etc. soup for Duce soup for Eurpoe soup for all except dead bo etc. (c) Wicked partition planned by 3 powers conference Outraged niggers massacre bo etc. great soup for League and Eden DUFF PM Of course the best thing would be great massacre of Balfour and Chronicle chap Bo escapes to tell tale Eden soup league soup Duff sir GARNET great success of bloodcurdler book great prestige hero of pix-ton. That may happen on account three never failing talismans gifts of dutch girl Katharine and M Herbert. It is bumbles for D MAIL to say it is quick &easy to type. T You never said if you read Campion £if you liked it was that just that you forgot or is a beastly bad book to tou

i hope you are having a lovely time with all you ur chums and jaggers. the secret of the art ofv typewriting is neverto try to use the little fingers only disaster lies that way. Have you read a book named Uncle SILas?[5]

Please give my v best love to katharine

X X X X X X X
Bo

---

[1] The journalist Stewart Emeny. The *News Chronicle* was very much opposed to Italy's colonial ambitions in Ethiopia, and in *Waugh in Abyssinia* (1936), Waugh wrote of Emeny: 'I did not know it was possible for a human being to identify himself so precisely with the interests of his employers.'

[2] 'All Sir Garnet', meaning everything is as it should be. An army phrase that came into use during the Egyptian campaign of 1882, under Sir Garnet Wolseley (1833–1913).

[3] Pixton Park, Dulverton, Somerset, Laura Herbert's family home, had been given to her father Aubrey Herbert by his father, the 4th Earl of Carnarvon. Waugh became a regular weekend visitor to Pixton from late 1934.

[4] Anthony Eden was Minister Without Portfolio for League of Nations Affairs at the time, and became Foreign Secretary in late December, following the resignation of Sir Samuel Hoare. Duff was then Financial Secretary to the Treasury.

[5] *Uncle Silas* by Sheridan Le Fanu, a haunting Victorian thriller published in 1864.

Evelyn to Diana

DEUTSCHES HAUS ADDIS ABABA   [13 September 1935]
[Typed]

darling Diana

well I have chucked the Mail it was no good they sent me offensive cables twice a day & i took umbrage & they wanted me to stay in Addis & I took despair. It is the most awful town in the world tin roofs constant rain bitter cold & colder shoulders on all sides forbidden the legation on account the book I wrote[1] suspected of being a spy on account of being slappers with the wops 74 journalists mostly american all lying like hell & my job to sit here contradicting the lies they write. then it is the altitude too which makes umbrage come easy so I shall be a free man in 2 weeks then off to Harar among decent mahomedans to wait for wop gases. iI got two scoops the first happened the same day as the Rickett concession[2] & I was away so all I got was abuse for not getting that. Sad because I was slappers with Rickett. The second happened on a saturday so the other journalists had 24 hours to catch up the telegraph clerks sell the news so I thought to be clever and sent it in Latin[3] but no one in the mail office knew that language so I got abuse for that. discouragig. Two days ago it was new year 1928. I got plastered with Egyptian first secretary and a Belgian brewer and an armenian whore & the brewer kept giving us tins of lobster. So yesterday i felt ill just like when we went to trent. I have got an abyssinian picture for J Julius. P Balfour has the depression worse than me because he is homesick Im not that yet. I say send us a letter care consulate Harar [in eastern Ethiopia] do it would be cheering. Have you read my life of E Campion? I suppose if this war is worlders i mustv come home to fight. How about this card

XXXXXXXXXXX X

Bo

---

[1] It was widely believed that Waugh had based the family of the British minister in *Black Mischief* on the family of the real-life minister, Sir Sidney Barton (1876–1946), who was Minister Plenipotentiary to Abyssinia 1929–37.

[2] Waugh's big scoop was that the French Consul in Jijiga had been thrown into prison for passing information to the Italians. However, this was small beer compared to the Rickett story. F. W. Rickett had negotiated a valuable oil concession between the Emperor and an Anglo-American firm. This caused grave embarrassment to the British Government, which denied all knowledge of the deal. (Martin Stannard, *Evelyn Waugh: The Early Years 1903–1939*, p. 402) The story broke on 30 August, and Waugh did not get back to Addis until four days later.

[3] The Italian minister, Count Vinci, appreciated the support of the *Daily Mail*. He told Waugh he would soon be withdrawing his staff. This must have been ordered by Rome; and Waugh realised that Mussolini was only waiting for the end of the rainy season to begin the invasion. This was the hot news in the Latin cable; but by the time that had been clarified, everybody knew.

Evelyn to Diana

[?Deutsches Haus, Addis Ababa;   *[September 1935]*
typed]

SO the daily mail sent a chap to Djibouti but the Abysssinians wont let him in as they feel just the same way I do about the 'Daily Mail' He is sitting there in great distress and a chap who came up 2 days ago says he is going bughouse & thinks he is a lepper. So now on account of my great honour I cant chuck the mail & i shall die in harness.[1] We had a great dinner at the palace & the lights went out five times & everyone had good taste & went on talking as if nothing had happened expect P Balfour who was so drunk he did not know it was dark and was laughing at a dirty joke A spaniard had made but all the Americans were horrified at his ill-manners. There are 83 journalists here now and it is too many. when we were drunk that night we locked the Times correspondent in his room & an Indian locksmith liberated him too late to catch a very important train. C M Gaskell[2] has gone away sad. i have got to hate the ethiopians more each day goodness they are lousy & i hope the organmen gas them to buggery, it is quite without romance or heroism to be here but it will make a funny novel. I say wish you would write me a letter sometimes to deutches haus addis ababait seems the railway wont be syksed untij Oct 20th. You would love the wop minister here he is named Vinci[3] prettier than grandi[4] & he rogers the english minister's daughter who married rival wop[5] so he tried to murder her, failed, shot himself, failed & now has gone home he was very nice too then Vinci had the servant of the other wop speared on account he alone knew the great truth re shooting & strangling but this servant slept the other way up & was only speared in the thigh so all those deaths left everyone still alive.

XXX
Bo

---

[1] According to Martin Stannard (*op. cit.*, p. 404), this is not exactly true. The reason that the *Daily Mail*'s replacement, W. F. Hartin, was stuck at Djibouti was that the Abyssinians would not allow him to proceed until Waugh had left the country. Waugh, however, decided to stay on, since he expected the fighting to begin at any moment.

[2] Charles Milnes-Gaskell. In a letter to Katharine Asquith of 5 September, Waugh wrote: '. . . another chum has turned up named Charles Milnes-Gaskell so now there are three of us who can enjoy it [the war]. Charles has no job here on account he is rich.' (*Letters*, p. 98)

[3] Although the Abyssinians blustered and threatened, they could never do Count Vinci any real harm without plunging their country into war. Vinci knew this, and enjoyed the dangerous thrill of provoking them to the limits of their patience.

[4] Count Dino Grandi, Italian Ambassador in London 1932–9, and one of Diana's most enthusiastic admirers.

[5] Sir Sidney Barton's daughter, Marion, was married to a member of the Italian Legation, Muzio Falconi. Falconi had attempted suicide in late August.

Evelyn to Diana

[postcard]   *[28 September 1935]*

I got a letter from you with some hair and I was very glad. So I am still with the *Mail*. Hand to plough.

It is very dull indeed here and now they say it will be three weeks before the bombardment.

Today there are great celebrations for the cessation of the rains. It is hailing.[1]

X X X X X X X
Bo

Evelyn to Diana

[no address, typed]   *[early October 1935]*

Darling Diana

so the war has begun[2] & all more cheerful except the americans who have been swaggering about since we came here armed to teeth & talking like E Hemingway tough guys lumber jacks hunting bear canoes rockies all that well these americans are scared blue now on account of they think to be blown up and W R Hearsts chaps[3] have bought a great mansion next door wop legation and have a lorry full of the sort of food americans eat ready with sleeping chauffeur . what is more one of them died yesterday of fever . He was a very dull chap & at the meetings of foreign press association he resigned on account of the great levity shown by me & my great friend balfour & Steer he is the times corespondent , when a french journalist who is a 5 to 2[4] complained he was called cochon francais by a nigger . Well this american went to maskal in a stove hat and tale coat & did he get wet yes sir so he is dead and we bought a wreath from the bosche legation garden and some of us have black ties and some not but all will be at the funeral. now it seems as though the wops will lose this war as i sagely said all along. Perhaps we shall go to the front but they dont like me these ETiopians so they think me a spy. Now all the wops are in prison in there legation & i have no friends left. how I wonder is miss laura Herbert. she is no writer well her art is the STAGE . I have bought a very lowspirited baboon & he masturbates all day we took him to the Peroquet

---

[1] The Abyssinians celebrate the Finding of the True Cross, and the end of the rainy season, with a great feast called Maskal.

[2] On 3 October the Italians bombed Adowa in the north. The great war drum was heard in Addis Ababa. By 7 October, the Italians had invaded from Eritrea and occupied Adowa and Adigrat.

[3] The star of Hearst's International News Service in Abyssinia was H. R. 'Cholly' Knickerbocker.

[4] Jew (Cockney rhyming slang).

that is our 43 [nightclub] last night and he pulled a whores hair and she put brandy on the wound on account the late king of greece died in similar fashion and this whore was greek but when I speak of whores you must not think I am leading a dissolute life quite the reverse except for being drunk a lot well that is the altitude just a few drops go straight to the nut. but it is a chaste life perhaps the altitude too & the great ugliness and illness of all women here it would not do to die in mortallers or yet to come back alive and marry miss herbert & give her a dose . such a nice man came as general organizer of lod lugards great ambulance. he said last time we met you gave me your hat i said i was drunk. chap. yes you gave me half a crown too. self. where was this. chap. at the bobbin i was cloak room attendant there. he knows all misses merrick[1] and michael lafone[2] & all my underworld chums and Raymond [de Trafford] & all my kenya chums such as gerry PRESton kikis husband now dead. It was a great pleasure to see this man he sang some scottish songs and then cried it made him so homesick then he cheered up a great deal and got a dead fish and put it in bed with balfour who was in alcoholic stupour. that same evening he put a table cloth as a flag from a pole and he stole the page boys hat from mon cine.[3] steer had moved to a house from hotel that night and was proud of that house so we locked him in and gave the key to madam georgitis who keeps mon cine. and this chap was 50 years old and had been a magistrate in Somaliland besides bobbin hatstand and also a farmer in kenya also a captain black watch what an interesting life. there is a comic count named du Berrier an american his plan is to bomb massawa but I have no sympathy with the killing of wops on behalf of niggers, Still he is amusing and it is nice sometimes to see ones who are not for the press. I do my work very badly all the others beat me on all news. that makes me depressed otherwise it is all sir garnet. it is partly laziness and partly incapacity but a lot is due to the great unpopularity of self and mail over which i have no control

XXXXXX
Bo

Evelyn to Diana

Harar [typed]   *26 October [1935]*

Darling Diana

   I got your letter. it said more pep in my messages more fantastic stories fewer place names etc. well you are quite right. But it is true that now and

---

[1] Mrs Meyrick, owner of the '43' club.

[2] Michael Lafone, like Waugh, was a regular customer of the '43'. Also a captain in the King's African Rifles.

[3] Mon Ciné was presumably the name of the local cinema.

then I send something with a point. then the d mail cut it out. They are a
drab lot to work with. There seems no chance of getting near the front so I
shall come home soon. anyway for Xmas. I look forward very much to
seeing you again and will not be ungrateful for some time for the good
friends god has given me.

Charles m gaskell has been expelled as a spy. Balfour my great friend
has gone to Aden so I am alone with a fat American. he is the author of
what price glory? also Big parade.[1] He is very afraid of bombs. He is often
drunk. it is something stronger than he.

So there is to be a General election. and me not there to help duggan.
well god knows i am not much help to anyone.

chiefly i am writing to show you my new writing paper i have had
made to plague the blacks. in case you do not know it i will tell you that
the lion is the L. of Judah.[2] C Russell said he heard people whose opinions
were good say they were in favour of E Campion. I was very pleased
thinking perhaps he meant D Cooper

all love
XXXXXX Bo

Evelyn to Diana

Addis Ababa [typed]   *12 November [1935]*

Darling Diana

I get all your letters. They havent syksed the railway yet and possibly
wont so please keep writing and tell me about the general election and
who is sleeping with whom and so on.

Things are a little better here and there is every chance of our being able
to move into camp this week within reasonable distance of the fighting.
The Mail now takes all its war news from a chap at Jibouti; he doesnt
speak French, has never set foot in Abyssinia or met any Abyssinians
except consular officials who refused him admission. He sits in his hotel
describing an entirely imaginary campaign - 18,000 abyssinians and
500,000 sheep killed by poison gas, a Bouer war lord invading Jubaland,
ton weight bombs raining down and destroying seven mosques in a place
he found on the map which in point of fact consists of one brackish well
and a dozen huts and so on. So i feel absolved of any obligation to take the
job seriously, particularly as he dates his despatches from places inside the
country. The heaviest fighting is among the journalists. The Times

[1] *The Big Parade*, a silent movie of 1925, was by Lawrence Stallings. *What Price Glory?*, a play of the
early 1920s, was by Lawrence Stallings and Maxwell Anderson.
[2] Ethiopian writing paper, reproduced on front endpaper.

correspondent a very gay South African dwarf - is never without a black eye. some say it is the altitude more than the bottle.

Last week a Frenchman and an American got leave to do an espionage flight over the Italian lines in a red cross plane. The other journalists took this badly but the Frenchman explained that the red cross had been the crest of his family since the time of the first crusade.

I gave my servants a fortnights wages in advance before leaving for Dessye[1] so the chauffeur is now in jug for shooting up a brothel.

The minister of Commerce has announced that from November 18th Abyssinia will take economic sanctions against Italy.

I have made friends with a very nice South African nigger who represents a worldwide society for the extermination of the white races. he has seven uniforms - honorary major in the Liberian army, colonel of the black guards of Harlem etc. all red plush and gold lace. The Emperor wont let him wear them. He says the Emperor is on his black list as not being a real negro. He has a thirty-six hour plan in that time all whites in South and East Africa will be chopped up. He is not sure if Nigeria is really loyal to him. His wife is an enchanting little Basuto first time out of the krall. She keeps letting him down by boasting that her grandfather met Queen Victoria.

all love
Bo

Evelyn to Diana

Addis Ababa   *5 December [1935]*
[typed]

Darling Diana

Well we are all getting recalled and I am very glad. I didnt realize how much I hated this job until I got the cable. Now I am deliriously happy. I suppose it is priggish to despise ones job but there it is. I felt ashamed all the time.

Now I am going to Bethlehem for Xmas and soon shall be on the steps of Gower Street. I have made a great number of resolutions first among them to be deeply loving to you and all my friends and not ungrateful any more. Then I am going to give up the snobbish attempt I have made for some years to be low-brow and to be just as fastidious as my nature

---

[1] Waugh organised the trip to Dessye, the Emperor's northern headquarters. On 13 November he set off in a lorry, with William (later Lord) Deedes of the *Morning Post* and Stewart Emeny of the *News Chronicle*. They were arrested a hundred miles from Addis Ababa by a native chief, and sent ignominiously back to the capital.

allows, to read books again and so on as I used before my 1928 debacle.[1]
Then to get a fixed abode. Then to be sober often and always two days
before doing anything with you. Remind me of these if you find me
falling.

all love and xxxxxxx

Bo

Evelyn to Diana

British Consulate   *[January 1936]*
Damascus
Syria

Darling Diana

So now the Pope says to come to Rome and perhaps he'll divorce me,
so that is the happy end of a very happy return journey. Jerusalem, Petra,
Amman, Bagdad, here.

I did a thing at Bagdad that only happens in nightmares and went to
stay in the wrong house. I met a woman in London whose name I didn't
hear and she lived, as I thought, in Bagdad, and was a diplomat's wife and
she said do come and stay with us. So when I get here I said who is a pretty
fair haired woman married to a diplomat in Bagdad and they said that's
easy we can tell you in one she is Tita Clark-Kerr. Well that sounded a
likely name, so I sent a telegram to say I was coming to stay and arrived to
find two totally strange people and my real hostess lives in Tehran.[2]
However after the first very grave shock it was O.K. and they laughed a
lot and I had quite a funny week-end. But my it was a shock and after a
sleepless all night journey across the desert in a charabanc full of Jews.

Back fairly soon full of love and respect

Bo

Grand about Duff in cabinet, though it's a shameful one.[3] Will he get me
into the Secret Service? seriously.

---

[1] A reference to his first marriage to Evelyn Gardner. They were married in 1928, and separated in
the summer of 1929, after She-Evelyn had fallen in love with John Heygate (1903–76).

[2] Waugh had been invited to stay by Peggy Mallett, wife of Victor (later Sir Victor) Mallett, who at
that time was Counsellor at the British Legation in Teheran. The Ambassador in Baghdad and his wife,
to whose residence Waugh had mistakenly invited himself, were Sir Archibald and Lady Clark-Kerr.

[3] Duff, who had been Financial Secretary to the Treasury, was appointed to Baldwin's Cabinet on 22
November 1935 as Secretary of State for War.

⟩⟩ *Waugh returned from the Holy Land via Rome, where he met up with Diana, and obtained an interview with Mussolini. He was impressed by the Duce, though his fling with fascism did not last long and he never felt any admiration for Hitler.*

Back in England, he shut himself away from all distractions to finish Waugh in Abyssinia. *'If the book bores its readers half as much as it bores me to write,' he wrote to Lady Acton, 'it will create a record in low sales . . .' (Stannard, op. cit., p. 481) This was perhaps why he was depressed and, as seems all too evident from this letter, frequently drunk.*

Evelyn to Diana

[Bridgewater Estate Office   *[Spring 1936]*
Ellesmere]

Darling Diana

Well I live in Ellesmere now. A cosy flat in a drab little town with good country round – a numer of lakes and miles of canal. It is named Bridgewater Estate Office, Ellesmere, Salop. P[eregrine] Brownlow lent it to me. A very unintellectual woman named Mrs Whitefield cooks for me and is my only company. I peg away with *The Times* X-word and a dull book about Abyssinia and every now and then fall into apoplectic seizures with rage at the correspondence columns of *The Times*. I come to London next week 5–7 to see L. Herbert – perhaps I shall see you too? Last Sat–Mon I went to stay with a young couple named Acton[1] near Bridgnorth where we had such difficulty with our luncheon Manchester–Brum. I thought they were neighbours on account it was the same county but the journey took 4 hours. I was sick Saturday night on account I drank too much. On Sunday we motored to Aberdovey to see a wop and I was nearly sick again. Are you eating again? Mrs Whitefield makes a very fair treacle tart. There was a man in the *Daily Express* was like you and believed in fasting and thought he would float to the top of Everest but it didn't come off and he is dead. Hope D. Cooper is having D. Shepherd unfrocked.[2] There was a man at Aberdovey where the wop works called

---

[1] Sir John Lyon-Dalberg-Acton (1907–89), 3rd Baron Acton, and his wife Daphne, daughter of the 4th Baron Rayleigh. They married in 1931, and were devout Catholics.

[2] On 23 March, the Dean and Chapter of Liverpool Cathedral had refused to say prayers for the Cabinet during Evensong, as a protest against British support for the French occupation of the Rhineland. Duff attacked their 'sloppy, irrational, nonsensical pacifism' and said: 'It was rank heresy to say that the army was anything but a noble profession . . . The attitude of some of these clerics . . . makes me feel some sympathy with Henry II, who in a moment of haste expressed an opinion which led to an unexpected vacancy at Canterbury.' It was not D. Shepherd, but Canon H. R. L. (Dick) Sheppard, who protested in a letter to *The Times* about a similar speech a month later.

Mr Mason he has crackers at luncheon every Sunday and embezzled the money of the slate quarry. Well he went to London for the first time and wanted to see Mme Tussauds so he asked the way of a lady in the street she took him there and they spent the afternoon together. 'And do you know who she was? – The Duchess of Rutland! I've written to her a lot since but she never answers' Which?

Hope J.J. is O.K.

XXXX
Bo

Evelyn to Diana

The Manor House   *[June 1936]*
Mells
Frome

Darling Diana

It is very very sad for me that we never meet. I wish I could come to Bognor but you see I have to get my beastly book re Abyssinia done by July 1st as I've promised to start work on the great Juliet–Bernstein play and then I probably go back to Abyssinia for August and then perhaps I shall be married in September. Please come to the wedding but perhaps it is early days to issue invitations as neither Pope nor L. Herbert have yet made up their minds.[1] It has been a very happy summer so far living in seclusion at Perry's office in Ellesmere and going away for occasional jaunts to see L. Herbert and loving her a lot and she being exquisitely unDutch. Goodness she is a decent girl here is a picture of her. I bought 48 for 2/6 and then I had them enlarged and put about the room – it makes Graham[2] very interested.

Katharine has lent me her cottage on account R. de Trafford said he would come and stay with me at Ellesmere. So I gave a dinner party in honour of M[ary] Herbert and she got a bit drunk and it was a success I think. It was a very kind thought to think of Dunn's[3] ball but no I must work and I had all last week with L. Herbert. Please don't think I don't try and see you a great deal. I ring up 2 or 3 times a day when in London but it never works.

So I lectured on Sunday to undergraduates but instead of undergradu-

---

[1] Waugh heard on 7 July 1936 that his first marriage had been annulled by the papal courts. He and Laura announced their engagement in January 1937.

[2] Alastair Graham (1904–82), diplomat, and later recluse in Wales. They were intimate friends at Oxford, and Waugh drew on his memories of Graham for the character of Sebastian Flyte in *Brideshead Revisited*.

[3] Philip Dunn (1905–76). Son of the 1st Bt., he married Lady Mary St Clair-Erskine in 1933. They were divorced in 1944, and were remarried in 1969, by which time he had succeeded as 2nd Bt.

ates it was Sir Ned Lutyens and Mr Algernon Cecil etc.[1] and my lecture was a great failure on account I dined first with R. Knox[2] and there was too little to drink but later there was heckling and I was jolly good so everyone went away thinking it had really been a success. Don't say anything about my going back to Abyssinia in August as it isn't fixed and I haven't mentioned it much to L.H. It is her 20th birthday on the 20th and I got her an expensive box thinking the Hawthornden Prize[3] was £200 but it is only £100. Not that the box cost 100 or nearly that still it was more expensive than if I had known if you see what I mean.

Then Maimie's brother is to be married next Tuesday[4] and she says I must come to that and I will stay in London at St James's till Fri. Saw ruptured [Conrad] Russell Saturday. Knox also ruptured seemed better recovery. Then on 24th I get presented with Hawthornden Prize. So perhaps in all these days there will be one when I shall see you.

Those exercises you taught me for the stomach are wrong I think. You ought never to throw it out. It stays out if you do – at least mine does.

There is the same picture of a flower in this room as I once gave you. The Night Blowing Cereus.

A book of short stories of mine[5] is to come out soon but don't read them as all except 2 are very common. The Abyssinian book is quite honourable and readable but no one will want to read about it by the time it comes out. I suppose it is always the Opera and the American courtiers[6] for you now. Saw Jackie Hance at Horse Show also Bartleet. Love and Loyalty

Bo & Wu

This was Waugh's first Christmas at Pixton. Although the engagement was not announced until January, he was there as Laura's fiancé, honour-bound to be amiable to his future in-laws. He felt ill and there was too much of what he called 'Family Fun' for his

---

[1] On 7 June Waugh addressed the Newman Society at Oxford. In an undated letter to Katharine Asquith (Letters, p. 106), he wrote: 'Had expected only pimply undergraduates, to horror saw (a) chums . . . (b) distinguished guests'. Among the latter were the architect Sir Edwin Lutyens (1869–1944), and the historian Algernon Cecil (1879–1953).

[2] Monsignor Ronald Knox (1888–1957). Scholar, convert to Roman Catholicism, and Catholic Chaplain to the University of Oxford 1926–39. Waugh admired him enormously and wrote his biography in 1959.

[3] In May 1936, Waugh heard that he had won the Hawthornden Prize for his biography of Edmund Campion. The Hawthornden is awarded for 'a work of imaginative literature by a British author under forty-one'.

[4] William Lygon (1903–79). Married Else Schiwe, widow of Direktor Dornonville de la Cour of Copenhagen on 16 June 1936. Succeeded his father as 8th Earl of Beauchamp in 1938.

[5] Mr Loveday's Little Outing and Other Sad Stories was published in early July.

[6] Perhaps a reference to the hangers-on of Mrs Simpson.

taste. But the discovery of Piers Court, near Stinchcombe in Gloucestershire, just before Christmas gave him and Laura much to think about.

Evelyn to Diana

Pixton Park   *[late December 1936]*
Dulverton

Darling Diana

How very nice of you to send me two embroidered handkerchiefs. Alas I have nothing for you except my love and that's cheap and shop soiled. Tell you what I'll send you the *Tablet* every week for a year. Would you like that?

Laura and I have found a house of startling beauty between Bath and Stroud, so that is where we shall live.

All love and Xmas greetings.

Bo

Evelyn to Diana

Easton Court Hotel   *[February/March 1937]*
Chagford

Darling Diana

I was delighted to get a letter from you as that is a real sign of love and lately I was getting scared that I'd lost your love in some way.

Well a lot has happened since the new reign began.[1] I have got engaged to L. Herbert and am to be married on April 15th. She has brought me a lovely house in Gloucestershire[2] and my head is spinning with plans for its decoration. In fact I don't think of much else. The main objection to the house is the lack of water, light and gas and all the chief rooms face due North. Also the snow gets in through holes in the roof.

I have to write a Cinema film and a novel before April 15th.[3] Also

---

[1] King George VI had succeeded King Edward VIII on the latter's abdication in December 1936.

[2] The house was in fact a wedding present from Laura's grandmother, Lady de Vesci.

[3] He hoped to complete them before the wedding (which took place on 17 April, not 15th). Alexander Korda had commissioned him to script 'a vulgar film about cabaret girls'. (*The Diaries of Evelyn Waugh*, ed. Michael Davie, 20 November 1936, p. 413.) It was called *Lovelies Over London*, and was never produced. The novel was *Scoop*. On 15 October 1936, his diary records 'made a very good start with the first page of a novel describing Diana's early morning'. (*Diaries*, p. 409) Despite his hopes of dashing it off, it was not published until May 1938.

see Mary [Herbert] two or three times a week, solicitors, architect, electrician and so on, so it is busy.

I find new depths of beauty and sweetness in L. Herbert daily. I want to show her more to you.

I pass through London on Monday. I suppose you wouldn't make a day Tuesday and see my house? Also Friday but I think I have to see M. Herbert. Supper with Laura and me Fri night any use?

All love
Bo Wu etc.

Evelyn and Laura were married on 17 April, and spent their honeymoon in Italy. They were back in England at the end of May, but the work to be done at Piers Court meant that they could not move in until August. Once installed, Waugh hoped to get on with Scoop – *but the house, the garden, their position as owners of one of the larger properties in the neighbourhood, and an incipient baby all created distractions.*

Evelyn to Diana

St James's Club   *[September/October 1937]*

Dearest Diana

It was lovely seeing you like old times and after you left Wales everything was jolly sad both on account of your not being there and of there being no wine to drink when Duff left.

So Laura and I drove 12540 miles without licence or mishap and yesterday we took our driving tests in Gloucester and both failed which is very inconvenient as we have to hire a man to sit with us on the box whenever we go shopping in Dursley so it is just as simple to come to London so I came today and bought some ironmongery and copal varnish and caustic soda etc.

So Laura is to have a baby and she is very well and I am very pleased about it and we are repapering the nurseries literally.

If there is really a chandelier in a shop somewhere for us could you please tell them to send it as the electrician is just off. We haven't really thanked you for it but we will – trust us.

Please come and visit us soon. It is frightfully uncomfortable but very beautiful. We followed your farmer [Conrad Russell] all over England and it was upsetting for him to see us 3rd time.

I envy you the *Enchantress*. We heard the grimmest stories of your adventures[1] from someone unlikely. Ldy Crewe or the Vicar of Stinchcombe. Now I must catch train back laden with shopping and with hair cut. V. rural.

All love
Bo Wu

You used not to be able to read my writing and now it is worse from lack of practice. Please write to me. What about Mrs Bloggs?[2]

Evelyn to Diana

Piers Court   *[?November 1937]*
Stinchcombe
Gloucestershire

Dearest Diana

So our Mr Ellwood came in and said gloomily, 'There's a box full of broken glass outside for you'. Well that is his way; actually only a few bits were broken and we were able to put together enough of the chandelier to see how beautiful it must have been and how clever and generous of you and Duff to find it and give it to us. If we can get it mended it will be a superb ornament, in fact the whole of our hall and staircase has been planned and painted round it. I am in lively correspondence with the shop and the railway and hope one day to get it fixed, when it will be a constant delight and pride.

But please don't wait till that distant time before coming to see us. We have one comfortable bed-room and bath. You would not suffer too much and there is another more austere room for Conrad or any boy friend you would care to bring.

We are well and very happy indeed and the beauty of the house waxes daily.

Dearest love
Evelyn

---

[1] HMS *Enchantress* was the Admiralty yacht, put at Duff's disposal when he became First Lord of the Admiralty in early June. The Coopers' first trip aboard the *Enchantress* took place in September, when they sailed from Holyhead and around Scotland to visit the Fleet at Invergordon. The weather was very bad for the time of year.

[2] Arthur 'Bloggs' Baldwin (1904–78), who in 1958 succeeded his brother as 3rd Earl Baldwin of Bewdley. Waugh knew him as 'Frisky', and they had been in competition for the affections of Teresa Jungman; but as neither of them pursued her with any success, they were more companions in disappointment. Baldwin married Elspeth Tomes of New York in 1936. His publications include *My Father: The True Story* (1956), and *A Flying Start*, a volume of autobiography, in 1967.

Evelyn to Diana

Pixton Park   *[December 1937]*
Dulverton

Dearest Diana

I was so very sorry to see the news of your mother's death.[1] I am afraid it must have been an anxious and sad Christmas for you. I remember constantly the lyrical days with her and you and *The Miracle*. You must be overwhelmed with letters, but I want you to know that Laura and I are having a mass said for your mother and that you have all our love and sympathy.

Evelyn

Diana to Evelyn

[90 Gower Street]   *[December 1937]*

Darling Bo. I love you. Thank you for your sympathy and thank Laura, and thank you for the mass – you knew I would be grateful for that. I should not be unhappy, should I? She had the loveliest of lives, almost unclouded – no war – nothing but, interest in a 100 crooks who she never recognised as such – beauty once health – love given, love returned for 80 odd years – utter selflessness – what more can one ask for a beloved?

When will your child[2] appear?

Let me see you soon

Love and love to L.

Diana

She, my mother I mean, never could resist you, could she?[3]

---

[1] Violet Lindsay, Duchess of Rutland. She died on 22 December, in her eighties. Married Henry Manners, Marquess of Granby, in 1882. He succeeded his father as 8th Duke in 1906, and died in 1925.

[2] Laura was then expecting their first child, Teresa, born 9 March 1938.

[3] Diana wrote in her autobiography: 'Evelyn was splendid with my mother, who came for the Edinburgh and Glasgow runs [of *The Miracle*]. She was very, very fond of him, and more fond when he had had a stiff whisky-and-soda. She approved only of the sober, yet never differentiated them from the tipsy.' (*The Light of Common Day*, p. 112)

Evelyn to Diana

Piers Court   *[May 1938]*

Dearest Diana

It would be lovely to see you here any time. Bring Mr Russell or Dr Kommer. The place is a desert – a disheartening year to start on a garden – but inside the chandelier excites universal respect.

We go for a jaunt in Buda Pest on May 21st for ten days. Why not come before?

You would not notice baby or dog they are kept away.

All love
Bo Wu

Reviewers all say delightful enchanting brilliant Mrs Stitch.[1] They don't know ½.

Evelyn to Diana

Piers Court   *[April 1939]*

Dearest Diana

Your letter excited me so that this is the third attempt at answering. Getting like Bloggs was. What has happened to Spencelaye[2] – R.A., knighthood, commission for World's Fair? I missed it.

We long to see you here. Will you bring Conrad and needlework? We have nothing to amuse you, but we do very much want to show you what we have done to the house. In my first two letters I wrote a lot on this subject, but it all boiled down to please come and please expect to be bored.

Where will you be in the last fortnight of July? We shut the house then, Laura and her daughter go to Pixton. I thought of a spree in the Polish corridor. Will you come? Or architectural tour of N. England. I should very much like to do something with you for as much of that fortnight as you can spare me.

I bought Rossetti's *Spirit of the Rainbow* from the Pines for £10. My word it is ugly.

I finished a book today. About Mexico. Like an interminable *Times*

[1] Mrs Algernon Stitch, an unmistakable portrait of Diana, made her first appearance in *Scoop*, published in May 1938. She later re-emerges in the *Sword of Honour* trilogy.

[2] Charles Spencelayh (1865–1958), a painter whose attention to detail earned him the name 'The Human Camera'. He was famous for his pictures of old men in cluttered interiors.

leader of 1880.¹ People will say well Waugh is done for; it is marriage and living in the country has done it. But I have a spiffing novel in mind and they must think again.

I have bought a plaster cast of Westmacott's *Distressed Motherhood* from St Paul's Cathedral. Hideous.

I buy a lot of ugly things. I find I like them best and they are very much cheaper.

J. Betjeman comes tonight.

The Yeomanry won't have me because I am too old. I wrote to Humbert Wolfe² who is in charge of special services and offered mine. He said people of my kind presented a problem for which a solution had not yet been found. So I think I shall spend the war here.

I wonder if this letter smells of turpentine. I have been cleaning mahogany all day.

All love
Bo Evelyn

Have you read *Nollykins and his Times*?³

Evelyn to Diana

Piers Court   *[June/July 1939]*

Dearest Diana

It is very exciting that the day I have looked forward to for so long is really fixed and that I shall see you here on Thursday. The sad thing is that Laura has arranged a system of 'staggered' holidays for the servants which prolong their inconvenience to the maximum. We shall not have a proper housemaid at the end of this week and though I am sure you would not mind having your underclothes unironed, we should mind bitterly. So will you and Conrad come for the day and return to Mells to sleep?

The way is through Bath on the London road, sharp left posted to Gloucester, past Dyrham and Doddington gates until you find a post left

¹ Evelyn and Laura Waugh were in Mexico for two months in the autumn of 1938. Expenses were paid by the Pearson family, whose coat of arms is supported on one side by a Mexican peon – appropriately enough, since the Pearsons held huge oil interests in Mexico. These had been appropriated by the socialist government of General Cardenas. The Pearsons knew they could rely on Waugh for a critical, right-wing view of the country. The result was *Robbery Under Law: the Mexican Object Lesson*, published at the end of June 1939.

² Humbert Wolfe (1886–1940). Prolific author and, at that time, Deputy Secretary to the Minister of Labour.

³ Joseph Nollekens (1737–1823), English sculptor. 'His character, mercilessly delineated by his pupil John Thomas Smith in his biography *Nollekens and his Times*, is that of a grasping man only outdone in miserliness by his wife.' (*A Dictionary of Art and Artists*, ed. P. and L. Murray, Penguin Books, 1959)

67

to Wotton-under-Edge. Go through lovely country through Alderly and Wotton-u-E. Up and through Wotton main street and straight ahead to Stinchcombe, about 4 miles. You will not see much of the village that way, but will find the road branches; left hairpin posted to Stinchcombe Village, right to Dursley. Take neither, the white gate and palings at the corner on the left is our house.

We look forward eagerly to the day.

Best love
Evelyn

Diana to Evelyn

34 Chapel Street　　　　　　　　　　　　　　　　　　　　*[July 1939]*
Belgrave Square, SW1

Darling Wu – a line to tell you both with much love how impressed I was by the excellencies of your house. The ½ wasn't told me – Its dignity and beauty of surrounding – in fact all its parts are terribly covetable – comfort too and splendidly appointed.

When I think of the 'room at the top of the stairs' [at Bognor] I blush. Your daughter[1] is fascinating – like a Reynolds and very deep-probing with her eyes. I was really glad to see you so happy and so serene.

There is only one thing I cannot understand – will you at your leisure sit down and write me an explanation why a subject which by its nature must be constantly present in all our minds must be taboo. It is the same with Katharine – it is different with Maurice [Baring]. It creates an abyss between friends – (i.e. you and me – and me and K) which yawns in my face and at my feet and makes me unnatural and miserable. I fought it hard at dinner and was rewarded by a very nasty snub.

D　'How strange that we should be ending dinner without speaking of the world situation.'
E　grunt.
D　'With us it is always referred to as being so much in one's mind.'
E　'So I've noticed. Did you get the long word down in the + word puzzle?'

I saw both butlers blanch at your tone. Why is it Bo? I realised within the first ½ hour that I must forgo 'listening in' to the Halifax[2] speech which Conrad and I had been anticipating with great interest – and that the

---

[1] The sixteen-month-old Teresa.

[2] Edward Frederick Lindley Wood, 3rd Viscount Halifax (1881–1959), became Foreign Secretary after Anthony Eden's resignation in February 1938.

Radio must remain in the car – that did not matter – but I felt shy to ask you to Bognor on a weekend with David and Rachal [*sic*] [Cecil] in July – fearful of a refusal and fearful of an acceptance that would victimise you – by its international conversations.

Do explain it and forgive me for voicing my discomforts and grievances. I was never one for bottling. Do please write.

Love
Diana

On 3 September 1939, the Prime Minister, Neville Chamberlain, announced the declaration of war on Germany. Waugh listened to the broadcast, thus breaking his resolve never to listen to news on the radio. Towards the end of the month Piers Court was let to a group of Dominican nuns, who used it as a girls' school. In October Laura, now pregnant for the second time, moved to Pixton, and Waugh returned to his old haunt at Chagford where he immersed himself in his most enigmatic (but never completed) novel – Work Suspended.

Waugh was among a large group of men who were too young to have fought in the First World War, and too old for regular service in the Second. He was profoundly depressed by his failure to find a job, but his hopes rose in late October. In a letter from Brendan Bracken, Winston Churchill's Parliamentary Private Secretary at the Admiralty, Waugh learned that Churchill was backing his application for a commission in the Marines.

On 3 November, Waugh wrote: 'The Marines have sent me a long questionnaire asking among other things if I am a chronic bedwetter. It seems probable that I am going to get a commission there.' The endorsement of Winston Churchill was evidently a powerful talisman. On 24 November Waugh joined the Marines, despite having failed his medical.

*A few days before he received his commission, on 17 November, Laura gave birth to their eldest son, Auberon. Waugh was delighted: as Christopher Sykes put it, 'His desire for a son and heir could not have been stronger if he had been a reigning prince.' (*Evelyn Waugh: A Biography, *p. 197)*

For Duff Cooper, the autumn of 1938 had not been so satisfactory. He had always violently opposed Neville Chamberlain's policy of appeasing Hitler, and had resigned his post as First Lord of the Admiralty in September. He had little to do in the following year, and was too old for active service when war broke out. Since the prospects of his finding a job at home remained bleak, he accepted a long-

standing invitation to do a lecture tour in America. He and Diana set off in November and returned in March 1940.

Evelyn to Diana

Pixton Park   *Xmas Eve [1939]*
Dulverton

Dearest Diana

What can a Netherland Plaza be? I suppose a relic of the great Duke of Alba.[1]

It was nice to be thought of. My heart bleeds for you and Duff. I can think of no more painful time to be among Americans and to be obliged by your duties to pay attention to their ghastly opinions. My poor friend Father d'Arcy is in precisely similar circumstances at Fordham University N.Y. Do get into touch with him when you want to hear a civilized voice; it would be a great kindness to him.

You ask for news of myself underlined. Well I am having a spot of leave at Pixton; it is a rough transition from the comfort and order of barracks but there was no alternative, as Laura is still bed-ridden. She had the baby quite happily (a son) and was making a good recovery when she contracted pleurisy and is only now beginning to sit up for an hour a day. Pixton is full of slum children; eight professional spinsters, ironically termed 'helpers' sit down to dinner with Mary. I eat on a tray in Laura's room. It is all highly disagreeable.

Stinkers [Piers Court, Stinchcombe] is a girls school but the convent have taken it for only six months and unless we get some decent raids early in the new year I am very much afraid that they will not take up their option of renewal.

I had an unsatisfactory first six weeks of war flirting with embusqués [shirkers from active service] but am now in a very fine force which Winston is raising in order to provide himself with material for his broadcasts. It is called the Marine Infantry Brigade. We are in training, at present, at Chatham in charming befogged Georgian barracks, excellent cellar, tolerable and tolerant company, wholly delightful routine except for P.T. which is a degrading and deleterious business. We are to be used for what are called 'combined operations' and given posthumous medals but at present there is no suitable coast for us so it is very cosy.

Everyone I see, but that is very few outside the Marines, is enjoying the

---

[1] A reference to the name of Diana's hotel in New York. Fernando Alvarez de Toledo, 3rd Duke of Alba, was sent to reduce the Netherlands by Philip II in 1567.

war top hole. The high brows have split – half have become U.S. citizens, the other half have grown beards and talk of surviving to salvage European culture. It is true about the beards and very curious – even Algernon Cecil has got one. Robert Byron[1] and Michael Rosse have started a thing called Federal Union which consists of all the old figures of my adolescence in the '20s – Elizabeth Ponsonby,[2] Harold Acton,[3] Brenda Dean Paul[4] etc. – they have meetings together and publish a very serious paper under the editorship of John Sutro. Lady Kinross (Mrs Patrick Balfour)[5] has a salon for spies. Alfred Duggan is a private in the London Irish (a force recruited entirely from the race gangs of Battersea). He was asked by the chaplain to become his batman under the supposition that it would be a slightly more civilized job. He said he was very sorry but he couldn't afford it; he paid out his entire wages as it was to his corporal to clean his uniform and couldn't undertake anything more. He had a spot of Christmas leave too and telegraphed his mother[6] to meet him for dinner at the Dorchester. She came up to London, got some jewels out of pawn, bought seats at a theatre determined to do Alfred proud and sat from 8 until midnight waiting for him. At 4.30 she was awoken – 'Will Lady Curzon come at once to the Slip-in bringing £4.12 and remove Mr Duggan'. Hubert is as fit as a flea, hair short, smart uniform, sitting on court martials and examining meat rations.

Eddie Grant is A.D.C. to André Maurois.[7]

I have had to leave ¼ of a novel I was working on [*Work Suspended*]. It was very good indeed.

By the time you are home I shall be at Deal I think.

Would you like to have Stinkers for the duration at cost price – i.e. rates taxes gardeners wages about £5 a week in all?

Best Love
Evelyn

[1] Robert Byron (1905–41). Byzantine historian and traveller, best remembered for his book *The Road to Oxiana*. He was drowned off the north coast of Scotland when his ship was torpedoed.

[2] The Hon. Elizabeth Ponsonby (1900–40). Only daughter of the 1st Baron Ponsonby of Shulbrede, she was the model for Agatha Runcible in *Vile Bodies*.

[3] Harold Acton (b. 1904), novelist, historian and poet. The dominant aesthete of his generation at Oxford, he deplored the Georgian poets and championed the works of T. S. Eliot, Gertrude Stein and the Sitwells. He was knighted in 1974.

[4] Brenda Dean Paul (1907–49), daughter of Sir Aubrey Dean Paul of Rodburgh, 5th Bt. She was a cocaine addict, and a flamboyant member of the Gargoyle Club.

[5] Angela Culme-Seymour, who married Patrick Balfour in 1938. They were divorced in 1942.

[6] Born Grace Hinds of New York, she married Alfred Duggan, a Catholic of Irish descent who had estates in Argentina. After his death in 1915 she moved to London with her sons, Hubert and Alfred, and in 1917 she married the 1st Marquess Curzon of Kedleston.

[7] André Maurois (1885–1967), biographer of Marcel Proust and George Sand among others. In the first year of the war he was French Observer attached to British Headquarters. Major Allister Edward Grant, who married Laura's sister Bridget in 1935, was in charge of foreign journalists during the war.

PART II

1940–49

VERY FEW LETTERS SURVIVE FROM THE WAR YEARS, WHEN Waugh is writing almost exclusively to Laura; and there are none to Diana during 1940 and 1944.

Waugh's new career as a soldier took him to a number of different training camps in England and Scotland in the course of 1940, and he formed part of the British expedition which accompanied General de Gaulle in his humiliating attempt to take Dakar in West Africa. In November he joined the new commando force under his old friend Colonel Robert Laycock, an outfit that also included Randolph Churchill and David Stirling, who was to become the founder of the SAS regiment.

With John Julius evacuated to safety in Canada and the US, Diana's life was divided between London, where Duff had been appointed Minister of Information in Churchill's new government, and her cottage near Bognor. Here, with the help of Conrad Russell, she started a smallholding, and they wrote to each other every few days. Not only was he generous with help and advice, but he was the only one of her friends with whom she could share the delights and despairs of farming.

Robert Laycock's unit, known as No. 8 Commando, was told it would be going abroad early in the New Year. Waugh's last meeting with Diana seems to have been far from pleasant, and the stiff, aggrieved letter that follows is perhaps the only one that passed between them during 1941. By the time Waugh returned to England in October, Diana and Duff had left for Singapore.

Evelyn to Diana

St James's Club   *[late January 1941]*

Dearest Diana

I wanted to come and say good bye and then I thought that there was no hope of finding you alone and that it was better to write. Because I love and esteem you and so I cannot leave it unanswered that I am alarmist, pessimist, etc.

Your complaints (a) that I prophesy evil (b) that I rejoice in distressing others by doing so (c) that I am unchristian to expect evil, had better shoot myself if I do not believe in the providence of God, etc. These errors rest on false premises of different sorts. The simplest first (b). It is a duty as well as a pleasure to oppose folly and prick bubbles. With different friends I am provoked to prick different bubbles. With you it is the Yankee-rotarian-Priestley love of a belief in 'Progress'. The fact that exposure causes pain does not give it its relish. It is the prevailing of truth.

(a) This is too big to discuss generally. It has to be taken piece-meal. For six years now I have seen everything moving to disaster and I still see most things (not all) going very badly indeed. But that is a question for detailed discussion.

Duff, of course, is a responsible man and can't say his mind. Thus when he says something palpably silly such as 'I have no reason to think Ireland is in danger of invasion', I know that is because it would be wrong of him, in the know, speculating in public. But not us.

(c) The saddest error of all and fundamental. It embraces nearly every kind of rotarian folly e.g. that we, because we are living in 1941 and for no other reason, have the right to expect greater beneficence from God than men and women living in, say, 741.

There is also the neurotic error of saying that because one expects disaster one should despair; or rather, you define despair as the recognition of the probability of disaster. Despair is a sin and has nothing to do with intellectual conclusions resulting from observation. I could explain all this so easily if I ever saw you not in a crowd. You say 'Why not commit suicide if you expect the world to deteriorate?' But I live in a world which seems to me to deteriorate daily before my eyes and I am not tempted to suicide. And when things get very much worse indeed I shall not commit suicide; why should I at the expectation of them? You reason like the Yankee woman who murdered her children so that they should not risk being killed by the enemy.

What your argument really amounts to is the worst pessimism and ingratitude to God, saying that you find life tolerable only on the assumption that it will get a great deal better.

I love you so much and you shock me so continually and I believe I often shock you and I know I am right and that you are obscenely wrong on every point in the realm of thought.

Evelyn

Oh dear this is so illegible.

In the summer of 1941, Churchill sent Duff Cooper – who had recently been appointed Chancellor of the Duchy of Lancaster – to the Far East, to report on the situation. He was sent too late: on 8 December the Japanese invaded Malaya, and by the time he and Diana got back to England Singapore had fallen. The bad news *continued in the New Year. In the Western Desert, General Rommel had advanced to Gazala, stripping the Allies of two-thirds of their territorial gains.*

By that time, Waugh had suffered a great disillusionment. During the Battle of Crete in May 1941, Robert Laycock's commandos had formed part of the rearguard, which covered the Allied retreat to Sphakia on the south coast. Waugh had arrived on the island believing that the spirit of the British Army could turn men into heroes. But on the road to Sphakia, he saw that army disintegrate into chaos. By the time he returned home in October, he felt there was little left to admire in his country, or his compatriots.

Evelyn to Diana

5 R.M: *[February 1942]*
Hawick
Roxburghshire

Dearest Diana

I am overjoyed that you are back in England. The week that sees you home safely is no black week for Bo. Not that there is any hope of ever seeing you. Perhaps in the future when Senator Cooper is representing the State of Free England in Washington and I am teaching English syntax to a convent school in Quebec, we may meet at Niagara. Meanwhile I live in the past. I spent three weeks in Edinburgh lately, at the Caledonian Hotel. It was too overcast for the camera obscurer.

Perhaps at Niagara we shall find ourselves in agreement. Till then I suppose we are better apart. It seems we must fall out now when we meet.

I am back as a marine doing company training in the snow and glad to have a routine. I find the mess, and the new young officers and the wireless daily more vexatious. Bob Laycock's commando spoiled me for regimental life. I wrote a short novel in a troopship with twenty or so funny pages.[1] I will send it to you.

Laura was with me in Edinburgh – piercingly sweet. I do not mind the debacle except for her.

All love
Evelyn

---

[1] *Put Out More Flags*, Chapman & Hall, 1942.

Evelyn to Diana

5 R.M.   *[late February/early March 1942]*
Hawick
Roxburghshire

Darling Diana

I long to hear it all – at Niagara or before. I shall be silent. There is nothing for me to tell. My life is lived staring at an iron roof, lying under a rug away from Hi Gang and Happydrome

Do you understand now why I would have no wireless or talk of Central Europe at Stinchcombe? I have to lie and keep a jaunty front to a hundred men. Duff [as a member of the War Cabinet] has to talk to a hundred million. Are there corners where old friends can still talk as though they were free? If there are, they must say in those corners that there is nothing left – not a bottle of wine nor a gallant death nor anything well made that is a pleasure to handle – and never will be again.

The English are a very base people. I did not know this, living as I did. Now I know them through and through and they disgust me.

Officers get leave rarely here. I may be in London in two months' time. If so I shall seek you sorrowing.

Don't tell Wade how despondent I am. She would rejoice.

Love
Bo Wu or what you will

Evelyn to Diana

White's   *[late July 1942]*

Dearest Diana

It was a splendid spread on Sunday night. I loved the visit – you and the pigs, and John Julius[1] and the milk pail, and Venetia[2] and Progress,[3] and Duff and the Stewardship of the Manor of the Savoy.[4] Do keep him up to the appointment. I will guarantee to produce a monograph on the Manor Rolls the moment I get out of the concentration camp. Duff has told my

---

[1] John Julius had returned to England in May, and was going to Eton in September.

[2] Venetia Stanley (1887–1948), daughter of the 4th Baron Stanley of Alderley. She is best known for being the confidante of H. H. Asquith when he was Prime Minister. In 1917 she married the Rt. Hon. Edwin Montagu (1879–1924).

[3] Perhaps Princess, Diana's cow.

[4] A reference to Duff being Chancellor of the Duchy of Lancaster. The Savoy Hotel stands on the site of the palace of the Savoy, owned by John of Gaunt, 2nd Duke of Lancaster (1340–99).

chiefs at Combined Operations that I am very 'Red', so I hope to be a colonel soon.[1]

I hope when you start the Aldwick[2] Institute of Public Opinion I shall be allowed to have my say.

All love
Evelyn

Evelyn to Diana

S[pecial] S[ervice] Brigade H.Q.   *[28 September 1942]*
Home Forces
[Ardrossan
Ayrshire]

Darling Diana

You asked for something encouraging. Here I think is a work which will confirm all your fondest hopes for the future. Moreover it has illustrations by John Martin.[3]

There is an original J. Martin in the Kilmeny Hotel, Ardrossan. A small painting for *Paradise Lost* – the finger of God pointing at Adam and Eve in Eden.

There is every hope of this headquarters moving south when I hope you will let me come to Bognor again. All S.S. Bde staff very much cumblestruck and proud to meet you.

If you think that the only bad thing about civil war is its violence and that there is nothing in English life worth defending against bad Englishmen, why do you not feel that about international war?

So we went with a general and an Air Vice Marshal to our depot in the Highlands to review the passing out batch and the local laird [Cameron of Lochiel] arrived draped in Tartan looking very fine and large and said <u>he</u> would take the parade instead as he represented the King in those parts <u>as</u> Lord Lieutenant.

---

[1] According to Waugh's diary, Duff accused Waugh of favouring another form of totalitarianism. See *Diaries*, late July 1942, p. 525: 'I went to Bognor for a night and fell out as usual with Duff. Since then he has been spreading it about that I am pro-Nazi. I told him I could see little difference between Hitler's new order and Virgil's idea of the Roman Empire.'

[2] Diana's cottage was just outside the village of Aldwick.

[3] John Martin (1789–1854), a painter of religious visions and brother of the 'unfortunate lunatic' who set fire to York Minster.

Mrs Fellowes's yacht[1] is built for love in the Mediterranean rather than Atlantic swell.

All love
Evelyn

Evelyn to Diana

White's   *[August 1943]*

Dearest Diana

Lovely at Bognor – the ideal weather for a heliophobe, splendid wine and cheese and Bultitude[2] – only one row with Duff but I thought three near rows with you and I thought perhaps I was not a success. I applaud and deplore your wartime life of bedmaking and pig starving and radio twiddling. I would have you thinking only of beauty and wit and being loved and not fretting about coupons and John Julius's clean shirt and Mr Kelly's[3] sloth. <u>You don't give us the time to treat you right.</u>

Did you see Herr Whatshisname's joke quoted in today's *Times*?

I shall not know until the day if I can come on Wednesday but want to in spite of having disappointed you yesterday and will telegraph or telephone when I know.

Give us time to treat you right. Not in and out of the room and on the telephone and waist deep in the dung heap and upstairs and downstairs and never in my lady's chamber.

My love to Katharine and if you see him before I do, to Duff.

And of course to you in swill buckets.

Bo

After these brief glimpses of life at Bognor, the letters cease until 1945 – by which time Waugh and Diana, and the rest of the world, had changed considerably.

---

[1] Marguerite (d. 1962), known as 'Daisy', daughter of the Duc de Decazes and widow of Prince Jean de Broglie. In 1919 she married Reginald Fellowes (1884–1953). She was very rich, being heiress to the Singer sewing-machine fortune, and was often described as the best-dressed woman in Europe. Waugh boarded her yacht, the *Sister Anne*, at Glasgow on 19 September, 'and had a very rough trip to the Depot . . . All were sick except Bob [Laycock].' (*Diaries*, 28 September 1942, p. 527)

[2] The chief character in F. Anstey's *Vice Versa*, which the Coopers were reading aloud in the evenings; see *Diaries*, p. 546: 'Friday [6 August] I went to Bognor for the weekend. The Duchess of Westminster was the only guest; Wade the only servant. Diana with grimy hands fretting about coupons and pig-swill. Fine wine, *Vice Versa* read aloud, gin rummy. Only one row with Duff, but continuous friction with Diana.'

[3] The gardener at Bognor.

To his great disappointment, Laycock did not include Waugh among the officers of 8 Commando he selected for operations in Italy. Waugh transferred to Bill Stirling's 2nd SAS regiment, and for a while North Africa looked like his next destination – but at the last moment the orders were rescinded.

In September 1943, he asked the War Office for indefinite leave in which to write a novel. The War Office was flabbergasted by the request; but since there was not a great deal of demand for his services, they gave their conditional consent. Brideshead Revisited was written between January and May 1945, with an interruption in February when the War Office called Waugh back to be ADC to two successive generals – an appointment so unsuccessful that he was soon allowed to return to his novel.

He corrected the proofs in Croatia, where – at the special request of Randolph Churchill – he had joined the 37th Military Mission to Yugoslavia in September 1944. It was yet another non-job which achieved nothing, yet he could not come back to England until March 1945.

After the failure of his mission to Singapore Duff served as Chancellor of the Duchy of Lancaster. Then, in October 1943, he was appointed British Representative to the French Committee of Liberation in Algiers. The job carried the rank of Ambassador, and the prospect of going on as such to Paris.

Diana was miserable at having to abandon her smallholding for North Africa; but once they were installed in a lovely villa with a tame gazelle in the garden, Algiers in its turn became the home she could not bear to leave.

In September 1944, in the wake of the liberation, Duff and Diana arrived at the British Embassy in Paris. This beautiful eighteenth-century house in the rue Saint-Honoré had once belonged to Pauline Borghese, Napoleon's youngest sister, and much of its furniture and plate were hers. Diana's restoration of the house revived the light-hearted, elegant spirit of Pauline as well; and the British Embassy became a focal point in the social life of post-war Paris.

Diana to Evelyn

British Embassy   *18 January [1945]*
Paris

Dearest Wu – Delighted – so delighted to get your book[1] to delight in. I've read it with care and tenderness and find it poetical. The chapter of your love are [sic] beautiful. I hope many will praise it sincerely as I do.

'I'm ill at these numbers'[2] don't know how to criticise or laud an author – embarrassed by the situation – so forgive but believe the sincerity of the few words I can drag to the surface.

We've had C. Conelly [sic] for three weeks in the house being fêted as tho' he were Voltaire returned. He blossomed beneath the warmth, and regretted his *Unquiet Grave*[3] – a book of so heavy a mealancholly that reading one half of its groan sent me to bed for a fortnight.

We are snow-bound – frozen stiff with cold – well loved (I think) by frogies who in their chaos of suspicion towards each other seem to give us a certain trust. Don't fail to lodge here if you come thro'. Write to me if you have time on your hands.

I have no idea where you are and what doing.

Love
Diana

Diana to Evelyn

British Embassy   *29 December 1945*
Paris

Dearest Evelyn – Bo – Mr Wu – all the dear names of different phases and memories – 'wooing Mr Wu'. You looked happy when I saw you, and I'm told by others that you are radiating goodwill – I'm delighted, and to receive a Christmas present from you endorses the rumours. Thank you darling Bo – It's a book after my own heart[4] – and just about what I

---

[1] *Brideshead Revisited: The Sacred and Profane Memories of Captain Charles Ryder*, Chapman & Hall, 1945.

[2] 'I am ill at these numbers: I have not art to reckon my groans' *Hamlet*, Act II, scene ii.

[3] Cyril Connolly (1903–74), author and critic, known to Waugh as 'Boots' – short for 'Smarty-boots', which was what Virginia Woolf called him. Connolly was editor and one of the founders of the literary magazine *Horizon*, which ran from 1939–50. He then became chief book critic for the *Sunday Times*. *The Unquiet Grave*, much of which is about French life and culture, was published in 1944.

[4] Waugh's diary for 21 December 1945: 'I sent off a dozen early Victorian albums and American *Brisheads* as presents.' (*Diaries*, p. 639)

can digest. Literature like *Yogi and the Komissar*[1] is too grown up for me.

Don't give me up –

Love
Diana

Evelyn to Diana

Dearest Diana

All loving wishes to you for the New Year, long service to the State or swift return to privacy poverty and the bosoms of your friends – whichever you prefer.

It was tantalizing to be within arms reach of you in London and not to come to grips. Yes, I am serenely happy, swathing myself in layers of middle age; the crisis over, the doctor's bag packed, I placidly doing cross-word puzzles at the bedside of the patient for whom all hope has been finally abandoned. After ten years' fretfulness I am quite reconciled to the decline of West.[2]

Piers Court is shabbier and more overgrown with weeds but much as you saw it in the days of the wireless. Poor Laura's life is one of drudgery, cooking, making beds, milking, feeding hens, all done vaguely but pertinaciously – so slowly that it takes all her waking hours. I have my two eldest children here, a boy and a girl; two girls languish at Pixton; a fifth leaps in the womb.[3] I abhor their company because I can only regard children as defective adults, hate their physical ineptitude, find their jokes flat and monotonous. Both are considered great wits by their contemporaries. The elder girl has a precocious taste for theology which promises well for a career as Abbess; the boy is mindless and obsessed with social success. I will put him into the Blues [the Royal Horse Guards] later; meanwhile he goes to boarding school at the end of the month with the keenest expectation of delight.

My faculties are unimpaired, except my memory which refuses to grasp any new face. *Brideshead* is having a disquieting success among the

---

[1] *The Yogi and the Commissar*, which came out that autumn, was a collection of Arthur Koestler's essays on Stalinism.

[2] Reconciled perhaps, but still preoccupied. On 27 December he wrote to Robin Campbell: 'It is entirely historical to believe that cultures decline and expire. I believe Western culture to be in rapid decay and that Picasso and Stein are glaring symptoms.' (*Letters*, p. 215)

[3] Evelyn and Laura Waugh had seven children in all: Teresa (b. 1938), Auberon (b. 1939), Mary (born and died December 1940), Margaret (1942–86), Harriet (b. 1944), James (b. 1946), and Septimus (b. 1950).

Yanks so I am writing a novel about the Empress Helena which will put the kybosh on that. Here is the first chapter. Do read it and tell me if you like it. It is primarily a portrait of Penelope Betjeman. Ronnie Knox proclaims it the best novel about third century Britain of the last six months. Constantius Chlorus of course is Fitzroy Maclean who is said to be about to marry the widow Phipps.[1]

Do you remember Mr Moray McLaren (Edinburgh, Scottish-nationalism, oysters)? He suffered from demoniac possession last year – genuinely – and has been exorcized and has written a most interesting account of the experience which I have just read in manuscript and hope to have published.

Is Bloggs still with you? Did you hear Freddy [Birkenhead?]'s superb account of staying at Lord Baldwin's on the night of Lady Baldwin's death?

I have found a great new pleasure in the works of Horace Round, the genealogist. Do you know his great chapter on Fox-Davies in the second volume of *Peerage and Pedigree*?

Since Maurice's death[2] I have tried to reread his novels. It's no good. I don't think he had a concrete imagination – only a wistful compassion for human failure which is lovable in a man but not enough to make a writer. When he had to take charge of the plot he was childish. For instance the final incidents in *The Coat Without Seam*; why in god's name take a relic for a signalling flag? Why tear it up for a bandage? There are plenty of people about – none of them naked. All his writing was less than himself. I think it ought always to be disappointing to meet an artist; if his work is not something otherwise invisible in him he can't have the real motive for work. Artists to be heard and not seen.

I hear from all sides that Horace Round was unendurable.

Nancy Mitford has written half a brilliant novel about her childhood; the adult half is no good but do read the beginning – *The Pursuit of Love*.[3]

But I am writing as though you were in Java instead of which you are in the centre of things – Picasso, Sartre, Connolly dining nightly no doubt – and I am in the jungle.

I was greatly moved to hear of Duff's decision to abandon his library – Is *David* also among the cenobites?[4]

I am too grown up for Koestler.

---

[1] Fitzroy Maclean (b. 1916), created 1st Bt 1957. In 1946 he married the Hon. Veronica Fraser, daughter of the 14th Baron Lovat and widow of Lieutenant Alan Phipps RN.

[2] Maurice Baring had been an invalid for many years, and died in 1945.

[3] Christopher Sykes wrote that Waugh was responsible for 'some of the more felicitous details' in Nancy Mitford's best-known novel.

[4] Duff made a beautiful library in the British Embassy. It was designed by the architect Georges Geoffroy, paid for by the Ministry of Works, and stocked by him with some of the finest books he had collected during his life. *David*, a fictionalised biography of the biblical king, was written between his appointments to Singapore and Algiers. Waugh did not think much of it.

I am very very grown up. All growing pains over. Only prostate ahead.

I have thought and thought about your statement 'everyone always thinks they have always been right' and find it balls.

Tomorrow I have to go to Bristol Pantomime.

Someone told me the airman who did ju-jitsu with his son, was dead. Your friends do pop off.

All my love
Bo

I like that name best.

Evelyn to Diana

Piers Court   *17 March [1946]*

Darling Diana

I am following in John Julius's footsteps to bait the fallen politicians at Nuremberg in the first week of April.[1]

Would you like me to stay a night with you in Paris on the way home – probably about the 5th or 6th? It would be a great treat for me to see you again.

If I would be welcome then, would you write and invite me so that I can show the officials evidence in applying for a visa?[2]

No news. A serene life of desultory writing. Enormous prosperity from America. A pig killed on Wednesday last so a full stomach for several days ahead. Ferocious altercations with the Rural District Council.[3] Immersed in the third century A.D. [*Helena*]. An occasional glance of ghoulish satisfaction at the *Times* newspaper.

All love
Evelyn

[1] In January 1946, John Julius had attended the Nuremberg trials as the guest of one of the English judges, Sir Norman (later Lord) Birkett (1883–1962).

[2] *Diaries*, 30 March 1946: 'Diana answered my letter of self-invitation: "Oh yes please Stitch." This was not very helpful as confirmation that I was asked as a guest of their Excellencies. I secured only a two-day transit visa.' (p. 645)

[3] *Diaries*, 18 March 1946: 'I have started legal action against the Dursley RDC for failure to supply water.' (p. 644)

Evelyn to Diana

Piers Court   *10 April 1946*

Darling Diana

Here is the last copy of the first edition of 'B.R.'[1] and the first of the latest. If you ever reread any of it, please read the last. There are several changes – I believe for the better.

The visit to Paris was a delight. The corporate mercies – from Duff's loan of pyjamas on the first night to your present of cheese on the last afternoon (Ly. Anglesey's[2] cheese duly delivered yesterday) through every stage of abundance and elegance – were tremendous. Still more the aesthetic joy of seeing you in your proper setting of luxury and splendour. Still more, and incomparably more, the happiness to know that you have kept a warm place for me in your heart all through my ice age. I love you.

An easy return journey, civil customs men, a morning at White's, then home to find everything bright and leafy, a pile of inane letters from America, children home for the holidays.

I hope Quennell has recovered from his palpitations.[3]

All love
Bo

Diana to Evelyn

British Embassy   *[April 1946]*
Paris

Darling Wu. You've been most loving and generous with the books. I am most truly and most lovingly grateful. Love envelops us. The visit [Waugh was in Paris from 3–8 April] was a great success I thought – funny too and made of elements rarely shaken up together. The character of the grouping has changed a lot – in place of the vigour of Amery[4] and

---

[1] Waugh's private edition of *Brideshead Revisited* numbered 50 copies, which he distributed among his friends in December 1944. The Chapman & Hall edition appeared in spring 1945.

[2] Marjorie, Marchioness of Anglesey (1883–1946). Diana's eldest sister, she married Charles, 6th Marquess of Anglesey, in 1912

[3] Peter Quennell (b. 1905), writer and one of Ann Fleming's closest friends. A published poet before he left Oxford, his books include biographies of Lord Byron, John Ruskin and Alexander Pope. Editor of *Cornhill Magazine* 1944–51, and *History Today* 1951–79. Waugh and Quennell were among Diana's guests at Chantilly on the weekend of 7–8 April, during which time Quennell suffered palpitations of the heart. Waugh claimed they were brought on by sexual excess.

[4] Leo Amery (1873–1955), statesman and journalist. Secretary of State for Dominion Affairs between the Wars, and Secretary of State for India in Churchill's wartime government. He was in Paris with his son Julian (b. 1919), who in 1945 had been Churchill's personal representative with Generalissimo Chiang kai-Shek. He later became Secretary of State for Air 1960–62, and Minister of Housing 1970–72.

Huxley[1] and Waugh we have languid Miss Clarissa Churchill[2] dressed charmingly as a Borgia – and the still more languid F.O. boys Jebb[3] and Sammy Hood.[4] Bevin[5] will pep it all up I hope.

I went to Lourdes and cured my dead leg – I saw where the Popes lived in Avignon and in Geneva where the giant stone reformers are lined up against a wall. I bought Foie gras in Foix and lunched on the frontiers of Spain looking across the Bidesoa at Fontarabia (a magic name!) The holiday was a success – God bless you and come back. Don't only like me in gilded cages.

love
D

Evelyn to Diana

Piers Court   *30 April [1946]*

Darling Diana

I thought it would rankle, that bit in my letter about 'your proper setting'. It was written with five grains of malice thinking of the Sunday trousers[6] (and the poor lame tart[7] looking like St Tropez 1930). But it was sincere too. It <u>was</u> an aesthetic treat to see you sumptuously housed for the first time. (I never liked the Admiralty bed.) Every year I like fewer things more and more intensely. I hate Freda-gadget chic and I hate proletarian sans-gene and the bakelite picnic set and I love all that is elaborate and gorgeous and your beauty in the yellow silk Borghese salon

---

[1] Julian (later Sir Julian) Huxley (1887–1975), biologist and writer. He was Secretary of the Zoological Society of London 1935–42, and at the time was Director-General of UNESCO 1946–8. Waugh baited him throughout the weekend with questions more properly addressed to keepers: 'What do you feed parrots on?' 'It must be awfully smelly looking after elephants' etc.

[2] Clarissa Churchill (b. 1920). Only daughter of Winston Churchill's brother, Major John Strange Spencer-Churchill. In 1952 she became the second wife of Anthony Eden, who was created Earl of Avon in 1961.

[3] Gladwyn Jebb (b. 1900), later 1st Baron Gladwyn. Deputy Foreign Secretary at the Council of Foreign Ministers, which was then convening in Paris. Ambassador to France 1954–60.

[4] Samuel, 6th Viscount Hood (1910–81). Private Secretary to Duff when Minister of Information, and now member of the UK delegation attending the Council of Foreign Ministers. He became Minister to Washington 1957–62.

[5] Ernest Bevin (1881–1951). The illegitimate son of a Somerset village midwife, he became a trades union leader, Labour MP, and statesman. He had been Minister of Labour and National Service in Churchill's wartime government, and was now Foreign Secretary in Attlee's post-war Labour Government. Bevin had a soft spot for Diana. He taught her old music-hall songs, and they would do the 'Lambeth Walk' down the Embassy corridors.

[6] *Diaries*, Sunday 8 April: 'A luncheon party, Diana in trousers after wrangle.' (p. 648)

[7] Louise de Vilmorin (1906–69), poet and novelist. She married Count Paul Palffy in 1937. Waugh, who usually refers to Louise by her married name, disliked her intensely and thought she had a sinister influence on Diana. But to those who fell under her spell, Louise was brilliant and enchanting. She was one of the few of Duff's mistresses whom Diana genuinely loved and admired.

was a unique joy and I was grateful for it and said so. Gilded cage my foot.

Jebb is a prig. I don't know Hood. Bevin is ingenuously adored in England by the conservatives. It is funny to find Frank Pakenham and Co. as fanatically anti-Russian as I was at the time of Stalingrad. Whitsun will show.[1]

I met Commander Campbell of the Brains Trust[2] at Chapman and Hall's board meeting. I said: 'I met your colleague Julian Huxley last week – a horrible fellow.' 'Yes, he's the only one of us who's had his head turned.'

My children are home for the holidays – merry, affectionate, sadly boring. My son (aged six) told me a detailed story of how an elder boy named Mock-Lavery had taken his ten shillings journey money, torn it in two, pocketed the pieces and given Bron the piece of wire inside saying that it was gold and that that was the valuable part. For a week I was in doubt whether I should take action in the matter. Then Laura discovered that the story was an entire lie.

Laura has a minute tractor and ploughed everything up to the windows. It looks horrible.

I lead an idyllic life rereading books like *South Wind* [by Norman Douglas], seeing no one, doing no work, except desultorily on *Helena*. Very funny book called *Prater Violet* by Isherwood.

I suppose Quennell died of his sexual excesses and Duff read the burial service over him in the Embassy grave yard.

Randolph is said to be on his way to Paris. That should be meaty enough for all.

Since I told Auberon Herbert I liked him his benefactions to me have quite ceased. Till then I got a little something every month.

I asked Bloggs to stay and got back a dismal catalogue of grievances against the socialist state. Persecution mania. I have written a funny essay advocating the establishment of 'native reserves' for those who can't enjoy the modern state, but no one will print it.

All love
Bo

---

[1] 1946 was the year when Stalin revealed that the Yalta agreements were worthless.

[2] *The Brains Trust*, a BBC radio quiz and discussion programme, was first broadcast on New Year's Day 1941. Its triumvirate panel consisted of Julian Huxley, then Secretary of the Zoological Society; Commander A. B. Campbell, a bluff and omniscient sea-dog; and Dr C. E. M. Joad, head of the Philosophy Department at Birkbeck College. Dr Joad attributed the extraordinary success of the programme to 'the accumulated fund of unexpended seriousness' in the listening public.

Evelyn to Diana

Piers Court   *2 June [1946]*

Darling Diana

That was a uniquely gruesome photograph.

I shan't be in London till July. I shall certainly study the Spencelayhs. Last year it seemed to me his invention was flagging a little though his great talents were unimpaired.

A direct consequence of the declaration of love for Auberon which you forced from me, was a visit from him last week. Very balmy.[1]

I go to Salamanca in a fortnight for a fortnight so please persuade Duff's communist chums to postpone their invasion.

I went to Oxford to speak at the Eights Week debate. The young men treated me as the incarnation of Michael Fane.[2] Most gratifying.

Stinchcombe Parish Council under my chairmanship has decided not to observe Victory day with any rejoicings.

I am much concerned about deciding what sort of hat I should wear in Spain as a delegate to an international Catholic congress. If I were taller it would be so easy – the boater. Perhaps something wide, black and clerical.

Father d'Arcy has written a very important book on Love. Heavy going in parts, full of detailed criticisms of authors I have never heard of, but a definitive treatise on the subject.

Yesterday Laura announced to me that a stone vase had fallen from a pillar on the head of one of my workmen. 'Oh dear is it badly broken?' 'It's bleeding profusely.' 'No no I mean the vase.' This came out quite instinctively. How to reconcile this indifference to human beings with the obligations of Charity. That is my problem. But I am sure that Dickensian geniality is as far from Charity as my indifference.

Extract from American letter to *Life* about me: 'It is unfortunate that *Life* should so glamorize an antediluvian relic of the fascist mentality'. Raimund[3] has a woman named Reeves[4] whom he sets on to write like that.

---

[1] Although his eccentricities did not endear him to his brother-in-law, Auberon Herbert was a charming, generous, and impulsive man. He was declared medically unfit by every major Allied army he attempted to join at the outbreak of war, but was eventually accepted by the Poles. From then on, the Poles had his undying loyalty. His London house was a haven for many Poles, and later Ukrainians, trying to find a place for themselves in post-war Europe, and Auberon campaigned vigorously on their behalf. He used to hold his cigarette in his fist, like a child with an ice-cream cone.

[2] A character in Compton Mackenzie's novel *Sinister Street* (published in 2 vols., 1913–14).

[3] Raimund von Hofmannsthal (d. 1974), son of the poet and librettist Hugo von Hofmannsthal. In 1939 he married Diana's niece, Lady Elizabeth Paget, and for much of his life he worked for the Time-Life Corporation.

[4] Mrs Reeve of *Life* magazine had written to Waugh in January, telling him that she was planning 'a photographic feature dramatizing character and scenes from your novels'. Waugh's reply (see *Letters*, p. 221) was brief and scathing.

Have you read R. Knox *God and the Atom*? Not at all abstruse and very comforting.

Complete silence from Mells. My boy is at school 2 miles away and Katharine has not once been to see him. Helen comes on tour of schools to within a mile of Stinchcombe and never calls. Very odd.

Candidates for the Foreign Office are now psychoanalysed by A.T.S. for three days at Stoke d'Abernon. It is the only way they can stop public school boys coming out top of the entrance exam.

Did you notice Bill Deakin[1] who came to luncheon with you some time ago? A very clever, heroic man. Roumanian wife.

What a dull letter. I am sorry. Any chance of seeing you in London in July?

E

Evelyn to Diana

White's [mid June 1946]

Darling Diana
    The Spencelayhs
    Ed [Stanley of Alderley] and I went to examine them. All are sold or in our after luncheon mood we would have celebrated the great inflation by buying you one. All three exquisite. One just junk called *Grandfather's Treasures*. The other two of the old man who features so often in his later work, with the familiar red bandana handkerchief. One *The Passing of Time* with a photograph album, grandfather clock in background, apples ripening on top of door-case. The masterpiece of nomenclature and symbolism is the old man seated with hands folded on calf bound Bible, look of earnest faith in his eyes, an oleograph of Christ behind his head, AN EMPTY BIRD CAGE. The title *Not Alone*. I would dearly have liked to have that.

Just off to Salamanca.

Love
E

---

[1] F. W. (later Sir William) Deakin (b. 1913). Before 1939 he was a tutor in Modern History at Wadham College, Oxford, and Churchill's research assistant. He joined SOE, and led the first British Military Mission to Tito in May 1943. Between 1945–6 he was First Secretary at the British Embassy in Belgrade. In 1943 he married Livia Nasta of Bucharest.

Evelyn to Diana

Piers Court   *13 December [1946]*

Darling Diana

Here is a dingy little rechauffé which I beg you to accept with my love. Part of it is already yours as I commemorate in the dedication.[1]

Over a year ago I ordered a dozen special copies on hand-made paper which I hoped would be ready for Christmas, but they are not. So please regard this as a book-token, to be redeemed later, not as a book.

I am just back from house-hunting in Ireland where Laura and I propose shortly to settle. A grave decision. We had fixed on a grim and haunted castle [Gormanston] on a desolate stretch of Meath coast and all but bought it when Mr Butlin[2] bought a property a mile away to set up camp. Perhaps you would have relished this souvenir of Bognor but not me so at the last moment I cancelled the purchase. However it is only a matter of months before I shake off the dust of England. I have to go to U.S.A. in the New Year. Then I shall start an intensive quest for castles.

Rats leaving sinkers: birds of delicate plumage migrating to a more genial climate: could it have been the food, sir?[3] What you will.

But Ireland is in easy reach of France without touching the accursed soil, so perhaps we will meet again one day.

I hear strange rumours that Duff is sending his son as a hostage to Stalin's court[4] but do not believe them. I saw him (the boy) at Eton, where, at his invitation, I went to preach. A master told me: 'Guinness[5] has turned the corner.'

At the castle I nearly bought, I said to a man working on the estate: 'It's sad to think of this place changing hands after so many centuries.' He said: 'Ach, His Lordship never came here but to kill somebody.'

I dread U.S.A. and am going simply to give Laura a treat. She has not been away since 1938. We go as the guests of the Californian firm Metro Golwyn [*sic*] & Mayers.[6]

---

[1] *When the Going was Good*, a collection of excerpts from his travel writings (1946). It was dedicated to the original dedicatees: Bryan Moyne, Diana Mosley, Diana Cooper, Perry and Kitty Brownlow, and the memory of Hazel Lavery.

[2] Billy (later Sir William) Butlin (1899–1980). He introduced the dodgems to British fairgrounds in 1928; the first of his famous Butlin's holiday camps was set up in 1936.

[3] Serious suggestion made by David Ormsby-Gore (later Lord Harlech) as a boy at Eton, during an inquiry into the reasons for the suicide of another boy in the same house.

[4] Diana was trying (unsuccessfully) to arrange for John Julius, who was learning Russian, to go and stay in Moscow with a Russian family.

[5] Jonathan Guinness (b. 1930), son of the 2nd Baron Moyne by his first wife Diana (now Lady Mosley).

[6] Metro-Goldwyn-Mayer wanted to discuss the possibility of filming *Brideshead Revisited*.

Christopher Sykes has written a lot of balls about the late Robert Byron but brilliantly about his own great-uncle.[1]

Love
Bo

Diana to Evelyn

British Embassy   [December 1946]
Paris

Darling Bo. I am delighted with your book, and rejoice in being part-dedicatee. It rereads well – my part I was giggling over thro' last night.[2] Waugh is much in Vogue at the Embassy – *Decline and Fall* has been grabbed from John Julius' hand by many other hands. Introduction of Mrs Stitch [in *Scoop*] was read aloud, and considered a 'frappant' likeness. Thank you very much dear Mr Wu – you write a great deal better than Mr Conelly [*sic*] – a phrase in *Horizon* (from his pen) struck me just now – he writes on the subject of an artist requiring £5 a day – 'if' he says 'he is prepared to die young of syphilis for the sake of an adjective he can <u>make do on under</u>' (sic) ça tombe très mal. Incidentally if the man of letters, fond of the bottle and leisure starts with £1600 a year his output will be meagre – Ld Byron disproved this supposition – and may be the meagerer the better. Take Vermeer. Cyrell's an ass.

I'm sorry about Ireland because I shall see even less of you – and Laura will be desolated – you'll get cream and meat and service and wit and a stab in the back when you least can stand it – except for the perpetual rain (see Ireland thro' tears) it is an amusing place. What will happen to Stinkers – shall I buy? or long lease it from you?

You have had a good year – all my wishes that the next shall not fall short. I've had a bad one, but have no real right to think it. Sister Marjorie's illness, less her death[3] – nervous tension – perpetual fatigue due to uncongenial work.

I'll be in London week of 19th to 26th – I shall hope you are too.

Diana

[1] The essays on Robert Byron and Sykes's great-uncle, also called Christopher Sykes, appear in *Four Studies in Loyalty*, published earlier that year.
[2] The excerpt from *Ninety-Two Days*, dedicated to her.
[3] The Marchioness of Anglesey died on 3 November 1946.

Evelyn to Diana

Hospital of SS John & Elizabeth   *10 January 1947*
NW8

Darling Diana

It was delightful to get a letter from you. It reached me in hospital where I have spent the last fortnight in great pain and shame[1] and where I shall spend another week. I sail for U.S.A. on 25th and will certainly be about London sometime during the preceding week having thumb-prints taken – literally – by the American consul. So I hope very much to see you. I will telephone to the Dorchester Hotel.

As you say it has been a prosperous year for me – another son,[2] considerable wealth and the prospect of more, good health except for the self inflicted wound from which I now suffer, the resolution no longer bitter now it is firmly taken, of adjuring [*sic*] the realm, the beginning to enjoy Henry James – countless blessings. I grieve it has not been so for you. Marjorie's death of course I realized would be deeply sad but I did hope you had found a manner of life you relished. The brief glimpse I had of you in your glory seemed to confirm this; but perhaps that glimpse was not of your complete life. There was absent a powerful influence making for ill, maybe. God guard you from all evil spirits.

Abjuring the realm is a big thing. The only people I like are English people and all my roots go deep in British soil. I am not leaving for convenience. In fact Ireland is inconvenient in many ways. They suffer from most of the contemporary famines, all their skilled labour is seduced to England for high wages and infected with English theories, there are no servants except clods but fortunately my upper servants want to emigrate with me, I shall have to pay double American tax which more or less equalizes the difference in surtax – in fact it is not convenient. But it is beautiful and England manifests its ugliness of mind daily more and more, and it is Christian. You know how the French called the army of occupation 'the grey lice'. Grey lice are swarming all over England. They will get to Ireland in time I've no doubt but I hope for ten years' respite there to write two or three more books.

Yes it is all balls when Cyril Connolly preaches about the economic status of the writer. He is wholly absurd in his serious moments which become more and more frequent. I think he sees himself as a sort of Public Relations Officer for Literature, trying to coax likely young chaps into the industry and then feeling betrayed when the conditions he thinks necessary are not forthcoming. I am told he is now at work in America telling the Yanks of his sufferings. He is a droll old sponge at his best and worth six of Quennell.

[1] Although not strictly necessary, Waugh had decided to undergo an operation for piles.
[2] The Waughs' sixth child, James.

I spent Christmas studying *Diary of a Nobody* and comparing it with the original serialized version in *Punch* with some very interesting discoveries resulting.

This letter will be hard to read. I have not got full control of the pen yet.

Jolly sad if Duff's Jewish friends whip Trim.[1] If it happened to me I should change my name and go to Australia.

I have written what I think rather a funny short story about my trip to Spain last summer.[2] I will send it to you.

Never since the disastrous reconciliation with Auberon have I had a gift from him. Does he frequent your house still? I see no one so hear no news of you.

God guard you from evil spirits.

Bo

Evelyn to Diana

Hospital of SS John & Elizabeth   *12 January 1947*

Darling Diana,

I forgot to answer your question about Stinkers. Of course it would be lovely to think of you there but I don't believe it would really suit you. It is tiny – 10 bed, dressing <u>and</u> servants' rooms, 4 baths, no cottage, 50 acres, 3 new cow stalls, pig-stye. Garden in poor state except for kitchen garden, lawns and tennis court <u>very</u> poor. Some fine trees and a fine view. I have put it in the hands of Knight Frank & Rutley who advise me to ask £15,000 for it which is 3 times what it was worth in 1939. It has one fine room – the library. All modern conveniences main water, light, central heating etc. But I don't see you and Duff happy there. It is not a gentleman's sporting estate. It is the sort of house where 3 elderly sisters with 3000 a year between them ought to live modestly. There are no neighbours you would enjoy within 20 miles, as far as I know. Building developments are threatened from Dursley, Cam, Bristol. It would suit a Bristol business man. It is definitely suburban and not even a suburb of London. It takes three hours and ½ door to door by train and car to White's. There is good hunting but I don't think John Julius hunts does he? No one has any pheasants. I am leaving servants there while I am in U.S.A. who will show you over if you think it worth reviving memories of your visit but I do not believe it is your house. I found returning to it with many sentimental tremors that my love for it was quite dead, as so many soldiers found about their wives but not me thank God. Perhaps all

---

[1] From 1942–8, the Earl of Oxford and Asquith was Assistant District Commissioner in Palestine. Terrorist attacks were common at the time, and there had been a number of kidnappings.

[2] *Scott-King's Modern Europe*, published that year by Chapman & Hall.

my ex-service resentment got concentrated on the house unjustly. It is certainly very pretty architecturally.

I don't think I explained my need to go abroad or that I can. You shall remember that I was very patriotic though my patriotism took a different form from yours and Duff's, right up to 1942. Then I realized that there were two historically necessary wars going on – Russia v. Germany, U.S.A. v. Japan and that England had no part in either of them – or France who realized it too. I shall come back for the 3rd World War, aged 52, but quite capable of being administrative officer to the next commandos. Meanwhile I have my work to do and a family to bring up and England is no place for that. Most typical Englishmen have lived most of their active lives abroad.

You will see from all this that I have not got an absolutely clear conscience about it. But the alternative is to become a peevish White's semi-alcoholic full of *schadenfreude* (is that how it is spelled?) and quite idle.

All love
Bo

Evelyn to Diana

The Savoy Plaza   *[1–3 February 1947]*
New York[1]

Dearest Diana

So I came to see these buildings you told me of and they [are] absolutely negligible in everything except bulk. I will write at great length on the subject when I have seen more. At first look I should say that they bear the same sort of relation to architecture as distempering a ceiling does to painting. They are nothing nothing nothing at their best. At their worst, that is to say when they attempt any kind of ornament they are actively wicked. Compare them with the kind of things you have at your doorstep – Horseguards Parade, Banqueting Hall, Martin in Fields, Westminster Abbey – or what I have within a five mile radius of Stinkers. Think of the infinity of aesthetic problems which a real architect has to solve every yard – and then of these great booby boxes. Interiors all vile. Some brand new exteriors just tolerable like exhibition ground stuff.

I thought I should not like America having met Lady Cunard, S[exy] Beaton, and such but real Americans are much more barbarous. It is the most damned awful country. Filthy food and habits.

Bo

[1] So says the writing paper, though the Waughs seem to have been staying at the Waldorf Astoria.

Evelyn to Diana

Piers Court   *10 May [1947]*

Dearest Diana

I have just returned from Ireland to hear the news of Conrad's death.[1] I am afraid it will be a bitter loss to you and you cannot share Katharine's consolation that in his last lucid period he was received into the Church. I presume she has told you all about it and how he said 'I hope what I have done will give you pleasure but you must not suppose that I did it for that reason.' He is being deeply mourned everywhere – a unique man. Death seems to knock one of the props from under you every year.

I saw Iris several times in California – alive but sickly and cranky, living in a peasant hut in the hills with a goat and a giant[2] and a grandchild and two new motor-cars, teaching yokels to act Macbeth, like a Women's Institute but organized, without success, for profit. Her boy Ivan is a common brute but amusing. Ledebur very beautiful. Iris goes weekly to a magician. She is almost bald, so the magician cannot be very powerful. She took me to supper with Charlie Chaplin and we saw his new film [*Monsieur Verdoux*] which is full of brilliant acting. Last week in Ireland I met an English girl of 16, smart, on the spot, rich. She had never seen a Chaplin film in her life. That made one think.

Three Spencelayhs at the Academy – up to standard but not remarkable. The best, *The Empty Chair* – not Dickens's. *The Bread Ration*, an elderly artisan looking quizzically at his loaf, 'Give us this day our daily bread' on the chimney piece. Rather a poor *The Telegram*. Impossible to tell whether it is good or bad news – one assumes bad on general grounds, but the face is downcast and the line of moustache hides the line of the mouth. It could hardly be a son killed in the war. It might be football-pool success. He has changed his address from Manchester and now lives in a village in Northamptonshire – St Mildred, Bozeat, Wellingborough.

I have been twice in Ireland. Just returned from seeing three houses a day for ten days. The privations there are as acute as in England. The choice is now narrowed to a medieval castle in Tipperary, exquisite, slummy, stinking, gorge with waterfalls, oakwoods, altogether beautiful and impractical and a prosaic Early-Victorian seat in Carlow, spacious, collegiate flat pastures and the Fitzwilliams next door. This house is not yet sold. Do you still think of it? I'll take 12,000. But I don't believe you would really be happy here.

I got obsessed by morticians like so many other visitors to U.S.A. and am starting on a short novel about them.[3] I met and made something very

---

[1] Conrad Russell died on 27 April.

[2] The Austrian Count Friedrich von Ledebur. He and Iris Tree had a son, Christian (known as 'Boon') in 1928. They were married in 1934.

[3] *The Loved One* (1948).

like friends with Mr Howells of Forest Lawn who gives the 'personality smile' to the embalmed corpse.

Trim is due back to marry a queer girl who looks up at you so that you always see white below the iris which I suppose fascinates him.[1] He will wear Lord Acton's (2nd Baron, not historian) frock coat and grey top hat. I think he will look absurd.

I was very much distressed to hear Duff had been so ill.[2]

It is no good being anything but a saint and we can all be saints. That is my new plan anyway.

Love from
Evelyn

Evelyn to Diana

Piers Court   *25 June [1947]*

Darling Diana

It was a joy to get your post-card. I have tried to persuade myself that your neglect was due to indifference not to dislike but you know what persecution mania is. I thought perhaps some of your foreign friends got at the post bag and destroyed your letters before you saw them. That was a great feature of fashionable intercourse in your mother's day I believe. Then I thought of a beautiful play called I forget what about St George and some children and they went to a lotus eating dragon kingdom where a captive midshipman gave the dragon his letters from home unread.[3] Did you see it ever? Well I thought perhaps Mme Palfi [Louise de Vilmorin] exacted that tribute from you.

Of course I long to see you. I am never in London. I would travel to Isfahan to see you but not to the Dorchester Hotel unless I could be sure Lady Jones[4] would be absent. Could you not come here? It is so easy now by train and really quite comfortable by non-official standards. I even have the wireless now. I bought one on Monday on the advice of Sir Max Beerbohm[5] and have listened attentively for two days and been greatly

---

[1] On 28 August Lord Oxford married Anne, only daughter of Sir Michael Palairet. Sir Michael had recently retired as Assistant Under-Secretary of State, Foreign Office.

[2] On 8 April, Duff had a violent seizure which was followed by five days of high fever. Over the following week he was injected with over a million units of penicillin. It was the beginning of the seven years' ill health which ended with his death.

[3] *Where the Rainbow Ends* by Clifford Mills and John Ramsay, with music by Roger Quilter.

[4] Enid Bagnold (1889–1981), author of *National Velvet* and *The Chalk Garden*. In 1920 she married Sir Roderick Jones, who became Chairman of Reuters news agency. She and Diana met during the war, when they used to take the produce of their smallholdings to market in Barnham, Sussex. Diana referred to her for years as 'my new friend'.

[5] Sir Max Beerbohm (1872–1956), essayist, caricaturist and author of *Zuleika Dobson*. Waugh described him as 'an idol of my adolescence to whom every year deepened my devotion'.

confirmed in my resolution to emigrate. I will tell you an interesting thing. Do you remember I told you apropos of J[ulian] Huxley that our public men have their accents chosen in Moscow. Well J. B. Priestley[1] was talking in this wireless. When I first met him he was a Cambridge intellectual protégé of Hugh Walpole[2] and spoke like that. Then in the war he spoke like a Lancashire comedian – 'bah goom lad'. Now he is back where he started as a Cambridge intellectual. And another thing. I stayed in a house with B. Bracken[3] lately. Well, you remember he had a deep Stornoway House[4] accent once. Now he has a plaintive cockney whine.

I go to Ireland a lot and am negotiating now for a house in County Carlow – quite unromantic, a machine for living in, 1845 baronial tudor, granite, yews. A pretty name – Lisnavagh with the accent on the last syllable. The privations in Ireland are as bad as in England.

Liz[5] was put up to public auction and knocked down to Laycock for £40.

I am slowly writing a very good story about morticians.

Love from
Bo

Evelyn to Diana

Piers Court   *14 October [1947]*

Darling Diana

In the way things happen nowadays your summons for yesterday reached me today. I long to see you but I couldn't have come as I am prostrate with fibrositis, contracted in a damp bed-room at Mells. I think from the various descriptions you have harrowed[6] me with from time to time of your own sufferings, that they must be this fibrositis. Perhaps you

[1] John Boynton (J. B.) Priestley (1894–1984), journalist, critic, novelist and dramatist, first known for his novel *The Good Companions*. His rumbustious Yorkshire populism prompted Conservative MPs to put down a motion, in June 1943, protesting at 'the continuing practice of the BBC in giving preference to left-wing speakers such as Mr Priestley'.

[2] Sir Hugh Walpole (1884–1941), novelist. Born in New Zealand, the son of a bishop. He was conscious of being old-fashioned, and deeply offended by Somerset Maugham's portrait of him as Alroy Kear, a hypocrite and ambitious littérateur, in *Cakes and Ale* (1930).

[3] Brendan Bracken (1901–1958), later 1st Viscount Bracken, politician and publisher. He took over from Duff as Minister of Information in 1941.

[4] Lord Beaverbrook's London house off St James's Street.

[5] Lady Elizabeth von Hofmannsthal (1916–80), the second daughter of the Marquess and Marchioness of Anglesey, and Diana's niece. She married Raimund von Hofmannsthal in 1939.

[6] As this word was not very legible, Waugh wrote 'HARROWED not HONOURED' above it.

got it from the notoriously dangerous damp grass at your many picnics. It is very painful.

I find Mells very happy and busy – a finely inscribed memorial stone about to be set up at Claveys,[1] Katharine's aunt's house being sold up revealing fewer treasures than was hoped, Ronnie Knox a perpetual delight. Trim sober, fairly clean. He has taken all Conrad's clothes to be made to fit him, but they don't as his arse is too big and as Conrad's clothes were highly idiosyncratic they are most unsightly on the boy. The bride bossy and industrious. No fierce lust on either side I supposed but quite matey.

Eddie Grant[2] kicked the bucket and Bridget is very sorry about it. Lucky they were not at Porto Fino with you at the time of death.

Love from
Bo

Evelyn to Diana

Piers Court   *[?end of 1947]*
[postcard]

I have just come across the charming prophetic lines (Landor)

'Paris I know is hard to quit
'But you have left it; and 't'were silly
'To throw away more smiles and wit
'Among the forests of Chantilly

E

Duff had been Ambassador in Paris for three years when he received a letter, in September 1947, informing him that his appointment would end in December. He was sad, but not surprised. A Labour government had been in power since July 1945, and he had not expected to remain Ambassador for much longer – despite the considerable success that he and Diana had enjoyed in Paris.

They had no wish to return to England, so settled down in the Château de St Firmin, a beautiful eighteenth-century house set in the

---

[1] Little Claveys, Somerset: the home and farm of Conrad Russell.
[2] Major Grant died on 27 September 1947.

park of the Château de Chantilly. They rented it from the Institut de France, and had been spending weekends there since the summer of 1945.

Diana to Evelyn

Paris   [pstmk 23 February 1948]
[postcard]

Enjoyed *Horizon* for the first time.[1] Greatly disappointed not to have met you this time – rang White's daily – usual frustration. I hoped to follow up what I consider to be a renaissance of love. Back in a month or so – keep in touch – don't be put off by a cist the size of a cistern under my eye. Diana

[in the margins of the picture, showing a Mother and Child by Alfred Stevens from the Tate Gallery:]

Please tell me – are there 2 artists called Stevens. This one I know well, but in Paris there is another – same date, but I think different genre – nobody here will be bothered with the question. You are my picture criterion and know-all.

Evelyn to Diana

Piers Court   *26 February [1948]*

Darling Diana,
    There were two Alfred Stevenses flourishing in the sixties. The Englishman who designed the Wellington memorial in St Paul's and the staircase and chimney pieces at Dorchester House. He left some fine drawings but I do not know of any painting by him. The second Alfred Stevens was Belgian – slick fashionable painter of great charm, who did the picture you sent me.
    I have not been in London for weeks and shall not be until after Easter. I have foregone wine and tobacco for Lent and am best alone and at home in those conditions.
    I wonder if you went to Tring.[2] Connolly did and lost 1½ stone. Well that is a lot for a shortish man. It will all come back and depress him much more. The craving for leanness is one of the nastiest of America's contributions to modern folly.

---

[1] *The Loved One* made its first appearance in the February issue of *Horizon*.
[2] A health farm near Tring, in Hertfordshire.

I did not send *The Loved One* because I knew you subscribed to *Horizon*. A copy of the edition de luxe will reach you before the 'fall' but not perhaps before the fall of France.[1] Stuart Boyle's[2] drawings suffer in reduction and reproduction. I propose printing them in sanguine like Bartolozzis. The story is being a great success and has re-established my battered repute with the high-brows.

I loved seeing you in London. I feel you have to make much greater sacrifices of your habits of life than I to mine when we meet. Why do I say 'have to'? There's no 'have to' about it. It is just that you sweetly and munificently do. Your coming to London on Sunday for a beastly luncheon was splendid. But the moment your Fiend[3] touched English soil you were a changed woman.

On re-reading Lady Lovat's *Maurice Baring*[4] I was forced to admit high qualities in her part of it. By the way do not forget please your promise of your mother's drawing of Maurice, if it comes to light. I told the committee at White's there was a chance of it, and they were enchanted. I am sure Maurice would like to be commemorated there. Well who wouldn't?

I suppose that your income is doubled since they devalued the franc? Defy the Foul Fiend.

All love
Bo

Evelyn to Diana

Piers Court   *[February? 1948]*
[postcard]

You said 'Keep in touch' well I shall be in London Easter Tuesday for a week at Hyde Park Hotel. Any hope? I have joined a smoky little club ironically named 'Bon Viveur' solely in order to have somewhere to take you to dinner. Horrified by Duff's communist propaganda in *Mail*. It is just what Churchill and Eden thought at Yalta – that Stalin was just old

---

[1] December 1947 had been marked by Communist strikes in Paris. They were violently against France receiving Marshall Aid from America.

[2] When commissioning Boyle to illustrate *The Loved One*, Waugh described him as 'a hardworking, penurious draughtsman of great technical skill and little imagination or taste. Just what I want.' (*Diaries*, 1 December 1947, p. 691)

[3] An allusion to a line in the hymn 'To be a pilgrim': 'No goblin nor foul fiend/Can daunt his spirit' – see also his parting words. Waugh refers to Diana's melancholia.

[4] Two years after his death, Lady Lovat put together a book called *Maurice Baring, A Postscript* (1947). It consisted of a piece by Ronald Knox called 'The Effect of the Classics on Maurice Baring's Mind', a letter to Laura Lovat from Princess Marthe Bibesco, and Lady Lovat's own record of Maurice Baring's last days at her house in Scotland.

Tsar writ large. And it was that frightful mistake which has landed us where we shall be soon – odd sentence. Am reading Proust. He is MENTALLY DEFECTIVE.[1]

δαμν παλφι[2]

Diana to Evelyn

[early April 1948]

[written in the margins of a small photograph of herself:]

This what I have become – isn't it insect and horrible? It's not only physically I'm deterirating but the ice is breaking up on every side[3] – no London till about 16th April.

Evelyn to Diana

Piers Court   *10 April 1948*

Dearest Diana

Your post-card read very sadly, but the words were cheerful – 'Ice breaking up on every side' – what could be a happier augury of Spring. I believe that you are in for a decade of deep content and discovery. Maurice's strong prayers and my feeble ones are going to take effect. You've let yourself run out of breath lately. Tranquillity is round the corner.

If only you could treat friends as something to be enjoyed in themselves not as companions in adventure we should be so much happier together. Not that I don't love adventurers and relish all the excitement of Scotch bonnet chasing which you bring into my life, but I do wish sometimes you could just sit quietly, almost silently, and enjoy your friends' love instead of always thinking of something amusing to do. And if at the end of an evening you enjoyed desultory conversation, growing drowsy, instead of being ashamed to be seen in any condition that is not highly galvanized. Now the chance has come for you to learn the sweets of that sort of companionship. Believe me the best.

---

[1] At about the same time Waugh wrote to John Betjeman: 'Well the chap was plain barmy. He never tells you the age of the hero and on one page he is being taken to the WC in the Champs Elysées by his nurse and the next page he is going to a brothel. Such a lot of nonsense.' (*Letters*, February? 1948, p. 270)

[2] 'damn palfi' (Louise de Vilmorin).

[3] The recurrent line of a ballad by Hilaire Belloc.

Mrs J. Sutro is giving a subscription ball for you to meet Mme Massigli.[1] To one earnest student of the social scene that seems a particularly odd invitation in all ways. I shall not be there.

I went to Daphne[2] for two sleepless days. Jazz all day. Drinking till 3.30 a.m. A ground floor room and the children riding bicycles round the house with loud cries at 6.30. Henry reading the most disgusting passages from Malinovsky's *Sexual Life of the Savage* (and goodness they <u>are</u> disgusting) aloud at meals to his 17 year old daughter and 16 year old son.

Then, in marked contrast, to Mells for a night. Great discussion before my coming: 'Can we give Evelyn high tea.' Ronnie ex cathedra 'The last man in England to treat in that way.' Then tremendous drama 'We forgot to tell Nanny there was late dinner.' Ronnie plump and cossetted, much changed from the haunted creature at Aldenham. Very much the host 'Do you know the geography of the house?' i.e. W.C. with ingenious ways of making the cross-word puzzle harder to solve.

Then to London where for four days my life followed the usual graph of waning popularity. Great welcome at first, tepid geniality turning to disgust . . .

All my beautiful edition de luxe of *The Loved One* has been destroyed by the Bristol Fire Brigade.[3]

I have bought such a lot of odd things. The trouble in London is that after luncheon I saunter out with folie de grandeur and a cheque book. I now have a grey bowler hat, three tie pins, a quantity of Victorian radiators, a granite clock, a solid silver candelabrum as tall as myself, all the result of four days in London.

Budget day in White's was the greatest fun. All the men who to my certain knowledge have not £100 in the world roaring that they are ruined. The dozen or so really rich men smugly looking down their noses having become Costa Rican companies domiciled in Cuba years ago.

All love
Evelyn

---

[1] Odette, wife of René Massigli, who had been the French Ambassador to London since 1944.

[2] Daphne Vivian (b. 1904), daughter of the 4th Baron Vivian, and biographer of Rosa Lewis, Emerald and Nancy Cunard, and Iris Tree. In 1927 she married Henry Thynne, Lord Weymouth, who in 1946 succeeded his father as the 6th Marquess of Bath. They were divorced in 1953, and in that year she became Mrs Xan Fielding.

[3] *Diaries*, 10 April 1948: 'The printers in Bristol at work on *The Loved One* have burned down.' (p. 697)

Diana to Evelyn

Château de St Firmin [*November 1948*]
Chantilly
Oise

Darling Evelyn – no Bo –

I've just got back from Rome (where I was last with you) to find *The Loved One* most beautifully embalmed and coloured.[1] She looks even better that way but the bones are what count and hers are so well-proportioned. Thank you it joins the shining row of Waugh-books. I always hope to see you here or in London. I always make a bid – but no success. Can't I invite you to Chantilly or couldn't you invite yourself?

Randolph brings his bride[2] to lunch. What did either of them do it for – Is security so precious to her? of course it's not security. And he? Love doesn't seem to be a part of it all.

Do come.

D

Evelyn to Diana

Piers Court *31 December 1948*

Darling Diana

Just back from U.S.A. to find your letter of weeks ago awaiting me. Just off there again. The pleasure of New York is momentary, the posture ridiculous, the expense damnable,[3] but I seem to [be] deeply involved there commercially and one can get caviar and Oxford marmalade. Not Bromo. I traced the head of the firm who made it, Diamond Mills. It was only made for English use and will never now be made again. He was very funny about the despairing fan-mail he gets.

Conflicting reports about Randolph's honeymoon. Yours and Tanis's[4] agree but another school speaks of bliss.

I find no one in England talks of anything except Stokes's chariot. White's committee wish to expel him. I hope Sir Alfred [Duff] will use his

---

[1] One of a special edition of 250, signed by Waugh and the illustrator Stuart Boyle.

[2] Randolph Churchill's first marriage to Pamela Digby (later Mrs Leland Hayward, later still Mrs Averell Harriman), was dissolved in 1946. Two years later he married June, only daughter of Colonel Rex Osborne. They divorced in 1958.

[3] A quotation from one of Lord Chesterfield's letters to his son, describing the indignity of sex for money.

[4] Tanis Guinness (b. 1908). In 1937 she married the American librettist and writer Howard Dietz. They were divorced in 1958, and she later became Mrs Edward ('Teddy') Phillips.

influence to avert this injustice. To my simple mind a man may with perfect propriety be whipped by his own wife in his own woods.[1]

I still think New York sky-line ugly.

Sir O. Sitwell[2] has grown his hair like Einstein's. I said: 'Why isn't Sachie with you?' Sir O. 'He is High Sheriff of his county and therefore cannot leave England.'

There is a wonderful toy called the 'Beau Alarm' designed to protect ladies from rape. No bigger than a cigarette case and it <u>literally</u> makes a noise as loud as an air raid siren. I gave Edith[3] one and she took it to Boston and when Brahmins ask 'Dr Sitwell, do you consider free verse more truly poetic than epic?' she lets it off.

All my love for New Year and all other years

E

Raimund [von Hofmannsthal]'s eldest daughter very nice. Alice's new husband not so hot but better than Harding.[4]

Did E. Cunard cut up well?

Evelyn to Diana

Piers Court

Winter Solstice
[21 December 1949]

Darling Diana

I hoped for a tentacle from the octopus and it was softer than I expected but the note of bonhomie struck harsh (raspers). Never bright confident morning again[5] but perhaps a nudge in the dark. I love you and I don't want to see you. Well that's easy. I never leave home except to lecture. God how I hate lecturing. I made a penitential vow last Good Friday that for one year I would accept all popish invitations. Easy for three months as I had built up an iron curtain over twenty years of curt refusals. Then it got round and now I lecture three times a week to pious ladies. You must remember me well enough to know I don't like sound of own voice.

[1] Richard Rapier Stokes (1897–1957), the Labour MP for Ipswich and Minister of Works 1950–51, whose perversions aroused much interest at the time. He was not expelled from White's.

[2] Sir Osbert Sitwell (1892–1969), 5th Bt. Poet, novelist, and author of six celebrated volumes of autobiography. With his sister Edith and brother Sacheverell, he encouraged modernist writers and artists.

[3] Edith Sitwell (1887–1964), poet and critic. She lectured extensively in the U.S. after the war, and was made a Dame of the British Empire in 1954.

[4] Raimund von Hofmannsthal was married to Alice Astor 1933–9. Their daughter, Romana, later married the painter Rory McEwen. Alice Astor (who, pre-Hofmannsthal, had been married to Prince Serge Obolensky) was married to Philip Harding 1940–45, and David Pleydell-Bouverie 1947–53.

[5] A misquotation from Robert Browning's *The Lost Leader*; 'bright' should read 'glad'.

My unhappy country is in a worse case than ever. The Freemasons gave a huge motor-car to three blackguards called Trevor-Roper,[1] Forbes[2] and Quennell and these three drive everywhere together in dust with loud yells.

Except to lecture I never leave home (to be blessed in late summer by another pledge of my affections).[3] I have laid out a garden which may be pretty (belle laide – all ivy, ferns and Portugal laurel) in twenty years. I have grown stouter and worse tempered and more pompous.

Women don't understand pomposity. It is nearly always an absolutely private joke – one against the world. The last line of defense.

I am writing, a sentence a week, a masterpiece (unreadable) about Empress Helena.

Talking of masterpiece did you see P. G. Wodehouse's great coal of fire to Duff (whose tenure of office will only be remembered as the occasion of his hiring the basest of the socialist journalists to insult a great artist).[4] Gussie Fink Nottle, arrested, gave the name of Alfred Duff Cooper. When you think of the predecessors . . . '"The prisoner Aristotle", said the beak, "which I strongly suspect is an assumed name"' . . .

Lecturing, I went to Edinburgh. The socialists have painted all the mahogany doors in the Caledonian Hotel 'apple-green'.

All love from the antipodes

Bo

---

[1] Hugh Trevor-Roper (b. 1914), historian and academic. Became Baron Dacre of Glanton in 1979. Master of Peterhouse, Cambridge, 1980–87. In 1954 he married Lady Alexandra Howard-Johnston, daughter of the late Field Marshal Lord Haig.

[2] Alastair Forbes (b. 1918), journalist. Diana always maintained he was a spy, her evidence being that he reads a great many newspapers, speaks several languages, and knows more about everyone than anyone should.

[3] His son Septimus, born 1950.

[4] As Minister of Information, Duff had overridden the BBC to allow the journalist William Connor ('Cassandra' of the *Daily Mirror*) to broadcast a savage attack on P. G. Wodehouse, for his ill-judged wartime broadcasts from Berlin.

PART III

1950–59

THE FLOW OF LETTERS BETWEEN DIANA AND WAUGH *reaches its peak in the 1950s – both in quantity and quality. Two factors helped. Diana was abroad most of the time, either at Chantilly or staying in various friendly houses across Europe; and Waugh had the leisure to write more letters to his friends than ever before.*

Waugh published eight books in this decade. He bought pictures, travelled, took jaunts up to London, and there were christenings and marriages and funerals to attend. The shape of his life was established. He did not make many new friends; and communicating with his old friends by letter was perhaps more satisfactory than seeing them face to face. So often, the meeting long planned and looked forward to was a disappointment.

The two most important upheavals in this decade are his alarming bout of madness in 1954 and the move to Combe Florey in 1956 – and in both of these, he had Laura to help him. Absorbed in her family, her garden and her cows, she took little part in the world of these letters – yet her presence can always be felt at the centre of Waugh's existence.

Diana, on the other hand, underwent the saddest and most profound change in her life: she had to learn to live in a world without Duff. The black bouts of what she calls 'mealancholia', which had no cause in the late 1940s, seem heavy with foreboding as they lead up to Duff's death; and although her life was still full of picnics and parties, it is restlessness and a dread of being alone that drive her on. A new coterie of friends emerges – she has known them for some time, but they become closer after her bereavement: Patrick Leigh Fermor, Jenny Crosse, Judy Montagu and Iris Tree. John Julius became the focus of her life, and to others it seemed that she still had a lot to live for; and yet, as Noël Coward wrote in his diary on 3 June 1956, 'A lot of light went out of her . . . when Duff died.'

Diana to Evelyn

69 rue de Lille   *25 April [1950]*
Paris

Darling Bo –

Don't be so unforgiving. I hear you are coming to Paris, and I've no doubt will detour me. This letter is to charm you into my arms again. Do forget past jars. All my eruptions come from disappointment, so in a way they should please the man on whom their lava falls.

I wish I was in Rome: our last happy morning was there – you showed me churches in the earliest morning whilst Bloggs lay sickening in bed.

I learnt in Rome that Paris was Liberated, and remember to my shame the stab of personal anguish it gave me. Algiers over – the Post-War world begun. It's all very dull now (my life I mean). It's what you like – calmly planned – unhurried – no adventure, no milking, no interest to me at all. *I* am to blame, but – I was born and bred an adventurer, with a great zest for change and excitement – and retirement is like prison.

Katharine comes here via Lourdes on 18th May – I'll be away 12th to 18th. Nancy[1] keeps you in touch –

Diana

Diana to Evelyn

Château de St Firmin   *21 October 1950*

Dearest Evelyn. *Helena*[2] received in her immaculate white and twice read by me with keenest enjoyment.

It is a happy facet of that jagged stone – our relationship – that allows me to admire whole heartedly your every book. Duff's I read in terror, Maurice [Baring]'s too – Osbert [Sitwell]'s I am anxious to hide his faults from others – the same with Nancy [Mitford] – Louise [de Vilmorin]'s strange language stays criticism – but your pen, your jokes – situations, coloqualisms, inspired prayers all find me and leave me sure of you – impressed, touched and amused.

Thank you so much for sending me the beautiful edition – it will join the other gems. The inscription was a masterpiece of negativism

Auberon [Herbert] and the King of Italy[3] to lunch today.

God bless you Wu darling

D

[1] Nancy Mitford. She married Peter Rodd in 1933, a disastrous union which was not dissolved until 1958. Drawn by her hopeless love for Gaston Palewski, whom she referred to as 'the Colonel' or 'the Col', she moved to France after the war.

[2] Waugh always maintained that *Helena* was his best book.

[3] Umberto II (1904–83). He succeeded on the abdication of his father, Vittorio Emmanuele III, in 1946, and left Italy just over a month later. He retired to Portugal as the Count di Sarre.

Evelyn to Diana

Piers Court   *24 November [1950]*

Dearest Diana

Thank you so very much for your charming letter about *Helena*. I never thought for a moment you would like it. No one else does except Magdalen Eldon and Noël Coward and myself. I keep rereading it with unfailing joy. I have learned with distress that stirrups were introduced into the Roman cavalry by Justinian – otherwise it seems perfect. But the reviewers don't think so.

I am miserable to hear you are ill – or were ill. Perhaps – I do hope – you are quite well again. I have been in New York till quite lately and then here without remission and hear nothing of anyone.

New York was delightful. I have come round to your love of it – except the architecture which still seems to me quite worthless and the new UNO building worse than that. Laura and I have about six friends in New York now and we see only them and are happy with them. American men are beastly of course but I like the middle aged rich women, particularly if they are childless as they mostly are. And English people are much nicer there than at home. You should just see Gladwyn Jebb[1] living like the Great Gatsby. We ate nothing but caviar and meringues and saw English plays with English actors. We stayed at a 'home', which means a country house not a looney bin, where the host showed me his vines and said they were raspberry trees.

We lunched at Mells last Saturday. Conrad's absence is still like a great bomb crater in the heart of the place but Katharine has Trim and Anne home on leave and radiated happiness. Anne has grown into a great pre-Raphaelite beauty and is good as gold. We stayed with Billy and Per[2] as it is next door to my eldest boy's school [All Hallows], where they were having a prize day. Who should be among the parents but Baby Jungman – a neurotic spinster – with the most unpopular boy in the school.[3]

I dislike my house more and more every season. Now and then I buy a statue and that cheers me up for a few days but soon palls. But we have plenty of servants and plenty of food and that is more than most English can claim and I suppose it is rather a good place for children to grow up in. In the New Year I go to the Levant (Sykes in attendance). There is so much to see before the next war obliterates it all. I don't want to be caught again as I was in 1939 with so much not visited.

[1] Sir Gladwyn Jebb was at that time Permanent Representative of the United Kingdom to the UN, a post he held until 1954, when he became Ambassador to Paris. Created 1st Baron Gladwyn, 1968.

[2] Lady Perdita Asquith (b. 1910), youngest daughter of Raymond and Katharine Asquith, married William Jolliffe (1898–1967), who succeeded his father as 4th Baron Hylton in 1945.

[3] From 1940–45 Teresa Jungman was married to Graham Cuthbertson, a Scot in a Canadian regiment. They had two children: Richard (b. 1941), who died in a car crash in 1964; and Penelope (b. 1943), now Mrs Desmond Guinness.

I never go near London now or see Londoners. My few friends all live in scattered farms now and the women grow beards and the men paint Picassos.

Bloggs, not far off, comes here sometimes. He came the other evening and was splendid company.

Ronnie Knox has dedicated his magnum opus on *Enthusiasm*[1] to me. That set me up high.

What else can I tell you to beguile a minute of the sick-room? This letter seems all about me but that is because I do not doubt that you hear heaps of news about everyone else.

Osbert Sitwell is tremendously decrepid. Edith eating like a horse and acting Lady Macbeth at the New York Museum of Modern Culture.[2] My children are all pretty affectionate healthy and pious – three of them are clever. I am glad to possess them but get little pleasure from their use – like first editions.

Venetia's daughter Judy[3] rivals Sir Gladwyn as the most popular limey in New York.

Are you reading Mrs Leveson's novels?[4] A fine creation called Raggett in *Love's Shadow*. Just the thing for the convalescent.

Love from
Bo

Make a note of my address. You always write to White's where I rarely go. My chums there are all now teetotallers on their doctors' orders or else have killed themselves one way or another. The Duke of Beaufort has a photograph of Hubert in his lulu. Odd? I enclose a recent acquisition.[5]

---

[1] The full title of the work, published in 1950, was *Enthusiasm: a chapter in the history of religion with a special reference to the XVII and XVIII centuries.*

[2] On 16 November, Edith Sitwell took the part of her ancestress, Lady Macbeth, in a reading from the play at the Museum of Modern Art. (Macbeth was read by the writer Glenway Wescott.) Her age, spectacles and quavering voice did nothing for the part, and the critics were unimpressed. As for Waugh in New York, Osbert Sitwell thought he was overdoing his self-imposed role as crusty old-fashioned gentleman: 'He has even taken to leaving visiting cards instead of telephoning.'

[3] Judy Montagu (1923–72). Her mother was H. H. Asquith's confidante, Venetia Stanley, who married the Rt. Hon. Edwin Montagu (1879–1924) in 1915.

[4] Ada Leveson (1862–1933). Oscar Wilde called her 'the Sphinx', and she sheltered him during his trials. Her novels, which include *Love's Shadow* (1908), *Tenterhooks* (1912) and *Love at Second Sight* (1916) are set in fashionable London society.

[5] Waugh had sent Diana a photograph of *The Upturned Barrow*, a painting by W. A. Atkinson (fl. 1849–1867), a little-known London genre and historical painter. Diana pasted the picture into her album, and it appears among the illustrations.

Diana to Evelyn

Château de St Firmin   *3 December 1950*

Dearest Wu.

I was delighted to get a letter from you – Nancy [with] great honesty took a glint of the pleasure off by saying 'yes' to my question 'did you tell him to write?' No matter.[1] It was a long generous letter, the perfunctory, if there, didn't show.

Auberon has to join the Coward – Lady Eldon – Waugh group.[2]

I'm immensely intrigued by the picture and have given the leisured <u>hours</u> of bedridden life trying to solve its problem. Do write me your views – Could it be the foreground child telling her Mum – the owner of the barrow upset by ? – that the kind rich passers by will cover the damage. The wealthy and indegent dressed so richly – is the foreground child meant to be in tatters? See her petticoat show thro' a rent. Why does the older woman look so alarmed? not at all cross – just paniced?

I'm fervently interested in your collection. Spencerlaye [*sic*] was one of this harvest's grains – so I was in the sowing. Will you not make for friends an expensive bound slim volume of your pictures – with short explanations or imbroglios and blank sheets for future – no there could be vols II and III. Colour would revolt you possibly – but I should like it.

I'm up again just. Weak and cowardly – home for Christmas – N. Wales[3] for the Yule-log.

love
Diana

Evelyn to Diana

Piers Court   *12 December [1950]*

Dearest Diana

Unprompted by Nancy I wish you a very jolly Christmas. I am delighted to hear you are healed and home.

Duff had a great success at Oxford. I didn't go but heard highest praises of his Belloc speech.[4]

---

[1] In his next letter to Nancy Mitford, Waugh complained: 'You spoiled all my efforts to cheer Honks by telling her you instigated them . . .' (*Letters*, p. 343)

[2] As appreciators of *Helena*.

[3] With Sir Michael Duff, 3rd Bt. (1907–80). The only son of Lady Juliet Duff, he married Diana's niece, Lady Caroline Paget, in 1949. They lived at Vaynol Park, near Bangor, North Wales.

[4] Duff had been invited to address the Oxford Union on the motion:

'The subject's very much too wide,
And much too deep, and much too hollow;
and learned men on either side
Use arguments we cannot follow.'
Hilaire Belloc

The picture. There have been suggestions of a romantic theme – that the barrow woman is a former mistress and so forth – but though I hate socio-economic interpretations I have come to the conclusion that the drama is socio-economic. The poor family are coming into North London from Finchley or Edgware with their produce – not cut flowers but pot plants of some value. The father is a brute and the woman's consternation is the thought of the beating she will get on her return. The loutish boy is responsible for running into the fatal brick. He is so loutish that he just scratches his head and doesn't even try to find out what can be salvaged. The other proletarians have nothing but delight in their fellows' disaster. 'Look here, mates, here's a lark'. But the good rich man (why is he sauntering with his family in Sunday clothes and not at business? is it Sunday? If so, is there a reflexion on the iniquity of Sunday trading?) comes to the rescue. Moreover he trains his little girl in charity by giving her the two half crowns to give. The poor girl sees this and wakes her stupefied mother: 'Look, everything is all right. No beating. The good rich man has forked out'.

The painting is brilliantly coloured. Spring everywhere. Is it Easter Monday perhaps?

I went to London. I had heard terrible accounts of Randolph's violence and melancholy but met him at dinner at the Heads[1] (who were trembling in fear for what he would do) and he behaved modestly and calmly. But by all accounts this is unusual and he is losing his reason.

Connolly is married to a concubine of the Emir of Egypt's.[2] He had a seizure at the wedding breakfast and was driven straight to Tring where he is now strapped up in a cell being starved and hosed – well, you know the regime better than I.

I went to dinner at Faringdon from the Betjemans. The Mad Boy has installed a Mad Boy of his own. Has there ever been a property in history that has devolved from catamite to catamite for any length of time?[3] It would be interesting to know.

Every post brings piles of American Christmas cards. The most refined have no ornament and are printed in copper plate like wedding

[1] Antony Head (1906–83), created 1st Viscount Head in 1960. A Conservative politician, he was Secretary of State for War 1951–6.

[2] Barbara Skelton, whose relationship with King Farouk, among others, is recorded in her memoirs *Tears Before Bedtime* (1986) and *Weep No More* (1989). From 1956–61, she was married to the publisher George Weidenfeld.

[3] Lord Berners lived at Faringdon House with Robert Heber-Percy, 'the Mad Boy', who was just as eccentric as his patron and a good deal more capricious. Heber-Percy, to whom Lord Berners left Faringdon House on his death in 1950, had recently invited Captain Hugh Cruddas to join their ménage.

invitations: Mr and Mrs Cuydam Hogheim have the honour to wish you happiness . . . Well I expect you get them too.

Anything I can do you can do better.[1]

Love from
Bo

There is a terrible Mr Wu going about the papers now.

Evelyn to Diana

British Embassy   *23 January 1951*
Rome

My dearest Diana

I have today had delivered to me a letter from you written on April 25th last year. I don't expect you remember what it said. I shall never forget and I am appalled to think that through the kind of mistake which I thought only happened in Hardy novels you should have thought for nearly a year that I had left it unanswered. It is one of the most charming letters I have ever read – certainly the most charming ever written to me – and I thank you with all my heart.

I am on my way through Rome to Jerusalem, Antioch, Aleppo etc. Almost certainly I shall pass through Paris in early March when I will lie on your doorstep night after night in penance for the beastliness of not having written.

I don't think it is any good trying to tell you an address where you might tell me where to find you because I shall be on the move from now on and if Victor[2] can't get a letter forwarded from Rome to Florence, it is absurd to think he could send one to Damascus or somewhere really difficult.

I'm not staying with Victor but with John Russells.[3] But I will telegraph from Athens to Chantilly when I am set for Paris and <u>long</u> to see you. I loved the Rothenstein[4] glimpse.

Love love love love
Bo

---

[1] 'Anything You Can Do I Can Do Better' was the title of a song in Irving Berlin's musical, *Annie Get Your Gun*.

[2] Sir Victor Mallet (1893–1969). Knighted in 1944, he was Ambassador to Italy 1947–53.

[3] John (later Sir John) Russell (1914–84), only son of Sir Thomas Russell Pasha. In 1935 he married Aliki Diplarakos of Athens. A professional diplomat, he was at this time First Secretary in Rome. He was later Ambassador in Ethiopia (1962–6), Brazil (1966–9), and Spain (1969–74).

[4] John Rothenstein (b. 1901), knighted the following year. Art historian, and Director of the Tate Gallery 1938–64.

114

Evelyn to Diana

Hotel de Paris   *2 June [1951]*
Monte Carlo

Darling Diana

The motor tour was awful. I had not realized how uncomfortable and
noisy our poor old car had become. We landed in late afternoon at
Dunkirk and drove for hours in rain among war-graves and coal mines.
All the main roads were closed and we drove round enormous diversions
among shell holes. At last reached Bapaume aching and miserable, too
tired to go on. Next day we got as far as Meaux (good luncheon Soissons)
and left the car there and took the train here since when we have been very
happy. General Popski is most kind to us and sends you his love.

Plans. Laura sails from Calais noon 13th. I shall see her safely off and
then head for Chantilly arriving that night or next day. Could you be very
kind and tell the hotel this?

Is the hotel called quite simply 'du Chateau' or is it the 'Chateau de la
Tour'.[1]

Please answer this as I have to arrange about sending things there.

We leave here on 10th by train, go to collect motor at Meaux and make
for Calais dropping my luggage at Chantilly on the way.

I seem to remember more carpets and orchestras and fewer motor
bicycles. Otherwise Monte Carlo seems quite unchanged. I will come
and live here as soon as my children are off my hands.

Nancy says you won't be at Chantilly much in the coming weeks. Do
please try to be.

All love
Bo

Evelyn to Diana

Piers Court   *12 July [?1951]*

Darling Diana

I will write this large so that you will not have trouble in decyphering it.
The trouble is that the misspellings will be so prominent.

Cool, dingy, enclosed. That is how Stinkers seems – overgrown, pitch
dark, rather solid, damp, small. Silver very bright, good gloss on the
mahogany, grass bald and piebald, jungle weeds everywhere, all flowers
dead and untrimmed; finest corn in the county, people come miles to see

---

[1] The Hôtel du Château, Chantilly. 'This hotel is *very* modest. No hot water or pillow case. Very
simple digestible food . . . In fact just what was wanted.' (Letter to Laura Waugh, *Letters*, p. 351) It was
here that Waugh began work on *Men at Arms*, the first volume of the *Sword of Honour* trilogy.

it, excellent green peas very large and sweet, Laura pleased to see me. I miss the great watery expanses of Chantilly the bread and the circuses. Most of course I miss you. Well it was jolly decent being chums again. May it last till death parts us. It was a wonderful long visit – well it was more a residence than a visit. Thank you so with all my heart for all your rare sweetness – is rare right? no.

I hope you had a lovely ball at the Palace[1] and that your crown outshone all the heirlooms. I wasn't asked. No one asks me to parties except people who don't know me like Mrs Hulton[2] and Mme Massigli. Once they see me it is enough. Since I met Queen I have been struck off the list.

I have written to your Mr Battersby[3] to ask him to make a trompe l'oeil for me.

Do try and visit us here one day. I know you can't this time but try to remember us when Duff lectures to Cheltenham.

Here is a pretty picture of a bearded mother.

All love
Bo

I sent you two little reprints to read in trains. Try *Trivia*[4] a bit at a time, not cover to cover.

Diana to Evelyn

chez Oggie[5]   [15 July 1951]
14 Chesham Palace

Thank you so very much for the books Bo darling. I haven't broached them yet on account of still being in a whirl of successful frivolity. The description of your return home sounded happy enough – no disasters – no list of depreciations [in] fertile field and hugs.

Shakespeare talks of the 'dark house and the detested wife'[6] – the line

---

[1] The ball was to celebrate the Festival of Britain, which had been officially inaugurated on 20 March.

[2] Princess Nika Yourivitch, second daughter of Prince Sergei Yourivitch. In 1941 she married the magazine publisher Edward Hulton (1906–88), whose most famous publication was *Picture Post*. He was knighted in 1957.

[3] Martin Battersby (1913–82), Cecil Beaton's assistant set designer in the late forties and a master of *trompe l'oeil* painting. His series of panels on copper for Duff and Diana, illustrating their lives, was reproduced on the endpapers of Diana's three-volume autobiography.

[4] *Trivia* (1902) by Logan Pearsall Smith (1865–1946), who was brother-in-law of Bernard Berenson and Bertrand Russell.

[5] Olga Lynn (1882–1961), singer, teacher and lifelong friend of Diana's. Her career was hampered by her stout and diminutive figure.

[6] '. . . war is no strife
To the dark house and the detested wife.'
All's Well that Ends Well, Act II, scene iii

always makes me shudder for what might have been. I shan't miss you to the full till I return to Chantilly – I quite dread it, not the return for itself but for the missing of you. I enjoyed it with the gusto of earlier decades.

Do come back one day.

The Palace ball was resplendently beautiful – my crown deceived and stupified. Mrs David Niven[1] and Mrs Timothy (Clifford Jones)[2] were the belles – also our Debo.[3] Duff spent a good hour at supper with the Queen – other partners joined and hoped he'd relinquish his coveted place but he [stopped] them out and went out with his bat.

Since this great diversion it's been Dots [Lady Dorothea Head] and Pams[4] and company so brilliant and light and spirited that weren't listed in France.

The streets too I don't yet tire of. The changing guard – the trees – the bright buses – and the not being insulted and the calm grace of bobbies – even Duff who hates to conceed this point has been deeply struck by the Englishman's desire to help.

It's lunch with Auberon today – he had a cocktail for Ukrainians yesterday – J.J. attended. I was the winter's tale – we cried like Niobes. Tomorrow the feast of music at Glyndebourne – next Beaton day – Tuesday Hulton night – couldn't you both come – I could perhaps fix dinner, and it will be a memorable sight.

Wednesday my new friend Lady J[ones] shows what she can do at the Arts Theatre. The description of the farce's first night at the Comedy Theatre makes me quake and quail for Enid and Cecil.[5] Thursday and Friday are lull days. Saturday begins the trek home in a limping motor-car, lying for two nights at a duchess's en route for the sea and over.

Fond love
Diana

[1] Hjordis Tersmeden, David Niven's second wife.

[2] Pandora Clifford (d. 1987) had married Timothy Jones, son of Diana's 'new friend' Lady Jones, in 1948.

[3] Nancy Mitford's sister Deborah. In 1941 she married Lord Andrew Cavendish (b. 1920), who in 1950 became 11th Duke of Devonshire.

[4] Lady Pamela Berry (1914–82), daughter of the first Lord Birkenhead. In 1936 she married Michael Berry (b. 1911), later Chairman and Editor-in-Chief of the *Daily Telegraph* and *Sunday Telegraph*. He was created Baron Hartwell in 1968. Lady Pamela liked to think that her dark beauty was due to gypsy ancestry, and her parties were filled with journalists and politicians.

[5] Diana's alarm was caused by the reception of the celebrated flop *Storks Don't Talk* by Charles Lincoln, at the Comedy Theatre on 11 July: there was booing in the gallery by the end of the first act. *The Gainsborough Girls* by Cecil Beaton opened at the Theatre Royal, Brighton, on 16 July, but never came to the West End. Two days later *Poor Judas* by Enid Bagnold opened at the Arts Theatre.

Evelyn to Diana

Piers Court   *2 August 1951*

Darling Diana

Big writing from a big heart.

I am on the Goller regime shedding all the weight deliciously assembled in France. Hungry, thirsty and petulant all day long. Tring must be a place of gormandizing compared with my dining-room. Bones pricking through the skin like asparagus in spring.

My book gets fatter though. I have a sad suspicion that it is very dull – all detailed descriptions of military training and mess tippling. A dry prig of a hero.

Yesterday I had the Master of the Chantilly Bar [Martin Battersby] here. I liked him very much. Your descriptions did not make me expect anyone so mature and ascetic and well informed. I had looked for a pink and gold theatrical flibbertygibbet. Did you know that he was brought up and disinherited by a grandmother, that at the age of eleven he could recite by rote the whole of the first three gospels, that he has written a learned treatise on French ormolu?

He is going to make a panel for me in imitation of yours – works not life and habit.

I have also had Mr Eurich here – the man Rothenstein spoke of who painted the sailors on the up-turned boat. He is going to do a companion piece to my railway pictures – an aeroplane full of flames and roasting passengers.[1]

I am also negotiating for the purchase and re-erection in the garden of a neighbouring church. If this coup comes off I shall be completely ruined.

I am being sued for 3000 dollars by an American editor for a story I never wrote though he paid me in advance. There is no legal way of restoring the money since I acquired it illegally. Prison gates yawn for me.

Katharine Asquith went to Lough Derg – the grimmest pilgrimage in Christendom – so Ronnie Knox came here and spoiled the Cross Word with intricate private rules. He has become very slow of speech.

In three weeks I send all the children and alas Laura to Porto Fino. The children are particularly odious. I have never met them quite sober before – I mean when I have been quite sober. I used to get tipsy before family luncheon and then be rather jolly with them. Not now in the shadow of Dr Goller. I snap at them like a turtle.

Your friend's play sounded a flop.

Hugs and kisses
Bo

[1] The painter Richard Eurich. The 'railway paintings' which the aeroplane was to join were *The Pleasures of Travel 1751* and *The Pleasures of Travel 1851* by Thomas Musgrave Joy: these compared the discomfort of travel by stagecoach with the comfort of travel by rail.

Diana to Evelyn

La Reine Jeanne   *[August 1951]*
Bormes-Les-Mimosas, Var

Darling Wu

I took a great delight in your letter – the purplest patch being – the children thro' sober eyes. Don't flesh down to the bone I think a certain Portlyness suits you and sweetens. Certainly you were a 'fruit comfit' at Chantilly – not a turtle-snap in you.

You will smile to read that his Grace of Brissac[1] – the proud Duke who bored us fabulously and who you maliciously misled in a matter of English translation is with us here and he has two young victims – a Cubitt of 24 whose family builds houses, and a[nother] equally young who travels in Gillette razors and whose Papa was jailed for international imbezzlement. These unfortunates – chained supporters – are kept grinding bad English from dawn to dusk. I am appealed to now and again and mislead without malice.

I motored down alone with Pierino[2] in the Camionette, springs breaking beneath the Bestigui ball Paraphanalia.[3] We boiled up on a hill – and he told me I was to blame for driving too fast. I reboiled and said I didn't pay him to tell me I'm wrong – that I know when I'm wrong thank him – he said he could get more money anywhere else as a valet chauffeur. I said (only I didn't know the words) he didn't know a plug from a carboretta – then we didn't speak again for ½ a day.

The roads showed democracy at its worst; when young I loved democracy – but I never saw it, except on bank holidays in Belvoir Castle gardens, and the children (us) were kept indoors so as not to catch diseases and lice – but the French roads showed them up in their monstrous white nudity – general immodesty – car bonnets agape – cars behinds yawning and dribbling out horrible tuck-baskets, nappies, rubber tubing and the like. Picnics on the dusty verge – cars by the million left to cool while owners flame up in the bushes. Some being sick – some so unlearnt as to stop traffic. Never again a Sat–Sun in August on that popular road. Here, completely out of touch, it's lovely.[4] My sun is dimmed by John Julius not arriving and one of those boring Clifford girls[5] (not his) has a sun stroke so we must wait her recovery – why can't she wear a straw hat like us.

---

[1] Pierre de Cossé, Duc de Brissac.

[2] Pierino Chitto was chauffeur, valet or handyman as the need arose.

[3] Diana was the centrepiece of the great ball given on 5 September by Charles de Beistegui in the Palazzo Labia, Venice. She was dressed as Tiepolo's Cleopatra, who adorns the walls of the palazzo.

[4] The Villa Reine Jeanne, summer retreat of Paul Louis Weiller, industrialist, philanthropist and one of Diana's closest friends. The villa is set between two curving beaches at the edge of a forest of pine and cork trees, and is one of the most beautiful and unspoilt estates in the South of France.

[5] Anne, Pandora and Atalanta, the three daughters of Sir Bede Clifford and his American wife, Alice Grundy. John Julius and Anne had recently fallen in love, and were married the following year.

My bedroom has of course its private terrace and broad private stairs that lead into the water – the house among its twisted pine trunks – 'old phantastic roots' is invisible to a passer – not that there are any as there is a 10 kilom. isolation ground. Across the way are the Isles d'or on one of which is a nudist colony. Jacques Février[1] or second best frog friend – (Palffy [Louise de Vilmorin] No 1) is a professional pianist who 'delights us' never 'long enough.'[2] Duff joins me in a few days – no telephone. Post office too far so no news of John Julius' arrival. I fret. Your letter a strange windfall here, and none the worse for surprising me.

Nancy not twenty miles away – living so blithely in a sink of drugs and sodomy.

I wish so much you were with me – you'd hate it I fear. The young scream exultantly on their water-ski – Sir Charles Mendl[3] creeps around like a tortoise robbed of its shell, terrified of his 82 year old heart stopping and clinging for life to his kind young wife. Drinks and cigarettes are hard to come by – all to the good. I have a diet, of course – hair treatment – morning exercises – purges and massage – a little dentistry – eye pads and the rest – against the Bestigui ball – but I have no male interest (i.e. a male to interest me or to interest) not that I ever do in this country that's why I loved yr sojourn in France.

Come again and write – 17th Aug San Vigilio. Garda. Lago di Garda (if called on business to Milan – call in before 25. Terrestrial Paradise – and yours). 26th Hotel Gritti Venice.

God bless you

Diana

Evelyn to Diana

Piers Court   *[September 1951]*

Big writing for Baby's big dim eyes.

Big welcome for Baby at one o'clock October 2nd. Feast of the Guardian Angels.

Remember STINCHCOMBE – the key word for finding this house.

Go from Winchcombe to Andoversford, then Birdlip, Stroud, Nailsworth, Dursley. 35 miles. At Birdlip do not turn left: go on. At Dursley go straight through town due West. Wherever tempted to turn,

---

[1] Jacques Février, pianist and member of 'la bande' – the intimate coterie who gathered in Diana's Salon Vert in the British Embassy in Paris.

[2] 'You have delighted us long enough' – Mr Bennet's words to his daughter Mary in Jane Austen's *Pride and Prejudice*, chapter 18.

[3] Sir Charles Mendl (1871–1958). Press Attaché to the British Embassy in Paris 1926–40. In 1926 he married the American interior decorator, Elsie de Wolfe. She died in 1950, and he married Yvonne Reilly the following year.

Evelyn Waugh

Diana Cooper

West House, Aldwick, Diana's cottage near Bognor. From a painting by Rex Whistler.

Waugh in the garden of West House.

The wedding of Evelyn and Laura
Waugh, 17 April 1937.

Diana as the Madonna in
The Miracle.

Gower St. _him for W_

The Secretary of State for War leaving Gower Street, 1935.

Duff, with Diana in her
Admiralty Yacht cap.

Smallholding days, 1941: Diana
with her 'Khaki Campbell'
ducks.

The Manor House, Mells, 1937.
Seated: Katharine Asquith, Conrad Russell, Lady Gwendoline Churchill, and Julian, Earl of Oxford and Asquith. Standing: Clarissa Churchill (later Lady Eden), and John Sparrow. [Courtesy of Lord Oxford.]

Daphne Bath and Conrad Russell.

Pamela Berry and Diana.

Hilaire Belloc, as sketched by Conrad Russell.

Monsignor Ronald Knox, by an unnamed monk from Downside Abbey.

Maurice Baring.

The Château de Saint-Firmin.

John Julius and Nancy Mitford in the park of Chantilly.

Waugh on the terrace.

Duff and Louise de Vilmorin (Countess Palffy).

Waugh in Diana's hat and sunglasses.

bear left. After 2½ miles you will see inn called Yew Tree and avenue. At end of avenue cottages. At end of cottages roadfork. Take neither fork. In private parts of fork is shabby white gate. Mine. From me to London is 110 miles. Your tour would be simpler, more comfortable, safer, cheaper swifter in the train. But I expect you won't go that way.

Longing for you. If more than you and Sir Alfred [Duff] please give estimated number of party.

Bo

Diana to Evelyn

[from London,   *[October 1951]*
written on two postcards]

'Babies subscribe to this anag.' I expect it was. I never told you the unfortunate interlude re Baccarat the man of glass.[1] When I was at Monte Catini part or all of the order arrived at a Paris station and a paper was sent to me to collect with cheque. Not being

[on second postcard:]

there to receive the 'faire par', after a few days they returned it to the shop and now it all has to begin again – but I'll hope to bring them election week. I adored the visit[2] – we all did – including organ, ivy resistance – the silver fruit tantalus and the wallpaper Betjeman bought and funked – love to Laura – thanks for lovely meal – come back to Chant.

Evelyn to Diana

Piers Court   *[pstmk 3 October 1951]*
[postcard]

Your king-fisher flash was a joy.

We can only make Subscribe out of Curse Bibs. Is it some recondite joke about Lady Plymouth? Come again, please, when the sun is shining and you have time to look at some books.

Bo

[1] Waugh had ordered a set of wineglasses from Baccarat, engraved with the legend 'In Vino Caritas'. Diana had undertaken to transport them to London.

[2] In a letter to Nancy Mitford, Waugh wrote: 'Honks and party came to luncheon. It was very difficult to get her in or out of the dining room. She won't be led only driven. She admired my moss on unweeded paths. "You can't grow that in France."' (*Letters*, 29 October 1951, p. 358)

Evelyn to Diana

Piers Court   *9 October [1951]*

Darling Diana

London spies tell me you have suspicions I have apostasized. Why? Not true.

It is most kind of you to burden yourself with Baccarat set. I think that what you left uncollected at railway must be single specimen. That was how I left it with Contessa Palphi. But if they have set incontinently to work on the whole boiling, and if you can possibly endure the boredom of lugging it to London, I should bless baby and baccarat and [Louise de Vilmorin] too. Can pay in any currency but more difficult now I am in concentraggers. Nancy holds one of my hoards but mostly in forms that need signature – not that that protects them from Prod [Peter Rodd]'s expert penmanship.

I shan't be at any of the Press Lords' Election feasts.[1]

Book gets longer and more and more facetious. Practical jokes now and chemical closets and clap. Ever read Hay's *First Hundred Thousand*.[2] Like that.

I have been brought to ruin by court of law pronouncing all my recent financial jiggery pokery illegal.

Great treat the other morning. Letter from Edinburgh (not Duke, city) 'Dear Sir I enclose these copies of correspondence between my wife and your brother Alec because they expose him as an unmitigated blackguard'. Then pages of such smut I never read before. Genuine too.

All love
Bo

Diana to Evelyn

Château de St Firmin   *[October 1951]*

Darling Bo. What a scream about your brother – strange that the outragee should appeal to the outrager's brother, isn't it? Vengeance not redress I suppose.

Glasses – they have all arrived – 6 doz. of them – Can you have ordered that number? Parties at White's? Falstaff friends? careless hands? over the

---

[1] Many of the press barons gave election parties, but it was most chic to be seen at that of the Berrys, held at the Savoy Hotel. The year before, the party had been somewhat muted, as Labour had scraped in by a narrow majority. October 1951, however, gave cause for jubilant celebration, as the Conservatives under Churchill were returned in triumph.
[2] Major-General John Hay Beith (1876–1952). His novel *The First Hundred Thousand* (1915), written under the name of Ian Hay, was one of the most celebrated novels of the Great War.

shoulder toasters? I shall bring them in my own way – a doz at a time – so Patience to your rescue.

Poor L[ouise] is to have her hip-joint opened and re-stiffened next week to enable her (say they) to walk without excruciatingers. She is then if she survives to lie 4 months in Plaster of P.

I'm coming for my fevers to London 22nd – two nights rollicking at meetings with Pam Berry – then two parties – then Pam's for ½ the weekend – Bog. my new friend [Enid Jones]'s for Sunday night and France on 29th. If you are in London 7348 Slo finds me. Did I tell you the luxury *Loved One* turned up? Spirits not so bad – never been as bad since you came to Oise. I've had to take the family photograph off its mount to stick into my book.

Love
Baby

> *Waugh sometimes wrote larger than usual as a concession to Diana's failing eyesight. Yet her complaints evidently persisted, and this is the first of several letters which Waugh wrote in capitals.*

Evelyn to Diana

Piers Court   *[?October 1951]*
[postcard]

I HAVE ASKED NANCY TO SEND YOU A SWEETENER ON MY BACCARAT DEBT. REST MUST WAIT UNTIL I CAN SIGN PAPERS. WHEN WE MET IN LONDON I DID NOT RAISE QUESTION OF YOUR IMPUTATION OF APOSTASY. SO FREUD[1] NOW TAKES PRINCESS MARGARET OUT DANCING IN YELLOW SOCKS. AWFULLY BAD HISTORY OF WHITES. TWELVE EIGHT FOOT CAESARS IN MARBLE BUSTOS ONLY LARGER THAN LIFE ON PEDESTALS FOR SALE NEAR HERE I HOPE TO BUY THEM. EVERY BODY LOVES MY BABY.

Evelyn to Diana

Piers Court   *[pstmk 25 October 1951]*

When I heard Baby's plans I changed mine. Dining Ann, then for a bit to Savoy Hotel. Would like to take Baby on tiles from there but don't know

---

[1] Lucian Freud (b. 1922), painter and portraitist. He was made a Companion of Honour in 1983.

roof geography any more. Free but probably crapulous next (Fri) after-noon and evening.

Awfully decent of you re glasses.

Bo

Piers Court   [undated, 1951]
[postcard]

Is this not an ingenious labour-saving device? I answer all correspondence with it – particularly bills and charitable appeals.

[printed:]

> Mr Evelyn Waugh greatly regrets that he
> cannot do what you so kindly suggest.[1]

Evelyn to Diana

Piers Court   24 December 1951

Sweet Baby

Thank you for the post-card reminding me of my enchanted summer.

Thank you even more for your great kindness and patience in trans-porting more charitable glass. I cannot think of a more tedious service. I will try and go to London as soon as my poor aching limbs allow, and collect them (are they in danger of seizure by Miss Olga's creditors?)

It is Christmas Eve and I shall join Maurice and Conrad in the prayer that you may one day find kneeling space in the straw at Bethlehem.

Sir Duff's kindness to Laura and Polly Grant[2] at Lady Rothermere's[3] ball was deeply appreciated.

My novel [Men at Arms] is very near its end and I am sick to death of it. I think that is a good sign perhaps.

I face the new year with deep gloom. Poverty (artificially induced by politicians) knaws. I cannot with the utmost economy live on less than

---

[1] This versatile printed reply appeared in the Daily Telegraph, 25 October 1951.

[2] The daughter of Laura's sister, Bridget Grant.

[3] Ann Charteris (1913–81) was the eldest daughter of the Hon. Guy Charteris. In 1932 she married the 3rd Baron O'Neill, who was killed in action in 1944. The following year she married Esmond Harmsworth, 2nd Viscount Rothermere (1898–1978), owner of the Daily Mail.

£5000 a year and I have to earn £62,000 to spend that and I am getting too old and downcast to earn it.

I went to a splendid luncheon of old war comrades and all we talked of was our aches and the stupidity of our children.

But I am comforted by the thought of you in your cosy retreat with your Wonderland gardener planting lilies with her file. Please have a very happy year there and turn your thoughts now and then from all your dagoes and levantines and sodomites and think of poor rheumatic

Bo

Diana to Evelyn

Château de St Firmin   *16 January 1952*

Darling Evelyn – You wrote me a line so beautiful about Maurice and Conrad and the straw in Bethlehem, that my heart quickens when I say the words. I hope too their prayers may be answered. One cannot embrace something so serious as the church, for a whim, a love for another – (not God) or as an experimental medicine. I must wait for the hounds of heaven – or some force – some instance – that is irresistible – no reasoning is any good (a) I'm incapable of the process (b) I don't believe reasoning counts any more than it does when explaining music to the tone deaf or rainbows to the blind.

Despair may take the shape of the necessary force. Yet I have made giants of it – and here I still am, without (outside) the walls – not hof-fähig, if you know what that means – Court-worthy (King's court not tennis-court or Earl's-court or court yard).

Nancy's hatred of Captain Carlsen[1] is exaggerated. I will keep Mauriac's letter, attacking Jean Cocteau – considered Bossuet-fähig – for you – I'll bring it to London on the 24th. It's strong alright – strong with God's help and his own wickedness.

How far are you from Dulverton? I have a beau of over 90 years – hatter-mad – and I must one day visit him. I can't stay at Pixton – I suppose I could, and prepare for the 'Camps' of the next concentration.

love from your
X X X Sweet Baby

---

[1] Captain Kurt Carlsen, the Danish skipper of the American cargo ship *Flying Enterprise*. The ship was damaged in exceptionally heavy weather on 29 December 1951. Carlsen ordered the crew to evacuate, but insisted on remaining with the ship as long as he could. When he felt it too dangerous to stay on board any longer he abandoned ship, and was given a hero's welcome at Falmouth on 12 January 1952.

Evelyn to Diana

Darling Diana

Can't write Baby because I have been troubled lately by letters from Paris from a lunatic who gives her address as 'Chez Baby'.[1] I thought at first could it be the lady who plants with a file but the letters have become too American for that.

[Very large writing from here on] Damn I forgot about baby's poor misty eyes. What I wrote above wasn't any interest but <u>don't</u> ask your gardener to read it to you.

Dulverton is 108 miles from here. The only mad old man I know there is Mr Green. You will have a scramble to reach him as he has lately barricaded himself in with granite boulders. It is no time to visit Pixton – very cool and leafy in June and still first class asparagus but death to baby in Jan.

I have had a change of life and sacked all the servants and I am going to become extremely bohemian like the Laird and Little Billy and resign from presidency of the Stinchcombe Silver Band and never again sub-scribe to Treloar's cripples.[2] Part necessity because of the politicians of my country who never stop begging and spending; and part sheer boredom of seeing their faces and hearing their horrible voices.

You speak of being in London on 24th. Details please. I have to be in Derby that night at a popish gathering but could come to London by afternoon Friday 25th or anywhere during Saturday. Any suggestions?

There was a jewess (friend of Sir Alfred's I expect) called Weil whom everyone is making a silly fuss about at the moment. She kept saying 'God will call me when he wants me. I must take no action but wait humbly on his will'. Well he didn't call her and she died unbaptised in all her pride and sloth, leaving behind a lot of pretentious lectures.[3]

Don't let that happen.

I sleep night of 24th at Midland Hotel, Derby – one of the few

---

[1] Letter to Nancy Mitford, 14 January 1952: '. . . You know I call Honks "Baby"? Embarrassing but true. Anyway I got a mad letter the other day of the kind one gets most days. High brow madness typewritten in English. The odd thing was that the address was "Chez Baby" 16 Rue de Condé, Paris VI. It began "Dear E.W." and was signed "Mary O'Connor". Is Chez Baby a nightclub.' (*Letters*, p. 366)

[2] Lord Mayor Treloar's College is a co-educational school for severely handicapped children, near Alton in Hampshire.

[3] Simone Weil (1909–43), an unconventional left-wing religious philosopher who could not fit into any church or political party. She served with the anarchist column of Buenaventura Durruti in the Spanish Civil War, and joined the Free French in London after the fall of France in 1940. Her death was hastened by the fact that she refused to eat more than the average ration available to workers in occupied France. Waugh reviewed her posthumous collection of essays, *Waiting on God*.

provincial hotels not associated with *Miracle*. Send <u>telegram</u> there if you want me to come to London. Otherwise I shall be going straight home.

All love
Bo

Diana to Evelyn

[postcard] *[pstmk 26 January 1952]*

Miserably disappointed – so is Pam – don't again – plan and fail. I'm too old and easily bruised.

I leave for Changtilly on 31st ferry boat – could meet you 30th if convenient – write plain and big to your loving dim-eyed B.

Evelyn to Diana

[Piers Court] *28 January 1952*

DEAREST BABY

THE CAUSE OF YOUR MELANCHOLIA IS VERY PLAIN — EGOCENTRICITY INSTEAD OF BEING HARROWED TO LEARN THAT I AM IN PAIN YOU ARE ANNOYED THAT THERE IS ONE MAN THE LESS AT BERRY'S TABLE. I DO NOT UNDERSTAND HOW <u>YOU</u> CAN BE TOO OLD AND EASILY BRUISED FOR <u>ME</u> TO FALL ILL.[1]

I AM AFRAID THAT I CAN'T RISK THE FREEZING STREETS OF LONDON THIS WEEK. IT WOULD HAVE BEEN LOVABLE IN MY OLD FRIEND IF SHE HAD POPPED INTO THE TRAIN AND COME HERE WHEN SHE HEARD I WAS ILL. WELL MR GREEN CAME FIRST AND WILL PROBABLY GO FIRST, SO HE HAS FIRST CLAIMS.

PLEASE GIVE MY LOVE TO OLGA AND THANK HER AGAIN FOR HOUSING MY GLASS. IF YOU VISIT MR BATTERSBY GLANCE AT MY COPYCATTING.

I FIND FORD M. FORD'S WAR BOOKS[2] TAKES MY MIND OFF MY DISTRESSES. <u>VERY</u> GOOD AND PUZZLING.

LOVE FROM
BO

---

[1] Letter to Nancy Mitford, 15 February 1952: 'While I lay in bed in agony I had to break an engagement in London with Honks . . . Do I get a letter of tender sympathy? Not at all. A scolding saying: "Never do it again – plan and fail. *I* am too old and easily bruised" (my italics). There is egocentric mania there.' (*Letters*, p. 368)

[2] Ford Madox Ford (Ford Hermann Hueffer) (1873–1939), grandson of Ford Madox Brown in whose honour he changed his name in 1919. He wrote *The Good Soldier* in 1915, the same year that he volunteered for the Army; he was invalided out in 1917. He also wrote the tetralogy *Parade's End*, which appeared between 1924–8.

127

Diana to Evelyn

69 Rue de Lille   *[early February 1952]*

Darling Bo – of course I didn't go to see my Mr Green and I would have loved to come to you. I see no reason to be scolded because you have fibricitis. I had bronchitis, was three days in bed in England – and am still abed here. Do try and keep last summer's gallantry alive. You should have written 'BELOVED BABY – alas too ill – my loss.'

I suggested the dinner with Pam because she was pressing it. I thought not only of your poor worn pocket but also humbly of my powers of distracting you. I can live happily with you, but an isolate meal gives me fears, even with you. I've confidence in myself in adventurous, active and illicit conditions – backgrounds of forest glades, or dark Arab alleys – the darkened cinema – but I have very little in my conversational powers.

The vino caritas-es accumulate – Oggie can scarcely see over them – the flat tinkles. I must hope that some foreign mission will bring you out again or I'll never see you. I shall go to London – if better – and see the King's last ride to Paddington but I guess I'll stay only 1 or 2 nights.

It's Sir Deaf Cooper now. He's had a cold as chill and as chronic as the ice age – can't hear my rasp. He's gone to London to visit the Queen.

Strange, I remember how funny it was saying 'God Save the King', and Nanny saying 'Mr Brown will be K.C. now, not Q.C.'.[1] I hope the II has the heart of a King.[2]

Souless Nancy's just left my bedside – her laugh is that of a mermaid. Poor Louis [Paul Louis Weiller] came in with an unsolicited box of 1st class sandwiches – knows I never eat if alone – only Poor Louis does those winning things . . .

Baby

Evelyn to Diana

[Piers Court]   *[early February 1952]*

I HAVE BEEN WRETCHEDLY UNWELL SINCE I LAST WROTE BUT TODAY HAVE DRAGGED MYSELF FROM BED TO TABLE TO SAY: DID YOU NOTICE THE COINCIDENCE THAT THE KING DIED[3] (SO FAR AS ONE KNOWS) AT THE VERY MOMENT WHEN PRINCESS ELIZABETH WAS DONNING 'SLACKS' FOR THE FIRST TIME. I HOPE YOU WILL BE WARNED AND PASS ON YOUR NETHER GARMENTS TO THE LADY GARDENER. I FORGIVE YOU FOR SCOLDING ME FOR BEING ILL. I

[1] King's Counsel, not Queen's Counsel.

[2] 'I may have the body of a weak and feeble woman, but I have the heart and stomach of a king, and of a king of England too.' From Elizabeth I's speech to the troops at Tilbury, 8 August 1588.

[3] King George VI died on 6 February.

ACCEPT IT AS C. CHAPLIN DID THE BUCKET OF WATER FROM THE BLIND GIRL. W. CHURCHILL MADE AN EXCRUCIATING SPEECH ON BBC ABOUT KING'S DEATH. PLATITUDES ENLIVENED BY GAFFES. THE MOST PAINFUL WAS (ROUGHLY) 'DURING THE WAR I MADE A POINT OF KEEPING THE KING INFORMED. HE SHOWED QUITE AN INTELLIGENT INTEREST. I EVEN TOLD HIM MILITARY SECRETS AND HE NEVER ONCE BLABBED.'

WE ARE IN FOR THE UNDOING OF ALL THE WORK OF RECENT HISTORIANS WHO HAVE EXPOSED THE WICKEDNESS OF ELIZABETH TUDOR.[1] IT HAS BEGUN TODAY IN ALL WEEKLY PAPERS. REBUNKING.

LOVE FROM

BO

Evelyn to Diana

[Piers Court]   *[February 1952]*

'BELOVED BABY' ALL RIGHT HERE. COULDN'T WRITE IT UNDER EYES DERBY CONCIERGE. 'MY LOSS' NOT MY LINGO. ANYWAY BB AGAIN. OUR LETTERS XED. THIS IS ANSWER YOURS UNDATED. DO NOT PLEASE WEAR INEXPRESSIBLES KING'S FUNERAL. I HATE MR CHURCHILL SO BITTERLY FOR HIS PANAEGYRIC. RAIMUND COULD BETTER HAVE EXPRESSED HEART OF ENGLAND. OR POOR POOR LOUIS. I EXPECT BEING BLIND HELPS YOU LIKE A LOT OF PEOPLE. BLINDNESS AND MADNESS IN WOMEN HAS ALWAYS HAD PRODIGIOUS EROTIC APPEAL FROM EARLIEST ROMANCE TO OUR DAY. CHARLIE'S HEROINE (LATER LADY JERSEY WITH EYES NO GOOD) CITY LIGHTS AND M. ARLENS LILY CHRISTINE (I THINK) IN MY DAY QUO VADIS OR LAST DAYS POMPEII HAD BLIND HEROINE. HAVE YOU READ 'BLINDNESS' BY MY FORMER FRIEND YORKE [HENRY GREEN] ONLY RECENT GOOD NEWS ANN'S LIBERATION FROM LOUT ROTHER-MERE.[2] I LIVE SO OUT OF WORLD TIMES ANNOUNCEMENT KNOCKED ME ARSE OVER TIP AS IF WITH FEATHER. I WILL NEVER SPEAK OF MONEY AGAIN (EXCEPT PAYING FOR GLASSES STILL NO BILL HAVE RECEIVED 20) IF IT MAKES YOU TOO SHY TO EAT WITH ME. WELL I DIDN'T KNOW I WAS RUINED IN SUMMER WHEN YOU INSISTED LUNCHING AT BARGEES SHACK AND I WAS SICK. IT'S NO GOOD SACKING SERVANTS NOW THEY JUST WON'T GO THEY BELIEVE THEY WILL BE SENT TO KOREA. I HAVE TO BE IN LONDON 29 ANOTHER POPISH MEETING HOW I HATE THEM. ANY CHANCE YOUR BEING THERE 28th OR 30th I MEAN 1st. RE

---

[1] The accession of the young Queen provoked a rash of articles on the theme of a second Elizabethan Age. In a letter to Nancy Mitford of 15 February 1952, Evelyn sets out the 'wickedness' of Elizabeth I: 'She was jockeyed into place by a gang of party bosses and executed the rightful heir Mary Stuart. All the newspapers are full of the glorification of Elizabeth Tudor, the vilest of her sex.' (*Letters*, p. 369)

[2] Ann and Esmond Rothermere had agreed to part in October 1951. The divorce was announced in early February, and became absolute on 24 March 1952. On that day, in Port Maria, Jamaica, she married Ian Fleming.

ROTHERMERES IN MY DAY IT TOOK MONTHS TO GET DECREE NISI. HAD SUIT ALREADY BEEN FILED WHEN THEY GAVE XMAS PARTY? I HOPE MR BELLOC IS TOO BARMY TO NOTICE AND MIND THE VILE ROPER WORK EVERYWHERE REBUNKING ELIZABETH TUDOR. I KNOW I SHOULD NOT HAVE BROUGHT YOU SANDWICHES. ALL LOVE IN BRIGHT LIGHTS NOT ONLY CAVERNS AND GLADES. ALL LOVE IN NEONS.

Evelyn to Diana

Piers Court   *[?February 1952]*
[postcard]

PAINS SO ACUTE MUST SEEK SUN. THINK OF COMING PARIS SAT MARCH 1st (PERHAPS WITH A MR MCDOUGALL IN ATTENDANCE) TO COLLECT SUPPLIES FROM NANCY. THEN IN TEN DAYS TO BE IN PARIS CURED AND CHEERFUL. SOUTHERN DESTINATION NOT DECIDED — PALERMO? SEVILLE? DOES ANY OF THIS INTEREST YOU. BB FROM BO

[on reverse, in Diana's writing:]

suggest you and attendant come direct Chantilly

Evelyn to Diana

Hotel Excelsior   *[?March 1952]*
Naples

BELOVED VAGABOND I SAW MR GILES[1] AND SAID YOU WANTED A BUTLER AND WIFE HE SAID I HAVE JUST THE THING SO WRITE DIRECT TO HIM IF YOU STILL NEED THEM.

I HAD A LOVELY NIGHT OUT IN ROME WITH MY FRIENDS RUSSELL AND A LOT OF WOP PRINCESSES AND WE SANG.

I FELL DOWN HARD LATER.

WHAT KINDNESSES YOU SHOWERED ON ME IN THE TAXI LINE AND THE

---

[1] Frank Giles (b. 1919). After a year as Private Secretary to Ernest Bevin he joined the editorial staff of *The Times*. In Paris he was Assistant Correspondent in 1947, and Chief Correspondent 1953–60. He was Foreign Editor of the *Sunday Times* 1961–77, and Editor 1981–3. In 1946 he married Lady Katharine Sackville, daughter of the 9th Earl De La Warr.

SKIRTS AND ALL YOUR RARE HOSPITALITY. I WAS VERY SORRY TO SEE YOU SO
ILL AND PRAY YOU ARE WELL.

I LIVE FOR THE GLORIOUS 31st OF MARCH.

I DON'T LIKE NEAPOLITANS.

THIS HOTEL IS FULL OF NOISY YANKS. FROM TOMORROW BOHEMIA AND NO
YANKS UNLESS SODOMITIC.

POOR RANS BALLS.

DEEP LOVE AND THANKS AND ANTICIPATION OF FUN TO COME

BO

ROME $\left.\begin{array}{l}\text{ICY}\\ \text{ICEY}\end{array}\right\}$ COLD WHEN SOBER

Evelyn to Diana

[no address]   *18 March [1952]*

SWEET SUGAR BABY

SICILY WAS A FLOP. COLD AND RAIN I EXPECTED. I DID NOT FORESEE THAT
THE ISLAND WOULD BE CHOCK-A-BLOCK CRAM FULL OF SCANDINAVIAN
TOURISTS, TIELESS MEN, WOMEN IN TARTAN TROUSERS, ALL WITH STREAMING
COLDS, SO THAT THERE WAS LITERALLY NO ROOM TO BE GOT IN ANY HOTEL
ANYWHERE EXCEPT A HELLISH RESORT NAMED TAORMINA WHERE I SPENT
THREE DAYS AND FLED.

FAR AWAY AND THE HOPE OF A JAUNT WITH YOU GLOWS, BUT IF ANY
IMPEDIMENT HAS ARISEN OR IF YOU HAVE THOUGHT WORSE OF THE PLAN FOR
ANY REASON, NOW IS THE TIME TO TELL ME. I WILL BE AT MONTE CARLO
STATION ON 31st IF THAT DATE STANDS FIRM. IF NOT I WILL COME NORTH AT
ONCE AND COLLECT THE BAG I LEFT WITH YOU AND RETURN TO PROOF
CORRECTING ABOUT WHICH MY PUBLISHER WRITES FRENZIEDLY AND TO
LAURA WHO WRITES WISTFULLY. WILL YOU PLEASE WHEN YOU GET THIS
TELEGRAPH AT ONCE TO ME CARE RUSSELL VIA PARCO PEPOLI XV ROME TO SAY
WHETHER OUR PLAN STANDS.

ALL LOVE
BO

> *The plan was that Diana should join him in her car in the South
> of France, and that they should drive back as far as Chantilly
> together, stopping a few nights on the way.*

Evelyn had been staying with Somerset Maugham, and he describes an uncomfortable moment at the Villa Mauresque in a letter to Harold Acton of 14 April 1952:

'I spent two nights at Cap Ferat with Mr Maugham (who has lost his fine cook) and made a great gaffe. The first evening he asked what someone was like and I said: "A pansy with a stammer". All the Picassos on the walls blanched.

'Diana joined me in a motor at Nice. We went to visit the Matisse public lavatory cocktail bar chapel at Vence and drove slowly to Paris through snow and hail.' (Letters, pp. 371–2)

Waugh felt he had not been on very good form, and was afraid that he had bored Diana with Men at Arms. *He had the book with him in galley proof, and evenings were spent reading it aloud.*

Evelyn to Diana

Piers Court   *8 April [1952]*

Sweet Baby

Here are some notes about Leo X's elephant.

I was sad to leave you in your famous fur coat, full of good wine as I was. I was sad our treat was over. Such a treat to me who take my few pleasures so sadly and am doomed to disappoint those I love. Try and forget my dullness at Vezelay and my sharpness at the Polignac Arms. Try and forget those tedious pages of military fiction. Remember instead your own great sweetness and patience with me, the sun at Vence, the Hospice de Beaune by the trout stream, the existential sandwiches. May your shells never lack pearls.

It is bleaker here than at Aix en Provence. Many welcoming children, ragged, muddy but polite.

Jenny Graves[1] is said to have provided herself with a most unsuitable successor to the late Mr Clifford.

Tomorrow I go to Downside for the end of Holy Week. You will not be out of my thoughts for long.

Do have plenty of treats and forget my phlegm in more volatile company, but don't quite forget me.

Love love love
Bo

[1] Jenny Nicholson (1919–64), daughter of the poet Robert Graves by his first wife Nancy Nicholson (it was she who decreed that while her sons should bear their father's name, her daughters should bear hers). A journalist herself, Jenny's first husband was Alexander Clifford, war correspondent for the *Daily Mail*. After his death in 1952 she married Patrick Crosse, who was for many years the Reuters correspondent in Rome. Jenny and Patrick Crosse were among Diana's dearest friends in the years immediately following Duff's death.

Ulrich von Hutten[1] wrote:

You have all heard how the Pope had a great animal called the elephant which he held in high honour and dearly loved. Know now that this animal is dead. When he was sick, the Pope was woeful. He called many doctors and said: 'If it be possible cure my elephant.' They examined the beast's urine and gave him a great purgative weighing 500 ounces. But without effect; he died and the Pope grieved. They say he would have given 5000 ducats to anyone who cured the elephant for he was a remarkable animal with an enormous nose. And he always knelt in the Pope's presence, crying 'Bar, Bar, Bar.'

[The inscription on the elephant's monument reads:]

BENEATH THIS ENORMOUS MOUND I LIE, THE HUGE ELEPHANT. KING MANUEL, CONQUEROR OF THE EAST, SENT ME PRISONER TO THE TENTH LEO.[2] I WAS AN ANIMAL NOT SEEN HERE FOR A LONG TIME AND THE YOUNG MEN OF ROME ADMIRED ME BECAUSE IN A BEAST'S BODY I HAD A MAN'S INTELLIGENCE.

FATE ENVIED ME MY HOME IN FAIR LATIUM AND WOULD NOT PERMIT ME TO SERVE MY MASTER FOR AS LONG AS THREE YEARS. THEREFORE, O GODS, ADD THAT TIME WHICH DESTINY SNATCHED FROM ME TO THE LIFE OF GREAT LEO.

HE LIVED TO BE SEVEN YEARS OLD, DIED OF ANGINA PECTORIS AND WAS 12 PALMS HIGH.

THIS MONUMENT WAS PLACED HERE JUNE 18th 1516 BY GIOVANNI BATTISTA OF AQUILA, PAPAL CHAMBERLAIN AND HEAD KEEPER OF THE ELEPHANT. RAPHAEL'S ART HAS RESTORED NATURE'S LOSS.

Diana to Evelyn

Château de St Firmin   *10 April [1952]*

Darling Wu. I waited with impatience for your letter because you being so unpredictable I had not a sure belief, in what spirit it would be written. So you will see how glad it made me when it came this morning. I do not want to forget the book. I'll try and wipe away the tears. I'll hold tightly

[1] Ulrich von Hutten (1488–1523), a dynamic German humanist and satirist.

[2] King Manuel 'The Happy' of Portugal (1495–1521). Patron of Vasco da Gama, he opened up the sea-road to the Far East and launched missionary enterprises in Africa and India. He was famous for the magnificence of his embassy to Leo X (reigned 1513–21), son of Lorenzo the Magnificent, humanist scholar and patron of Raphael.

133

to my heart the cheer of your pink smile and pinker carnation on the Nice platform – the streaks of sun – jokes at Willie's and at his catamite[1] – the flowers and sea, Villefranche and the Golden Lion – the window open to the moon – the Eno's and the orange sticks. Remember Polly – forget Australian Morric of the abeye – forget le bon roi René. Remember baby, cream buns, and the beauty of Sir T. Moore's full face. Forget the drawing of Ingres's lady's throat – the snow on our lashes, the Mistral – the escape from one another to bedrooms on the Avignon afternoon – the tidged up restaurant. Remember again 20 to 10 and too much cheese in the bar – and the reading aloud running thro' all. Forget, O quite forget 'however-long-the-journey' let's get back in a day for poor baby's health – no more readings no more jokes no more of the jaunt. Forget 'Chanel' tho' not its fish and floods.

Rochefort the castle with the patterned roof that stood so nobly, nobly – then there was the narrow escape. I forget where no-room-at-the-inn was and the dear Mill and Mme Bertier[2] the sauce and the wine – jump straight from there to snacks in Bohemia – Rue Monsieur,[3] Monsieur Piebald Palewski[4] – forget the book ended, the first of the winding-ups. Forget my exhaustion and remember Isaiah[5] (remember now and then thy Creator) and his embarrassing discretion – but perhaps you can't remember anything after that bottle drunk at a gulp.

We had the blizzard and our neurotic spoilt natures as luggage and I am ready to pack them up again and stuff it all into a snail's shell that must be well-shaken before using – and be off to the south, pointing out fewer things, leaving guide-books behind, taking only good resolves and the second vol's galley proofs.

Can one say more? dearest Wu – Harold Acton says you're mad – I agree but I like it that way. The Elephant's epitaph delights us all – 'nose' is the operative word.

I'll come to London 6th or 7th for Laurian Jones's wedding to 'un Monsieur tres Bien'[6] ('Is he well?' 'I haven't the slightest idea; I hope so' 'But I thought he was the son of a very well peer')[7]

I shall leave by ferry after the ceremony and festivities with June (Capel

---

[1] W. Somerset Maugham (1874–1965). Playwright and novelist, he trained as a doctor in London before starting to write. Among his best-known novels are *Of Human Bondage* (1915), and *Cakes and Ale* (1930). Alan Searle joined Maugham in 1945 as his secretary, and looked after him devotedly until the end of Maugham's life.

[2] Madame Bertier was the *patronne* of the Moulin des Ruats, just outside Avallon – one of Duff and Diana's favourite hotels.

[3] Nancy Mitford lived in rue Monsieur.

[4] Gaston Palewski (1901–84), General de Gaulle's *chef de cabinet* and the love of Nancy Mitford's life.

[5] Isaiah (later Sir Isaiah) Berlin (b. 1909), philosopher and President of Wolfson College, Oxford, 1966–75.

[6] On 8 May 1952 Laurian, only daughter of Sir Roderick and Lady Jones (Enid Bagnold), married Rowland Winn, later 4th Baron St Oswald. They were divorced in 1955.

[7] 'Bien' in French can be used as an adjective meaning 'well-born'.

Osborn)[1] and her mother Westmorland[2] and dear dwaff Oggie – those are
my plans –

Love
Baby

Evelyn to Diana

[from Downside Abbey]   *[Easter 1952]*

DEAREST BABY

EASTER GREETING I HOPE ST FIRMIN'S BONES CREAK WITH THE ALLELUJAHS OF JEWS FREE-MASONS ATHEISTS AND OF THE INVINCIBLY IGNORANT.

I ASKED ALL THE MONKS AT DOWNSIDE ABOUT MARY MAGDALEN. THE MATTER HAS BEEN IN DISPUTE AMONG THE HIGHEST AUTHORITIES FOR 1800 YEARS AND NO DECISION YET. BEST AUTHORITIES SEEM TO FAVOUR TWO MARIES TWO POTS OF OINTMENT TWO SIMONS BUT IT IS ALL RUM THERE IS 0 TO CONNECT MAGDALEN WITH OINTMENT IN ANY GOSPEL.

ALL LOVE
BO

I AM DUMBFOUNDED THAT H. ACTON SHOULD THINK ME MAD. WHAT WAS CONNEXION BETWEEN BACCHUS AND WIDGEON?

Diana to Evelyn

Château de St Firmin   *27 April 1952*

Dearest Bo – Thank you for my pretty Easter card and kind words – ever since you left me thro' sleet – the sun has shone with undimmed violence and my successful spring beds of all the flowers that fell from Dis's waggon – are burnt to sad cinders for the Amateurs des Jardins to gasp at next Friday. If it could have been otherwise! – our week warmed and this one cooled.

I think from report that we were quite liked at Maughams – considered rum, but alright. The Doctor [Maugham] is in bitter mood – he says Daisy [Fellowes]'s face is deformed by her strokes but the cattamite has

[1] June Osborn, née Capel, was first married to the pianist Franz Osborn. After his death Cecil Beaton proposed to her, but she turned him down in favour of Jeremy Hutchinson (later Lord Hutchinson of Lullington) whom she married in 1966.

[2] Diana Lister, daughter of the 4th Lord Ribblesdale. In 1923 she married the 14th Earl of Westmorland after the death of her second husband, Captain Arthur 'Boy' Capel.

trundled him off to Switzerland for his circulation's sake. The Lees-Milnes,[1] par contre, proclaim themselves as never so happy before.

Bad news for Bo. Listen – no you can't – rather mark and digest. I shall go to Bruxelles with Duff's Wagon-Lits colleagues on Monday 5th. I'll follow the Villette relics and take a boat from Antwerp that will toss me to London at dawn on Wed 7th. I shall have my wig fixed and lunch with Oggie and have a jaunt with you in the afternoon if you are in London. I shall dine with Pam Berry that night. She would love you too – if you cared to join. I shall bring some glasses.

Much as I appreciate the script that is so easy on Baby's dim eyes – I fear the effort of it disinclines you to a longer letter. I'd rather unravel it with a lens than see in a flash so few lines.

In the house lie Paddy Lee Firmur [Leigh Fermor] (just sent for two alka-Selzas) and his Joan,[2] Susan Mary and Bill Patten.[3] To lunch came 'Pug' Ismay[4] – 1st Lord of NATO, and member of White's. Mr James of Verriere with daughter and nephew – a wop Princess – Orson Welles,[5] Charles Mendl, Ali Mackintosh[6] – Christ have mercy!

I wish you'd been here. The Austrian giant[7] always enquires for you in a swimmy-dreamy way.

Hugs and xxx
B

---

[1] James Lees-Milne (b. 1908) had the previous year married Alvilde, née Molesworth Bridges and formerly Viscountess Chaplin.

[2] Patrick Leigh Fermor (b. 1915), writer and traveller. He spent much of the war fighting alongside the Cretans, as British Liaison Officer in Crete. In 1944, he and William Stanley Moss led the band which kidnapped General Kreipe, commander of the German division on the island. In 1968, he married the Hon. Joan Eyres-Monsell, daughter of the 1st Viscount Monsell and previously Mrs John Rayner.

[3] The American diplomat William Patten (1909–60) married Susan Mary Jay in 1939. His work, first with the American Embassy and then with the World Bank, kept them in Paris from 1944 until 1960, and they became great friends of Duff and Diana's. In 1961, Susan Mary married the American columnist Joe Alsop.

[4] General Hastings Lionel, 1st Baron Ismay (1887–1965). He was Churchill's Chief of Staff in 1940, and in 1952 he took on the five-year appointment as Secretary-General of NATO. In *The Fringes of Power*, John Colville wrote that he was 'universally known as Pug, for he looked like one and when he was pleased one could almost imagine he was wagging his tail'.

[5] Orson Welles (1915–85) was working on the final cut of his film of *Othello* in Paris, which he showed at the Cannes Film Festival later that year.

[6] Alastair Mackintosh (b. 1889). Equerry to Queen Victoria's youngest daughter, Princess Beatrice. He married first, Constance Talmadge; second, Lola Emery (later duchesse de Talleyrand). His autobiography, *No Alibi*, appeared in 1961.

[7] Count Friedrich Ledebur.

Diana to Evelyn

Château de St Firmin   *[Spring 1952?]*

Dearest Bo – Beloved Bo

Do you know 'Gran Grins's'[1] (as he is here called) address. Could you forward enclosed – it's asking him about his house in Capri – and if he'd care to let. I brought you no glasses last time on account of I forget what but I'll come again the 4th till 6th laden with charities. I dine with Judy Montagu 4th or 5th – I troop the colour 5th a.m. Scrum lunch with Pamberry. Dance in my finery or rather observe the dancing at Mereworth the Palladian on the 6th and fly home 7th a.m. Prix de Diane at Chantilly 8th. Ran Antrim[2] and Lambtons[3] will be here and I shall wave them to the course. Always wish you were here –

Love and hugs and x x x
Baby

Evelyn to Diana

Piers Court   *[June 1952]*

DEAR BABY

WAS IT YOU IN THE PARK? ANGIE [Laycock] MADE EVERYTHING ENMERDÉ (CORRECT USE?) THAT MORNING.

DEEP CONDOLENCES ON YOUR TERRIBLE FALL IN PRECEDENCE FROM PUTATIVE DAUGHTER OF DUKE TO WIFE OF LOWEST VISCOUNT. YOU WILL HAVE TO GIVE PLACE TO LADIES CAMROSE AND KEMSLEY NOW. IT IS SAD, TOO, HAVING TO CHANGE YOUR NAME WHICH YOU HAVE MADE ILLUSTRIOUS. THE ONLY WAY OUT IS FOR SIR (ALFRED) DUFF TO BECOME LORD DIANA.

LADY HELEN JESSEL INSISTS ON RETAINING HER STYLE AFTER HER HUSBAND'S SUCCESSION[4] BUT ALL AUTHORITIES CONDEMN HER.

ALTOGETHER AN ENJOYABLE HONOURS LIST – BEACHCOMBER, MACKENZIE,

---

[1] The novelist Graham Greene (1904–91). He had been an Oxford contemporary of Waugh's. They admired each other's books, and argued a great deal about religion.

[2] Randal, 13th Earl of Antrim (1911–77). Chairman of the National Trust. He succeeded his father as 13th Earl in 1932, and in 1935 married Angela Sykes, daughter of Colonel Sir Mark Sykes, 6th Bt.

[3] Antony Lambton (b. 1922) disclaimed his peerage for life for a career in politics, but was allowed to sit in Parliament using his courtesy title of Lord Lambton. He married Belinda (Bindy) Blew-Jones in 1942.

[4] Lady Helen Vane-Tempest-Stewart, 3rd daughter of the 7th Marquess of Londonderry, married Sir Edward Jessel, Bt., in 1935. When he succeeded his father as 2nd Baron Jessel in 1950, she became – technically – plain Baroness Jessel. In the same way, Duff's elevation to the peerage made Diana the Viscountess Norwich. She followed Lady Helen's example, and insisted on remaining Lady Diana Cooper.

LUNN AND BEST OF ALL CAROL REED.[1] HE IS MY EMPLOYER JUST NOW. WHAT I FIND VERY ODD IS THAT HE IS QUITE UNOBSERVANT. ONE WOULD EXPECT THE CAMERA EYE. ALSO DISCONCERTINGLY IGNORANT. BUT WE ARE GOING TO THE SEA-SIDE TOGETHER. HE REALLY ONLY WANTS SOMEONE TO TALK TO.[2]

GREENE'S ADDRESS IS 5 ST JAMES'S STREET. MAKE A NOTE.

NANCY'S LETTERS NOW CONSIST ONLY OF EXTRACTS FROM FAN MAIL. ODD.

SIR CAROL AND I MAY MAKE DOVER OUR HOME.[3] IN THAT CASE YOU MIGHT VISIT US IN PASSING. BREAK THE JOURNEY AS IT WERE.

I WANT TO SEND MY DAUGHTER AGED 14 TO FRENCH HOME FROM 1st SEPTEMBER TO 20th DECEMBER. I KNOW IT ISN'T AT ALL LIKELY THAT YOU WOULD HEAR OF DISTRESSED GENTLEFOLK (NOT MASONS) WILLING TO TAKE HER IN, BUT IF BY ANY CHANCE YOU DO, PLEASE REMEMBER

BO

Diana to Evelyn

Château de St Firmin   *20 June 1952*

Darling Wu – it was me in the park shouting at you – you dressed to kill – I never grasped Angie – I saw your group again plunging into Green Park and moped for the rest of the day because you didn't try to get in touch.

No you can't say Angie made everything ENMERDÉ I don't think – it would translate 'Angie made everything shitted' – but you can say Angie made ev.th. enmerdant – or better elle enmerdait tout le monde. I accept your condolences on my terrible fall – it's hell. I who walked before Lady Pembroke and Montgomery and the Derbys. I'll survive, won't sit so often next the holders of those titles, but my name to me is a limb – I can't imagine myself not Lady Diana yet alive. Marriage couldn't change me – and of all names NORWICH is the most horrible. Duff suggested 'Marrington' a nice plain English name not owned – invented entirely for his hero in what Nancy calls Op. Sickmake.[4] J. Julius and I both decried it

---

[1] This was the first Honours List of the new reign. J. B. Morton ('Beachcomber') received the CBE; Arnold Lunn, 'for services to British ski-ing and Anglo-Swiss relations', became a Knight Bachelor; Carol Reed, film director and producer, received a knighthood; and Duff Cooper was created 1st Viscount Norwich.

[2] In May 1952 Reed had asked Waugh to turn a story of his into a filmscript – a thriller called *The Tangiers Story*. Waugh wrote to his agent, A. D. Peters: 'C. Reed keeps coming here in a motor-car. I think he is disposed to employ me. All he wants really is a listener. I will listen for £250 a week but I think it is essential to have a contract signed.' (Nicholas Wapshott, *The Man Between*, p. 254)

[3] In fact Reed took Waugh to Brighton to work on the script, as he had done with Graham Greene. Waugh seems to have enjoyed the work as well as the money, but he had little respect for Reed's plot and did not want his name associated with the film.

[4] *Operation Heartbreak*, Duff's only novel, was published in November 1950.

– and scoffed at Aldwick. I aimed too high: Ld. Ldy Diana, or Unicorn, or Lackland, Sansterre, Erewhon – all good. St Honor (Honoré), St Firmin, St James, St George – even Duff or Duff Cooper would have been better than Norwich – better Porridge – Man in the Moon better still – tho' cause me being Diana the Moon – I mustn't think about it or I shan't sleep.

I went to see the rehearsal of Nancy's sketch – also Violet Trefusis's which deals with des filles Siamoise très bien: well-born S. Twins. Nancy's weighs about the same but these bubbles need highly experienced old sligers to blow them up in irridescent. The poor untaught bust them with their first puff. Both authors thought their pieces rollicking.

Read Duveen's life [by S. N. Behrman].

Love your BABY

and come back soon

I think of going to England 18th-ish and might take a western tour – Stratford from Warwick or Stanway – will Waugh be in residence? Then there's the spectre of Mr Green re-seen. Please write. Grey hairs, furrows and lost enthusiasm weigh me down.

Baby

Evelyn to Diana

Royal Crescent Hotel   *[?June/July 1952]*
King's Cliff
Marine Parade
Brighton

Sweet Baby

I hear hideous accounts of Norwich. Apparently it is in American occupation and is a mixture of Coney Island war-time Foggia.

DAMN. I'VE BEEN WRITING TOO SMALL. I LIVE WITH A SHY NEW KNIGHT WRITING A SIMPLE TALE OF ADULTERY AND MURDER.[1] ALL MY MOVEMENTS DEPEND ON HIM. WORTH IT FOR 250 A WEEK AND EXPENSES BUT I CAN'T PLAN. IF I EVER FIND MYSELF NEAR YOU I SHALL COME LIKE AN ARROW.

I LIVE AMONG TOURING ACTORS AND ACTRESSES HERE AND PINE FOR MR BOULBY. SPLENDID SCENE WHERE DUVEEN GIVES FORD ALBUM. JUST REREAD AFTER 28 YEARS GENTLEMEN PREFER BLONDES,[2] AWFULLY GOOD. IT IS EXPECTED THAT W MAUGHAM WILL DIE AT OXFORD AS DESMOND DID AT CAMBRIDGE.[3]

---

[1] Sir Carol Reed's *The Tangiers Story*.

[2] By Anita Loos (1925).

[3] Desmond MacCarthy (1877–1952), literary critic of the *Sunday Times* for many years during the thirties and forties, and a brilliant conversationalist. On 7 June he died unexpectedly in Cambridge, where he was about to be awarded an honorary degree.

MY SON BRON HAS WON A SCHOLARSHIP AT DOWNSIDE.

ALL LOVE
WU

P.S. YOUR LETTER ALL QUITE NEW TO ME.

Evelyn to Diana

Piers Court   *[July 1952]*
[postcard]

[newspaper clipping:]

CHURCH RUINS DANGER. Three medieval churches in Norwich, St Michael-at-Thorn, St Paul's and St Benedict's which were all damaged in the war, are being demolished because the ruins are considered to be dangerous.

The anti-God campaign has begun, I see.
Katharine has been here, as gay as be damned. She is giving the first cocktail party ever held at Mells and longs to go to New York.
I saw John Julius's engagement[1] with satisfaction that the honours of the House of Norwich will descend to Catholics.
Gloucestershire very enervating after Brighton. I think I go to Tangier with Sir Carol this week.[2] I take it you are in Mr Guinness's[3] yacht being photographed all day long. He has 'interests' in Tangier I think. Why not steer him there?

Wu

Evelyn to Diana

Piers Court   *[pstmk 6 August 1952]*
[postcard]

[newspaper clipping:]

Recently the Norwich local education authority disallowed the following religious teaching books from the routine requisition of the

---

[1] John Julius and Anne Clifford announced their engagement on 8 July, and were married less than a month later on 5 August 1952.
[2] Reed decided against the trip. Instead he arranged a lunch party with Waugh and the producer Sir Alexander Korda of London Films.
[3] Group Captain Thomas Loel Guinness (1906–90).

Catholic secondary modern (aided) school: Catechisms; *Catholic Schools Assembly Book* by Fr. Drinkwater; and *Teaching the Religion Lesson* by Fr. Cronin.

The persecution gathers speed.

Evelyn to Diana

Piers Court   *Assumption [15 August] 1952*

Darling Diana
[newspaper clipping:]

> The Rev. G. A. H. Cooksley, rector of Lopham, Norfolk, died in Norwich yesterday from infantile paralysis.

Germ warfare now.

. . . I have been given a new pen named 'Kalligraph' guaranteed to make the worst handwriting legible. I hope it is working according to specification.

I hope you are having a lovely August. I am tied here in ceaseless rain, entertaining priests and Americans. My children are extraordinarily good – affectionate, bright and helpful but I yearn for adult company.

Next week I will send a copy of *Men at Arms* to remind you of water logged Polignac Arms with angry fists beating on the wall to silence tipsy reading. People who have read it seem to like it – I can't think why. It would be a great convenience if it were a commercial success.

I parted from Sir Carol Reed wistfully and from Sir Alexander Korda with bitterness.[1] The latter showed a very hairy heel in his cups. The former lapsed into complete juvenility. I don't think the film we 'worked' on will ever come to anything.

I have several projects for writing in the autumn. A 'Reflexions at Vence', a highly pretentious essay on modern painting which will entail another journey to Nice; a long short story about a girl with a beard; another about a man called, as it might be, 'Gregory Peck' whose life is ruined by the appearance of a film star with the same name; a second volume of Operation Lifetime. All this must wait until the house is clear of children. At present I keep an unstable good temper with the aid of gin and bromides.

---

[1] Waugh wrote a screenplay for Sir Alexander Korda in 1936 (see page 62). Although never filmed, Waugh and Korda got on well. But at a lunch party given by the Reeds, 'Waugh was thoroughly objectionable to Korda, making pointedly offensive, largely anti-semitic remarks'. (Wapshott, *op. cit.* p. 257) His behaviour must have contributed to the decision to drop *The Tangiers Story* project.

My Battersby is up and looks very well and fills me with tender memories of St Firmin.

Laura has at last secured justice in a long and, to her, very worrying litigation with a tennant farmer. So in all that sort of way my life is full of blessings.

Just looked up 'tenant' in dictionary. Should be so spelt. Why are English peoples' names always different from occupation names? Batchellor for instance. Very worrying for bad spellers.

Have you read [Paul] Claudel's[1] *Seigneur apprenez nous à prier*? Awfully good.

Snake Head[2] withdrew his offer of giving me a tour of Germany. I am rather glad.

Ann Fleming has a son.[3] Perhaps you saw. Most satisfactory for Mr. F.

I go to Cambridge to buy shoes on Monday and proposed dining with Mrs Walston.[4] She says by telegram 'Must warn you I have 150 dining that night'. Who? How? Why? Particularly, How.

Love from
Wu

Evelyn to Diana

Piers Court   *8 September [1952]*

Darling Baby

Long silence. I wonder if you got a letter of mine about a month ago. Not that it 'required an answer' but usually you send a post-card or letter in return and it occurs to me that it may have gone to an hotel where the 'Diana Cooper' you demand was not put among the Norwich mail. It began with a press cutting about the masonic persecution of the Church in Norwich . . .

New paragraph. There is a suggestion that the BBC should do a long programme about Maurice Baring. You know the kind of thing better than I do. Various voices piping up with personal opinions and memories. If this comes to anything, would you take part?

I am a pure busy-body in the matter. I have no share in it at all. As you know I barely knew Maurice and, alas, don't admire his work as I should,

---

[1] Paul Claudel (1868–1955), French Catholic poet, dramatist and diplomat. The work above was an example of the 'Verset Claudélian', a verse poem inspired by the Bible.

[2] Antony Head was at that time Secretary of State for War.

[3] Caspar Fleming was born on 12 August 1952.

[4] Catherine Macdonald married Henry Walston (1912–91) in 1935. She was the mistress of Graham Greene. Her husband was a farmer and Labour MP, who wrote several books on agricultural development and was created 1st Baron Walston in 1961. She died in 1978.

but my advice would be accepted a little in the matter, and we don't want another Laura botch.[1]

John Julius wrote a perfectly charming letter in thanks for a silly little wedding present.

You know that Trim has an heir?

I emulate [St Thomas] More in giving a paternal school course to my children who don't enjoy it at all.

Are you going to Tring soon? My corpulence has become altogether too much and I should like to shrink with you.

What an excellent – really good – review Norwich wrote of Churchill's last volume.

My unhappy novel is having the reception it deserves – large sales and sharp criticism. I am coupled always (greatly to my honour) with Hemingway as a 'beat up old bastard'.

All love
Bo

Diana to Evelyn

Hôtel du Park et Regina   *17 September 1952*
Montecatini

Beloved Bo. I'm glad you missed my scrawls – I'd been writing to you in my head, a kind of letter – so loving yet so full of thorns that I hesitated to pen it. San Vigilio is the most beautiful and restful plot of land and water imaginable – and I thought and wondered how it would suit you; and feared that my – no anyone's recommendation would taint it for you. The owner [Leonard Walsh] is an English drunk of 70 – there is no telephone – he has left orders at the exchange 3 miles away to answer to enquiries for rooms (there are only 7) and for banquets (sic) 'No'. It's growing on him – this year he puts up 'Chiuso' on the entrance door from 2 till 6 and we have to creep atiptoe out of the kitchen exit. Tourists are diverted that way to a tavernetta and the inn is unmolested.

The food and wine – taken under chestnut trees on a terrace walled-in-on-3-sides-with-stone and oleanders, the 4th being sheerly on the lake – is prodigiously good. Freshest, tenderest – nursery-gourmet – butter – trout – red beef laid on and in Belvoir brightness of linen and silver. Your bedroom has an open loggia on the water that acts as yr sitting room. Occupations are mountain walks – which I take alone – swimming straight out of your bedroom – expeditions to Trent (Council of), Verona, Mantua, or Catullus's Sirmione by boat. 3rd Programme 'spetacoli' of Shakespeare – Goethe – Goldoni and opera in various arenas,

---

[1] A reference to Lady Lovat's memoir, *Maurice Baring: A Postscript.*

Roman theatres or medievil strongholds that are dotted round the lake. If I took you there you'd get fat and you'd notice the ghastly motorbicycles that ruin Italy with their open exhausts, and drunken Walsh might irritate you, and the luxurious simplicity you might find austere. I don't know.

It would be less of a risk of pain than for you and me to go hand in hand to Tring. I don't see how the frailty of your nerves and love of me could weather the strain of rain and turnip-juice and higher irrigations. I forget if you've been and know what the torture is like. I love it but I don't get up for more than two hours in the afternoon to take a walk as far as the bus in order to scour curiosity shops or visit the cinema – other patients slip off to a blackmarket tea house where they charge 4/- an egg. The rest of the long day consists of treatments, generally finished by 11 – books, embroidery and the radio – sleep – radio till midnight. If you were there we could have reading aloud – but then the regime might keep you in too great a rage. Anyway it's a tremendous challenge to me, and I'm prepared for a week or 10 days – it would be better perhaps to join you after the first 2 or 3 days and stay a week more.

I get to England mid-October and stay probably 3 or 4 weeks – for Norwich to fulfill and enjoy his duties in the House of Peers. I should like to combine it (Tring) with something else so secret – could I put you under oath and rest happy and secure of your faith?

I'm at a cure now – but here I come at fabulous expense for Duff's sake tho' I have to pretend it's for my good. I lie in black mud and enjoy much what I hope is breaking down the reumaticks. I can't drink the waters, which are the strongest purge to others and cement to me. Duff derives such benefit and has lost nearly a stone – his ankles are like racehorses – his temper sweet and his face aglow – but it's hard work to keep the spirits up at Montecatini, tho' with the help of Tuscany and a car we've succeeded. I write from Ravenna which I must now (7.50 a.m.) get up and visit for the 3rd time in 45 years.

I hope to be a grandmother in earliest May 1953. No time has been wasted by the young lovers. They are over come with gratitude and delight at the present you sent them – indeed I too am impressed – thank you so very much. They've had (it is the fashion) dreadful presents, and few. The Aga sent an ice bucket – they'd hoped for a cooker. The F.O. up to date has only given J.J. a book on table manners.[1]

---

[1] Waugh had given them his collected works, signed – a treasured present of lasting value. An ever-warm, coke-burning 'Aga' cooker would have been, too – but the Aga Khan said it with ice rather than fire. As for the rest of their wedding presents, Diana was doubtless comparing them with her own, some of which are listed on p. 107 of Philip Ziegler's *Diana Cooper*: 'The King and Queen gave a blue enamel and diamond brooch bearing their own initials; Queen Alexandra a diamond-and-ruby pendant; the French Ambassador a gold ewer for incense-burning; the Princess of Monaco a diamond ring; Lord Wimborne a William and Mary gold dressing-case; King Manuel a gold sugar-sifter; Lord Beaverbrook a motor car; Dame Nellie Melba a writing-table . . .' The list goes on and on, occupying 88 pages of a large notebook from the Army & Navy Stores.

Please if you have a chance see them when you go to London – the Allies Club or for the moment the shameful address of The Welbeck Suites 16 Welbeck Street (single bed-sitters) finds them . . .

I wish you could teach me to write. I'll be at Paris Chantilly 24th – come over – bring Laura? – and there I'll stay training a septugenarian wop butler and looking for a cook.

Hugs and x x x
Baby

Evelyn to Diana

Royal Crescent Hotel   *Michaelmas 1952*
Brighton

Darling Baby

Your letter from Montecatini has just arrived here where I have taken Laura for her annual convalescence after the summer holidays – a humble successor to previous jaunts by Queen Mary to the Plaza.

I have never been to Tring. Besides corpulence I suffer from melancholy and aches and pains. I am told the treatment is beneficial for these particular troubles but the chief motive would be a time of solitude with you. If I had less than ten hours a day of your company it would not be worth it. I celebrate my birthday – grand climacteric on Oct 28th. I have to lecture in Nottingham on Nov 7th. These dates seem to make the cure hopeless unless it could begin on Nov 8th. What is the shortest period that would work a change? Would the fortnight before Oct 28th suit you at all well? If so will you please tell me how to obtain entrance. Say Oct 16th to Oct 26th?

All secrets safe with Wu.

I went yesterday to visit Belloc, by elaborate prearrangement. Two civil and pretty grandsons received us. Sherry in the hall. Then a long wait for Belloc. Shuffling and stumping. Then an awful smell like the wolves at the zoo, then entry. A tramp, covered in garbage. A sweet, wise, mad face. An awful black growth like a truffle under one eye. First words: 'Old age is a curious thing. It leaves a man crawling like a beetle while his mind is as strong and young as ever.' Second words (rather disconcerting, because I have met him twenty times or more since you first introduced us; stayed with him often at Pixton and Juliet's. In fact knew him quite well): 'It is a pleasure to make your acquaintance, sir.'

Then he sat down and said to Laura: 'You greatly resemble your mother'. Wu: 'Her mother is taller'. Belloc: 'All Englishwomen and Englishmen are quite enormous. Why?' Wu: 'I am rather short'. Belloc: 'Forgive me, sir. I am unable to judge relative magnitudes'. Then a

145

grandson, who had been taking a festive swig at the sherry, clearly a rare commodity, brought him a glass. Rapturous pleasure and rhetorical praise of wine. Then: 'Nancy (Astor) used to ask me to dinner without my wife. Poor woman she was quite unfamiliar with European decencies'. Wu: 'Lord Astor is dying'. Belloc: 'Forgive me, sir, I forget the subject under discussion'. But he was very happy with his wine, though greatly troubled by attempts to light his empty pipe. We stayed 20 minutes. I believe he enjoyed the occasion though he never discovered who we were.

I am delighted to hear John Julius's good news. You saw that Trim has an heir?[1]

Deep love
Bo

[in margin of first page:]

I think you have Ann Fleming with you. How is she? Her letters seem sorrowful. Is the baby all right?[2]

Diana to Evelyn

Château de St Firmin   *4 October [1952]*

Dearest Bo

Laughed a lot about poor Hilary [Hilaire Belloc] – the smell! O dear – you don't mention the dreadful Regan – horrible Goneril has shuffled off.[3]

Re Tring. Everything us made un-easy by the celebrations of your birthday. What happens? Choose your own lunch? Sit up to devise presents? the children with addresses in verse? No it's not the birthday it's the lecture that intrudes. Suppose then that you came the 10th – having fasted as much as possible before – (it's easy when you have Tring ahead) (and the cutting off of days there.) I could stay till 15th, that's only 6 days – but we'd see . . .

---

[1] Raymond, Viscount Asquith, was born on 24 August 1952. He had two elder sisters: Mary Annunziata and Katharine Rose.

[2] Caspar Fleming was well, but Ann was suffering the after-effects of a painful Caesarian section.

[3] Belloc had far more in common with King Lear than his daughters did with Regan and Goneril. Belloc's elder daughter, Eleanor, married Reginald Jebb in 1922. She and her family moved into his house, King's Land, so that she could look after her old father (her mother had died in 1914). Some thought that Eleanor was over-protective of Belloc; but it was she, and not his friends, who had to cope with his ill-health and exhaustion after his jaunts to London. Belloc's younger daughter, Elizabeth, was a natural vagabond. She would occasionally appear, half-starved, on the doorsteps of her father's friends – as she once did with Duff and Diana: she devoured a loaf of bread without saying a word, and then vanished into the night.

Everything has changed – I got my dates muddled – I could stay till 20th. Will it rend in twain the frail veil that covers us? I would like to think you had vol II to read aloud – failing that you must think of a choice of books. I'd take Helena again or Campion.

My London season starts next Wednesday. I shall be staying at Miss Lynn's. I want a nice Sunday and will propose myself to Berry (Pam) or Head. I have Paddy Leigh Firmur [*sic*], Mr and Mrs Rowland Winn (Laurian Jones), E[lizabeth] von Hoff in the house and no cook. Sunshine – a ghastly cold – perennial mealancholly and listlessness in my opinion are never to be shed except for a minute under the influence of wine or <u>Love</u>. Religion and causes could help but doubt hangs around representing the two brutes.

Tring veils them a bit and keeps them veiled as long as you keep Tring up – but once in circulation again among friends and bores and chores and fears one relapses into fat and gloom and drink and paliatives.

God bless sweet Bo

B

Evelyn to Diana

Piers Court
[postcard]

Please find enclosed stamped and addressed card for your completion.

All love
Bo

Evelyn to Diana

Piers Court   *[pstmk 9 October 1952]*
[postcard]

Can trace no reply to my recent esteemed communication. Presume too late now make arrangements Tring. Shall be in London 15th–17th inst.

Bo

[in red ink below:]

Your letter just arrived. Dates still seem muddled. I shall be at Hyde Park Hotel until 10 a.m. on Thursday 16th and about all that day. Ready for anything.

Evelyn to Diana

Piers Court   *22 October [1952]*

Sweet Baby

Pearson tells me you left parcels for me at White's. I take these to be glasses. Thank you. Thank you. I can only repay you in love for all the trouble you take with them. But there is a material debt you have never disclosed. How much? Can I pay in sterling or is it not true you are coming to England to live?

Do you feel that communications are ceasing – not between us two thank God – but generally with most people. No one listens or wants to understand anything that anyone else says. That was what upset me in U.S.A. Now it seems to be here. I return from my rare trips to London feeling as if I had spent the time in a diver's suit trying to shout at other divers at the bottom of the sea – and no treasure to salvage. Only coral bones.

All love
Bo

Evelyn to Diana

Piers Court   *[November 1952]*
[postcard]

BABY HAS BEEN FIBBING. IT WAS HER SUGGESTION TO GO TO MEREWORTH MY ONLY COMMENT WAS THAT THE PLACE WAS ONE OF PAINFUL ASSOCIATION.[1] I FROWNED CONTINUALLY AT BABY IN LOOKING–GLASS INDICATING DISAPPROVAL. ALL ENCOURAGEMENT CAME FROM NICOTINE MANIAC AND HIS GIRL.[2] BABY KNOWS THIS VERY WELL AND SOUGHT TO EXCUSE HER LATENESS BY BLACKENING MY CHARACTER

WU

[1] The Hon. Peter Beatty (1910–49), younger son of Admiral of the Fleet the Earl Beatty, had been one of Waugh's fellow-commandos under Robert Laycock. Unable to come to terms with blindness, he threw himself from the sixth floor of the Ritz on 26 October 1949. In a letter to Nancy Mitford of 9 November 1949, Waugh describes the weekend before Peter's death: 'I got an SOS from Baby Jungman to come to Mereworth where Peter Beatty was in despair . . . He had asked a party about as comforting as a cage of parrots . . . We chattered away and Peter wandered in and out of the room hardly aware of us.' (*Letters*, p. 312)
[2] Patrick Leigh Fermor and Joan Rayner.

Diana to Evelyn

Train to Bognor   *12 November 1952*

Beloved Bo – I'm always delighted when I see your writing and today leaving Belgravia at dawn I kept my expected treat (undated) for this train. What a disappointment! I never said you'd encouraged me to go to Mereworth – I said (it escapes me where) that I had suggested it, that I found it too late once the turn was missed, that the chimney and his girl, pressed me against my will to find the dome – (I had a reason of my own to want to go – something difficult – but for all the selfinterest I was rattled by the shortness of time.) I said you had stayed in the car – I did not know why – that you had said you had spent the last weekend before Peter Beatty's suicide, uncomfortably in the house – adding that I had asked you if you had liked Peter and you had said '– no –' (I could not guess that this last visit would affect you in the same way as Lady Derby's ordeal that has left her unready to visit Knowsley.)[1] I said, I think that you did it to be difficult – tho' it had embarrassed the callers it was as well – as I was able to get away the quicker by saying that 'Waugh would be in a wax' if we did not hurry. I do not know to whom I told the story nor who was unfriendly or common enough to take it hot foot to you – whosoever it be I hope you will quote this scrawl. You know perfectly well you have no Baby as loyal as this Baby and that if you believe anything else you are very foolish. I thought, if you want to know, that you did it to irritate – or rather from Irritability's possession. It's an unexorcisable demon. The embarrassment of explaining your action to the Trees[2] I rose above.

O dear how sad it all is.

B

P.S. I never saw the frown in the mirror and you know it.[3] And I was not late – luncheon was at 1.30 – so had no cause for excuse – in fact I do not think I mentioned the weekend at lunch.

---

[1] Lady Derby, the wife of the 18th Earl of Derby, had been shot and wounded by a schizophrenic odd-job man working on the estate at Knowsley, Merseyside. The man also attacked the butler and under-butler.

[2] Michael Tree married Lady Anne Cavendish, sister of the present Duke of Devonshire, in 1949. Peter Beatty left Mereworth to them after his death. Michael Tree writes: 'I do recollect the incident as it was so singular . . . Waugh, who I or my wife did not know at the time, refused to enter the house and sat in the car during the visit. He did not speak when I saw your grandmother into her car.'

[3] Diana once told Patrick Leigh Fermor that looking in the rear-view mirror was 'common'. A great many things were common – the list included catching colds, going to the loo in the interval of a play, saying 'bye-bye' instead of goodbye, and tomatoes.

Evelyn to Diana

Piers Court   *Friday [?early November 1952]*

Dearest Baby

I wish I were spending Sunday with you in Rex's best parlour instead of carrying a cold to Cambridge.

Please forgive my cross post-card. My chief sorrow at the moment is that, as all epigrams get attributed to Ronnie Knox, all rudeness gets attributed to me. Beasts come to me and say: 'I heard something so amusing you said the other day' and then recount an act of hideous boorishness without the shadow of reality. So when I got one of these blows (as it seemed) from you, I was sad.

By the way it was <u>you</u> who disliked Peter. <u>I</u> said I liked him very much tho I couldn't quite tell why.

You see what I mean by despair of human communications and divers trying to talk at the bottom of the sea.

Happy canasta
Bo

Evelyn to Diana

Piers Court   *Immaculate Conception*
                                                   [8 December 1952]

Sweet Baby

I am just off to Goa. I have longed to see it all my life and suddenly I thought any day now will be too late. I know it is no good saying Come too. So I can't come to Chantilly Jan 1st as you said I might and as I longed to do. But I will be back in London, alas, Jan 14th to be best man (ha ha) to Alf Duggan. I say why <u>not</u> come to Goa. 'Air India' all black line stops at Paris France 16th Dec 1255. Reach Bombay 17th Belgaum 18th 9.30 a.m. Then 50 miles canoe bicycle or bus. Deserted city in jungle St Francis Xavier's feet to kiss. Tarts opium gambling baroque Hindu temples in classical style. Come on. Was Aldwick Lodge where Rossetti stayed 1876 your house?

I will send you silly Xmas present printed by Fleming.[1] I wrote a mockery of A. Eden the other day. No paper would print it except *Sunday Express*. A. Eden's comment: 'so Beaverbrook has bought Waugh for his campaign against me'. Doesn't that show the politician's mind? Never occurred to him that he might have aroused genuine indignation by his

---

[1] Ian Fleming was on the staff of the *Sunday Times*, and commissioning editor of the Queen Anne Press. Both the paper, and the Queen Anne Press which specialised in fine editions, belonged to Lord Kemsley. The Queen Anne Press was publishing Waugh's book *The Holy Places*.

preposterous Tito-love.[1] They have forgotten the Chinese partisans whom Mountbatten brought for the Victory March, who all went straight back to Malaya to murder planters.

Won't Norwich join the Eden rag?

All Viscounts I meet are very anxious about their chances of getting into Abbey.[2]

All love
Bo

My paper says your boy J. Julius is promoting an obscene play.[3]

Evelyn to Diana

Portuguese India   *29 December [1952]*

Darling Diana

I wish you had come to Goa. It is really a very singular place and may soon disappear altogether. At the moment it is full of pilgrims from all over India and Ceylon – the descendants of people Francis Xavier preached to without knowing their language. He just landed, taught them three prayers phonetically, baptised them and went off and they have remained staunch Christians for four hundred years in spite of frequent persecution. A happy contrast to June Capel [Osborn] and Clarissa [Eden] and Pryce-Jones.[4] Did you know that when F.X. went to Japan he asked the word for God and they told him the Japanese for cock so he spent weeks preaching phallic worship without knowing it.

When I left Europe they said it was the coldest November for a century. Here they say it is the hottest December.

Except for a handful of pale dim Portuguese officials there are no white men in the country. I am quite a curiosity. People stop me in the street to ask my advice about their daughters' piano lessons. There are awful conversations with graduates from Bombay. 'Of modern writers do you most admire as a thinker Shaw or Wells?' A charming Brahman priest

---

[1] Waugh thought Tito no better than Stalin: both were treacherous, repressive, and persecuted the Church. But whereas Stalin was treated as an enemy by the British government, Tito was an honoured ally. The President of Yugoslavia was to come to England in March, and be received by Prince Philip, Churchill and Anthony Eden. Waugh protested vigorously in articles, lectures and letters to newspapers and magazines.

[2] For the coronation of Queen Elizabeth II, planned for June 1953.

[3] *The Frog* by Edgar Wallace. This perfectly respectable play was being restaged for the Invalid Children's Aid Association. The leading roles were taken by Lord Porchester (later Lord Carnarvon) and Elizabeth Winn. Princess Margaret was also involved, although she did not appear on stage.

[4] Alan Pryce-Jones (b. 1908). Journalist, critic, author, and Editor of *The Times Literary Supplement* 1948–59.

who said 'Here there is no courtship or love as in America. There are three questions for the parents – caste, dowry and siphilis'.

Today I was taken four hours drive to see the only 'nobleman' in the country. A major of artillery in the present Indian Army. He lives in a bungalow next door to a temple full of photographs of rajahs to whom he is related but is not allowed inside the temple his mother built because he is low caste. Indian class distinctions are perplexing and fully maintained by the Goans after 450 years of Christianity. It is the main subject of conversation after Shaw and Wells.

A man woke me up in the middle of the afternoon to show me Mr Churchill's autograph. He has published a life of Churchill in Portuguese. He wondered whether if he got it translated into English the BBC would buy it.

F.X.'s body is very dry and grey now. It remained absolutely fresh and bright for 150 years (constantly being exposed and having juicy (literally) bits carved off it) and then suddenly in 1708 began to mummify. This may be the last time it is opened. One of the great threats the Portuguese hold over the people is that they will carry it back to Lisbon if they try to secede to India.

Now I am moving on to see filthy sculptures in Mysore. In London for Alf Duggan's wedding[1] on 14th.

I asked John Julius his views on religion. He said he did not consider we were meant to think about it. He should come to India.

All love
Evelyn

Diana to Evelyn

Chateau de Laaken[2]   *[January 1953]*
[written from St Firmin]

Are you back, beloved Bo?

You gave me no chance to come with you beyond an invitation – you witheld the airfield from me and John Julius who was under telephone orders to discover it – so that I might at least speed you well at a stage. I got your letter: it sounded well worth the displacement, as the frogs say.

I displaced myself to this fabulous palace and am back home, the stationary stolen still intact. Betty Salisbury always writes to me from Balmoral or Sandringham – but she at least scribbles from the actual royal roof – which means her days there must be devoted to letters.

---

[1] Alfred Duggan married Laura Hill in January 1953.
[2] A palace of the Belgian Royal Family.

I have quite a saga – about the Congo brought to Belgium – the Crystal Palace banana glades – the player King – the playing for a fall – the over-excitement of Poor Louis – the old and young princesses – but it will have lost vividness before I see my pretty Bo again.

Will it be soon – I fear the hols are over and you are happy at home. The house is warm and there are no guests for bed or board. You could do your Tring here – no cook, no maitre d'hotel, no one who can read or write. Pierro who puts 'CRI' for gruyère. Jaqueline – my life, my memory – is off with a garagiste to be knocked about by a frog husband, her place is taken by a Tchack [Czech?] child – utterly unlearned. Antoinette, the Polish milker, is in command – she can't even make herself plain – but cooks with originality and charm. If you come all this shall be bettered.

Louise has had her lung out and is like a roebuck in spring. Phyllis [de Janzé], and my dearest sister Marjorie, to say nothing of Viola Tree and Clarissa's mother, might all have been saved most hideous deaths [from lung cancer].

I have no life, no beckoning delights – no admirers (there's the rub). Duff scribbles[1] – and I am left to *Mrs Dale's Diary* or the Benvenuto Cellinism-cum-too-old-for-me of the Third Programme.[2] In Paris one can't even visit the theatre, cinema or concert hall – the geolers are too rude to allow museums any relaxation. We aren't asked out – thank God – save by Indians or Paul Louis. Nancy is Pompadoured[3] out of currancy. Daisy and Reggie Fellowes sit dying fast on each side of a dying grate.

There is no sap in Nature – nor in me. Spiritless, not in pain or acute melancholy I languish chilly – not happily resigned. Laaken was an outing – I shouldn't grizzle – no England in sight.

Love to Laura – write again – I think it's all I look forward to in my post.

X X X
Baby

Evelyn to Diana

Piers Court   *17 January 1953*

Darling Oh Forgot eyes

I mean Darling Baby. Just home to find all the children laid up with mumps and my table deep in undecypherable letters from enthusiastic

---

[1] He was writing his autobiography, *Old Men Forget*, which was published that autumn.

[2] *Mrs Dale's Diary*, a radio serial about a provincial doctor's wife, which ran for many years on the BBC. At that time, the Third Programme was the most cultural and highbrow of the BBC's three radio channels.

[3] Nancy Mitford was working on her biography of Madame de Pompadour, the mistress of Louis XV. The book was published in 1954.

Jugoslavs. I must stay and support Laura who let me go uncomplaining but must now have comfort.

I am full of strength and start the year with resolution of unremitting toil. India was very nice and old fashioned dust, famine, tear-gas, grovelling servility. The only human relationships I abide are intimacy, formality and servility. What is horrible here and in America is familiarity. That doesn't exist in Asia. The filthy sculpture was most disappointing – so small. All an invention of Aldous Huxley really. I came tearing home by air to be best man to poor old Alfred Duggan; had every arrangement made to step straight from aerodrome into top hat. Of course aeroplane was held up 36 hours in Rome. Dined with Mrs Russell. Freya Stark had gravy poured on her head by a footman and it fell in cascades on elaborate new evening dress while a lot of polite wops pretended not to notice.[1] Then I despaired of fog lifting and took train. Oh the joy of settling in a sleeper and swaying down the passage to the restaurant after the claustrophobic hell of air travel and the plastic trays and the smiles of 'hostesses'.

Things seen in India. Communist slogan painted on wall: 'Please vote for Comrade Kosalaramadas B.A.'. At Madura railway station 'Gentlemens Lavatory' 'Gentle' painted out and 'Upper Class' substituted. Christian housekeeper at rest-house, hearing I was back from Goa – would I give her some water from F. Xavier's well. Very sorry I had not got any. Please just a little. I have none at all. Just two drops. She had such a stomach ache. So I gave her a handkerchief with a portrait of Xavier printed on it. She put that on her stomach and went away much relieved. Englishman in Bangalore said: 'The Hindu religion is all Sex. But they don't look on it as you and I do as something disgusting.'

Ian Fleming's idiot printing firm [the Queen Anne Press] made a great balls of a little book of mine [*The Holy Places*]. Did you ever get your copy? Most seem astray.

I saw no elephants in India. The women were lovely, beautifully dressed and so female they make all Europeans look Lesbian. Don't understand 'Benvenuto Cellinism' in your letter.

All love. Please keep writing to me.

Bo

Have you made a study of Juliana of Norwich? Miss Undset's favourite writer. I must have told you about my dinner with her (Undset) and 'July Nortch'? No?[2]

---

[1] Freya Stark (b. 1893), explorer and travel writer. She stayed at the British Embassy in Rome from 9–16 January; but her letters, perhaps not surprisingly, do not mention the incident. She was made a Dame of the British Empire in 1972.

[2] On 25 August 1947, Waugh recorded his meeting with the writer Sigrid Undset in Oslo: 'She never spoke except to ask if I had read "Julie Noitch" (Julian of Norwich, it transpired), drank a lot, and looked like a malevolent boarding-house proprietress.' (*Diaries*, p. 688)

Evelyn to Diana

Piers Court   *[pstmk 1 February 1953]*
[postcard]

I sent out two dozen copies of Ian Fleming's Press's horrible arts-and-crafts misprinted book named *The Holy Places* and have had only 10 acknowledgements. Could you please assist my investigation by telling me whether a copy ever reached you? I suspect coshes.

E.W.

Diana to Evelyn

Château de St Firmin   *2 February 1953*

Darling Bo. Nothing to say – except thank you for your letter. Duff delving into his archives read me a lot of letters from such men as Bobbity Cranborne, Brendan [Bracken], and Harold Nicolson[1] written in 1940 when we were lecturing in America. I, deep in the 'belles lettres' of the French 18th cent. found them infinitely more interesting, spicily flavoured, individual and equally polite – less formal – with more variety and fantasy in their construction than any of Mad. du Deffand's[2] Jeremiads or M. et Mad. de Choiseul's[3] epistals. These last are exiled and in disgrace in the Touraine and hold a court of anti-du Barri partisans at Chanteloup (a Pagoda which I'll take you to see was erected there to commemorate the guests. It's all that remains of the huge Palace and appendages.) A great day was when 100 rare cows arrived (on the hoof of course) from Switzerland – beribboned garlanded with their calves at heel, and numerous Swiss attendants of both sexes in gala national costumes. The house-party (never less than 30) were beside themselves.

A queer custum, fortunately obsolete, was that in great Society, when you were ill, in ratio to the gravity of the complaint your friends arrived to <u>camp</u> either in town or country. They came for the duration of anxiety – 40–50 strong – the intimates had a right to the sickroom, and the others disposed themselves in various salons and antirooms – their effects were scattered everywhere – they brought their maids, valets, and if it was far

---

[1] The Hon. Sir Harold Nicolson (1886–1968), author and critic. He resigned from the Diplomatic Service in 1929, went on to a career in politics, and published more than thirty books. In 1913 he married the writer and poet Vita Sackville-West (1892–1962), and together they created the gardens of Sissinghurst Castle, Kent.

[2] Marie, Marquise du Deffand (1697–1780). Celebrated for her correspondence with Horace Walpole and the Président Hénault, among others.

[3] The Duc de Choiseul (1719–85), soldier, diplomat, and patron of philosophers. Voltaire was among his correspondents. He was flagrantly unfaithful to his wife, the Duchesse de Choiseul (1734–1801), but she adored him nonetheless. A friend of Horace Walpole and the Abbé Barthélemy, her letters were first published in 1866.

from Paris their lovers *au besoin*. The patient's household had to feed them and the distraught wife to amuse them, or howl with them.

You see I have nothing to say – I have to quote from my books. The plans are London on the 11th, and I've suggested dining with Pamberry – but received no answer. 12th to visit Salisbury – no, Bath (to see a house) for the day, then dinner in London – maybe – with son and Anne. Friday lunch with Violet Wyndham[1] ('Auntie Nose' to Nancy and others): one who loves me out of reason till it hurts her and me – a Limpet of Love – and home here that night on the ferry boat. Next – quietly here watching the first shoots of spring then a fortnight of Tring in middle March. The pageant of the spring in April and May here, which brings us to the High Jinks of the coronation – Do you fit in?

Meanwhile and at all times I love you –

Diana – Baby

Evelyn to Diana

Piers Court   *[?February 1953]*

Darling

I suppose the postman got coshed. I got persecution mania when no one thanked me for my little Christmas present. Then I thought perhaps they were so horrified by the misprints they could not write. I have corrected this copy for you. 'Paddy the next best thing'[2] had a copy for review and a very pretentious review he wrote.[3]

If you are really going to Bath on 12th please note it is only an hour from here and that there is now no decent place to lunch there and it is too cold for picnic so do please consider lunching here.

I shall shun London during the tourist season of June.[4]

All love
Bo

---

[1] Mrs George Wyndham. She wrote biographies of Ada Leverson, the Duke of Monmouth, and Madame de Genlis.

[2] Patrick Leigh Fermor was often called 'Paddy the Next Best Thing', which was the title of an old music-hall song.

[3] Patrick Leigh Fermor thought some of Waugh's references to the Orthodox Church unfair. He cannot now find the review, but remembers writing something like: 'Mr Waugh attacks in the manner of French boxing, and the shanks and shins of his opponents are jarred by many a deft kick below the normal target area'.

[4] The coronation of Queen Elizabeth II was set for 2 June.

Evelyn to Diana

Piers Court   *[?mid-February 1953]*

Darling Baby

Was our evening out hell? I was looking forward to it so much and what must I do but get pissed. I am so awfully sorry and ashamed. What did we talk about? Your house in Bath? Denton Welch?[1] Tito? I have a memory of a candle-lit upper room somewhere and then arriving at my hotel in the middle of a Caledonian Ball with pipers in the lift and you telephoning and my thinking it was the pipers. I had so many things to ask and tell you. Oh Dear Oh Dear. I have given up all sleeping draughts for Lent so have plenty of time for reading and am fascinated by D[enton] Welch a little dying pansy describing pathetic picnics in the rain – rye-vita and milk chocolate – and tiny two bob antiques and then when he meets the great Eddie Sackville-West,[2] Mrs Nicolson,[3] Herbert Read,[4] Sickert,[5] Osbert Sitwell etc the most frightening penetration. He met only one woman he thought perfect – S[ybil] Colefax. Try his *Journals* for size.

Yesterday I was offered a seat in the Abbey for coronation + £250 for sitting in it as a journalist, but had to turn it down for sheer boredom. I would be much happier if I could get interested in the topic of the hour but I can't. I am so bored with Tito and next week I go to Glasgow to inflame the criminal classes against him. Oh Dear Oh Dear.

I have been concocting very pretty pictures for a silly little book[6] and I have begun Vol 2 of Magnum Opus[7] and taken to composing music.

Lady Curzon [Alfred Duggan's mother] is really a very gruesome woman. She lives in a little St John's Wood style house in the park of Bodiam which is a fine and roofless house full of magnificent huge remnants of past splendours – so is her conversation. Lady Milner for luncheon. Lady Milner's grandson to dinner.[8] Harold Nicolson for tea. Coronation talk. 'I have been asked as <u>myself</u>.'

---

[1] Denton Welch (1915–48), writer. He was going to become a painter until a bicycle accident in 1935 made him an invalid for life. His most important work is the autobiographical *A Voice Through a Cloud*, which appeared posthumously in 1950.

[2] Edward Sackville-West (1901–65). Novelist, critic and musician. He wrote *The Sun in Capricorn* (1934) and *A Flame in Sunlight* (1936). He succeeded as 5th Baron Sackville in 1962.

[3] Vita Sackville-West.

[4] Herbert Read (1893–1968). Art historian, writer and critic, he was knighted in 1953.

[5] Walter Sickert (1860–1942), painter. With Wilson Steer, he was the most important of the British Impressionists.

[6] A drawing of *Cupid and Psyche* by Canova was undergoing transformation to illustrate *Love Among the Ruins*.

[7] The second in the *Sword of Honour* trilogy.

[8] The Viscountess Milner (1872–1958). She was first married to Lord Edward ('Nigs') Cecil, author of *The Leisure of an Egyptian Official*, who died in 1918. In 1921 she married the 1st Viscount Milner (1854–1925). Lady Milner was Editor of the *National Review* 1932–48. Her grandson George Hardinge (b. 1921), later 3rd Baron Hardinge of Penshurst, was a senior editor at Macmillan, publishers, 1968–86; but at this time, Waugh described him as a 'starving young publisher'. (*Diaries*, p. 716)

Please forgive me for spoiling one of your rare London evenings. Please trust me not to do it again

All love
Bo

Your friend Lady Jones asked me to dinner. Why?

Diana to Evelyn

Château de St Firmin   *28 February [1953]*

Darling Bo. What islands we are – never knowing what's going on in other's lands. I thought our dinner delightful. You were tremendously foxed at 'Time & Life', as was Ed. Stanley and others. I feared for our evening – but you were docile and deigned to be led to Wheelers. There you sat in a corner in discreet light and you ordered a sole *Pavé* (pronounced excellent) and a bottle of Traminer. Before their consumption I'm rather sorry to say you sobered completely. Conversation alas! I forget as it's nearly always ear-in-ear-out with me. I cried only once not from pain but emotion because you assured me so very many people dead and alive were praying for me. You suggested, without enthusiasm, following the evening up with a bottle of Pop at the Hyde Park but there is something throttling to me in its atmosphere of respectable gloom – and of the liner – without an escape to a seascape – that I said it was better not.

When I got home Oggie was still out, and feeling my song ½ sung I called you to give thanks, and for reminisance, and love's sake. I got a very sharp 'These are Mr Waugh's appartments' and a 'hang up', a viscious one, because I laughed. Ten minutes later, pride successfully swallowed, I tried again, only to get 'Put me immediately onto the manager'. 'It's only BABY,' I whined and pleasant good nights were said. You never spoke of Denton Welch to my memory. I can't read in your letter what I should read of his. 'Try Goivnals far rize' you write. I can't decypher.

I wish you'd go to the Abbey [to report on the Coronation]. You say you can't bring up the pretty chickens on what you make – but £250 for four hours pageantry and reportage surely helps if paid tax free or in kind (by arrangement) as would giving up oyster snacks at Wilton's before going to lunch or dine with friends.

What of the bewitched child? – an individual keeper will be another expense. Is it the raggle taggle gipsies O? or the death wish so to the modern fore in Child Psychology.[1]

And my friend Lady Jones asked you to dinner – 'Why?' you say. It seems clear as day to me – big link I am – fellow author – known for wit – not yet known for sulks. Many other friends shared, i.e. Conelly.

Enough now of answers to your letter, but then I've nothing of my own to tell you. Duff's had 'flue for two weeks. He might have had lock-jaw from the way I carried on – ear to the keyhole all night – prayers of Panic. He has improved but it's slow still – invalid life – bed for dinner in cactus-hot room – then I read my letters to Conrad from the 1941–42 world trip.[2] I paint the upper floor in the afternoons – the dirt up there – where I seldom go as all the servants keep their doors locked and I can't see if they are warm and dry – is Augean – it's never had a spider's web destroyed – Revolting. I discovered that that criminal Jean (maitre d'hotel) had a master telephone laid on to the third floor servant's lu – the only one in the house that was able to frustrate Abetz's[3] splendid German inter-outer coms that could not be overheard. That's where he spent his day.

I shall go to Tring next month for ten days then back for the real spring – tho' it's begun already – snowdrops withered, crocuses partly up. Will you come back with me about 23rd for a few days? Duff will be racing at Aintree old style – and I'll be lonely.

I love you
B

Evelyn to Diana

Piers Court   *2 March [1953]*

Darling Baby

JOURNALS OF DENTON WELCH published by H. HAMILTON [1952]. Just the thing for Tring.

I am hugely relieved to hear that I was not entirely obnoxious in the candle light. Wine takes all my memory away.

I long to spend the Grand National with you but, alas, can't. I am 'seeing' a little book 'through the press' which in this case – me doing illustrations which go back and forward to photographers daily – does

[1] On 27 January, Waugh wrote in his diary: 'I suggested to Mother St Paul that Harriet should remain here this term if they would remit her fees. The nuns leaped at it, remarking that many little girls at the school are terrified of her.' (*Diaries*, p. 714)

[2] Diana's letters to Conrad Russell had been returned to her by his executors.

[3] Otto Abetz (1903–58), Hitler's Ambassador to France during the occupation. An art teacher by profession, he was a passionate francophile who had married a Frenchwoman. He gave elegant parties in the German Embassy in the rue de Lille, and used the Château de St Firmin as his country retreat.

mean daily attention. But I will swiftly respond to any appeal after Easter if you are left solitary.

There is no way of getting payment tax free or in kind in this country except in the real criminal world. My financial troubles are not from lack of earnings. Anyway what could one possibly write about the Coronation that would do for Empire syndication?

Damn Tito and Eden. I am involved in a dozen tedious controversies. Sad about Paris *Daily Mail*.[1]

Our papers hardly mention the case of Jews who are trying to kidnap the Christian orphans. Is Norwich behind it?

Since I gave up narcotics for Lent, my Sundays are spent in a stupour.

It is a great delight to do the pictures for my silly story. I haven't the guts nowadays to do an original drawing but by the time I have finished with paste and scissors and Chinese White and Indian ink they are really all my own work. It is like Cinema producers who have to have a story to start on and then gradually eliminate it.

All chimneys are smoking today and my eyes are full of tears.

I go to Mells on Wednesday and then to Glasgow without Wind in the Willows (to harangue mob on Tito). Did you have a dog named 'Willow'? Did you know Bloggs was called Willow by his aunts?

I am so happy it is all right about our outing. Those men in kilts on top of everything made the reason totter.

All love
Bo

Evelyn to Diana

Piers Court   *18 March [1953]*

Darling   I don't live at White's. Do try and remember my address. The servants at White's are usually drunk and most of the members are thieves so that it is very risky to write there. For once however they have forwarded a post-card (no possibility of enclosed cheque) and what a very pretty one. Where is Chateau de Pierrefonds? Never heard speak. Looks lovely.

I sorrow for you starving in this exhilarating spring. Everything is very well with me. I got a prize last week – not usual in middle-age, unknown in my youth – £185 free of tax. I have to earn about £800 to get that. I have ordered six shirts and six pairs of shoes and still have £70 left for a picture or a trip to Chantilly.

---

[1] The *Continental Daily Mail* might be described as a popular version of the present *International Herald Tribune*. It began in Paris after the war, and had just been closed down by Lord Rothermere.

I am <u>very</u> pleased about the fiasco of Tito's visit. Clarissa's social ambition to entertain the criminal classes is thirty years out of date. I remember Driberg[1] first made fashionable friends by taking them to visit a gangster chum called 'the Hoxton Horror' in a cellar in Greek Street. *Punch* was going to publish this (enclosed) but I have withdrawn it as the politicians have made fool enough of her already.[2] But I am very tired of the campaign of mockery and shall never again venture into public controversy. Oh, the morning's post the last two months. At Glasgow over 3000 people paid cinema prices to proclaim their disapproval. It was rather a gruesome visit though. I suppose I am a very bad guest – often complaining I don't get enough to drink. In Glasgow a 'double whisky' was thrust into my hand literally every five minutes of the day and I didn't like that either. But they sent me a crate of Gourock kippers afterwards and that is something.

Then I am very pleased too about the Apotheosis of Art Nonsense at Sir (ha ha) Herbert Read's great exhibition of the 'Unknown Prisoner'.[3] Did you see it? All pure balls and at last even the critics are ashamed.

I have done some very pretty decorations for a short story (enclosed one). Luxury edition will reach you at Coronation time.

I have begun the second volume of Magnum Opus and it starts well – White's in an air raid with Archie Groom[4] as hero.

How boastful all this is. Well I am so often in the dumps and write whining so please forgive cock-a-hoop for once. Perhaps it wasn't kind in your present situation to mention the kippers.

Who are Messrs Carr[5] and Grimond[6] whom Clarissa asked to her Tito banquet? F.O. stooges?

Nancy takes Pompadour with proper seriousness. All her letters now are about the Bull 'Unigenitus'.

No hope of your coming here for blow-out after fast? Pretty new pictures to show you including a fine Augustus Egg.

---

[1] Tom Driberg (1905–76), journalist and politician. From 1928–43 he was on the staff of the *Daily Express*, where he was the original 'William Hickey' gossip columnist. From 1949–74 he served on the National Executive of the Labour Party. He wrote biographies of Lord Beaverbrook and Guy Burgess.

[2] While in Yugoslavia during the war, Waugh and Randolph Churchill reached the conclusion that Tito was a woman because he never seemed to shave. From then on, they always referred to Tito in the feminine form between themselves, and Waugh developed the joke into an article.

[3] An international competition had been held for a sculpture of 'The Unknown Prisoner'. The winning entry, a mildly abstract piece by the British sculptor Reginald Butler (b. 1913), was put on show and almost immediately vandalised.

[4] The hall porter at White's.

[5] Robert Carr (b. 1916), created 1st Baron Carr of Hadley in 1975. From late 1951–April 1955 he was Personal Private Secretary to Anthony Eden, then Secretary of State for Foreign Affairs. Under Edward Heath, he was Home Secretary 1972–4.

[6] The Rt. Hon. Joseph Grimond (b. 1913), created 1st Baron Grimond in 1983, lawyer and politician. He was MP for Orkney and Shetland 1950–74, and leader of the Parliamentary Liberal Party 1956–67.

I enjoyed *Madame de* very much. Also Norwich's review of Virginia Cowles's book.[1]

I say what about Fleur Cowles coming to the coronation? Takes the gilt off a bit and adds to the guilt, doesn't it?[2]

All love
Bo

Diana to Evelyn

[Château de St Firmin]   *[March 1953]*

Darling Bo

I think your picture most lovely – immensely talented – much better than dear foolish Cocteau[3] – would you like it put on a silk square for your wife's head? (kerchief) – or squares for your friends? What a wealth of laughs this week has given us from the art front. First the £4,000 'Unknown Prisoner' together with its distruction and its promise of restoration in under a week – then Picasso and Stalin and Aragon – I've taken your letter <u>au pied de la lettre</u> which has quite another meaning to the one I mean.

1. Re addressing you at White's – I very rarely do but sometimes the whim takes me to have you think of me in London. If you had happened to be there that day you'd communicate perhaps and we'd meet half seas over. I only err when I'm in England and promise not to again.

2. Pierrefonds is not far from Chantilly. Enormous – Violated by Duc Chateau-fort[4] – I haven't been inside. I've got a perfect new guide book with a page devoted to ruins, abbeys – chateaux in our region – you in mind when I bought it, and Vezelay and tears.

3. You don't say what the prize was for? the spending of it ever so masculine – poor Missus and the kids!

4. Eyes see what they hope for. From what I gather from telephone, Radio and general gay attitude – experimental and sans soucis that the Titto visit is far from a Fiasco. Not that I'm keen on his success. Could

---

[1] *Madame de* is a novel by Louise de Vilmorin, in which a pair of diamond earrings trace a woman's relationship between herself, her husband and her lover. The writer Virginia Cowles (d. 1983) married Aidan Crawley, politician and Chairman of London Weekend Television 1967–71, in 1945. Her latest book was *Winston Churchill: The Era and the Man.*

[2] The young Fleur Cowles (married to a cousin of Virginia Cowles) was the creator and Editor of *Flair* magazine and Associate Editor of *Look* magazine. President Eisenhower appointed her an ambassador to the Coronation in preference to older women, such as the Republican hostess Virginia Bacon, and Elizabeth Arden, a heavy contributor to his campaign fund. According to Fleur Cowles, this fomented great jealousy and a 'whispering campaign' against her.

[3] Jean Cocteau (1889–1963), writer, playwright, film-maker, poet, artist and designer.

[4] i.e., a *Château-fort* much restored by Viollet-le-Duc.

Punch have published your laugh? I'd have been staggered and subscribed in future. Randy always refers to 'her' – I can hear him and you gathering the legend up, triumphing with a new endorser – Randy's delight I see and hear.

Pipe down on Clarissa and concentrate your mockery on Eden. Clarissa baiting smacks to many of thwarted love – I never liked her much but am able now to wish her well.

5. Chantilly has the Battersby bar – 'Take it or leave it' clinks the tray – 'I'll soothe you' says the mint – 'I make a change' says Absinthe – 'But I'm Bo's boy –' smugs whiskey. Result that you have always been an admirable guest – ever to helping me with St George[1] and pleasing my difficult Duff – now much deafer than you. The thing is I'm told, to wear a so-called 'aid' – a bogus one, and people no longer mumble but concentrate and speak to you and clearly at that. People are sensitive about wearing their Umbilical like cords in their ears. I'm not. I suffer dreadfully to see Duff more out of the conversation – bringing up a topic or quotation just finished with, the echo having touched enough subconscious to bring it new to his mind. I detest age. G. F. Watts[2] should have painted Age and the Senses – fleeing wraiths watched by a resigned draped tottering figure. I should paint a poor woman like me groping for spectacles to look for her trumpet to see her tasteless food.

6. Who are Carr and Grimond? Carr – no-can-do and Grimond successful lawyer M.P. Lib. I think – married to a daughter of Lady Violet Bonham C. (Chief Whip Lib. just seen in paper.)

7. Nancy! O! my poor Nancy.

8. No hope of blow-out in Gloucestershire Master Shallow.

9. What's an Augustus egg.

10. So pleased to hear about *Madame de.*

I still have a glass mountain for you in Paris. I'll dole them by degrees. I've contributed nothing of me to this letter – there is nothing – I am always happy here – in spite of a black eye due to a bathroom fall. I'm not doing a total starve for fear of looking too ugly – not because of hunger pangs. I've read

(A) Paddy's book on monastries [*A Time to Keep Silence*, 1953] fully bound in Morocco – I should like your criticism.

(B) a new book on Browning – a subject that cannot cloy for me.

(C) a sensational French book by d'Erlanger (not Leo) about Villiers, duke of Buckingham

(D) a novel by my chum Pamela Frankau with a life-like portrait of Max.

---

[1] The gala dinner on St George's Day in Paris.
[2] George Frederic Watts (1817–1904). One of the last painters of those grand allegorical or historical scenes that the Victorians were so fond of.

Now it's to be a book recommended by Quinel [*sic*] – I don't think it's going to be any good for me – then *God, Graves and Scholars*.[1]

Please tell me what your picture illustrates? I'll leave here Monday, and to France Tuesday.

Love to Laura –

Hugs –
Baby

Evelyn to Diana

Piers Court   *23 March [1953]*

Darling

(a) Augustus Egg R.A. a great but little known early Victorian painter. The first academician to encourage Millais and Hunt. The only one, besides Dyce, whom they admired. I have three lovely ladies in a punt picking rushes.

(b) Prize rather odd – called 'James Tait Black' after Scottish benefactor. In the gift of the Professor of Rhetoric at Edinburgh University. Given to *Men at Arms*.

(c) Deafness no trouble in tête-à-tête. It only prevents me going to dinner-parties. Anyway no one except Lady Jones and someone I don't know called Mrs Hulton ever asks me to anything.

(d) I hate whisky.

(e) How peculiar the arrangements seem for Graham Greene's play.[2] Four first nights. They hated it in Glasgow. 'The kind of thing' they said, 'that goes down well in Edinburgh'. I am all for Edinburgh since James T. Black.

(f) Why not the DENTON WELCH JOURNALS as advised by yours truly.

(g) Eden is such a chump he is not fair game. You can call it thwarted love with Clarissa – I call it scales falling from eyes.

(h) Picture represented gentleman fucking bearded lady. The figures are from Canova's *Cupid and Psyche*.

(i) I wish my eyes often saw what they want to find in newspapers. Usually it is quite the opposite with me. I saw only a terrified police force, a sycophantic protestant primate, the probability of an arranged betrayal of Italy over Trieste, an army threatening mutiny – all that seems to me a fiasco.

---

[1] *God, Graves and Scholars: The Story of Archaeology* by Kurt Marek Ceram (1952).

[2] Graham Greene's first play, *The Living Room*, put on by Donald Albery at Wyndham's Theatre in London.

(j) More Reg Butler fun in today's newspaper – solemn protest by American sculptors. Who is the lunatic donor?

(k) Horrible children returning prematurely this week. I go to Downside for Holy Week. I long to visit you at Chantilly. Would you accept me on 17th of April? Or a day or so earlier. I have promised Graham to go and applaud his first night but don't know which first night he means. I should like to come on the day after it, which may be 14th, 15th, 16th or 17th. He is in Jamaica so I shan't know until he returns.

(l) Sweet Bridget Grant is here. For her Dursley is a great emporium and centre of civilization. She has her toe nails cut and buys china and other refinements for the home.

(m) It isn't so much the wires – it is the button in the ear that revolts me. Bob [Laycock]'s mother left a number of ear trumpets. Angie has promised me one.

Oh, dear I have been writing small again. Very sorry indeed. Must I copy out? Please not.

All love
Bo

Evelyn to Diana

Piers Court   *Easter Monday [1953]*

Darling Baby
   Damn. Starting small again.

Darling Baby I mean.
   I will come to Paris on the Golden Lion on 17th. Longing for it. Could you be very kind and tell me the time and point of departure of the train for Chantilly. Same station as Lion? Or if you will be at 69 [rue de Lille] so that I may meet you. But perhaps you will be in train – best of all.

Graham has asked Laura and me to his fourth first night – 16th. He is giving a cocktail party at Claridges before it so I take this to be the chief celebration. Tickets are said to be scarce so you should claim at once. He lives at 5 St James's Street. He is not available after performance.[1] Laura

---

[1] Waugh was not very impressed by *The Living Room*. In his diary he wrote: 'Went to play in high spirits which the performance failed to dispel. More champagne between acts. With result that I was rather inattentive to the final scene which presumably contained the point of the whole sad story.' (*Diaries*, 16 April 1953, p. 718)

and I will be dining alone after the performance. Huge treat if you and Norwich (or other escort) would dine with us.

All love
Bo

Arrow of course not Lion

Diana to Evelyn

Château de St Firmin   *8 April [1953]*

Darling Bo –
  Of REAL IMPORTANCE.

CIRQUE PINDAR

comes to Chantilly 17th so for pity's sake arrive before then – as soon as possible in fact. Has G. Greene's play got a date? We have a moveable on to lunch with Nancy at Versailles.

Flowers that bloom in the spring Tra-la are with us – I do hope the tipsy, in-the-know Rajah is in the Parade still – and the snake charmers or were they fire-eaters? I'll take a lot of ringsides.

I've got a lump on my jaw the size of an egg and made of stone – I fell on the bath and got a black eye which faded normally two or three weeks ago – the jaw has not blacked but I am told it will over the course of months and the lump will be absorbed – meanwhile I look an ass in a wimple.

love
Baby

P.S. Letter from you received since writing. This is therefore to emphasise that you must <u>not</u> leave London (Vic) later than 10 a.m. arriving Paris 6.08 p.m. where I will meet you – I think it safer. The idiotic Lion doesn't get to Paris till 9.30 p.m. when there is I imagine no train to Chantilly (the station is Gare du Nord for and from England and Chantilly) and too late for the Rajah. There's hourly air service – but I don't hold to it, still I could meet you at Le Bourget – not Orly.

I shan't be able to go to G.G.'s play – gathered it was here, stupidly.

Love again
and again
B

Evelyn to Diana

Piers Court   *13 April [1953]*

Darling

Real Importance indeed. Will that little girl be able to fit into the box? Will they have a larger box and canon or a new girl?

I thought that luncheon train <u>was</u> the Golden Arrow. Anyway that is the train I will take and arrive at Paris FRIDAY 18th APRIL at 6.08 and sit on the platform of that train until you come. If any change telegraph Hyde Park Hotel tel. address 'Highcaste' not Highclere. Looking forward to it all <u>awfully</u> I've a jolly good mind to try standing on the horse on the end of the rope.

All love
Bo

This visit to Chantilly was not a success. Too much wine and too little food ruined the circus evening and forced Waugh to leave halfway through, and on his return to England he wrote: 'My dreariest trip abroad since Christopher [Hollis] and I went to Paris together.' On 18 April, Waugh recorded that 'Duff had alarming outburst of rage and hate'. Waugh and Duff had often lost their tempers with each other, but this occasion evidently unleashed more venom than most. The row was patched up by Diana; but it re-merges in these letters in July.

Another point of grievance was that on 21 April, in the middle of his visit, Diana hurried to London for the birth of her first grandchild, Artemis. Evelyn spent the three days of her absence in Paris, returning on the 24th. 'Much against my will,' he wrote on 24 April, 'I had agreed to return to Chantilly to help them with Douglas Fairbanks, who was guest of honour for St George's dinner.' (Duff was Chairman of the Parish branch of the St George's Society.) (Diaries, p. 719)

Since the trip had been such a disappointment to him, Waugh could think of little to say in thanks. But with his 'Collins', he sent a copy of a remarkable letter to Penelope Betjeman – presumably passed on to him by the recipient.

Evelyn to Diana

Piers Court   *29 April [1953]*

Dear Remorseless Baby

I thought of you with love untainted by envy during the evening of Sir Douglas's gala. I wondered how I could show my gratitude for my two visits to Chantilly and decided to send you a rare document – a copy of the letter sacking Mrs Betjeman from the village organ-loft. It is the work of the present Dean of Wells, but worthy of Jane Austen. Every sentence which he starts amiably ends with a sharper reproach. I hope it brings a smile.

I did not find the moment to tell you how deeply happy I am at the news of your grandchild. I am sure that she and her successors will fill all the empty places in your heart.

It is very cool and flowerless and moist here – no americans or jews or dogs or divorcees or free masons or film actors. Just Margaret's inflammatory smile. The green drawing room looks very fresh and suburban in a nice 1909 way.

Remember pray that if you ever want to see me I am here with open arms.

Bo

[enclosure]
Balking Vicarage   *7 May 1940*

My dear Penelope

I have been thinking over the question of the playing of the harmonium on Sunday evenings here and have reached the conclusion that I must now take it over myself.

I am very grateful to you for doing it for so long and hate to have to ask you to give it up, but, to put it plainly, your playing has got worse and worse and the disaccord between the harmonium and the congregation is becoming destructive of devotion. People are not very sensitive here but even some of them have begun to complain and they are not usually given to doing that. I do not like writing this but I think you will understand that it is my business to see that divine worship is as perfect as it can be made. Perhaps the crankiness of the instrument has something to do with the trouble. I think it does require a careful and experienced player to deal with it.

Thank you ever so much for stepping so generously into the breach when Sybil was ill; it was the greatest possible help to me and the results were noticeably better then than now.

Yours sincerely,
F. P. Harton

Evelyn to Diana

Piers Court   *[pstmk 4 May 1953]*
[postcard]

The Bristol recluse about whom you enquired was found drowned last week in the river.

Funny about our new KG[1] saying 'Better to be bribed than killed'. True to 1912[2] and all that.

Bo

> 🌿 *Duff had cut down his intake of wine since 1951; but a lifetime of over-indulgence had already done considerable damage to his liver, and he had not been feeling well since the beginning of the year. On 2 May, when he had just finished the last chapter of his autobiography,* Old Men Forget, *he suffered a severe haemorrhage. He was rushed to hospital in Paris where, thanks to the skill of the doctors and massive blood transfusions, his life was saved — but there was no question of his attending the Coronation the following month.*

Diana to Evelyn

Château de St Firmin   *[May 1953]*

Darling Bo

I've very few friends and I've let them fade, or rather let myself fade in their hearts on account of Duff's illness having incapacitated me more than him. I've thought of you a lot — bringing you into my non-stop prayers as a sort of supporter. This to me is despicable and in concequence such a weight. Welcome death to be rid even temporily of one —

Exaggerater of deep ends: the old girl on the flying handle — and you will have thought from my long silence that I love you less — not true — but it's been so horrible — the anxiety and apprehension and imaginings and magnifyings. Today it's better and I see my beloved not (to my eyes) so ashen.

Duff has had to renounce the Coro (without a pang) but I shall come from June 1 to June 6 — hoping to leave him in the uneven hands of

---

[1] Winston Churchill had just been made a Knight of the Garter, the highest order of chivalry in Britain.

[2] In April 1912, David Lloyd George (1863–1945), the Chancellor of the Exchequer, bought 1000 shares in the American Marconi Company. His purchase was badly timed, for the Postmaster-General was concluding a contract with the British Marconi Company. The affair provoked much public criticism, and was investigated by a select committee of the House of Commons.

Daphne and Xan[1] – who propose escape from England and might be ideal in making a gay, self-sufficient background to his sorties from a chaise-longue, his milk-drip.

I don't suppose I've any hope of seeing you in those few London days – the sadder for me. Annie [Fleming] asks me to lunch 3rd or 4th.

Do write love and sympathy

X X X
Baby

Evelyn to Diana

Piers Court   *Whit Sunday [24 May] 1953*

Dearest Diana

The *Daily Mail* announced and Susan Mary [Patten] confirmed the distressing news that Duff had gone into hospital. My heart was with you in your anxiety. It is a great relief to learn that he is well enough to be left with Daphne and 'Xan'. What is Xan? Can it be the name of some new Next Best Thing for poor Daphne?

On Friday I sent you a pretty little book [*Love Among the Ruins*]. I hope it arrives safely through all the strikers. It is something I began 3 years ago and is now not very timely except as an antidote to the Coronation. I drove down most of the main streets of London and saw the decorations – admittedly not complete – but banal common feeble. Perhaps they will be better at night. The most offensive feature is the line of parabolic girders down the Mall. I pray that your dear dim eyes will be shielded from too clear a vision of them.

I certainly shan't be anywhere near London during the cosmopolitan invasion. My treats are (1) A cocktail party here for the Dursley Dramatic Society of which I have been president 15 years without ever meeting one of them (2) Huge influx of little girls – both mine and strangers with parents in Burma and Ireland (3) An evening mass (4) Susan Mary (5) Tea with Lady Violet Benson[2] (6) *Antony and Cleopatra* at Stratford.

You seem to have been taken in by the untenable mid-Victorian craze into supposing that Death can extinguish personality. If that were true we would all jump off the Eiffel Tower in a bunch. Even Hindu heathens

---

[1] Daphne Bath's divorce was then in progress, and once it was settled she married Major Alexander ('Xan') Fielding (b. 1918). He had fought with the Cretan Resistance in the White Mountains, which provided the subject of his first book, *The Stronghold*, published that year.

[2] Lady Violet 'Letty' Manners (1888–1971), Diana's surviving elder sister. Her first husband was Hugo Charteris, Lord Elcho. They married in 1911, and he died in action in 1916. In 1921 she married Guy Benson.

know better than this and think extinction the huge, ultimate reward that can be earned by life after life of increasing selflessness.

Oh Dear I have forgotten and written small. Will you take a reading glass to page one?

I went to examine a possible school at Lechlade for home-sick Margaret, and went to tea with the Jungman sisters. Their state of destitution has been much exaggerated.

I've read Freddy's life of Eleanor[1] with great amusement. Never an intimate of mine but a crony in the early thirties at boxing matches and supper parties. The lowering figure of F.E. in the background is the best part. Freddy quite misses the point of Eleanor's very vehement religious life and treats it as part of her gypsy-circus craze.

I do hope the Coronation is fun for you. I expect it will be. You always find plums in pies bless you.

Most disgusting. Laura has not been asked to present mugs, judge sports, light bonfires or take any part in Stinchcombe revels. The omission reveals unsuspected unpopularity.

I have suffered a severe attack of fibrositis and have been hobbling on two sticks in great pain. You would have laughed fit to bust your pants.

All love
Bo

Diana to Evelyn

Darling satyrical Rogue – you've written, for me (and Duff who laughed aloud) a miniature masterpiece [Love Among the Ruins]. I've read it twice, on account of bolting such gems from yr pen – swallowing whole, panicking with anticipation – no mastication. The second time I take Mr Gladstone's 30 chews a bite, and savoured it as a conaisseur. O dear! O dear it reconciles one to one's natural death of cancer or whatever – I've been near death more than usually because of Duff's dread hemmorage – my confidence is undermined for the years left us. I prayed – you will be glad to hear, unintermittently – but then I generally do – but panic prayers followed by cool and provisional thanksgiving seem unbalanced and of no good. Duff's recovery from what may have been a nose-bleed (not from the nose) left him as bleached as a plaster cast. His blood was all lost –

---

[1] *Lady Eleanor Smith – A Memoir* by her brother Frederick, 2nd Earl of Birkenhead. He also wrote the biography of their father F. E. Smith (1872–1930), who became the 1st Earl of Birkenhead in 1922. Lady Eleanor Smith (1902–45) wrote books about ballet, flamenco and gypsies, and was a Roman Catholic convert.

but he's put it on with the help of a Red-man (brought from his own cedar tree) and now he looks hardly frail.

I left him with fear and misery to visit the Queen – and dear Daphne took over. So good and consciensious she's proved (she's now a little wistful and uncertain, the stammers gaining, and the beauty improving from lack of means to buy spirits).

The stone in my heart lightened in London where I could not be forever listening to Duff's breathing, watching his appetite, listening outside doors for snores; and with the help of encouraging telephonic reports I managed to adore my Coro.

I would love to write you some sagas – but I know how I can bore good friends and lovers – so I'll wait till I see your face's reflection of their recitals and thus know when to abridge or stop. Susan-Mary was 1st class about her outing – adored it. Told her tale with herself as the booby – I wonder how much 'mauvaise plaisanterie' was in you – I hope none . . .

Terrible about yr unsuspected unpopularity! (I quote from yr long ago last letter unanswered till now because of the torment (mine) . . .

I shall come to England the 24, dine at the Gages,[1] Glyndebourne, listen to an opera – sleep with my new friend Lady Jones whose son has just passed the most advanced of his law examinations, and return next day by Newhaven to Duff. No hope of seeing you alas and alack. I want to hear and tell stories of Ava[2] and Lady Mowbray[3] in the Abbey – and of the 'children's' party on Debo's boat – a death trap for the drunk in 2 senses. The toddlers called one of the death holds below the drunk room as lightly as one talks of the pump or cloakroom.[4]

Your best friend Patrick Balfour put me into *Punch*. Tell him if you see him how overjoyed I was. 'Who's the lovely dressed as Eleanor of Aquitaine?' Curious coincidence, as she was exactly the fashion I wanted to represent. I wore a gold wig and glass crown.

When will it be? that you'll return I mean – not till the holls? then these holls dissipate families and groups – what are friends doing? We shall go to Garda mid April for two weeks, and for three weeks there is no plan afoot. You wouldn't want I know to visit a Paradise near Toulon belonging to Poor Louis where I'll go 2nd week in Aug Duff's health permitting. You don't know what a pain I carry in that I have to write such a phrase. The solid earth fails beneath my anyway faltering feet.

[1] Henry, 6th Viscount Gage (1895–1982). In 1931 he married the Hon. Alexandra Imogen Grenfell (d. 1969), known as 'Mogs'. In 1971 he married Diana Campbell-Gray.

[2] Ava, née Bodley. In 1925 she married the diplomat Ralph Wigram, who died in 1936. She became the second wife of Sir John Anderson PC (1882–1958) in 1941. He was Home Secretary 1939–40, Chancellor of the Exchequer 1943–5, and was created Viscount Waverley in 1952.

[3] Sheila Gully, who in 1921 married William Stourton. In 1936, her husband succeeded his father as the 25th Lord Mowbray, 26th Lord Segrave and 22nd Lord Stourton.

[4] The Duchess of Devonshire does not remember children being invited to this party on a Thames boat, though people were asked to come in boating clothes. The mention of a 'death hold' was curious, however – for the boat was *The Marchioness*, which went down with the loss of 57 lives in May 1989.

Since I started this letter the blood-count analysis is not quite so high – quite normal to have variations they say – but I'm back on the rack.

Do write –

D. no, B.

Evelyn to Diana

Piers Court   *23 June [1953]*

Darling Baby

I heard of your high jinks in London and rejoiced vicariously. I understand half the nobility are still picking splinters of glass from your tiara out of their hands and arses. I saw the very robe you wore. It bore the air of a good-time too. I am delighted at your renewed high spirits and pray that Norwich's health gives you no further anxiety.

Coronation here was all children and peasants. There was no shade of mockery in our welcome to Susan Mary. Stanway[1] was indeed rather a disappointment to me. It is clearly a place that needs sunshine and children – nothing fine enough to attract in the rain, empty with host and hostess kind but quite worn out by London, all alone with a steam kettle. Stratford was hell[2] but I felt it my duty to take S[usan] M[ary] there as she had taken me to fireworks at Versailles. I have kept the child Margaret at home with me for the rest of the term. She is an intense pleasure. I took her to Belton[3] last Sunday where Annie Orr Lewis[4] fell into a strange passion for her. We drove to Belvoir[5] but found it all barred and deserted. Poor Perry [Brownlow] talks incessantly of all the details of Kitty's sickness, death and burial, and is producing very painful plans for her tomb. Every topic turned to Kitty in two moves. He has found a charm of hers, depicting a lady's drawers in diamonds, and wears it as a tie pin. Margaret did not approve but she wandered from portrait to portrait of Kitty developing a poetic love of her.

My poor little book has been greatly abused in the Beaverbrook press – or rather I have, but it sells quite briskly. I don't think it is as bad as they say. I am <u>delighted</u> it amused you.

All love

Bo

[1] As the widow of Lord Elcho, Lady Violet Benson held a life interest in Stanway, Gloucestershire: one of the loveliest Elizabethan houses in England.

[2] Waugh wrote in his diary that 'Michael Redgrave's performance of *Antony and Cleopatra* not all it is cracked up to be'. (*Diaries*, 4 June 1953, p. 721)

[3] Belton, near Grantham, Lincolnshire: the family seat of Waugh's friend Lord Brownlow.

[4] Phyllis Ann Allan (née Bibby) married Sir Duncan Orr Lewis, 2nd Bt., in 1940.

[5] Belvoir Castle, Lincolnshire, the seat of the Dukes of Rutland. Diana was brought up here after her father succeeded to the dukedom in 1906.

Evelyn to Diana

Piers Court   *[July 1953]*

Dearest Baby

I telegraphed to the address on your postcard asking if you wanted my company at Belloc's funeral.[1] No answer, so I presume you are going with Norwich. So I shan't go. But I will go to the Requiem (date not yet promulgated). Perhaps we could meet for luncheon after that. Otherwise, of course, I shan't be in London.

But you will be very welcome here if you cared to come. Every house has different sorts of discomfort. Mine, I think I can claim, has all. But there would be open arms.

All love
Bo

Evelyn to Diana

Piers Court   *[?July 1953]*
[postcard]

Oh dear, peevish again, baby?

What, pray, is 'cavalier' in inviting you to stay with me? I have no London house and prefer to entertain my friends at home, as you do. I take it from your silence that my invitation is refused. Cavalier? Or just plain round head?

My telephone has been struck by lightning.

I go to Mells tomorrow and then remain at home until July 31st when I go to visit Randolph at his new country place.

Belloc's Requiem is on the 6th. I presume you will have left the country by then. How very odd of you not to go to his funeral. I shall think it most cavalier if you cut mine.

Bo

Diana to Evelyn

5 Belgrave Square   *24 July 1953*
[Chips Channon's house]

Beloved Bo – You see I don't go to funerals – I couldn't explain because like you the storm isolated me in a strange house – no telephone, no

---

[1] Hilaire Belloc had died on 15 July.

village for a P.O. I went to my father's funeral only to hold my mother – I did not go to hers. Public ones I grace, i.e. King – Generals de Latre [de Tassigny] or Leclerc by official duty – but not the burials of those I love, therefore not yours if I survive you – which I hope is unlikely.

I shall not go to Duff's if he dies first – except that one is uncertain of one's acts in great emotion. The idea jars upon me – exhibition of grief – the society duty side does not, in my heart, fit.

You won't see what I feel and I don't expect you to, but I do expect you to love me – and my affection for you brings out the peevish. We are both spoilt babies – you are deathly proud – I'm not, but I'm vulnerable to lack of spoiling. Someone long ago said to me in Italy – 'God repudiates old women'. I don't suppose he does but most men do not unnaturally.

You'll see Duff at Randy's on 31st. He – Randy – asked me and I would have swallowed June, line and sinker to see you – but I am taking my children to Chantilly that day and we motor down France on Aug 2nd. I should love an occasional word – (O do spoil – I spoil you.)

San Vigilio, Lago di Garda, Verona will find me from 15th Aug to Sept 1st.

Be gentle with Coo [Cooper].

It's difficult to 'do' on two glasses of wine, as we all know.

God bless you
Baby

Evelyn to Diana

Piers Court   *29 July [1953]*

Baby mustn't use words she doesn't understand. Grown ups do not use expressions like 'deathly proud' unless they wish to provoke permanent enmity, or else feel impelled to denounce mortal sin wherever they see it for the good of the souls of others (and such an impulse is itself often a symptom of pride).

The statement, 'God repudiates old women', is fatuous and blasphemous. I cannot believe an Italian made it or anyone with any knowledge of God.

I am afraid I shall not have the pleasure of meeting Norwich at the week-end, nor will he have the pleasure of meeting June [Mrs Randolph Churchill].

The chief reason, of course, for attending funerals is to pray for the soul of the dead friend. The other reason is courtesy to the surviving relations who like to think that their 'loved one' was loved enough for his friends to inconvenience themselves slightly by making a public demonstration of mourning. If baby studies her lesson books she will find that the custom is ancient and honourable in all civilizations – not merely a popish quirk.

I have had many treasured tokens of your affection. I can think of no case of spoiling except your discontinued habit of bringing me wine glasses. If you had accepted my invitation to come here you would have experienced a very much more tender entertainment than I recently received at your hands. I should neither have left you alone in the middle of your visit nor have permitted Laura to insult you at my table. But of course she is incapable of such behaviour.

E

Diana to Evelyn

5 Belgrave Square   *July 1953*

Baby stupidly assumed that you would recognise Belloc's 'deathly proud' ('Godolphin Horn was nobly born'[1]) and in that light spirit the words were used, though she has no recollection of writing them or in what connection since her scrawls are more of a planchette than anything reasoned. She would love to think your letter (just read) was not so coldly aimed to wound – arrows heavy as lead curare tipped.

She can't think that she subscribed to the woman's dictum about God and old women? did she really? She never had lesson books but her upbringing taught her to pray, as you know, tho' not necessarily in public. 'Popish quirk?' – no suggestion of such an idea in what she meant. As to the 'inconvenience' of the funeral outing believe me a day spent with you in a kind mood presents no inconvenience. When the mood is not good difficulties present themselves, but it was not for that reason that she left you for two days when you came to stay, and you know it. Duff has a well known weakness of uncontrolled rudeness – we all have grave weaknesses – Baby's is melancholia and cowardice. You have some too – and she is shocked that, following on your suggestion of not returning to Chantilly as you felt yourself to be on her nerves and Duff's – you believed her denial – coming back to an appreciative and warm fold for a week – you should now bring the story up in a deformed way.

Of course Laura would not have been rude; as a fellow girl Baby is not rude – but both men in this story are exceptionally rude in cups. But since recriminations are the note, neither B. nor D. would have told all and sundry that their hosts were trying to poison them both in town and country.

She will not write again – it's too painful to face the leaden answers devoid of understanding or love.

[1] 'Godolphin Horne, Who was Cursed with the Sin of Pride, and Became a Boot-Black'. See Hilaire Belloc's *Cautionary Tales for Children*, first published in 1906.

Evelyn to Diana

[telegram]   *[received 30 July 1953]*

DEEPLY REGRET DEPLORABLE FAILURE RECOGNIZE BELLOC QUOTATION = BO

Evelyn to Diana

Piers Court   *[? August 1953]*

Darling Diana

I am torn between quoting Patmore and saying 'Come off it', but neither would do. All I can say is 'Why?' It must be my fault I know. There must be a dozen nuances I coarsely miss when I begin to offend until, splosh, I stand dashed and dazed under a Niagara of rage.

Some friends – Randolph and Co – put it about that it is funny for me to be offensive and no doubt I sometimes basely indulge them – but never with those I love, except always with you.

> [. . .] Much against my heart
> We two now part
> My Very Dear.
> Our solace is the sad road lies so clear
> It needs no art
> With faint, averted feet
> And many a tear,
>   In our opposèd paths to persevere.

It had to be Patmore, you see, there's no coming off it.

With unalterable love

Bo Beaverbrook

[in a separate letter, also undated:]

Darling Diana

The poem ends:

> Perchance we may,
> Where now this night is day
> And even through faith of still averted feet,
> Making full circle of our banishment,
> Amazèd meet;

177

The bitter journey to the bourne so sweet
Seasoning the termless feast of our content
With tears of recognition never dry.[1]

Beaverbrook

Diana to Evelyn

Château de St Firmin   *2 August 1953*

Really Bo. What is this I hear? That you chucked Randy because Duff was of the company? It's hard to believe – if you took exception to our exchange of rudeness, why did you stay on my return from the baby's birth in London for another 4 or 5 days and nights, apparently on the best of terms with both of us? 'I'm afraid I am on Duff's nerves and yrs' you said to me but you believed my emphatic denials. All was happy again – I also for a change – and now crash! Can't meet Norwich – too rude – and again, these stories of attempted poisoning. Please do write and say it's rot exaggerated.

You must not lose friends so deliberately – you'll find it hard to lose me – you've tried, but it's possible to succeed, though I shall be miserable.

I'm so miserable anyway. Duff is better and now John Julius looks really like death and my anxieties are as dreadful as ever.

Love
Baby

Evelyn to Diana

White's   *7 August [1953]*

Dearest Diana

I thought you might like to read Ronnie's panegyric [for Hilaire Belloc]. The congregation at Westminster was astonishing – Belloc silent and invisible for 15 years and more, most of his books out of print, the first week in August – and yet the whole huge Cathedral packed.

I am very sorry that John Julius looks ill. Is it the best thing to take him to the enervating South? Surely the grouse moors would be more restorative.

Yes, it's true that I chucked Churchill because of Duff. Typical of him

---

[1] Coventry Patmore (1823–96). Waugh quotes from *The Farewell*, a poem inspired by the illness and death of Patmore's first wife.

178

to blab. As you know Duff and I have never hit it off. He wrote me an awfully funny Mr Bultitude[1] letter.

I don't know how much you remember of your ooja board writing. Lately you called me very aptly leaden. A solid, soft almost incorruptible metal, useful to keep the rain from your head, to make a sound shot to defend you, a lining for a coffin.

Also <u>please</u> don't forget Portia's casket.

All love
E

Diana to Evelyn

San Vigilio　　　　　　　　　　　　　　　*26 August 1953*
[Lake Garda]

Darling Bo – I have not received 1 letter since I left Paris on August 2nd. I dread the day when they will avalanche in – outmoded and confusing. I shall look if there are any from you but without much hope – Randolph has cooked our goose to a cinder and I shall find it hard to forgive him tho' his complete lack of sensitiveness and sense, common or otherwise, mantles him with a pathetic innocence.

Duff told me from memory what he had written to you – and of course I deplored a letter that can never be taken back or obliterated. The worst 'repeatings' are showing written words and what an unconscious brute is Randy to show Duff your letter! He of course would think nothing of reading or writing it, but he should have learnt, if he can't feel, to be cautious.

It is sad for me, because I don't suppose you'll ever come to our house again – since <u>you</u> can neither forget or forgive. It is sad for Duff who said wistfully telling me the story – 'It's funny I didn't start by liking Evelyn much – but I'd got very fond of him'. I ragged him about the White's link-of-love – but he repudiated this reason. You will see when you read his new book how good and true Duff is and sensitive enough for your letter to wound deeply and your chucking of Randy's weekend because of his presence to come as a st . . . burnt[?] shell.

I suppose I'll not see you again except in the houses of Pam – or whose? It's tragic for me – with only 4 men friends left – one of which I'm forbidden to see, another is the-next-best-thing, Raimund who I brought up, and Paul Louis – O Evelyn Evelyn how can you have done it to me.

I'm hating my holiday – acute and increasing melancholia – the pleasures of drink cut off because of Duff.

[1] The chief character in F. Anstey's novel *Vice Versa*, Paul Bultitude was a Colonial Produce merchant. 'His general expression suggested a conviction of his own extreme importance, but, in spite of this, his big underlip drooped rather weakly.'

It's raining today. 'Row me out to Degenzano'. Where Catullus lived – there give me an enormous cup of Hemlock, or reliable news of a new milenium – Nations at peace – Bo's without arrows and Duff well and well-disposed. Back to Chantilly mid-September I suppose –

World-weary
Baby

Evelyn to Diana

Piers Court   *29th August [1953]*

Darling

Yours of the 26th inst. to hand.

There must be a letter of mine somewhere in the strikers' hands, enclosing a copy of Ronnie's beautiful panegyric on Belloc. I hope it turns up.

I am very sorry to hear that Duff was surprised and grieved to learn that I have detested him for 23 years. I must have nicer manners than people normally credit me with.

Twice before this we have come near a quarrel; each time after an outburst from Duff, when I have despaired of ever being able to keep it up and the result has been a trivial squabble with you, suddenly swollen out of all sense.

It would be tedious to go into the rights of my squabbles with Duff. With regard to the last I see nothing odd in my avoiding him. We have never done anything together or spent five minutes alone together. It was when Randolph accused me of upsetting a party 'built round' myself (total strangers and Duff) that I went idiotically too far in what I wrote.

I thought it funny (ha ha) that Duff should offer to teach me how to carry my wine and funny (peculiar) that he should accuse me of sponge-ing on him.

I look forward to reading his account of himself.

I do hope you will come and see me here often. It isn't very attractive at the moment. I am starving and light as a feather and writing hard and the child Margaret, whom I love, away from home.

Oh another funny haha sentence in Duff's letter: 'I consulted various other guests whether I had gone too far and they all agreed that my rebuke might prove salutary'. Guests were Miss Fahie[1] and Master Hart-Davis[2] and, as far as I remember, no one else.

---

[1] Norah Fahie, who for many years was Duff and Diana's secretary in France.
[2] Rupert Hart-Davis (b. 1907), author, editor and publisher. Son of Richard Hart-Davis and Sybil Cooper, Duff's elder sister. He founded the publishing firm of Rupert Hart-Davis Ltd in 1946, and went on to edit the papers of Oscar Wilde, Siegfried Sassoon and Max Beerbohm. Between 1978–84 he published six volumes of his correspondence with George Lyttelton. He was knighted in 1967.

I have not been to London since Belloc's requiem. Laura and I may go to Brighton next month.

Nancy is a hard worker you know. I wish I were. I am hacking away at the war novel. Not bad but so little done and so much to do. I shall feel I have got out of prison when the last volume is finished. It will have fewer and fewer readers as it goes on and when it is all complete a lot of young prigs aged 12 today, will take it up and write studies of it and I shall be given the OBE by Lord Mountbatten.[1]

All love
Bo

Duff Cooper to Evelyn Waugh

[Château de St Firmin] *4 September 1953*

My dear Evelyn – Your undated letter, delayed doubtless by the French postal strike, reached me only today. There is much in it that surprises me. You have never, you say, regarded yourself as my guest except when I was living at the British Embassy. You give no reason for making this solitary exception and you detract from the grace of it by insinuating that as a taxpayer you were entitled to all you received. You are quite wrong, thank God, in assuming that the Government provide the Embassy with wine. The Government pay the Ambassador and give him an entertainment allowance, facts that do not in my opinion, although they apparently do in yours, give to all taxpayers the right to demand free meals at the Embassy.

I am ready to admit that one is occasionally obliged to accept hospitality from people for whom one has no very high regard, but it is a very different thing to become a regular visitor at a man's house, to make long stays, to propose oneself with the certainty of being always welcomed by somebody whom one cannot tolerate. To justify oneself on the ground that one finds the intolerable creature's wife charming seems to me the conduct of an adulterer rather than a gentleman.

If I have been rude to you occasionally during what I believed was a long friendship, I am sorry. I am hot-tempered and I fear that few of my friends have escaped it.

As you have never regarded me as a host I must assume that you neither regarded me as a guest and I suppose that I must ask you to thank Laura for the excellent luncheon I once enjoyed in your house. The old-fashioned code in which I was brought up taught me that man and wife were one, and that on entering their house one became the guest of both. I

---

[1] Lord Louis Mountbatten, 1st Earl Mountbatten of Burma (1900–79).

cannot follow your modern subtleties. I am sorry to have lost your friendship, but sorrier to learn that I was deceived when I thought I had earned it.

Yours ever
Duff

Duff Cooper to Evelyn Waugh

Château de St Firmin   *14 September 1953*

My dear Evelyn –

I find your letter of September 8th very magnanimous; and I accept your apology gratefully. I shall not mention it to any of those who have enjoyed our quarrel more, I suspect, than we have. I shall say that the incident is closed and that we are on the same terms as we always were.

The word that really offended me was not 'intolerable' but 'always'. Had you written 'Duff was so rude to me last time we met that I don't care to meet him again' I should no doubt have been willing to apologize to you. I think I did express regret in my last letter. But it hurt me to feel that on many occasions when I had enjoyed your company the pleasure had been entirely on one side. You say it would now be absurd to offer your friendship. If that is all that stands in the way of the offer I shall consider it as offered and can answer that it is accepted. I have never been afraid of absurdity as no doubt this correspondence has proved.

Yours ever
Duff

Diana to Evelyn

Château de St Firmin   *17 September 1953*

Dearest Bo – I got a Bo as a signature last letter, tho' not a Baby as a start – so in the black skies there's quite enough blue for dutch pants (Baby's) but soon with bonne volonté there'll be light enough to guide you back to Chantilly. What I should like of all things is to have vol II of Magnum Opus (or is it opus magnus) read aloud as vol I was. We could go and see another hideous church or the caves with bulls all over them in the Dordogne.

Thank you for sending me Ronnie Knox's Pangyric. It is quite wonderful, I think – and so must all. I can't quite accept that loss of good fellowship and craftsmanship is entirely the fault of the Reformation –

Chinese hands are still cunning. There's good fellowship in the U.S. There are no nastier people than the frogs who were little affected by it – while the Scandinavians are comparatively pure, less wily than wops less cruel than Spaniards – I think I'm out of my depth – 1 foot from shore too.

I had a new low in mealancholia and hypercondria for others, followed by a 10 days taste of Paradise in the highest Dolomites and good still Switzerland – both resorts chosen for noiselessness. Duff had a meta-mophosis I don't know whether from Pity or not. Picnics every day – (he bought the basket for 2 as a birthday present), a love of music began – and to make the change complete he became a bit stingy in marketing.

I'll be in London 22nd till 24 p.m., so make a sign if you happen to be there.

Love
Baby

Evelyn to Diana

Piers Court   *19 September [1953]*

Darling Diana

I have apologized to Norwich and he has accepted my apology, so that is O.K.

I am afraid that the second volume of magnum (neut.) opus is far from finished. I write slower and slower now with many revisions and I find it hard to concentrate on my work when I am constantly aware of domestic responsibilities. It has been a cruel summer for the English, with crops of hay and corn ruined by storms, our own notably so.

Now at last the children are beginning to go back to school. I am taking Laura for a short holiday in Belgium (care to join us?) in the first fortnight of October. After that I must settle down to very hard work to finish this volume.

What has the fiend Randolph been doing about pornography? I keep coming on allusions to him and it in *Punch* and *Tablet* but can't make out what he has done. It seems to be something creditable.[1]

I liked in your letter '1 foot from shore'.

You mustn't think that frogs are a Catholic nation. Those you meet are the fruits of the Masonic regime at the beginning of the century. They continue however to produce individuals of high sanctity who don't appear at your Sunday galas. Scandinavians are bores with the highest

---

[1] In September 1953, Randolph was invited to be Chairman at a Foyle's literary lunch, in honour of Hugh Cudlipp's *Publish and be Damned* – a history of the *Daily Mirror*. Instead of confining himself to a few innocuous words about the book (which he had not read), Randolph seized the occasion to denounce the irresponsibility of the popular press, which he claimed was wallowing in a morass of crime and pornography. His book *What I Said About the Press* came out shortly afterwards.

suicide rate in the world – and lowest birth rates. But these are not the reasons that keep you or anyone else from God. I remember your appalling dictum (not 'dictus') that you had never experienced remorse. That is the cause of your melancholy, not increasing age.

I am afraid I have quite given up going to London. Laura and I would love to see you here. I feel you have a shyness of her which must be overcome if we are to see as much of one another as I ardently desire. Horrible cooking[1] – but you could choose us as a resort for starvation. Clean beds. Constant hot water. No frogs.

I hear rather sad accounts of Katharine. Did she visit you on her way back from Porto Fino?

Legal worries. It seems that the legacy from my aunts, which I relied on to put my affairs in order, is going to be seized by an unknown cousin in Tasmania.

Poor Maimie awfully crazy.

All love
Bo

Diana to Evelyn

Château de St Firmin   *[?October 1953]*

Darling Bo. My chilly blood froze when I saw the word Laeken scratched big on the back of my pad (book not foot) and I realized I'd forgotten the introduction and that I didn't know where to find you in Villette. The only Bore-geous's that I know there are Willy de Grünne and Madame de Lambert who would never have furthered a visit to the ex king, so I could not even give them the office to find you for that purpose. I do feel remorseful – what mitigates it perhaps is that La Belle Princesse sans Mercie and her deposed husband were not there (at least I'm told they are here) but you would have liked the house – not I think that anyone is shown round. I hope you saw the Congo brought to Belgium in the conservatory – that treat is allowed a paying public. Do forgive.

I was happy to feel at ease with you again – and am in hopes of other outings between 26th inst. when I hope to go to Tring for inside a week and middle Nov.

My hands are too numb to write – and too mean to put in my pocket for money to start the heating. Also heating is goodbye to flowers in vases. There's a house in Victoria Sq – it reads a bargain! I've asked Annie to 'peck' at it. But how can we leave this pretty house and all that has been so

---

[1] Waugh often complained about the food in his house, but according to Frances Donaldson, it was very good.

laboriously dug into it and its garden, its veg. and fruit, and stocked shelves etc. – but to think of the friends and jokes and gossips and interests of arts which I can't cope with here at all – to think of English banter with tradespeople and at the P.O. makes me cry out with nostalgia.

Keep in touch.

Much love
B

Evelyn to Diana

Antwerp   *[pstmk 11 November 1953]*
[postcard]

Wiertz was rather disappointing. <u>Beautiful</u> ideas[1] but he couldn't paint for toffee.

Laura and I are greatly enjoying the food and pictures. Expense appalling.

All love
Bo

Evelyn to Diana

Piers Court   *[19 November 1953]*
[postcard]

Love to Godfrey Winn[2] and Mrs Hemingway[3] – I don't think.

All is well. No return of sciatica. It is indeed kind of you to bring more loving cups. It is sad that you have been twice to my country and not come to see me. Now the time for country visits is passed. All is damp and misty and cheerless here. Only my heart is warm.

I was so glad to hear that the Norwich Confessions[4] sold well. Have you read a fascinating book about buggery named *Heart in Exile*.[5]

[1] This particular postcard shows a picture by Anton Wiertz entitled *Hunger, Madness, Crime*. An impoverished mother, with one breast bare and a mad grin on her face, is about to stab her baby to death.

[2] Godfrey Winn (1908–71), star columnist for, successively, the *Daily Mirror*, *Sunday Express*, and *Daily Mail*.

[3] Martha Gellhorn (b. 1908), journalist, novelist and war correspondent. She and Ernest Hemingway had lived together for four years before their marriage in 1940. They were divorced four years later. Martha had met Diana in Algiers in 1943, but they did not become close friends until Diana moved to London in 1961.

[4] Duff's autobiography *Old Men Forget* came out that autumn, to excellent reviews.

[5] By Rodney Garland, published that year.

Evelyn to Diana

Piers Court   *26th [?November 1953]*

Darling Baby

·Here's something to make you fart with laughing. Ever since we met I have been in <u>acute</u> pain – old leg trouble something itis. Anyways it's too bad so I am flying (I mean sailing) to Ceylon. Shall be at Kandy which I am told is very pretty 22nd Feb. Queen's Hotel. Awful suspicion that Queen Herself will be there too then. Join up?

I hope all your Alis[1] are obeising abjectly. I'm with them at your feet.

Bo

Duff and Diana had been invited to stay in Jamaica by Lord Brownlow. Duff's health had rallied since the haemorrhage in May, and his doctors thought the Caribbean would do him good – but he was not feeling well when they boarded the Colombie. *The bleeding started at about noon on 31 December, and he died on board ship shortly after midnight on New Year's Day, 1954. Diana never got over his loss, or the agonising hours she had spent at his deathbed, made worse by the cruel sounds of New Year revelry. She accompanied his body back from Vigo to England. Diana did not attend Duff's burial at Belvoir Castle on 6 January; but she was at the memorial service the following day, at St Margaret's, Westminster, where she and Duff had been married thirty-four years before.*

Evelyn to Diana

Piers Court   *2 January 1954*

Dearest Diana

All my poor prayers are for you and Duff.
If there is any service anywhere that I can do, command it.
If my company would be at all comforting, call for me.
Believe in my true, deep love.

Evelyn

---

[1] Alastair Forbes, known to many as Ali.

Kind as it is, this letter did not touch Diana's heart as it was meant to. Three days later, Waugh wrote: 'Ed Stanley told me that Diana was desperately seeing everyone she could. Sent her note by his hand. He told me later that she said she hadn't the patience to open it as I had showered her with letters of condolence beginning "My dear Diana" and signed "Yours sincerely, Evelyn Waugh".' (Diaries, 5 January 1954, p. 723)

When Diana did open the note delivered via Lord Stanley (now lost), she found that it was to 'Darling Baby' from 'Bo'. She telephoned Waugh immediately and asked him to come and see her.

Waugh was about to escape the English winter by taking a trip to Ceylon, which he hoped would restore his health. He felt unwell much of the time, and suffered rheumatic pains – which may have been brought on by his reckless intake of a strong sleeping draught containing chloral and bromide. In order to ease his pain he started taking the chloral and bromide during the day, as well as at night; and by the time he left for Ceylon, he had absorbed the mixture in such dangerous quantities that it began to affect his mind. On the ship out to Ceylon, he became prey to a series of nightmarish hallucinations which he could not shake off – as the following letter, written to Diana from Ceylon, makes clear.

On his return to London, the chloral was diagnosed as being the root of the trouble, but Waugh preferred to believe that he had had a taste of real madness. It was also an experience he was far from regretting, for it gave him a marvellous subject for a novel – which appeared as The Ordeal of Gilbert Pinfold in 1957. Christopher Sykes observed that Waugh never lost the dread that he might write all the stories out of himself: 'He told several friends that the Pinfold experience . . . had come, like an unexpected legacy, to increase the capital sum on which his safety depended.'

Evelyn to Diana

[Grand Hotel Nuwaraeliya   18 February [1954]
Ceylon]

Darling Baby

Ink? The first letter you have ever written to me with a pen. A very sweet letter too. I can't write with the tenderness I feel for a very odd reason. There is a group of psychologists a thousand miles away who read every word I write over my shoulder. As I write this I can hear their odious voices repeating it word for word. You will think I have finally

187

gone out of my mind and am suffering the wildest aberrations of persecution mania, but this is the strict truth. I fell victim to them on board ship when I was ill and full of drugs. It began with an elaborate series of practical jokes during which I was convinced I was insane. My sufferings were exquisite but now I know that it is merely a trick of telepathy. I will tell you the whole saga when we meet. I can't say in the presence of these eavesdroppers how much my heart and prayers are yours. They break into cackles of laughter at any expression of that kind.

I wish I could come to Athens with you but I am slinking home at once. This trip has been a most painful failure.

Ceylon is lovely but densely crowded – film companies and international congresses filling every hotel and rest-house and I am very lonely and low spirited so I should be poor company. Well that's rather silly because of course if we were together I shouldn't be lonely, should I?

Oh, dear, you will think me insane or possessed by devils. Perhaps you have something there.

Darling Baby I will write again when these fearful voices are silent.

All my love
Bo

Diana to Evelyn

M/V George Potamianos   *1 March [1954]*
Athens bound

Darling Bo. I was happy indeed, to get your letter – but it alarmed me a little – surprise no, but anxiety. It's no use to ask you to expatiate – this cackling of ultima thule laughter will begin and the eavesdropping and peeping Toms will stay your hand – but when I see you – soon soon – will your voice be safe? from scoffers? What can it all be? Allied (by all that's ridiculous) to practical jokes on a ship? 'Possessed' – you've got something there perhaps – my poor boy. It will teach you not to travel alone. We have a lot in common (or rather in uncommon) one of the lot is not to be alone. <u>Change</u> – not solitude. 'Busily moving in perpetual change' is what I'm after to allay pain and dread of my empty home. This old smouldering-out torch is being passed on from one kind hand to another's. I have often spoken to you about losing friends – beware, beware! They have done so much for me. Susan Mary is carrying me for the moment after a careful kindling from Jenny Nicholson-Crosse[1] on the

---

[1] Jenny Nicholson (Mrs Patrick Crosse) lived in Rome, in the Torre del Grillo – the Tower of the Cricket.

top of a tower in Rome. S. Mary is what she would call 'dear' and like me in youth, having docked at Corfu for two hours and taken a drive, is planning to buy a villa – 'good for asthma' and all.

What shall I do to be saved? I'd so love not to wake when at night I sleep with aids. Mary Paget – mentally arrested – pointed at Juliet [Duff] and said 'What's that lady for?'

I'll be in Greece maybe two weeks then back to Rome or Venice to take train to London. Write me yr. plans please to Chantilly – to be forwarded by air. What about you and Laura and a few children coming over? I'd love it – or you, or her alone. I imagine I'll be back earliest April to see the flowers, planted for the last time, blossom –

I'm less strange – than when you saw me last, but standing firm from instinct and upbringing – desperately needing of help for all that.

Yours – as for so many years –

Diana

Evelyn to Diana

Piers Court *6 March 1954*

Darling Baby.

Yes, I have been quite mad. A very disturbing experience. It came on quite suddenly on board ship and was acute for a week – constant violent hallucinations – then gradually grew feebler. Now I am restored to my senses. My alienist thinks that the attack was brought on by excess of chloral and is not constitutional. May never recur. I don't know whether it was better to have been alone or not during the period, but I shall never think of going anywhere alone again.

How right you are about not losing friends. You have stuck by yours heroically – me especially despite every sort of provocation. I lose mine fast. Not I think from not loving them but from expecting them to be different. You find something agreeable in almost everyone. I am put off by anything not wholly agreeable. Wiser and happier baby.

I would love to come to Chantilly and help pack in early April. Have to to be back on 14th for Holy Week. Could come any time in first fortnight or after Easter if I should be more use then.

I have just read Nancy's *Pompadour*. Very prettily done. All written like an intimate gossiping letter about people she is living with. A very happy knack of picking out the funniest anecdotes. But all make-believe. The facts keep undoing her theories, just as they do in her life of Parisian make-believe now. She tries to present a fairy-land of exquisitely elegant, good humoured, witty, polite people living wholly for pleasure, while half the time they are playing brutal guttersnipe jokes on one another – secreting disgusting lampoons in table-napkins, bouncing about overhead to keep one another awake etc – and pursuing ambitions as grossly as F. E. Smith or Simon.[1] Also she is never clear about the moral sentiments involved, speaks as though endless adulteries were accepted as normal while it is plain that great opprobium attached to them in half the court at least. I don't believe at all in the huge sexual virility she attributes to all her heroes – octogenarians fucking twice a day. Also it is plain that the court was really acutely monotonous. The very fact that Pompadour owed her success to her gay little fireworks and theatricals shows that most of them were stiff with boredom most of the time. Levées, hunting, couchers – All the same it is a most readable and informative book and I am sure it will have a success. How innocent and modest the Pompadour's extravagances were compared with Miss Horsburgh's.[2]

My fond love to Susan Mary if she is still with you. I have always wanted a house in Corfu – staged a scene there in my first novel.[3]

Per (Hylton) leaving Mells after mass. Magdalen [Eldon] staying there runs after car. 'Per, Per, do stay five minutes. I never see you'. Per: 'Oh dear I can't. The butler has lit a lovely fire in my sitting room and I must get back to it'.

Those who have seen the first half of my work in progress speak well of it [*Officers and Gentlemen*]. Insanity has held it up, but I hope to get back to it next week.

Randolph tremendously patronizing since a lunatic gave him £3000 to write the life of the late Lord Derby.[4] 'You must study the market Evelyn. It is no good writing to please yourself'.

I bought an elephant's foot in Ceylon. Enormous difficulties in getting permission to export it. The Game Preserve Dept wanted to know where the other three feet were. Ceylon was a great failure. Lonely and haunted by hallucinations all the time. But a pretty place.

If you go to Crete please retain photographic memories of the road from Suda to Sphakion (the scene of our retreat in 1941) which I need to describe in work in progress.

All love
Bo

[1] John Allsebrook Simon PC (1873–1954), Viscount Simon. Lawyer, Secretary of State for Foreign Affairs 1931–5, Lord Chancellor 1940–45, and author of *Simon's Income Tax* in 5 vols.
[2] The Rt. Hon. Florence Horsbrugh (1889–1969), who became Baroness Horsbrugh in 1959, was the first woman to serve in a Conservative government. Churchill made her Minister of Education in 1951, and she held the appointment until 1954.
[3] Margot Metroland had a villa in Corfu in *Decline and Fall*.
[4] Randolph Churchill's *Lord Derby, King of Lancashire* appeared in 1960.

Evelyn to Diana

Piers Court   *2 May 1954*

Darling Baby

So I went to London and they told me there that you are staying in France and resuming your Sunday galas. I don't believe you would have been at your ease for long in modern England – but then it would not have been the same modern England with you here. Brighton would have been the place, perhaps.

Three Spencelayhs in the Academy. Compositions as beautiful as always and many familiar details – the red and white spotted hand-kerchief, the guinea, the fiddle but his old eyes are dim and his old fingers numb and there is not the fine finish of 25 years ago. None sold either.

Bitter cold here and the flowers without smell. Children at last going back to their schools and I going back to the ink pot and the story interrupted by my lapse into insanity. The little girl I loved immod-erately[1] is losing her charm for me. My alienist said this might happen when I regained my wits.

Graham Greene has received an official rebuke from the Grand Inquisi-tor for what do you think? – *The Power and the Glory*.[2] A much graver scandal than the suppression of the Worker-Priests.

Miss Felicity Attlee[3] reported a motorist for dangerous driving and who should it be but Mr Bevan.[4]

Saw Katharine over Easter – very thin and lame.

Mrs Fleming thinks she is an octopus – in the way modern little girls think they are horses. No one will publish H. Charteris's second book.[5] C. Connolly cannot finish his book.[6] He spends his days wandering from silversmith to silversmith examining objects he cannot buy, and his evenings teaching his wife Greek. My book is all right but going slowly.

Please tell me if there is ever a day or two when you will be <u>alone</u> and in need of company.

Saw Deirdre very pink and plump with a fetching debutante daughter.[7]

---

[1] Margaret Waugh (1942–86), Evelyn and Laura's third daughter. In 1962 she married Giles Fitz-Herbert, by whom she had five children. She also wrote *The Man who was Greenmantle* – a highly-acclaimed biography of her grandfather, Aubrey Herbert.

[2] *The Power and the Glory* (1940) was condemned as 'paradoxical' by the Holy Office.

[3] Felicity Attlee (b. 1925), daughter of Clement Attlee (1883–1967), 1st Earl Attlee.

[4] The Rt. Hon. Aneurin Bevan (1897–1960). The son of a coal-miner, he became Minister of Health in Clement Attlee's post-war Labour Government.

[5] Hugo Charteris (1922–70), novelist. His second book, *Marching in April*, was published in 1955. Brother of Ann Fleming and Laura Canfield (later Duchess of Marlborough). He took a sour view of his privileged family, many of whom appear in his novels – which was why he had difficulty finding publishers. In 1948 he married Virginia Forbes Adam.

[6] Cyril Connolly's next book proved to be *Les Pavilions* (with Jerome Zerb), which did not appear until 1962.

[7] Duff's niece Deirdre Hart-Davis, then Mrs Ronald Balfour, with her daughter Susan Balfour.

Everyone seemed awfully drunk in London – not yours truly. I think a lot of my recent drunkenness was half chloral poisoning.

I have been introduced to an interesting new thing like a water pistol for washing the teeth instead of a brush. Most invigorating. Plain soda water at high pressure. Very messy. My boy had as his report from Downside 'Very messy'. I read it as MERRY and was delighted. It proved to be MESSY. Not so good.

All love
Bo

Diana to Evelyn

69 Rue de Lille   *7 May 1954*

Darling Wu. Lovely to hear from you.

Would you come to me whenever you can or like. On the 18th an 'intimate' dinner is to be given for Nancy and Pompadour by the dedicatee. Dolly Rats.[1] I said I would go – but need not – they would love you. Pretty house, scrumptious food, and drive home to Chantilly afterwards, spend Wednesday – Thursday – Friday at Chantilly or on the road and be anyway at Chantilly Saturday 22nd to welcome Daphne and Xan Fielding on their way to the Barbary Coast. Stay on when they leave and read your work and write it.

Thursday 8 June is equally empty but too far off and too near the end. The house is let July 1st for 3 if not 4 months. It makes it possible for me to hang on for another year anyhow – Having faced the return I would now like to stay where the loveliest years, for Duff, were to have been spent.

It's long since I was with you – do come. The willow that made its pattern is dead. The cascade does not play. I try instinctively to keep the house and life as it was, but not successfully.

Do come –

Baby

Love to Laura

I think Pompadour a delight – far more delightful than anything she has written. Imitations of the approach are to be dreaded.

Evelyn to Diana

Piers Court   *13 May 1954*

Darling Baby

Everything you suggest sounds lovely but alas I can't do it. Absurd engagements – Margaret's Confirmation, the visit of a German fan, the

---

[1] The dedication to *Madame Pompadour* is to 'Dolly, Princess Radziwill'.

visit of Anne Fremantle[1] (Duff's old socialist opponent, now a chum), presenting prizes at a school – something every three days. Damn. I long to see you. Perhaps you will be in England when you let your castle. I could settle in London and wait on you.

Belloc's collected *Verses* just come. Nicely arranged and printed but ghastly good taste – Katharine's? – makes it far from complete. Lord Devonport has shown truly noble magnanimity and consented to the poem about his father, but Lords Wimborne, Swaythling, Rothschild[2] and Edward James[3] apparently less accommodating. Have you still got Miss Fahie? Do you think she could type the expurgata for me? It would be a great boon.

How I wish I had foreknowledge in my soul of your true sisterhood with heavenly things. Darling baby, isn't all this living in changing crowds a narcotic? Isn't this the time for solitude and reflection? No? Can't grief be turned to good account? You say you try 'instinctively' to keep house and life as it was. Don't trust that false instinct.

I don't look forward to visiting Ascot (girls' school) staying in hideous cheerless, very expensive hotel and entertaining large parties of little girls. I feel false as hell beaming at the head of the table. My unnatural passion for Margaret has subsided. She is very happy at this new school. I am but with melancholy people.

Re-reading Belloc I am greatly struck by how un'Bellocian' (in the vulgar sense) he was. Almost nothing about beer and hiking. Lovely classical lyrics predominating. I'll send you a review I am writing.

My heavy luggage, sent home from Ceylon by Cooks, has arrived painfully light. Everything of value stolen and no compensation, it seems. Owners risk.

All love
Bo

Diana to Evelyn

Château de St Firmin   *17 May 1954*

Darling Bo – I love you and yet you have the power to hurt me so – that is the reason of course. That dreadful word 'Narcotic' made me feel guilty in your eyes.

[1] Anne Huth-Jackson (b. 1909), journalist and author. She married Christopher Fremantle in 1930 and wrote over thirty books, including a biography of Father Charles de Foucauld, the Saharan missionary.
[2] Belloc's offensive verses about Lords Swaythling and Rothschild appear in A. N. Wilson's 1984 biography of Belloc.
[3] Edward James (1907–84). He inherited a fortune, and became patron and friend to countless poets, writers, composers and Surrealist artists. In 1971 he founded a college of arts and crafts on the family estate of West Dean, Sussex. From 1931–3 he was married to the Austrian ballet dancer, Otillie (Tilly) Losch.

You have never, I think, known real Grief – panic, melancholia, madness, night-sweats, we've all known for most of our lives – you and me particularly. I'm not sure you know human love in the way I do. You have faith and mysticism – intense inner interests – a diverting, virile mind – gusto for vengeance and destruction if necessary, a fancy – a gospel.

What you can't imagine is a creature with a certain irridescent aura and nothing within but a beating frightened heart built round and for Duff. I have no 'sisterhood with heavenly things' not for want of praying and trying to feel it. 'The instinct' that you call false 'to keep life as it was' is protective against madness and despair, the bottle or the pills. I have had as you can imagine since January a lot of the solitude that you advise. The 'reflection' alas! is as it always has been – morbid, unedifying, vain and dangerous unless made healthy by the company of friends. For two days I am quite alone – in these empty rooms with one thought one prayer – 'let it end now' – an absurd feminine desire to die in the same way exactly as Duff. The 'good account' grief has turned me into is fearlessness of death – so let it come now before custom of living disinclines me for dying. The summing up is that one survives as best one can – either by spiritual or worldly ways, and I imagine as a rule by one's habitual way. My way has always been friends and distraction – you have always disliked it and condemned it – but in these dreadful days one must be thankful and lenient to the Way found – for really there is no choice. Cynics call Religion Narcotic – and reading is a dope too. I want to think Duff is helping and protecting me. Bridget McEwen weaves me such lovely designs and comfortable pictures of how he guides and knows and helps.

So don't criticise me – in your heart I mean. I'll ask Norah Fahie for the Belloc expurgation if she has it – I don't quite know what you mean, the actual poems – Swaythling – Wimborne, James etc?

Don't forget to send me the review. I'm sorry no plan was acceptable – it seems to me you are the 'changing crowd' boy. Perhaps England will bring us together.

Six people, the last H. Belisha,[1] have sent me Father Jarrett Bede's[2] prayer. I say it twice a day. I do try.

Baby

I don't think this letter makes sense, now that I re-read. It's the end of a very bad day. My education is tags, my mind ever spastic – forgive and remain fond.

---

[1] Leslie Hore-Belisha (1893–1957), lawyer and politician. As Minister of Transport 1934–7, he brought in a number of road safety measures – including the amber globes at pedestrian crossings.
[2] Father Bede Jarrett, a Dominican.

Evelyn to Diana

Piers Court   *22 May 1954*
[in red ink]

Written in heart's blood.

O Darling, O God, what a shit I am! How I don't want ever to hurt you! I am an insensitive lout. Please forgive me. Of course I have never experienced real grief or pain or for that matter 'panics or night sweats'. I am irritable and melancholy but a dull clod and I can't sympathize with high delicate creatures like you. I was just passing on at second hand what the experts agree in prescribing as the noble acceptance of sorrow, provoked to the impertinence by Belloc's sonnet. Well I did it all wrong I see and I am truly contrite. It's the fatal pen always turning kind thoughts to offence. Talking is the thing, face to your dear face.

All love
Bo

Diana to Evelyn

Château de St Firmin   *[late May 1954]*

Darling darling Bo never did you write me a letter as touching and loving. O do remain as that minute of writing found you – cleansed and kind. I hope I wrote nothing to hurt you – my 'spirit-writing' leaves no mark on my memory and so I tremble sometimes for the irretrievable words.

Thank you – thank you. I'll be in London for three days next week – and then for all of July – we might go to Stratford together – I've a lot to say and hear.

Baby

Evelyn to Diana

Piers Court   *15 July 1954*

Dearest Diana

Laura says it takes 2 and a half to 3 hours to drive here from Stratford, knowing the way. We will provide a cold collation so that you need have no anxiety about dinner spoiling, and will be on the look out from 8 p.m.

You leave Gloucester by the Bristol Road and travel for about 10 miles. There are only 2 serious left turns. The first to Stroud. Don't take that.

Continue on main road until, 2 miles later, you reach the village of Cambridge – an inn with a Wellingtonia, an island, and left turn labelled 'Cam and Dursley'. Turn left there. Do not go to Dursley. Turn right in the Village of CAM. I think the road is labelled 'Wotton-under-Edge'. This road leads through a Macmillanville[1] of new houses, incline right when in doubt. Seek the Yew Tree Inn. At the Yew Tree take the avenue which leads to Stinchcombe village. This house is at road junction.

Katharine expects you and jewels and me to tea on Sunday. You and me to dine and sleep.

All love
Bo

Diana to Evelyn

[postcard] *[pstmk 20 July 1954]*

Watch values. It isn't the class of carriage that counts, but the destination of the train. Mine was bound for Portsmouth and the London puff. was at 12.20. Luckily a kind guard got me out at Westbury – a station like the one where R. Knox says his office where I must wait 1 hour 40 mins. No bookstall no village – I tried a walk, but the heath was too blasted. The only bother is my London appointment – fortunately I'm long-suffering – and am sitting hard-A. over a cup of Bovril and sherry after writing to Laura.

[on front of postcard:]

2 o'clock Monday
Don't tell K. my misadventure as perhaps she looked up the train.

X X X

Evelyn to Diana

Piers Court *[pstmk 28 July 1954]*
[postcard]

Oh dear what a ghastly thing to happen just when everything seemed hunky-dory. All my fault. I looked up and <u>found</u> that train. Shall never forgive myself or forget.

Bo

---

[1] Harold Macmillan (1894–1986), Prime Minister 1957–63, and later 1st Earl of Stockton. Between 1951–4 he was Minister of Housing, and promised '100,000 new homes a year'.

Evelyn to Diana

Piers Court   *29 August [1954]*

Darling

O dear. The Athenian summer is fiery enough without having a Storrs done on you. My heart bleeds for you. Spring is the only time for Greece and quiet pansies the best company – not roaring Fermor in August and perhaps Sir Maurice too roaring back.[1] O dear.

It still rains here as it did when you took the train to Portsmouth. We had one fine day – thanks to Poor Clares – the day of the Great Fête in aid of the Popish presbytery in Dursley. That was a great success. Dense throngs from all parts. I managed to Stitch some publicity in the London papers. One crew-cut was waiting at the gates at 11.30 for the opening at 3. He had left Grosvenor Square at 6 and come in a series of buses. We brought him in and gave him luncheon in an out-house and then put him to work in the car-park. At seven he was still pushing cars out and had no way of getting home so I popped him in the last car. It held a drunk, homosexual apostate named de Hoghton and off they went together. No subsequent reports.

We had the house open and Miss Rose Donaldson (16 and very plain) as lecturer. She was splendid. 'Ladies and gentlemen, this is Sir Max Beerbohm's famous caricature of Sir Ernest Cassel. Pray notice the gross Jewish features so strongly transmitted to Lady Mountbatten' etc.[2] Lady Sibell [Lygon] judged the baby-show. My children ran a wood-louse racing racket. A good time was had by some and sharp at 7.15 the Poor Clares turned the rain on again.

People like you and Mary and Katharine can take such things in your stride. Laura and I have been discussing ours without stop ever since.

Frank Pakenham has given up politics and philanthropy and become a banker. Chairman of a bank with 80 million pounds.[3] Most peculiar. He came here young and jolly, just what he was 30 years ago all his socialism thrown off.

Snake Angie is off to the island where St Paul dealt sharply with snakes.

I peg away at Vol II and have jolly nearly finished it. It seems all right to me.

No further hallucinations.

[1] Patrick Leigh Fermor and Joan Rayner had been lent a house on the island of Hydra in the Peloponnese, by the painter Nico Ghika. Diana and Sir Maurice Bowra (1898–1971), Warden of Wadham College, Oxford, were among the guests that summer.

[2] The daughter of Frances Donaldson. Her mother wrote, 'He conscripted the children for various jobs and to my daughter Rose he gave the part of acting as guide to those people who wished to see his pictures. He rehearsed her very carefully in what she was to say and on the afternoon of the fete her childish voice was to be heard, echoing innocently through his house, voicing remarks of his invention. The effect was remarkably funny . . .' (*Evelyn Waugh: Portrait of a Country Neighbour*, p. 49)

[3] Frank Pakenham took up his appointment as Chairman of the National Bank the following year, but he did not desert socialism. He returned to government as Lord Privy Seal in Harold Wilson's Labour government in 1964.

What are your plans for Jan Feb? I must go somewhere warm. I don't believe Perry and Jamaica is really the best imaginable. Graham Greene (who really is barking. Did you see his preposterous letter in *Figaro Litteraire* about Colette's obsequies?) says the Shan States are the place but he thinks anywhere with opium all right.

Margaret is home. All my love for her returned with a bang not a whimper. My eldest boy much taller than I. I don't like that. Perhaps it's nice for him. Margaret saw the giant with the shaved nut[1] acting in Ireland – Iris's giant I mean – and fell in love.

I say do the Greek papers report the case of the New Zealand girls who murdered the mother? I long for a verbatim report. One funny feature was that the surviving mother is a member of the New Zealand Marriage Guidance office.

All love
Bo

Diana to Evelyn

Athens   *[pstmk 20 October 1954]*
[postcard]

My anchor, brains and hands captain and crew Norah Fahie has TB! Out for a year at least. So sorry for her and myself. Delightful life (in so far as it can be) with Paddy and Joan – Primitive beauty, silence and courtesy. Can't judge if you would love it. O dear unpredictable

D

Evelyn to Diana

Piers Court   *All Saints [1 November] 1954*

Darling Baby

November and still rain morning and evening as it has been since I was mad in Ceylon. Mushrooms and moss on all the buildings. Aches in the joints. My work nearly finished. Three weeks more and I shall have done the last chapter. Rather good though Mrs Stitch turns out rather unscrupulous and uncharacteristic. Thoughts of sun. I am going to Bermuda in what is said to be a comfortable ship named *Britannic* Jan 14th

---

[1] Friedrich Ledebur had shaved his head in order to play the part of Queequeg in John Huston's film of Herman Melville's novel *Moby Dick*.

tickets obtainable from golden hearted man named Mr Reed at the Cunard office in Lower Regent Street. Do come too. From Bermuda midnight-dawn aeroplane to Jamaica. Perry and Ann [Fleming] and (for you) countless other welcoming Jamaican chums. Do come too. Returning end of Feb in cheap not luxurious Elder and Fyffe ship. Do come too.

So I went with a rum lot of English to Rheims to drink champagne. Frogs awfully mean hosts. A comic Lord[1] wore a kilt and took snuff. I had one frog joke 'La soeur de ce Lord est devenu son frère.'[2] Went down O.K. except they think all English change sex often.

Poor Maimie is sunk in madness.

Graham Greene behaved very oddly on Rheims outing. Saw Pryce-Jones's name (the Welsh journalist whose grandmother's name you asked to discover – a most civil and inoffensive fellow) on list and said 'I won't go. I can't meet Pryce-Jones. He is too negative'. Luckily P-Jones wasn't air station going direct to aerodrome. Then it was too late for G. Greene to desert but he complained bitterly. Well that night owing to frog meanness we all went to bed about 10 o'clock and next morning we all met in the rain at 10 o'clock to drive to vineyards. G. Greene ghastly. 'G. what have you been up to?' 'Drinking Marc until 6.' 'Who with?' 'Pryce-Jones.'

Just read David [Cecil]'s most disappointing life's work.[3] Well of course it is entertaining because Lord M was a funny fellow but how sloppily written.

You will find your great friend Quennell if you come to Jamaica.

While I was at Brighton I bought 2 beautiful rolls of bread for Laura to eat with her supper at the hotel and suddenly whish a great swoop and they were snatched from her plate – Juliet [Duff].

Someone absolutely awful was at that hotel called Charles Morgan[4] – connexion of yours I think.

Awfully sorry to hear about Miss Fahie – for you and a bit for her too.

All love
Bo Wu etc

---

[1] William Francis Forbes-Sempill (1893–1965), 19th Baron Sempill. A Wing Commander in the RAF, he was a member of several aeronautical committees, associations and missions. In 1919 he married Eileen (d. 1935), only daughter of the painter Sir John Lavery.

[2] The Hon. Elisabeth Sempill (b. 1912), daughter of the 18th Baron Sempill, changed sex and became the Hon. Ewan Forbes-Sempill in 1950 or 1951. In 1952, he married Isabella Mitchell; and he succeeded his brother as the 11th Bt. Forbes of Craigievar in 1965. The crest of his coat of arms (matriculated in 1963) is a cock proper.

[3] The first volume of David Cecil's biography of the Victorian statesman Lord Melbourne came out in 1939, entitled *The Young Melbourne*. In 1954 he published the second and final volume, *Lord M*.

[4] Charles Langbridge Morgan (1894–1958), novelist. Now best remembered for his novel *The Fountain*. He was drama critic of *The Times* 1926–39, and a passionate francophile. In 1923 he married Hilda Vaughan. Their daughter Shirley married Diana's nephew Henry, 7th Marquess of Anglesey, in 1948.

Diana to Evelyn

Château de St Firmin   *[late October? November? 1954]*

My darling Bo. I was happy, proud and flattered by your invitation to the Caribbean. The first stab of thought 'How can I start a journey so ill starred as my last setting-out for the West-Indies – again?' But of course it's no harder than living here in its emptiness.

The long sea companionship would have been, I think, successful – I have a new method in pickle for dealing with our temperaments – but I hesitated to answer waiting to hear of J.J.'s posting. Having pulled every reachable string to get him to Paris – I have failed in effort. They are to be sent to Belgrade in Feb.[1]

I thought of going too – to install them with the help of my slav-talking maid – but we'd be incubi perhaps. Then I thought of going on to Bahrein whose Sultan you threw me with via the Talbot, Clifton Way – friends called Brooks Richards[2] are there 'en poste' but I don't know – I really don't know. An Atlas would have to be found to shoulder this house during my absence of 2 or 3 months. Pam Church[ill] might oblige. By time my mind is made up it will be too late to get a birth on yr. boat – anyway London sees me about 25th Nov or so, and I can better feel the ground and the bogs when I get there. My new friend Lady Jones asks me to join her on a trip to Basuto Land. Then I've anglo-frog pals en poste in Khartoum.

You'd laugh to see my daily meals à quatre: Iris, me, Rosamond Lehmann[3] and Betty Salisbury.

God bless you my dear Bo

Baby

Evelyn to Diana

Piers Court   *16 November 1954*

Darling Baby

I have finished my book at last and is O.K. although Mrs Stitch rather lapses from her high original and becomes a sort of Cleopatra of intrigue (not amorous).[4] It is a great joy to be done with the thing. What next?

---

[1] John Julius was posted to Belgrade from January 1955 to the summer of 1957.

[2] Brooks (later Sir Brooks) Richards (b. 1918), diplomat. He was on Duff's staff at the Paris Embassy, and was at this time Head of Chancery in the Persian Gulf Political Residency.

[3] Rosamond Lehmann (1901–90), novelist. Her books include *Invitation to the Waltz* (1932), *The Gypsy's Baby* (1946), and *The Echoing Grove* (1953). In 1928 she married the Hon. Wogan Philipps, 2nd Baron Milford, who for many years was the only Communist member of the House of Lords.

[4] At the end of *Officers and Gentlemen*, Julia Stitch saves Ivor Claire from a court martial for desertion in the face of the enemy in Crete. She also has Guy Crouchback, who knows the true story, sent back to England.

Belgrade in January would be unbearable, even in the company of your jewels. Bahrein presumably warmer but I believe awfully boring. Although he is the richest man on earth he has nothing to spend his money on and his only interests are child welfare and adult education. And the wealth is brand new so there are no splendid treasure houses – merely countless American motor-cars and TV sets and I suppose a few Picassos. Basutoland would be better. I've been to Khartoum – no great shakes. But you had much better think more about Jamaica. Remember the name of the golden character in Cunard office is Reed REED and the ship BRITANNIC. I am not sure about that second N sailing Jan 14th. Hotels cost £25 a day in Jamaica so we would have to sponge but I think there are multitudes of sponging houses.

Have you read Daphne's memoirs?[1] The childhood part delightful. The adult part oddly enough marred by discretion and good taste. It is rather as though Lord Montgomery wrote his life and neglected to mention that he had ever been in the army.

Last Saturday I went to Mells and found Katharine more robust than on our last visit. I did the round of [Christopher] Hollis and Powell[2] and greatly enjoyed the day. Since then alas the rheumatism has fastened on my knee – there are 2 months to go before the tropical sun.

Peter Rodd has gone awfully mad and is threatening Ed Stanley and me with libel actions.[3] The bore is that he can sue as a pauper at the public expense, lose his case and leave us to foot the bill. It may be necessary to have him certified but I feel a certain loyalty to loonies when it comes to facing a committee of alienists. My turn can't be far off.

People keep producing such silly patronizing books about Victorian Art. Two this week. I am having a smack at them in the *Sunday Times*.

Where do you spend Christmas? Jewels? I must be here with my cairngorms and moss agates. I do so dislike little boys. From boxing day I am free as air.

Freddy and Sheila brought a small girl here yesterday.[4] She could only talk of intestines. My Meg is better than that.

All love
Bo

---

[1] Daphne Fielding's *Mercury Presides* had just been published.

[2] Anthony Powell (b. 1905), novelist. After the war he embarked on his sequence of twelve novels, *A Dance to the Music of Time*.

[3] Waugh had reviewed Lord Stanley's *Sea Peace*, an account of various sailing expeditions – on one of which he was accompanied by Nancy Mitford's husband Peter Rodd. The main criticism of Rodd was that he could be tiresome company.

[4] The 2nd Earl of Birkenhead had married Sheila Berry in 1935. the 'small girl' was presumably their daughter Juliet, then aged thirteen.

Evelyn to Diana

Piers Court   *13 December 1954*

Darling Diana

I don't know where to post my Christmas Greetings – to the Congo it is too late, to Chantilly too early, to Athens just right perhaps. Wherever you are and whenever you receive this letter be assured of my deep love. A desperate and distracted year is over for you. Pray God next year is fuller and smoother. Life can't be the same of course, but it can be rich and peaceful in a different way.

My mother[1] died last week, very old and feeble, and in her last year greatly irked at being physically dependent on others. Nancy says the English always write of death as a 'happy release'. In her case it was and for her sake I am glad, but I am full of regret for failures in gratitude and patience and service and that has made me think of my failures towards all I love, and you come very high on the list – so ungrateful, so deliberately mischievous – well, you know worse than I. Please forget my constant failures and believe always in my love – not only at Christmas. And please be happy at Christmas, thinking of love and peace and hope reborn yearly at this dreariest season.

Bo

Diana to Evelyn

69 Rue de Lille   *1 January [1955]*

Beloved Bo – You wrote me so moving and sincere a letter written with your heart as well as your pen. I know you have a great heart but you hate to put it on your sleeve – rightly up to a point – but rather than let it sometimes fly there by its dear volition, you pin a grinning stinking mask on the site.

I am sorry for your mother's trials and for you in many ways – poor Bo. This day a year ago Duff was taken from me. New Year's Eve was the worst day I have known – the cruel sounds of merriment and carnival and popping balloons seeped into the cabin where he lay dying and I knelt praying and gasping – so although I sneer at anniversaries, deeming all days to be by nature the same – Those dreadful welkins and Auld Lang Synns will always bring the worst day back in a ghastly way – too horrible for my frailty – though it might have been a scene of your invention.

I've just read *Helena* again with intense enjoyment. I don't know Penelope.[2] I should like her, I know. No sight of you for too long and

---

[1] Catherine Waugh, née Raban. She and Arthur St John Waugh were married in 1893. She was an affectionate mother, but did not share the literary tastes of her husband and sons.

[2] The character of the Empress Helena is partly based on Penelope Betjeman – see Waugh's letter of 3 January 1946 (p. 83).

soon you will be sailing west. I left you a present of glasses at White's Club.

Will you be in London before you leave? and shall I see you? I'd like you to scrap all your plans and come to Rome – Malta and Bahrain with me at the end of this new month.

Your letter makes me glad to be your limpet –

5 Belgrave Square finds me from the 4th – Slo 8231.

Baby

Evelyn to Diana

Piers Court   *3 January 1955*

Dearest Baby

Greatly relieved to get your letter. Whenever I write from the heart I fear I have caused embarrassment.

Helena is my favourite modern book. I am so glad you like it. Few do.

I shall make a dash for London before the railways stop, perhaps keeping Epiphany there. My only hard date is luncheon on 7th. I have written to Ann Fleming proposing dinner 6th or 7th. Could we meet with her? What free hours have you? I can spend either or both nights in London. Many exhibitions to see.

An awful Christmas – all children and servants successively succumbing to mild but vexatious 'flu'. Now I have bought them a new motor-car and that has cheered them up.

I envy you Rome and Malta – not Bahrain. Tilly [Losch] hooked the ADC in traditional style.

How very kind of you to leave glasses for me. Lovely Christmas present. I hope those horrible hooligans in White's spare them for the horrible hooligans in Stinchcombe.

My children are extraordinarily nice to one another. Can't understand it.

Could you telegraph about London plans?

All love
Bo

Evelyn to Diana

Roaring River   *27 January 1955*
St Anne's Bay
Jamaica BWI

Darling Baby

Where will this find you? When? I wish you were here. It is a fine airy spacious house on a hill, full of secondary treasures exported from

Belton. Perry has cleverly cut away all the palms making a park very much like Pixton if you can imagine blue sea at the gates. He is in a very fretful mood – the jaguar has broken its axel, the jeeps have lost their gear boxes, the electric cocktail shaker has fused, Edward[1] has failed to get a commission in the Grenadiers, Sylvia Ashley[2] has accused him of sharp practice in land speculation, his agent goes in fear of assassination, Cuckoo Belville calls daily accusing him of neglecting his children. He takes all these tribulations very hard and drinks far too much whisky. His bride[3] is very garrulous and good natured and nonsensical. A party assembles next week, when I hope to go on tour of the island before Princess Margaret buggers things up.

The voyage out was stormy but delightful. I don't believe there is any comfort in this reduced decade comparable to a Cunard liner – none more congenial to me anyway. Agreeable company on board – jews for you, lords for me. By contrast BOAC from Bermuda was squalidly incompetent. I go home by sea all the way.

Some jews called Joel[4] were in the ship. They set out with a valet, maid and biographer, taking the biographer by train and sending the servants ahead with the luggage. Snow blocked the servants so the poor Joels were left with nothing for the voyage except emeralds and lipstick. Joel wore the biographer's clothes. Mrs J. got a few dresses flown from Paris to Le Havre. But they were in a sad condition. I found the biographer's manuscript in the smoking room. It is called *Solly the Magnificent*.

I am writing a record, whether for publication or not I can't yet say, of my recent lunacy [*The Ordeal of Gilbert Pinfold*]. An enthralling subject to me but not perhaps of much general interest.

Humming birds by day, frogs at night. I can't see anything through the goggles everyone wears bathing.

There was a lady here went to sleep on a mattress in a red bathing dress and all the vultures thought she was dead and bloody and tried to eat her.

Oh dear I have been writing too small again. You won't be able to read it. Damn.

All love
Bo

---

[1] Edward Cust (b. 1936), who succeeded his father as 7th Baron Brownlow in 1978. He went on to make a career in underwriting and insurance.

[2] Sylvia, daughter of Arthur Hawkes. Her first husband was Lord Ashley, son and heir of the 9th Earl of Shaftesbury, to whom she was married 1927–35; her second husband was Douglas Fairbanks Sr; her third, Lord Stanley of Alderley, and her fourth, Clark Gable.

[3] Lord Brownlow's first wife Katherine died in 1952; and in 1954 he married Dorothy Sands (d. 1966), daughter of T. S. Power of Virginia, USA, and formerly wife of the 2nd Earl Beatty.

[4] The Joel family had made their fortune as financiers and gold dealers in South Africa.

Diana to Evelyn

Train to France   *2 April [1955]*

Darling Bo. Annie is coming to Chantilly the Sunday after Easter – won't you come too? It's the hols and you like to absent yourself from felicity of children. You could perhaps stay on a little or I could take you for a jaunt to some monument or pleasure-dome.

I hope so much you'll come, and take back the last six charity glasses. Artemis Cooper is travelling with me – her nurse is a tender ogress. I'm not good at children really – when this little girl looks at me she whitens, petrifies, and then bursts into hysterical tears.

Always faithful –
Baby

Evelyn to Diana

Piers Court   *24 April [1955]*

Sweet Pug-Baby

Who will be reading this aloud to you – Quennell, Forbes, Jenny Crosse? They will see no good of themselves.

The classic Collins. First, the journey. Well, that aeroplane was flowing with free wine and I am beginning to think better of air travel. Secondly, the itemized pleasures of the visit. Of course for me the chief pleasure was the hours alone with you – just a moment while you answer the telephone – as I was saying the hours alone with you, your kindness to my story reading, your tremendous indiscretions about our friends. I have not divulged a word even to Laura but goodness I do brood about you know who. Then I enjoyed the party too – the clash of Fleming and Raimund, the infirmities of Judy and Marguerite [Daisy Fellowes?]. The Dutchman's lice I have taken as public knowledge and told my children who were delighted and suspect the cowman here now. Beaton's sneak eye was creepy and his poor bare head. Thirdly I should say I left something behind but I didn't thanks to your able servants – nothing but my heart and they couldn't pack that – it is so full of love it wouldn't go into the bag.

So I drove with my elder jewels 80 miles to a ball at Stonor[1] – ghostly, impoverished, candle lit halls and galleries full of delicious 16 year old convent trained girls and gawky youths in plastic shoes.

Then yesterday to the Hollis wedding at Mells. Katharine very merry in church but quickly tiring in the marquee. We are not used to so much social life and all rather out of temper as the result.

Read [P. H.] Newby's *Picnic at Sakkara* – awfully funny.

---

[1] Stonor Park, Oxfordshire: the home of Ralph, 5th Baron Camoys (1884–1968).

Perhaps it was officious of me. I hinted to K that it might be more fun for her to visit Chantilly on the way to Lourdes.

The Jerk [Anthony Eden] goes in fear of his life with doubled police guards. People (I presume Randolph) keep telephoning him with threats of assassination.[1]

Auberon [Herbert] has organized a canvassing party of negroes.[2]

All love
Bo

[postscript in the form of a postcard, postmark as above:]

P.S. I forgot section 4 of the Classic Collins: 'Comment on subjects discussed during visit.'
(4) I have consulted eminent authorities all of whom agree that *ossi bucchi* are shin bones.

Evelyn to Diana

Piers Court   *5 May 1955*

Sweet Pug

I have not been idle about Duff's portrait. By good chance one of the best firms of 'Art' printers is at Wotton-under-Edge near here.[3] They (and others) advise collotype as superior to photogravure. A false plate-mark can easily be added. Would you like me to go ahead with them? If so, what size? I suggest about 10 × 12 for the plate with three inch margins at side and four at bottom. I have asked for an estimate at this size. How many copies? The peculiarity of collotype is that the expense is mainly in the printing not in the making of the plate. i.e. 200 copies probably cost nearly double 100.

I take it you will want a title at foot. Simply: 'Duff Cooper, 1st Viscount Norwich, after the painting by Sir John Lavery' or more? or less?

At your command
Bo

---

[1] Winston Churchill, who had been Prime Minister since 1951, resigned in early April. He was succeeded by Anthony Eden.

[2] After the war Auberon Herbert stood as Liberal candidate for a number of parliamentary seats, but never won an election.

[3] Diana wanted a print made of Duff's portrait by Sir John Lavery, to distribute to his friends. Waugh suggests the Cotswold Collotype Company for the job.

Evelyn to Diana

Piers Court   *[May–June 1955]*
[postcard]

[newspaper cutting pasted at top:]

O MOST CHARMING PUG
'Ha! a pog, a very seldom dog.'

Sweet seldom Pog
  Will you pray put this ikon in Katharine's bedroom?
  'Art' printers telephone. I say I will be intermediary if needed. I thought you wanted perhaps copies of portrait for all subscribers (Waugh and Sherwood[1] abstaining) to Duff's Memorial Fund.[2] But you can have as few as you like. <u>No one</u> now can produce copper engraving. If by any happy chance you wish to visit Wotton-under-Edge printers, stay here please.

All love
Bo

Evelyn to Diana

Piers Court   *14 July [1955]*

Sweet Pug baby
  Hyde Park Gate? That smells of the Spencer-Churchills.[3] Have you yielded? O Pog. O Pog. Fie.
  Please can't you come here for luncheon between Stanway and Bulbridge? It is not far out of your way. If you have Forbes with you he can be given a tray in the business room.
  . . . Or failing all else I could come to London for the evening of 28th. But I should see you better in my own home and Laura would have that treat too.
  Funny your addiction to Stratford.
  I hope you got the copy of *Officers and Gentlemen* I sent. Try reading it again. It is much better than the reviewers believe.
  I go to Ann Fleming at Dover on 29th. Why not you too? From her I move to a seaside hotel to escape jewels and write about lunacy.

[1] Sir Hugh Seely, 3rd Bt. (1898–1970), who became Baron Sherwood in 1941. He was Joint Under-Secretary of State for Air 1941–5, a Liberal MP, and one of Duff's handful of friends in the Liberal Party.
[2] To Diana's delight, Duff's friends suggested setting up a fund to endow a literary prize in his name. Randolph Churchill was one of the prime movers in the scheme, but Diana's gratitude chilled a little when she met him in Monte Carlo that summer. He was blind drunk and had lost the list of subscribers.
[3] Sir Winston Churchill lived at 28 Hyde Park Gate.

Miss Spain[1] is said to practise unnatural vice too.

All love
Bo

Evelyn to Diana

Piers Court   *18 July [1955]*

Darling Pog
    Is Mrs Spencer-Churchill going the Edwardian whole hog and inter-
cepting my letters?
    Did you receive numerous suggestions for a meeting?
    Are you going to Ann on the 28th?
    Are you driving there in a motor from London? If so shall I come with
you?

Bo

Diana to Evelyn

42 Hyde Park Gate   *Monday 25 [?July 1955]*

Thank you so much for my day of sweetness and light – Laura so pretty
and lissom – you unpossessed and as you should always be – the dear
darling Papa pug, petted ragged and loved.
    Indeed indeed I loved it. My telephone is <u>2248 Western</u>. I'll drive you to
Dover – or would you rather legover legover?[2] Are we asked Friday or
Sat? Will they perhaps weary of us before Tuesday morning if we go
Friday?
    Write now your desires
    Love to all the children
        and loving thanks to Laura

Baby
X X X

---

[1] The journalist Nancy Spain was at that time literary critic for the *Daily Express*. She did not like
Waugh, and in her opinion his talent was overrated. On 21 June, just after the publication of *Officers and
Gentlemen*, she and Lord Noel-Buxton turned up at Piers Court. Waugh described the incident in an
article for *The Spectator* of 8 July: 'They attempted to effect an entry into my house and wrangled until I
dismissed them in terms intelligible even to them.'
[2] 'Leg over leg, as the dog went to Dover
    When he came to a stile, jump! He went over.'
                    (nursery rhyme)

Evelyn to Diana

Grand Hotel   *August 2nd [1955]*
Folkestone

Darling Pug

So it was KNOT not KNOB: knotty problem, see?

I pray that the agony in the tooth has abated.

Thank you for driving me about in your motor-car and bringing me here. Folkestone at this end of the town is very prosperous and genteel. Proles to the East. The servants in the hotel are excellent – all save the cook, alas.

They showed me into a fine suite containing a grand-piano and I thought well baby can't say I am being rooked at five guineas for all this. Then they came and said I wasn't to play the piano or even to go into the parlour.

It has been lovely seeing so much of you lately.[1] I wish it was to be me and not Giles in your schooner.[2]

I do hope poor O'Neill[3] has perked up a bit now we have gone. I liked the sodomites. What a rotten housewife Ann turns out to be.

All love
Bo

Evelyn to Diana

Piers Court   *October 19 [1955]*

Sweet Pug

I kick myself that I am not with you in London today. It is all that devil telephone. When I use it I feel absolutely isolated and loveless – no sense of contact and communication. So like a booby I have missed the treat of seeing you for I don't know how long. Damn damn damn.

I misunderstood too about 'U' and 'you' and only hours later realized what you were saying and how I agree. Nancy has inflamed a most unwholesome appetite. My article is all about heraldry and the incomes of Dukes. Except that I expose her as a hallucinated communist agent, there is nothing she can mind. I will send it to you in December.[4]

[1] He and Diana had spent the bank holiday weekend with Ann Fleming at St Margaret's Bay.

[2] Stavros Niarchos had lent Diana a yacht, the *Eros*, in which she was shortly to cruise the Aegean in company with (among others) Frank and Kitty Giles.

[3] Raymond O'Neill (b. 1933), Ann's son by her first husband Shane O'Neill, 3rd Baron O'Neill. Raymond succeeded his father as 4th Baron in 1944.

[4] Nancy Mitford had written an article in the magazine *Encounter*, entitled 'The English Aristocracy', which observed that a person's social class was immediately revealed by the words and phrases he used. The terms U and Non-U, denoting Upper-Class and Non-Upper-Class usage, were coined by Professor Alan Ross, a philologist from Birmingham University. Waugh's response to the article, 'An Open Letter to the Honble Mrs Peter Rodd on a Very Serious Subject', appeared in the December issue of *Encounter*. The following year Hamish Hamilton published a book – *Noblesse Oblige* – which pursued the subject further. It included pieces by Nancy Mitford, Evelyn Waugh, Professor Ross, Peter Fleming, Christopher Sykes, and a poem by John Betjeman.

I have ordered your treatise on Oggie from the library and look forward to it.

Laura's cowman has broken his leg and she has a cold and has to milk twice a day.

Did you ever come across an American named Caresse Crosby? I have just had her autobiography for review. She seems to have known several of your friends. Can't write for toffee but fucked a lot.[1]

I am trying to get someone to pay for me to go for a long warm journey this winter but so far no takers. Where will you be in January and February? How about India for us?

I can't drink claret any more. Very odd and inconvenient as I have a cellar full of it so I am swapping for Burgundies – laborious

Fifty two next week. Going to Ascot to dine with Margaret for my treat – my daughter I mean not the fallen princess.[2]

All love
Bo

Diana to Evelyn

Château de St Firmin   *23 [?October 1955]*

Rab's Roy Jelly – nothing like it in our time – Thank you very much. I'd missed it. The comment too wonderfully suited.[3]

If only I could get someone to live here Feb and Jan – pay their food and drink and half the wages so the servants did not rot – I'd gladly – so gladly venture again to wilder shores with you. Minemum of flying – suggest Ceylon as an assignment.

No jungle grass has grown under my feet since your last letter. Spying the Aga Khan, I asked him what princes were left – 'Only Gye[4] is much

---

[1] Caresse Crosby (1892–1970), née Mary Phelps Jacob, wife of the American poet Harry Crosby (1898–1929). She was Mrs Richard Rogers Peabody when she and Crosby eloped to Paris, where she changed her name to Caresse and he set up the Black Sun Press. They were married in New York in 1922. In December 1929, Harry Crosby – who had always been obsessed with the mysteries of love and death – shot himself and his lover, Josephine Bigelow, a young bride who had run away from her husband to be with Harry. Caresse Crosby's memoirs were called *The Passionate Heart*, and not published until 1968 – so Waugh must have been going over an early draft.

[2] HRH Princess Margaret, the Queen's younger sister. It was no secret that she wanted to marry Group Captain Peter Townsend; but because he was divorced, the match was forbidden. On 14 October, the Palace had issued a statement saying that 'no announcement concerning Princess Margaret's personal future was being contemplated'. In 1960 she married Antony Armstrong-Jones, who was created 1st Earl of Snowdon in 1961. They divorced in 1978.

[3] In a letter to Ann Fleming of 1 October, Waugh wrote: 'The photograph of Butler, stuffed with royal jelly, reeling up the steps of his house, was one of the keenest pleasures of last week.' (*The Letters of Ann Fleming*, ed. Mark Amory, p. 163) He sent the newspaper cutting to Diana, who pasted it into her scrapbook (see illustrations).

[4] The Maharajah of Jaipur (1911–70), 39th ruler of the Indian State of Jaipur, known to his friends as Jai.

210

good now' he said and he rules the rulers. He said he'd write at once. I think only princes, tigers and temples are of any good – Indian fly ridden Hotels are impossible. To stay in towns like Calcutta however near the Delhis and Agra (Taj Mahal) is monstrous and dear.

There's an eccentric writer called Jane Bowles, her husband is called Paul[1] – he writes too I think – they have a rotunda or octaginal house in Ceylon that I would borrow. Martin Russell of Mottisfont Abbey has lived there years.

I write seriously. India – i.e. Delhis and Kashmir are <u>cold</u> in winter – I've done it – but Ceylon might be clement.

What of the Mauritius? Seychelles? I have friends in Bahrein – (Talbot Clifton's sultan) called Brooks Richards – but Bahrein is a far cry and dead end.

Get the gen on Damascus – too cold I fear. Diabeah? Upper Nile with crocs and Osimandias his works? avoiding Shepheard's – These visions of Mount Abora swiftly vanish but as I set them down I nearly revive.

Paddy is here but ailing so that next best thing – also Judy [Montagu] blind of one eye – and a cultivated humorous Belgian name of Staerke[2] – catholick. You might like him – but you are unpredictable – I'm uncertain.

X X X
A hug from
Pug

Diana to Evelyn

Château de St Firmin   *30 October 1955*

Darling Wu. Collotype writes that my reproductions are ready. It seems all important that I should be able to take the canvas back with me to France on the 16th especially as I have a car. My plans are the following. I come to London 14th or maybe I go on that day straight from the coast to Stratford-on-Avon where they are playing *Titus* which Poor Louis *insists* on my seeing; and as he lends me a car there and back and I want to export from England a garden of forbidden roses, I have inclined to his will. That night I shall get to a friend or a hotel and leave at earliest dawn for London – chores – collect plants etc – I shall watch the youth and fashion dance that 15th night of Nov at the U.S. Embassy. The Ambassador Aldrich[3] is so drivelling with love for my niece Liz and this party is one of his testimonies.

I've written to Collie Type – no, to Mr Frith to ask him if he can get the

---

[1] Paul Bowles (b. 1910), novelist and music critic, born in New York. In 1955 he had just published *The Spider's House*. Jane Bowles, his wife, was an American fiction writer and playwright, who suffered from bad health.

[2] André de Staerke, Belgian Ambassador to the UN.

[3] Winthrop Williams Aldrich (1885–1974), US Ambassador to the Court of St James 1953–7.

picture and prints either to Stratford 14th or 15 Connaught Square 15th. I have also said that I would ask you if by any chance you were coming to London and would bring them up – by careful hand – to White's say? You will see if it's possible and communicate with him.

The Pug fancier has just left the house – all passion a little cooled. I tremble for her reason – so indeed does she – but I think her domestic situation warrants madness. Write dear Bo –

to your most loving
Baby

Are you still thinking of wilder hotter shores – I am.

P[ug]

Evelyn to Diana

Piers Court   *All Saints [1 November] 1955*

Sweet Pug

All very well. I have to go to London for a popish luncheon at the Hyde Park Hotel on 14th. I will leave the portrait with the porter there before one o'clock. O.K.?

I have been to Ceylon, the time I went mad. It is very pretty but nothing to see except a field of ruins and Buddha's tooth. India is teetotal and uncomfortable but full of Great Works of Art which may be closed to us soon. I want to get an editor to pay for my trip in which case I could help put down in baby's cot and cream in her saucer. If I pay for myself I shall have to live cheap and bohemian. No editor shows zeal at the moment.

Or I would settle with pug in a pension in Teneriffe – 'caught the syph in Teneriffe and clap in the Canaries'.

Very cold here now.

I went for 52nd birthday treat to see Margaret at Ascot and found her full of new common tastes and greedy as a little boy.

All love
Bo

Evelyn to Diana

Piers Court   *7 November [1955]*

Sweet Pug

My kind intentions towards you have been frustrated. The Collotypists say they have had instructions from you to deliver their work and Sir John's to you in London and so won't let me take it.

212

I hope you enjoy *Titus* as much as I did. I wonder if you saw my fulsome praise of it – or rather of Lady Olivier – in the *Spectator*.[1]

Enjoy your yankee ball.

All love
Bo

Evelyn to Diana

Piers Court   *28 November [1955]*

Sweet Pug

I say can I interest you in Assisi? The Americans are paying me an absurdly large sum to write about St Francis. I must go to Umbria for four or five days just before or after Christmas. Must have chum. No chum like Pug. Americans would pay all expenses in whatever luxury is available. Do think of it. It was sad you didn't like [Stanley] Spencer[2] but you might prefer Giotto.

All love
Bo

The snag about Assisi, as I see it, is the evenings. Dark at 5 and nothing to do except sit in now very luxurious hotel.

Perhaps we could call on Lady Berkeley.[3]

Evelyn to Diana

Piers Court   *[December 1955]*

Well now sweet pug that is <u>very</u> nice. I should like to go on or about Jan 1st. My plan would be for us to take Rome express to Rome and there put ourselves in the hands of *Life* magazine to provide a motor-car and cicerone to Assisi, Spoleto, Rieti etc. It will be all ice and wolves. I don't think the servants with appendicitis or your own little bus are really much

---

[1] The actress Vivien Leigh (1913–67) had married Laurence Olivier (1907–89) in 1940. He was knighted in 1947. *Titus Andronicus* is the bloodiest of all Shakespeare's plays and includes a rape, five stabbings, a strangling, an immolation, two cut throats, several mutilations and an act of involuntary cannibalism – yet Waugh felt that Lady Olivier had played her part with some humour. In the *Spectator* article of 2 September 1955, he wrote that 'when she was dragged off to her horrible fate she ventured a tiny, impudent, barely perceptible roll of the eyes, as who would say "My word! What next?"'

[2] Sir Stanley Spencer (1891–1959), painter; his heavy figures did not appeal to Diana.

[3] Mary Emlen, née Lowell, of Boston, Massachusetts, widow of Randal Mowbray, 8th Earl of Berkeley (1865–1942). She lived in great style in a converted church in Assisi, and wrote a volume of memoirs called *Beaded Bubbles*.

213

needed. How would you like it if I took my daughter Teresa with us? She is no jewel but good sound rock. She would maid you and support our old limbs up the precipices to Francis's caves and it would be an educative experience for her – you and St Francis both.

It seems quite probable that she has passed her Oxford entrance. If so this jaunt would be a reward. If not, she will have to go back to her crammers. I shall know in a week or so. I haven't mentioned the project to her.

I was at Mells last Sunday. Katharine bed-ridden and in pain, I thought. The house full of rich gifts from you.

See *Encounter* this month – Waugh exposes the Mitford Imposture.

All love
Bo

Evelyn to Diana

Piers Court   [?*December 1955*]

O pug darling it is all off.

Those foul yanks having promised everything, now go back on it and say they won't send us to Assisi. Shits.

I was so looking forward to it.

I do hope you hadn't put yourself out and made any arrangements.

I grovel utterly humiliated

Damn damn damn all yanks.

Evelyn to Diana

Piers Court   *20 December* [*1955*]

Darling Pug

Well I will explain. *Life* said write an article about St Francis dollar a word. Yes I said, half as expenses in dollar cheques. That makes all the difference with taxes and for 5000 words I could have taken you and Teresa (who has got a scholarship) for a ripping treat. Then *Life* said, article first, then money. Not at all like their great and gracious ways. It is being argued now by agents in London and New York but it looks as if it is all off. There is just a chance that the Right may Prevail. If it does I will at once tell you and hope you are still free, but don't refuse any good offers as I think chances small.

A very happy Christmas to you sweet Pug Baby.

Mrs R. S. Churchill got a black eye from Mr R.S.C. last Thursday, during a quiet evening in her own home, not at Ann's charity orgy which I didn't enjoy at all. Some pretty girls but all the men looked quite awful. Next Best Thing very affable

Connolly's cuckolding[1] is a great bore. I dined with him and he went on and on. The guilty couple are making rings round him.

Here is a picture of a Jew because you love them so. Not so Connolly.

I say I visited Bobo's grave.[2] You remember how she died, with Hitler's name on her lips. Do you know what they put on her tomb stone? – 'Say not the struggle naught availeth'.

All love
Bo

[enclosed: postcard of a Rabbi holding a seven-branched candlestick; message reads:]

Christmas love from Bo, Laura, Teresa, Bron, Meg, Harriet[3] and Septimus

Diana to Evelyn

Château de St Firmin   *[December 1955]*

O Bo darling – I am so disappointed – and to think at this very moment you've got your nose in a flesh pot and I might have mine in the same one at Annie's board. I returned out of a sense of duty – to discover it was unnecessary – I'd thought with wonder and excitement about Assisi – the fanged wolf and the caves of ice, and Teresa I should have loved. Can't we do something else – I've got to get out of this for 4 to 6 weeks – it's cheaper to travel and the servants' wombs and livers are ailing. That's why I thought to take them to Italy, their home – to be dropped off not to serve us – and the little car was to save our four tickets.

I shall still do this about the 18th as I have to pause for a wedding in Switzerland on 21st – failing any better, more shining idea of yours.

England's good enough for me but my sands have run out for this year that has to limp on till April for tax purposes.

I'll be in London Tuesday or Wed next week to go to Vaynol, Bangor, Wales Fri. If you are in London Slo 7348 will know where I am.

X X X
Diana Pug

---

[1] Cyril Connolly's marriage to Barbara Skelton was falling apart. She was seeing a great deal of George (later Baron) Weidenfeld, whom she married in 1956.

[2] Unity Mitford, youngest of the six Mitford sisters. She became a passionate believer in fascism and hero-worshipped Hitler, whom she met in 1933. On the day war was declared, Unity shot herself in the head: the suicide failed, and left her mind and memory much impaired. She died of meningitis in 1948.

[3] Harriet Waugh (b. 1944), novelist and reviewer. In 1985 she married Richard Dorment.

Diana to Evelyn

Vaynol   *[January 1956]*
Bangor
North Wales

Beloved Bo

Cold and sickness pines the climb in N. Wales. But they're all very good and considerate to me and fill me up with comforting wine and spirits. It will end on Thursday and I shall go to Petworth, in my (now useless) pursuit of Harold Macmillan. I'd softened him wonderfully and now no longer can he help the posting of my only son.

From Petworth I shall try and get to Mells for a night – is there a hope of your meeting me there? Do try. It would make it much more agreeable for me and for Katharine and for Ronald.

It's disappointing about Assisi – being punch drunk I accept it. Perhaps an alternative may rise with new spangled or?

I shall return to France about 6th – I wish you would let me feed and warm and wash you when you want, for work's sake, to absent yourself from family. No assignments. I shall go to Rome for 6 weeks I think.

Pug Baby

Answer me to 5 Belgrave Sq re Mells
Matches for Laura

Evelyn to Diana

Piers Court   *[January 1956]*

Sweet Pug

When last seen Katharine was iller than either of us – but Ronnie robust. I have written to her to say I'll come if asked whenever you are there.

I went to Petworth last summer as a tourist and thought it hideous and – for a palace – meanly furnished. The famous art gallery <u>dreadful</u> and lay-out of park miserable. Some pretty carved decoration in the hall. I suppose Turner raised expectations too high.

Poor SORRY forgot about dim eyes. Poor Nancy is off her rocker about Aristocratic Usage. She has never distinguished between girlish chat and literary language and now she is deep out of her depth about Scotch and Scottish and Scots.

If you see poor bald Beaton do ask him what he thinks 'pristine' means. He uses it five times in his recent book. He seems to think it means 'new' or 'clean'. I suppose someone once said that a collar was not in its pristine state.

I have written a final personal appeal to Harry Luce about Assisi and don't absolutely despair.

216

Diana in coronation
robes, 1953.

Preparing to
abandon ship,
on Lake Garda.

Two of Waugh's enclosures:
R. A. Butler (see letter p210).

ROYAL CRESCENT HOTEL
(KINGS CLIFF, MARINE PARADE)
BRIGHTON.

TELEPHONE:
BRIGHTON 29272·6

Who's been at my
royal jelly?

The Upturned Barrow by
W. A. Atkinson (see
letter p111).

Dinner in Rome. Left to right: Judy Montagu, Patrick Crosse, Diana, Milton Gendel, Jenny Nicholson-Crosse.

Diana and Patrick Leigh Fermor, Delos.

Iris Tree, Rome.

Panel by Martin Battersby, depicting the works and interests of Evelyn Waugh. The long reliquary contains part of the rope that hanged Edmund Campion.

Waugh at Piers Court.

One of five panels
by Martin
Battersby,
commissioned by
Duff and Diana.
This one
represents Diana's
acting career in
The Miracle.

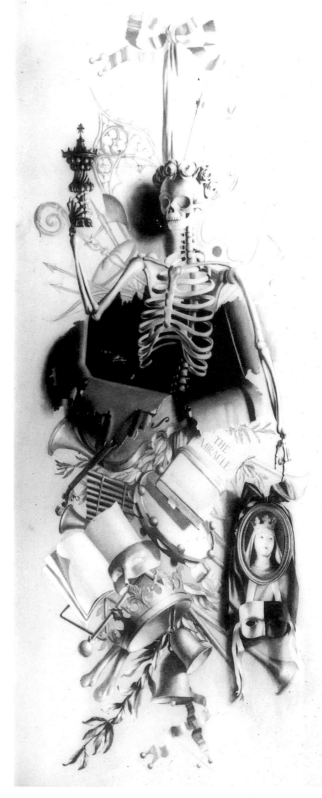

Announcement of the forthcoming
serialisation of *The Rainbow Comes
and Goes*, March 1958.

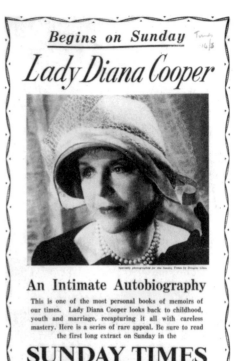

John Julius, Artemis and Anne in Beirut, 1957.

The Waugh family, c. 1965. Back row, left to right: Lady Teresa Waugh; Auberon
Waugh holding Alexander Waugh; Teresa d'Arms holding Justin d'Arms; Giles
FitzHerbert; Margaret FitzHerbert holding Claudia FitzHerbert; Harriet Waugh.
Front row, left to right: Septimus Waugh; Laura Waugh holding Emily
FitzHerbert; Mary Herbert; Evelyn Waugh holding Sophie Waugh; James Waugh.

Piers Court and Combe Florey, as they appear on Waugh's letterheads.

Diana on a donkey, in the Valley of the Kings, Egypt.

Laura is <u>delighted</u> with her pretty matches. You committed a criminal offence in sending them through the post, did you know?

Your jewels sent me a Christmas card. I was deeply touched.

Re matches in post do you know the story about Mr Nicholson the painter and the hamper on the uninhabited island? I will tell you when we meet. No good asking you here? My poor spastic Harriet is pug-like in her devotion to you.

Well anyway it is not very cold.

All love
Bo

Evelyn to Diana

Piers Court   *[?early January 1956]*

Darling Pug

No hope of Assisi left.

My 'Dear Harry' letter has been answered by the very man against whom I was protesting. Poor Luce lives like a Nizam surrounded by eunuchs.

Now I must sit at home and exploit my insanity to pay for Teresa's season.

As soon as the door shut behind you Ronnie insisted on my sitting down to play scrabble with him. I can't play for nuts but had wonderful hands. He kept the score. He made 10s to my 50s. At the end he totted up. 'You seem to have won' he said. 'Yes, I had all the luck'. 'You have beaten me by seven' said that tricky prelate.

All love
Bo

Evelyn to Diana

Piers Court   *26 February 1956*

Sweet Pug

What has become of you in the great cold? I read horrible accounts of wolves roaming the streets of Italian towns. Lucky we didn't go to Assisi. But are you alive and safe in your fur coat of shame?[1] I went to Brighton for a bit and to London for a bit where I took a liking to Daphne's Mr Zan [Xan Fielding]. It was what C. Connolly would call the manic-depressive curve; what I call going on a bust and sobering up. Then I came home

---

[1] Paul Louis Weiller had given Diana a mink coat. She revelled in the luxury, but the twinge of guilt she felt at accepting such a handsome present meant that it was always called 'the coat of shame'.

meaning to work but sat numb instead. I sent Teresa to a convent in Bonn where she is not at all happy.

I have just read a very poor book about Lord Beaverbook.[1] It says you originated the *Sunday Express*. O pug the things you have done.

Is there any truth in the statement made by a shady don named Blake that Duff was challenged to a duel for reviewing his (Blake's) life of Lord Haig?[2]

I saw the Wotton-under-Edge print of Duff in White's and thought they had done very well. I hope you liked it.

Bloggs's life of his father is very good [*My Father: The True Story*]. Also Bemelman's life of Lady Mendl.

So Daphne and I went to *Waiting for Godot* but we got there after the first act rather tight and could not grasp its deep meaning.

Teresa has twenty printed invitations to tea at the Hyde Park Hotel in March. Seems rum to me. Will you please grace her ball on July 5th?

Six foxes play in the snow under our windows. Lucky little Lord Gormanston[3] is not staying.

How could you have started the *Sunday Express*?

Mr G. Greene is making an ass of himself – first advertising an indecent book called *Lolita* [by Vladimir Nabokov] and then trying to organize a rag of the editor of your dream-child [Lord Beaverbrook] for mocking him.

Nancy's U and non-U has become the most boring topic. I went to Dublin for an evening and all the Irish were talking about it too. And now your great friend Hamish Hamilton is reprinting it all in a book. I will send you a copy to make you sick.

Your great friend Henriques[4] has written another book.

I say this is a dull letter isn't it?

All love
Bo

Diana to Evelyn

Torre del Grillo 5 March [1956]
Rome

Darling Bo I've survived the great cold – I endured it in 3 capitals. My hands turn a livid corpse colour and become incapable of action – to all

---

[1] Tom Driberg's *Beaverbrook: A Study in Power and Frustration* (1956).

[2] The historian Robert Blake (b. 1916), created Lord Blake in 1971. His edition of *The Private Papers of Douglas Haig* appeared in 1952. Two years before, he went to visit Duff at Chantilly to show him the draft and ask him whether he approved of Haig's francophobe remarks being published. Duff, who had written the authorised biography of Field Marshal Lord Haig (1935 and 1936), said he was all in favour. This provoked an outcry in France, and there were calls for him to resign as Chairman of the Paris Travellers' Club.

[3] Jenico Preston (b. 1939), 17th Viscount Gormanston. A schoolfriend of Auberon Waugh's.

[4] Colonel Robert Henriques (1905–67), *Red Over Green*. His novel *Through the Valley* won the James Tait Black Prize in 1950.

appearance dead even in mild winters – so it's meant a lot of suffering. All the Chantilly pipes and furnaces and boilers have what frogs naturally call 'claqué-d' – and on the 12th inst my grandchild Artemis arrives together with mother and Nanny – a cold welcome indeed. I come to London for two nights as I warned you. I might arrive and go immediately to Birmingham for the dress rehearsal of my great friend Lady Jones's play 20th; Oggie's beano – to which you are invited – is 21st, I shall expect return 22nd. The other jewel returns on Maundy Thursday – and we pray for a happy Easter fortnight of leave. Can you come any part of it. Next best thing and his girl Joan Rayner will I hope arrive bank holliday with Daphne and Xan.

I'm so glad to read you love the Fieldings. I do too – glader am I to hear yr. praise of Bloggs' book. It has given me, I cannot tell you how much pleasure – the book is noble, touching – incidentally very entertaining and I'm particularly pleased that he, who I love so much – should have triumphed over his indolence and lack of confidence – his embarrassment another obstacle. O I'm so pleased.

I'm now at *Surprised by Joy* by C. S. Lewis[1] – I can read childhood better than anything – it's very good. Wonderful picture of his father and his master. So I read a lot these days – all night since I never sleep because of trying to break the drug addiction. Then to pay for the 'claqué''d pipes I've agreed to write 4 articles for the *Sunday Times*. They will appear supposedly on that wide feature page that carries neuclear articles or a General's Burmese apologia or the like – well, the next 4 Sundays they get more bilge than they bargain for. More tripe that unfortunate Jenny must try to turn into onions[2] – it horrifies me. Bertha Lady Michelham said she was so horrified she wanted to put her head in a hole in the ground but that she had not the time.

Iris is a solace – Derek Hill was – D'Arcy Osborne also escorts me sometimes. My beau is Grandi but we drag each other down with constant moans over our broken mainsprings – my great friend Henriques's book I will not takle.

Delighted to accept your invitation to a ball. I told you not to send Teresa to Germany. Would you like me to give her a delightful contact there? Charles Ritchie,[3] Canadian Ambassador, as unusual as Bloggs.

I know nothing of Duff's being challenged by Blake, nor that Blake wrote a book about Haig. Lady Haig wrote one – *The Man I Knew* – there cannot have been room for a 3rd life of that good dull man.

[1] C. S. Lewis's spiritual autobiography, published in 1955.

[2] Diana had thought of asking Jenny Crosse to ghost her memoirs, but was persuaded that she could do it herself. However, Jenny Crosse gave Diana a great deal of help and support, both on her memoirs and the articles that accompanied them.

[3] Charles Ritchie (b. 1906), Canadian diplomat. He had met Diana when he was Counsellor in Paris in 1947, and she thought him one of the funniest and most charming men she had ever known. In 1948 he married Sylvia Smellie. He was Ambassador to Bonn at the time (1954–5), went on to become Canadian Ambassador to the US 1962–6, and Canadian High Commissioner in London 1967–71.

Poor Pug's a' cold – I do hope to see you soon – in London or better in Chantilly.

Hugs and kisses
D

Evelyn to Diana

Piers Court   *12 March 1956*

Sweet Pug

Rushed to *Sunday Times* yesterday but no balls from Baby[1] – only General Slim and the threat of T. Roper to come. I take it hard that you should go to Mrs Jenny for literary advice. Yes, I know, you and she went to the board school together. All the same I know better about grammar – not spelling, alas. I am jealous of Mrs Jenny.

So I have come out of the battle with Generals Janvier and Fevrier alive but battle weary. I shan't try fighting them another year. My heart bleeds for your sufferings among the wolves.

It is very kind of you to ask me to Oggie's jubilee but I should be a fish out of water, floundering on the bank of pansies.

It is kinder still to ask me to Chantilly. Would I be welcomed in Low Week, April 10th onward for a few days? Something I read in a news-paper gave the impression you would be touring in Spain then with the Fieldings, but the papers aren't any good for serious news.

Have you heard of the Abdy disaster? Diane still unconscious after ten days, Valentine possibly lame for life.[2] Bertie half out of his mind with anxiety. I hope to get him here. Diane is in Bristol, Valentine in Truro.

Teresa returns today to prepare for presentation. I wish I had known about your chum in Bonn. Too late now. Thanks awfully for proposing it.

Is it wise at our age to give up narcotics? I tried to emulate you last night. Not at all a pleasant experience.

Last Sunday I went to stay at Melbourne – Lord M's birthplace now somehow inherited by the Lothians. A little Queen Anne stone house on the edge of a lake near Derby. Very cosy and Catholic, called by the butler 'Will you be taking Holy Communion this morning, sir?' A lot of upper class ladies said: 'Do you actually <u>know</u> Lady Pamela Berry <u>personally</u>? What is she like? Very clever is she not?' 'No, a prize booby.' 'But doesn't she make a great deal of mischief?'[3] 'That is the nicer side of her character.' They couldn't understand at all.

---

[1] The *Sunday Times* began its serialisation of Diana's first volume of autobiography, *The Rainbow Comes and Goes*, on 16 March.

[2] The result of a car accident. Lady Diana never properly recovered, though she survived until 1967. Her son Sir Valentine is now the 6th Bt.

[3] Lady Pamela Berry liked putting sworn enemies next to each other at dinner parties, and enjoyed watching the results.

Pam has a grand new word 'dedicated'. She can only read dedicated writers. Nancy and I are not dedicated.

Colonel Henriques was here yesterday. Awful. Also Coote [Lady Dorothy] Lygon who is setting off to be governess to a Greek family in Constantinople. Her charge, aged 4, speaks 4 languages and her father thinks she needs someone to retard her development; hence Coote's appointment. She is forbidden to birch her.

Will you please let me know whether I may keep Low Week with you?

All love
Bo

Bloggs has done so well with his book that he has taken Elspeth for a holiday to the Grand Hotel, Torquay.

At the end of 1955, Waugh had decided it was time to move house. The local town of Dursley was, he felt, growing too close for comfort, and Piers Court seemed to have lost its charm. Perhaps it was simply that he was feeling stale and restless; at all events, Laura was willing to leave a house she loved, in the hopes that a move would give Evelyn a new lease of life. Much of the first half of 1956 was spent in house-hunting.

The choice fell, that summer, on Combe Florey, near Taunton in Somerset, which was only twenty miles from Laura's family home of Pixton. The Waugh children loved it, and his favourite daughter, Margaret, wrote a letter begging her father to buy it. Although more secluded, it did not have the architectural elegance of Piers Court, and was further from London – which meant fewer visits to the capital, and fewer people coming to stay; but Waugh seemed happy enough with Combe Florey, and lived there for the last ten years of his life.

Evelyn to Diana

Piers Court   *[23 March 1956]*

Dearest Pug

Today's *Sunday Times* was the best. How I wish there were more coming. It was a tricky thing to describe childhood after all the masters of the last fifty years have had a go at it. You were right up with them all the way. I only detected Mrs Jenny's touch once – where you used the abhorred expression 'U' – and once before when you wrote of [Alastair] Forbes.

I wish you sometimes wrote to me. Have you started that little girl on

221

prayers and little stories yet? Never too early. You don't want her to follow her aunts into apostasy, do you?

O dear I have been writing small again. Sorry. Could you read it at all? I was saying how deeply I enjoyed the description of your childhood with Mrs Jenny at Belvoir. Also, Artemis must pray.

Mary [Herbert] here last night. Arrived at 8.30 sat up with Laura till 1, early mass, off driving alone to call on an old lady's maid at York, then to Sunderland to help Auberon nurse his minority, then off to Porto Fino to take charge of horrible Pat Smith who has had a go of lunacy. She was covered in skin disease and ate like a hound puppy, but very noble.

People come in large numbers to see over this house. No one will buy it. They come for fun. Well who doesn't?

Nancy's disgusting book is being taken up by all the disgusting papers.

Meg is back at school so I can start work again on the account of my lunacy.

Randolph gave his sister Sarah – the only member of his family who ever liked him – a black eye the other day. St James's Club is doing big business with refugees from White's on the day Randy comes to London.

You know everyone over 40 is dotty in England now. I am sure they used not to be. It ought to ensure a sympathetic reception of my work in progress.

Do sit down now and start a real Life of Baby sans Mrs Picture Post.

Know cripple Hayward? I sent him Maria Pasqua.[1] His criticism almost identical with mine.

All love
Bo

Evelyn to Diana

Piers Court   *[March 1956]*

Sweet Pug

I have ordered a ticket for the aeroplane which boasts a 'gourmet's' or 'Epicure's' luncheon or something like that on April 10th.

Is there an attic room for my jewel Margaret – huge footed but very

---

[1] John Hayward (1905–65), bibliophile, writer, editor, and companion of T. S. Eliot from 1946. Waugh had sent him a draft of Dom Aelred Watkin's biography of his grandmother, Maria Pasqua, which was based on an earlier draft by his mother, Helena. Maria Pasqua, the beautiful daughter of poor Italian parents, was born in 1856. She went to Paris with her father and became a child model, until her father sold her to a rich and childless Englishwoman, the comtesse de Noailles. She later married a Norfolk doctor, who was a relation of Duff's. On 7 February Waugh had written to Dom Aelred Watkin to say that he thought the biography 'a charming book of reminiscences. But there is a unique and poignant story somehow lost in it.' Maria Pasqua's biography eventually appeared in 1979, by Father Watkin's sister, Magdalen Goffin. (*Letters*, p. 460)

dear to me? I should rather like to bring her on a course of refinement. But would a pubescent girl be a bore? They are said to attract poltergeists.

Have you read *A Legacy* by a writer who I think must be Nancy's colonel? Very good.[1]

I am suing Lord Beaverbrook for libel and hope for some lovely tax-free money in damages. He has very conveniently told some lies about me.[2]

Longing for glorious 10th.

All love
Bo

Evelyn to Diana

Piers Court   *20 April 1956*

Darling Pug

Well, that <u>was</u> a success, wasn't it? Or so it seemed to Meg and me. We thought you were enjoying it too and Meg said 'I believe Lady Diana really liked having us alone best'. You were heavenly to us, driving out cold and tired to show us palaces, falling asleep over the wheel at Senlis – that moved to tears. Thank you, thank you. I hope you had reward at Monte Carlo and that St Firmin is full of servants for you.

Everyone I have met in England is full of delight at 'Picnics'[3] and agog for more.

I went into White's, first time for weeks and was given a broken bottle addressed to you. They didn't know how long it had been there. It seemed to have had some sort of lotion in it. I hope [it] was not something you needed badly. It seems to come from a chemist in Cranbourne Street but the label is covered with plaster and hard to read.

Nancy gives whisky parties now to Lesbians and there was a man like a murderer with a horrible smile.

Pam gave us a fine dinner and took us to a fine film. Susan Mary gave us

---

[1] The book, which had just been published, was by Sybille Bedford (b. 1911). She had written several other novels and a biography of Aldous Huxley. 'I wondered . . . who this brilliant Mrs Bedford could be,' wrote Waugh to Nancy Mitford on 22 March. 'A cosmopolitan military man, plainly, with a knowledge of parliamentary government and popular journalism, a dislike of Prussians, a liking for Jews, a belief that everyone speaks French in the home . . . Then, of course, it came to me. Good old Col.' (*Letters*, p. 471)

[2] In the *Spectator* of 24 February, Waugh wrote that the *Daily Express* no longer had any literary influence. This was too much for Nancy Spain, the literary critic of the *Express*, who had already crossed swords with Waugh (see p 208). She retaliated in the *Express* on 17 March, and Waugh sued for libel. He claimed that her article implied that 'he was an unsuccessful writer who had made a false and malicious attack on Miss Spain'. Nancy Spain put in a counterclaim that his description of her and Lord Noel-Buxton's visit to Piers Court was also libellous.

[3] One of Diana's occasional forays into magazine feature-writing.

223

a fine dinner and asked the Gileses and Odette and we acted charades and it was very happy.

Versailles rather got Meg down.

I wanted to buy that Augustus Egg we saw in the *Sunday Times*. Price £950. So I turned tail and bought silver gilt spoons instead.

Hotel St James and Albany very friendly and cheap. Recommend it to poor English.

Shall I send you the book of shame? Nancy's U. It is very awful and artificial. I don't think you would like it at all. But yours for the asking.

Luncheon in English aeroplane better than Frog.

Did I tell you I was suing Beaverbrook? I told the parish priest here that I would give him 10% of the damages for his roof. He said quite seriously 'May I announce that from the pulpit?'

Maria Pasqua's grandson[1] comes tomorrow. Seriously, would you think of editing it [Maria Pasqua's biography]? No money, Love.[2]

Kitty Giles behaved very badly at Susan Mary's. Wouldn't act. Lady Jellicoe[3] whom I have not previously liked, acted vigorously. Giles was the best.

That Jewish lady paid her debt on the nail.

Good bye

All love
Bo

Evelyn to Diana

Piers Court [pstmk 30 April 1956]

Little Meg and I enjoyed 'Pleasures of Travel' even more than its predecessors.

Evelyn to Diana

Piers Court [?May 1956]

V. sad your coming to London sans Bo. I was celebrating Laura's damn forgot dim eyes liberation from milking stool by tour of Lowlands of Scotland. Jolly pretty except for R. A. Butler who was with but not of us.

---

[1] Father Aelred Watkin (b. 1918). Housemaster at Downside Abbey 1948–62, and Headmaster 1962–75.

[2] Diana was as fascinated by Maria Pasqua as Waugh, but did not take up his suggestion. On 7 June he wrote to Nancy Mitford: 'It is a most moving story of Beauty in captivity, very sad and full of authentic, bizarre detail. Not a plot for you or me, but it could be made a great work of art by someone.' (*Letters*, p. 472)

[3] Patricia O'Kane, the Canadian wife of George, 2nd Earl Jellicoe (b. 1918). They were married in 1944, and divorced in 1966.

I say you said you would come to Teresa ball on July 5th. Not holding you to it, but if you will grace same pray dine with us first. Did you read delicate tribute by Bo to M. Beerbohm?[1] Well what with you and me *S. Times* looking up, no?

All love
B

Diana to Evelyn

Château de St Firmin   *11 June 1956*

Darling Bo. Thank you for asking me – I'll try to come but as I can't be certain I think I must not engage myself for dinner. My life takes no shape let alone design. I come over for balls – it costs me £30 and so I get to the ball and hang about the buffet nibbling horrible kickshaws and sipping poison with my ears skinned for 'who goes home'. Then I prize out the goer and hitch-hyke. It's all wrong. Now I'm coming to Sussex (cheaper as I motor to Dieppe and get the Royal Suite on the boat – with Wade returning to thralldom at Bognor – for steerage tickets) for Lord Gage's ball at Firle – shall I meet you there? – on the 14th I shall sleep at Rottingdean with my famous new friend Lady Jones, on 15th with the Great Reaper-lover Ava [Waverley] – on 16th I go to my early treat Glyndebourne and sleep with Rhoda Birley[2] nearby and Sunday I shall return.

The 26th Dot Head sweetly begs me to go to her Chelsea Hospital beano – but then again bang goes £30. Then there's Bo's party on the 5th July.

If I could get Poor Louis asked to the Chelsea Hospital he'd bring me in a car – which would make it easier to come again so soon. I returned for good on the 15th-ish and shall do a Western tour – you? K.? Jubags [Juliet Duff]? Stratford?

Yesterday I won a prize for creating a vase of flowers (from my own garden) at the Frog Horticultural. So there were 60 amateurs judged by Florists – I was 2nd. To my surprise I got a prize. The same day I picked up a present from Le Palais de la Legion d'Honneur – a tiny, exquisitely beautiful Chinese boy – not too old to play with Artemis but considered good for a butler. His father owned huge properties in Shanghai and lost all – this child forfeited his education in the débarcle. He speaks faultless French – he's going to break his heart with loneliness. No other servant in the house after 6 p.m.

---

[1] Max Beerbohm died on 20 May.

[2] Rhoda, Lady Birley. She was of Irish descent, and in 1921 married the painter Oswald Birley (1880–1952), who was knighted in 1949. She was the mother of Mark Birley, founder of Annabel's club in Berkeley Square.

Write to me if you are not to stand up with me in Sussex and tell me what you thought of Randy's skit on *Time* Mag – not much fun to me – and Muggerage's [*sic*] coat of arms.

Love hugs and kisses and more love to Meg and all

B

Evelyn to Diana

Piers Court   *13 June [1956]*

Darling Baby

Very mysterious that your letter was posted in England. I agree with you balls are beastly. In fact I have chucked Mad Mogs [Gage] and am going to Meg at Ascot instead. But I shall see you at Dot [Head]'s hospital. Per [Hylton] has a ball the same night and Laura is giving a dinner-party for it so I shall have to look in there first. How about you hitch up with me for the evening, dining at Laura's, popping in on Per and then fun at Dots, sans P. Louis. Only other ball I am going to (Laura again giving dinner party, so must) is Norfolks. Should be imposing. Care to dine with us for it? Poor Laura is having hell of a time in London. She does hate it so. I stay here and show prospective purchasers over the house. At week-ends we hunt houses ourselves. Found an exquisite palace near Mells named Ston Easton – everything the heart could desire but all the land sold off. Bertie (Diane still unconscious) wrote that there was a house near him might suit. I wrote to the agent for particulars. This morning a volume weighing six pounds of catalogue and a letter saying reserve price is £550,000.

I don't know that I really recommend my ball as worth £30 – about a fiver at the outside. There will be frescoes by Lady Antrim.[1] But if you come you will cause delight and pride and I will lead you to a secret room full of vintage wine and old chums. Lord Sherwood is spreading it abroad that Mogs has ordered a tub of caviar. I don't believe it. Or might he be giving it to her.

Wait a mo. I see I am going to another pair of balls, both on June 28th – Tanis [Guinness] and Lady Nichols[2] – dining with Mrs Fleming. Also that I shall be loose in London all 27th. See you then?

All love
Bo

[1] Angela, daughter of Sir Mark Sykes, married Randal McDonnell, 13th Earl of Antrim, in 1934.
[2] Phyllis, wife of the diplomat Sir Philip Nichols. He was Ambassador to Czechoslovakia 1942–7, and to the Netherlands 1948–51.

Evelyn to Diana

Piers Court   *2 July [1956]*

Darling Pug

It is sad for us all that you can't come to Teresa's debut but I am glad really that you are not making a special expedition for it. That would have been a great responsibility and if it rained (as it will) and the tent fell down (as it may) I should have thought of Baby's thirty quid and her pilgrimage with agony. I hope you will be living in England by the time Meg comes out. By the way are you considering moving? Care to share a house? There is a palace near Mells called Ston Easton that tempts me. You could have a ball room and bed-room and parlour and bath in it and your own kitchen, your own staircase too and a latch key like any grown up. You would have to use our staircase to get to the ballroom which is magnificent though rather small for more than 50 couple. Use of water-fall.

This house is a cut above Laura and me alone. Our furniture and pictures would look mean in it.

It is very exciting finding a new house. Found a very fine 1850 domestic gothic, not baronial, mansion in Radnorshire but that is like living in Kenya.

Also an 1860 Tudor ruin-slum of great possibilities near Pixton but we have to be out of here in October and that would take a year to restore.

Bertie Abdy told me of a little place near him that might suit. I sent for particulars. Reserve price £550,000. Ten miles of fishing, its own harbour and 20,000 acres of mature timber.

Teresa is greatly enjoying her season and clearly is popular with both sexes and all ages. She dresses terribly and has spots on her back, but she is always cheerful and not at all blasée. That's what gets them, I suppose. I say to her: 'I am going to Max Beerbohm's funeral tomorrow at St Pauls. You can come too if you like': 'Oh, papa, may I really? What fun'. Well it's endearing.

Tanis's party was considered a huge success in White's. I was deafened and dizzy in the cramped little rooms.

I go to only one more ball, the Duchess of Norfolk on 11th. Laura has a dinner party for it. Why not come to that?

You spoke of a Western tour. When? Laura Bron and James go to Porto Fino for the first fortnight of September. Why not come and keep house for Meg and me?

Lord Beaverbrook is counter-suing me for libel. My lawyers say I must hire Sir Hartley Shawcross.[1] It will ruin me.

All love
Bo

[1] When the case was heard in February of the following year, Sir Hartley Shawcross QC represented the *Daily Express* and Lord Beaverbrook. Waugh was represented by Gerald Gardiner QC, later Lord Gardiner, who became Lord Chancellor in the 1964–70 Labour government.

Diana to Evelyn

Château de St Firmin   *Tuesday [late July 1956]*

Darling Bo – y – in other accents darling boy

Thank you both and all so much – the morning I motored to you was the happiest I've had this year – by <u>far</u>. I so loved the welcome and then there was the mescalyn mood.

It tore down to zero as it always must when I go to Mells. It makes me overpoweringly sad. Not that Katharine is not still a builder of all that's good and noble – with her I feel a whining worm – with Ronnie I feel alright – with you – can't be gone into . . .

I don't know when I'll ever see you again. My jewells write this morning that they won't get their hols this summer, so bang goes all I looked forward to – and I'm left with Poor Louis youth camp followed by the Lordly Ship[1] that my heart is fighting.

Last hopes of Rome contrecarréed by Mrs Jenny having her Mum.

I love you always – escape me never.

Perhaps you and Meg in October for forest strolls – or is she at school? I fear

P *or* B

I rather loved *Love's Labour's Lost* – but was too tired after 3½ hours' motoring to sup with Glen Byam Shaw who talked of you. He's the boss of Stratford now and delightful – beautiful – unchanged.[2] We got home at 2.

P.S. – important. I have a secretary – Daphne Wakefield[3] – I love her. She trains to be a teacher because she loves using her mind and hates house work – she's remarkable. Now she has to write a true documented paper for her examiner. Can I lend her Maria Pasqua – no one would read it but one man – I could tell it her of course when she comes to see me next Wednesday, but I can't do the documentation – Would there be any harm – I think not – no worse than writing it to a friend. If you can, let me have it for two days.

D

---

[1] Stavros Niarchos's yacht, the *Eros*.

[2] Glen Byam Shaw (1904–86). Co-Director with Anthony Quayle of the Shakespeare Memorial Theatre, Stratford-on-Avon, 1952–5; Director 1956–9. Married to the actress Angela Baddeley (1904–76).

[3] Daphne Wakefield (d. 1990), née Marler. She married Anthony Wakefield in 1940. She started working for Duff as a temporary secretary after his resignation in 1938, and soon became indispensable to both Duff and Diana, looking after all their affairs in England while they were in France. After Duff's death, Diana relied on her even more.

Evelyn to Diana

Piers Court   *2 August [1956]*

Sweet Pug

I have no copy of *Maria Pasqua* in my possession. Nor does the original draft now exist. The grand-son Dom Aelred Watkin of Downside would doubtless lend you his version which has many details lacking in the original, but, alas, has lost much of its charm. Fr. Aelred has decided to keep his manuscript until some Maurice Baring appears to rewrite it. I don't think he would object to a school mistress using it as a text for her exam. What sort of text do candidates usually provide? It seems an odd sort of exam.

I can't understand your dislike of Oxfords. He is eminently good and kind. Compares favourably with all other descendants of Mr Asquith whom I know – indeed with the descendants of all democratically elected politicians – Randolph, Freddy Birkenhead, Oliver Baldwin, Maclean etc. She is devout and dutiful and well informed. I think Katharine very much blessed in her jewels.

I shall be jolly glad if any of mine turn out so well. My only complaint against Trim was that he was 20 minutes late for dinner so that we were bustled through the meal and out of the dining-room in an unseemly way. But no doubt he is used to docile black servants.

A long wet expedition yesterday to show Bron and Meg Combe Florey – a modest house near Taunton. S[ydney] Smith was parson there and put antlers on the ass in his paddock. A pleasant backwater without the main-road horrors of Ston Easton.

Now there is a 13th century palace near Exeter to see.

I trust you have a full gaggle of Joneses to help you fast.

Meg has gone to Bridget for a week leaving me very lonely. If war breaks out in Mediterranean[1] come here first 2 weeks of September. October no good for Meg.

All love
Bo

Evelyn to Diana

Piers Court   *5 September 1956*

Darling Pug

Meg and I are alone here and wish you were with us. She is growing very fat.

---

[1] On 26 July, the fourth anniversary of the abdication of King Farouk, Nasser had announced the nationalisation of the Suez Canal. The crisis came to a head on 2 November, when British and French troops landed in Egypt.

229

At Portofino, if you arrive before 18th you will find Mary, Laura, Bron and poor mad fan Hatty.

Still no home. I have to be out at the end of next month. It looks like a winter in a boarding-house. There was a splendid house near Exeter 1226–1860 very like my old school Lancing which I thought was in the bag but we had trustee trouble and a Public Body outbid us.

It never stops raining and the lightning has destroyed electric lights and telephone. Don't mind the latter but I strain my old eyes reading *Pickwick* to Meg. What a dull book!

Meg and I went to stay with Pam. She has done up her house a fair treat hasn't she? <u>Very</u> pretty. The house I mean not the Bearded Wonder.

I saw your latest Jones[1] at Pam's on the Television (2nd time I have ever seen the device). He was <u>sickening</u>. He was flirting with Quennell and Muggeridge and all your set. Oddly enough Quennell came out quite dignified.

All love
Bo

Evelyn to Diana

Tetton House   *4 December 1956*
Taunton

Dearest Pug

Your kind invitation to the prize giving[2] did not reach me until today. I should have been a fish very much out of water among all those journalists, but it was a very kind thought to ask me. I was very sorry to see in the paper that the prize had gone to such an undeserving work. I thought you said it was destined for young Cronin and his wise man. [3] Mr M's *Gallipoli* is not the kind of book prizes exist to encourage. It had already had all the success it deserved. Well, it was not your fault, poor pug, so I must not say more on this topic. But to give a prize for <u>Literature</u> to . . .

Laura and I are staying here while we watch the vans bring our shabby furniture into Combe Florey. We sleep there on Thursday for the first time. I greatly enjoy the transition.

I went to the sale of furniture at Ston Easton. Few bargains. That Chinese Chippendale overmantel and chimney-piece made 1400 guineas.

---

[1] 'New friend', unidentified.
[2] The first Duff Cooper Memorial Prize, which went to Alan Moorehead for *Gallipoli*. The prize is awarded yearly to a book of history, biography, poetry or politics.
[3] Vincent Cronin, *The Wise Man from the West*.

The plain mahogany dining-room table £1000. But I got that prodigious 1860 side-board and cupboards for £4.

My new house won't be fit to show for 10 years. It won't be habitable for 2 but it has great possibilities and I have a lot of men at work knocking rooms together and partitioning them.

I spent 4 days at Mells. Ronnie painfully weary and slow. Katharine not sleeping and crippled. Their cigarette lighters broken. The dog's tail thumping the floor the only sign of life.

I spent a day in London but found they were all overexcited about the Suez canal – blows exchanged, families sundered.

Meg took poison – a great quantity of quicksilver[1] – and was stomach pumped by a negress in Windsor. She is very proud of the experience.

Laura's cousin Mervyn[2] – whose house this is – has made a great fortune and built a sky-scraper in Toronto.

Pixton – need I say it? – is overrun by a golden horde of Hungarian freedom-fighters (defeated).[3] Even Auberon cannot speak their language and they have been given most unsuitable clothes by the Lord Mayor of London – black overcoats with velvet collars and football boots.

All love
Bo

Diana to Evelyn

Château de St Firmin   *[December 1956]*

Dear Monster – don't you feel that to start a long-awaited letter to your poor Pug with 'I should have been a fish very much out of water amongst all those journalists' – being one yourself – is horrid? but incidentally among a hundred guests there were 2. Reuter's, because the house next [to] Winston's belongs to Sir Roderick Jones and the Australian Herald or Blade or something because Moorehead belongs to that country. The other 98 were exclusively Duff's White's Club, career, and lady-friends – mine, and yours.

As to the winner. I was sorry too – I had suggested Cronin but Rupert who published the book felt incapable of nudging it forward. I agree Gallipoli is not litterature – tho' an enthralling story, understandingly and charitably told. Bowra has written very often in the last year explaining how the prize should be awarded to an unknown struggler – I have always

[1] Margaret had accidentally sucked mercury through a pipette at school.
[2] Mervyn Herbert (b. 1926). His father, also called Mervyn, had died in 1929.
[3] Auberon Herbert was a passionate supporter of the Hungarian uprising. This had begun on 23 October 1956, and was brutally suppressed by invading Russian troops during the first four days of November.

answered, 'I said it first.' To make matters worse the *Sunday Times* awarded Moorehead their £1,000 ten days after our judges had spoken – To make it better the author has had very poor sales so it's inaccurate to say 'it had already had all the success it deserved' as no one wants to read of any war but their own – or Troy's.

We asked the S.T. if we could present it first – being first choosers and told them Winston would preside. They rather naïvely suggested that he might give both simultaneously. Well, we must hope for a subtler choice next year – and that you will get your invitation in time and be with me on that day at a party – which, if it is like this year's – will be one of the most delightful and moving possible to be at. Duff would have been so proud and happy and pleased to see the loved faces, and the limitless good champagne <u>given</u> by Odette Pol Roger.

So don't denigrate my effort and start me off on the joys of your letter with a frown.

I greatly regret Stinchcomb, but you are the best judge of your own surroundings.

I have been told to quit.[1] I refused to give Sam White,[2] the *Evening Standard* stringer in Paris any information on the subject – we had our classic telephone conversation:

'What, Mr White, will you never learn? You've never yet got a word out of me – why should I feed your paper?'

'Well Lady Diana, the E.S. is always very good to you.'

'Wrong again, Mr White – they've twice said I was having a face-lift, and put my age in brackets whenever they print my name.'

'O you're so amusing Lady Diana'

'Of course if you paid me Mr White – that would be on another footing, and more interesting. They pay you, don't they? What will they, or you, pay me?'

'O you're so amusing Lady Diana.'

'Good-bye Mr White.'

So it runs – but a few days later there was a big piece with information that I had not got – i.e., what rent I paid. I have discovered by his own admission that he got it from the Domaine de Chantilly – i.e., L'Institut de France. Well, I haven't accepted the dismissal yet, so we shall see. I want another three years – I want a notice of three years that I may not lay something down – some improvement – and then not be there to enjoy it.

[1] The Institut de France, which owned the Château de St Firmin, wanted a new tenant – but Diana did not move out until 1961.

[2] Sam White (d. 1988), a legendary Australian journalist who for many years was the *Evening Standard*'s Paris correspondent. He kept tabs on everything that was going on in that city, despite his elementary French and the fact that he never left the bar of the Crillon if he could help it.

I made a great investment in fruit and shrubs and regali lilies a month before this ejecting bomb.

I'm coming to London the end of next week – Christmas at Vaynol – more detail please about Meg's poisoning. I'll be at Channon's 'hot bed of cold feet' [as] London is called by Sparrow.[1] If you come to London we could meet.

Dear Bo –
Pug Baby

Evelyn to Diana

26 December 1956

Combe Florey House
Combe Florey
Nr Taunton

Darling Pug

It was jolly decent of you to send those fragrant hearts to my little girls. They were overjoyed.

Christmas was not quite as horrible as I feared. I don't particularly mind not washing and there is a blessed pause in the hammering of plumbers and carpenters. They return in force on Friday so I fly to London.

Can't remember your plans. Will you be there at all? I shall be on tap at Hyde Park Hotel for at least a week. Come and buy carpets with me.

In case we don't meet here's wishing you all the best in the New Year. May you rout the Institute of France, the Academy and the President of the Republic and preserve your corner of foreign field forever England.

The typography at the head of this paper is distressing and to be changed.[2]

All love
Bo

Evelyn to Diana

28 January 1957

Combe Florey

Sweet Pug

No address to write to. Will anyone forward this from Chantilly? You are very lucky to be in Rome. Nowhere to touch it. Pray for me at the tomb of the Apostle. Have you been down to the excavations? They look

---

[1] John Sparrow (b. 1906), barrister and Warden of All Souls College, Oxford, 1952–77.

[2] A skimpy, widely-spaced Gothic typeface which was replaced by a far larger and more authoritative one (see front endpaper).

fascinating in photographs. I hope you are keeping Mrs Jenny's Picture Post paws out of your book. Speaight's book on Belloc[1] has thrown my mother in law into gnashing rage. Can't see much wrong with it myself. The best part is the series of letters to K[atharine].

Ronnie Knox had an operation for cancer last week. I went to see him in City Road E.C.1 in a hospital which had painted across the front in huge letters FOR DISEASES OF THE RECTUM. He talks of convalescence and saying mass again. I could get no information at the hospital about his condition.

Randolph is shedding many crocodile tears about the illness of Eden.[2] I also overheard him saying earnestly 'All I have ever tried in life is to bring a little happiness to others'.

All my chicks have gone except Bron who sits about all day smoking cheroots and occasionally slips out at dusk with a gun and brings in a pheasant. I am seeking to transport him abroad. Also to take Laura for a week to Monte Carlo. We were offered a week at Hotel de Paris, all free, vin inclus, by Victor Gordon-Lennox[3] but why Victor should be able to offer this I can't explain.

Just been called to the telephone by Magdalen to say will I send champagne to Ronnie.

My ear trumpets are a great convenience and a great success socially. The mad book is at last 'finalized'.[4]

My first libel action against Lord Beaverbrook may be heard next month. I have lost interest in it and am concentrating on the second which I hope will pay for some of the prodigal expenses of plumbers and paperhangers here.[5]

Ann [Fleming]'s mad chum [John] Minton[6] took poison.

A chum of Teresa's is in prison in Buda Pest.

I long for you
Bo

---

[1] Robert Speaight, *Life of Hilaire Belloc* (1957).

[2] In October 1956, the Prime Minister Anthony Eden developed a violent and, as it turned out, recurrent fever. His doctors said he would never be free of it, and on their advice he tendered his resignation on 9 January 1957.

[3] Victor Gordon-Lennox (1897–1968), a grandson of the 6th Duke of Richmond. Political Correspondent for the *Daily Mail*, 1922–9, and Diplomatic Correspondent for the *Daily Telegraph* from 1935.

[4] *The Ordeal of Gilbert Pinfold*, published later that year.

[5] Waugh was suing the *Daily Express*, owned by Lord Beaverbrook, for an article by Nancy Spain on 17 March 1956 in which she alleged that Alec Waugh's books sold better than Evelyn Waugh's.

[6] John Minton (1917–57). The best-known graphic artist of his day, he taught painting at the Royal College of Art. On 20 January he committed suicide by swallowing a bottle of sleeping pills.

Diana to Evelyn

Torre del Grillo   *22 February 1957*
Rome

Clever Bo – to win a case, and against the press too – I'm completely delighted – what will you do with a windfall? Pay debts or blow it abroad?

I went to see the Pope[1] taking my jewel [John Julius] along – thought to be amongst a crowd and found ourselves alone sitting as one does in a doctor's consulting room across this bureau. Forgot to ask if he was deaf so John Julius's carefully thought up piece about the Church in Yugoslavia I do not think was understood – maybe he doesn't understand English as well as he speaks it. Everything was 'very difficult' – 'Yes it is very difficult, but not so difficult' 'It eesa difficult everywhere' 'Yes v. v. difficult' so we plodded on thro' our difficulties and it was a great success – because he sent a message to a man called Uttly[2] in the English Holy See by his chef de Cabinet to say how very highly he thought of the Giovanotto Inglese – 'anche la mama' – anche il Papa from our end. The invitation was addressed to me and Il Figlio [*sic*].

I took him a cross to bless – all I could find and not very suitable as it was made from the plaited hair cut from the crowned head of William IV, and his mistress Mrs Jordan, and his five illegitimate Fitzclarence children.[3] I prayed that I would not embark on a saga about it. John Julius could find nothing better than some round cardboard discs that fit into a plastic viewer and show a child of 4 ravishing pictures of the Nativity, Flight, Massacre and the rest of it. Going there he said – it was typical of the child in him – 'I wish I had brought the viewer too'. D'arcy Osborne advised against the disc blessing – so he had nothing but received instead a rosary for Artemis – and a really fine heavy silver medal for himself in a red case sanctified with triple crowns and keys.

The Pope is about the only person I've seen except Mrs Jenny and her husband, and Iris and a tame house–cat called Milton.[4] I stay in bed most days and try and write my book – Mrs Jenny has no interest in it you'll be glad to hear tho' not glad maybe when you read the purile farce. She neither approves nor suggests improvements. I feel a *bateau ivre* [drunken boat] among rocks. It is to be a monument of bad taste – that is what weighs on me now – I don't know why I have become so insensitive to what one shows and conceals. I've put in love letters – do you think that's appalling – Duff curiously enough wanted to in his book, and I restrained

---

[1] Pius XII (1876–1958). As Cardinal Eugenio Pacelli, he had been Papal Nuncio in Munich during the revolutionary upheavals of 1919. He was extremely conservative, and negotiated the Concordat with Nazi Germany in 1933. Crowned Pope in 1939.

[2] Thomas Uttley was permanent attaché at the British Legation to the Holy See.

[3] Duff Cooper's maternal grandmother, the Countess of Fife, was the daughter of the 17th Earl of Erroll and Lady Elizabeth Fitzclarence.

[4] Milton Gendel, American writer and art critic. He married Judy Montagu in 1962.

him – now he is dead. It seems right that so important a piece of my life should show in an autobiography – it doesn't shock me but my hands rush to my throat when I think of what you and Katharine will think and say – or not say. Paddy N.B. Thing is a triffling fear, but a fear.

I've enjoyed lying in bed with three panoramas of Rome round me, reading quires of old letters. I lived in them completely, especially those before 1915 and felt young and Duff not dead.

John Julius will <u>probably</u> be sent to Beirut in this summer – It's a bitter blow to me, miles and days away – only accessible by expensive air. Every form of Middle East restrictions on the Palmyra and Petra expeditions, let alone the dangers – Please write and tell me (A) you love me (B) you'll forgive my taste however bad – (C) your life and near future plans.

Love to Laura and my two girls.

Baby

Evelyn to Diana

Combe Florey   *24 February [1957]*

Darling Pug

My action was not as gay as the Montesi case[1] but it had some funny bits. It is merely the opening skirmish in a great battle against the *Express* by which I hope to secure my old age.[2] They have been teasing me for five years and they went too far. At any time in the last six months I would have settled for £500. At the end of the first day's hearing I would have taken a fiver. During the long deliberation of the jury my lawyers were apologizing for having led me into such a mess and hinting I should have to pay about £5000 costs. That would have meant New South Wales and a change of name. But it turned out O.K. and there was much champagne drunk in White's and the Hyde Park Hotel that afternoon.

I got through on prayer and prejudice. I told the priest at Dursley he would get a share of the damages and his prayers were answered dramatically. From the moment Shawcross[3] (a socialist but the most dangerous lawyer alive) took the case [for the *Express*] he was stricken

---

[1] A big Roman *dolce vita* scandal, which erupted when a girl called Wilma Montesi was found dead on a beach. The case was made much of in the British press.

[2] Waugh won £2,000 in damages from the case he describes – and before it came to court, Nancy Spain made yet another error of judgement. She reviewed a book which contained libellous remarks about Waugh – and quoted the offending passage in her column, while the case in court was still *sub judice*. The book had to be withdrawn, and the *Express* was obliged to pay Waugh a further £3,000 in an out-of-court settlement.

[3] Sir Hartley Shawcross QC (b. 1902), Chief UK prosecutor at Nuremberg, Attorney-General 1945–51, and Labour MP for St Helens 1945–58. In 1959 he was created a life peer.

236

with a series of Egyptian plagues culminating at the very moment when he had me under cross-examination and was making me feel an ass, with a well nigh fatal motor-accident to his mother-in-law. He had to chuck the case and leave it to an understrapper. The judge was a buffoon who behaved as though in Gilbert and Sullivan.[1] The jury were splendid, solid, prosperous citizens with a firm detestation of Lord Beaverbrook. They did not find the judge at all funny. While all the wigged and gowned lawyers rocked with laughter, they glowered. They were out to fine the *Express* for its rudeness to the Royal Family and didn't listen to a word about the rights and wrongs of me and Miss Spain.

Miss Spain perjured herself frequently but behaved in a gentlemanly way afterwards, gripping my hand and saying 'the better man won'.

I had meant to take Laura to Monte Carlo but alas, it is not to be. Ronnie Knox, slowly convalescent, is being left by K. who goes to hospital for treatment of her knee. So Laura and I have to take Ronnie to Torquay for three weeks.[2]

I am sure your book will be exciting. Stuff it with love letters. You have never been one for ghastly good taste, have you? It is the bastard in you – Edmund and Edgar constantly at strife.

I love you and long for you.

I have sent my boy Bron to Italy. If he turns up in Rome give him a smile.

All love
Bo

[P.S.] Pope does not understand one word of English. He has got into habit of not listening to it at all because Americans bore him so.

Evelyn to Diana

Combe Florey   *[pstmk 2 May 1957]*
[postcard]

[newspaper clipping:]

Nearby hangs a picture by a 91-year-old painter, Charles Spencelayh, who is going blind. The name of his work: 'My first painting and my last.'

It shows the interior of a room with his first painting on an easel. A guttering candle stands on a table.

---

[1] The 'understrapper' was Mr Helenus Milmo, and the judge Mr Justice Stable.
[2] Ronald Knox had undergone a major operation for cancer. Laura left Torquay after a while, to supervise the work being done on Combe Florey; but Waugh stayed on to care for his friend.

Evelyn to Diana

Combe Florey   *11 May [1957]*

Darling Pug

There is a fine house three miles from here in a beautiful park going practically free. Not for sale. It belongs to a policeman in Kenya who wants someone to repair and live in it. Classic 1830 with furniture, carpets, curtains etc. all made for it at that date. Are you interested? This is a <u>very</u> beautiful part of the county – of the country indeed. Do join us.

Will you be alone at Chantilly round the 26th of this month? If so Laura and I would love to pop in on you. We are going to Monte Carlo for a week leaving England, I hope, nothing booked yet, on 17th and going straight through by train. Hotel de Paris. Write there later this week if we may visit you on way home.

Pauper Kinross enjoyed himself top hole with you and says your book is the cat's pyjamas. I long to read it. I long to see you. Very sad about Spencelayh being alive still and blind. I hope he was prudent in his investments.

Ronnie Knox awfully ill and sad. Katharine went into hospital with one stick, came out on two, brave and saintly. I tell Sweet Alice Jolliffe[1] that it is her plain duty to leave Oxford and tend those two and I think she thinks it is.

All love
Bo

Diana to Evelyn

Château de St Firmin   *16 May 1957*

Job never had servant trouble – I could a tale unfold to him of worse plagues. But today with a clean sweep of them with my broom and a better job sweep of my cupboards, linen and store and cellar by theirs, I start anew – so let's hope all will be well by the 26th. You will find the house dense with Papists unless they leave that day and some of them must – McEwens en famille.[2] I hope you'll stay long to mitigate the invitation of poor dying Olga [Lynn] – who is coming, I fear, for the 'duration' – fortunately in bed. By duration I mean her Lizzie's sentence in Holloway.[3]

---

[1] Alice Jolliffe (b. 1937), daughter of Lord and Lady Hylton, married John Chancellor in 1959 and Richard Windsor-Clive in 1969.

[2] The painter Roderick (Rory) McEwen (1932–83), his wife Romana (Raimund von Hofmannsthal's daughter by his first marriage to Alice Astor) and their children.

[3] Maud Nelson, Olga Lynn's supposed former lover, had been jailed for attacking a young female lodger with a carving knife.

The house sounds just the thing – keep it empty for three years and I'll take it for duration of life. I must stick it out here or sweat it out travelling and storing this furniture for at least that long in order to salt that potential mémoire's money.

I'm in touch with K. It's dreadful dreadful – I saw her twice in the nursing home and she seemed almost dead to me. Ought Ronnie to be sad to her? I think he should spare her – she broke down talking of him because she thought he was so unhappy. I've tried and am trying to get a new miraculous Belgian pain killer but she says [he] has no pain. It all comes of surviving so long. My troubles too – I should be better if I saw you more often – or if you ever kept in touch without reason. As it is morale's bad and I've laid my book in dust for duration of Oggie.

Daphne Fielding comes the 11th. Care to come back?

Dear Bo – dear Laura. I'm glad you're coming.

Diana
Pug

Evelyn to Diana

Hôtel de Paris   *[May 1957]*
Monte Carlo

Sweet Pug

I have asked my publisher to send you a proof-copy of Pinfold so that you may know the worst before I arrive. This is for baby's blue eyes alone. Not to be shown please to Mrs Jenny or Master Paddy or Ali ha ha Forbes, but to be destroyed by fire when read.[1] A fine large paper edition will follow in mid-July.

All love
Bo

We went to Lady Jones's old play the other night and enjoyed ourselves there.[2]

Evelyn to Diana

Hôtel de Paris   *28 May [1957]*
Monte Carlo

Darling Baby Doll

Your postcard and telegram to hand. Your telephone irruption not understood. We (Laura and Evelyn Waugh) hope to travel to Paris

---

[1] Waugh was understandably concerned at the opportunity the book presented to anyone who disliked him. When J. B. Priestley reviewed it in the *New Statesman* he claimed that Waugh had been driven insane by his attempt to pass himself off as a country gentleman.

[2] *The Chalk Garden*, then in its second year at the Haymarket Theatre, London.

tonight, Tuesday 28th, arriving at Gare de Lyon Wednesday 29th. We shall then go to Gare du Nord and take first train to Chantilly. When we get there we will telephone your castle from the Queen Mother's café.

If you wish to intercept us this can be done at Gare de Lyon only, on the platform where Blue Train arrives. Laura seems to think you were her mother telephoning from Porto Fino. The telephone is a most subversive device.

All love
Bo

Evelyn to Diana

Combe Florey   *6 June [1957]*

Sweet Baby-Doll

Goodness it was decent staying with you. I wish we could have stayed on to see the unknown [Charles] Ritchie but it is lucky we left when we did. Crises of all kinds had occurred. Septimus (my youngest) was in hospital without his appendix. The letters you most kindly forwarded to me brought news of the deep disgrace and near expulsion of my poor Meg who has been driven into a Pinfold state of persecution by the nuns believing, perhaps truly, that the head nun is 'poisoning everyone against her'.[1] Also I found telegrams and urgent letters saying I must work on a film scenario – drudgery. We felt so smug about your servants, now most of ours have left. So it was proper to return but we do wish we were as we were this time last week. Darling Pug thank you for all your kindness and I will try to forgive your violent unkindness when Gaston came to luncheon.

Read *The Titchborne Claimant* by D. Woodruff.[2] Fascinating.

It was so kind of you to drive us to Paris that morning. Well everything was kind except your temper Ascension Day Luncheon. But Ascension as I told you is a day of mourning to me since 1917.

Love to that poor brotherless, friendless, Godless waif Artemis and to Oggie and Daphne and all your brilliant circle.

I did enjoy (and so much look forward to more of) Baby's Bouquet.

Bo

---

[1] Margaret, who was very unhappy at St Mary's, Ascot, left at the end of that term.

[2] Arthur Orton (1839–66), a Londoner, claimed to be Roger Charles Tichborne, the long-lost elder brother of Sir Alfred Joseph Doughty-Tichborne, 11th Bt. Orton was found guilty on two charges of perjury, and sentenced to fourteen years' imprisonment with hard labour.

Evelyn to Diana

Combe Florey   *14 July [?1957]*

Baby Doll

I sent you a fine copy of *Pinfold* to Chantilly. Then too late I heard you
were in London. How long?

Could you bear to come to a Foyles banquet (luncheon) in my honour
on Friday? Your august presence would be greatly appreciated. Chums
will be there – Miss Judy, Ann Fleming, Andrew and Debo etc. Horrible
food and very vulgar behaviour – but Pug never shrank from the
hustings.

I believe there is a grand ball to which I am not bidden on Thursday
night. If you are not going there, could we dine? I shall come to London
that afternoon. Could make it morning if Pug had time for me.

Bathroom is being prepared and will be ready at the end of next week.
Any chance of your coming to wash in it? Mells is in a sad way. Ronnie
going down fast.

All love
Bo

Evelyn to Diana

Combe Florey   *17 July [1957]*

Darling Pug

Not kind to reproach me. I wrote by return on getting your card. Miss
Foyle's beano is Friday luncheon but if as I suppose those Shakespearean
performances are at Stratford that's no good.

Pity you aren't going to Juliet earlier. You could visit a great carpet that
is being woven for me at Wilton, but the works close on 26th for weavers'
holiday.[1]

Did you see 'The Agony of Evelyn Waugh' by Driberg in the *Sunday
Dispatch*? That comes of getting tight with an old school fellow.[2] Can't
blame Driberg, only Bo.

Will you be alone at Chantilly or full of Forbes and Quennell? I long to
see you.

I suppose you wouldn't come for a night next week to see this house?
You can leave Paddington any day at 3.30 and find me on Taunton

---

[1] Waugh had decided to spend most of his legal winnings from the Nancy Spain cases on
commissioning a new carpet for his drawing room based on a design which won a prize at the Great
Exhibition of 1851. Christopher Sykes in his biography described it as 'a work of art of almost
inconceivable hideosity', although he had to concede that it was appropriate enough for Waugh's
collection of Victorian paintings.

[2] Driberg and Waugh had been at Lancing together.

241

platform at 6. Then, if pressed for you can take 9.25 next morning and be in London at 12.15. Not too bad. I do so want to show you what's going on here and have your advice.

I go to London tomorrow, Thursday, and leave 3.30 Friday.

All love
Bo

Evelyn to Diana

Combe Florey *[?late July 1957]*

Sweet Pug

It was jolly decent of you to send me a telegram at Foyles' luncheon. I am glad for your sake you didn't come. Mr Muggeridge made a long silly speech about the BBC and *Punch* and himself and told dirty stories about birth control. The only bright spot was a stark mad neurologist.[1]

I mind awfully that you won't come here.

You give no hint of what will be going on at Chantilly next week.

Margaret tells me that Gaston has got his post in Rome.[2] True? Is Nancy desolate? Does one congratulate or condole?

All love
Bo

Diana to Evelyn

Château de St Firmin *8 August 1957*

My darling Bo – I have arrived and the book was waiting in its classical spaciousness – and my heart brims with thanks. What a lavish and faithful boy you are – I do love you.

A glorious success *Pinfold* has had – its childhood and now its entrance must have pleased you. Gestation is pure pain to this author. I can only suppose the monster's delivery will be worse.

I went to see K. and Ronnie – most dreadful – how would it be to endure a husband's fate like his. I thanked God for Duff['s] too early but peaceful quick death – and Katharine – curiously enough more cheerful

---

[1] The chairman of that particular lunch was the Duke of Devonshire. The speakers were Waugh and the writer and broadcaster Malcolm Muggeridge (1903–90), who was then Editor of *Punch*. Among the guests of honour were Alec Guinness, Rose Macaulay, Frank Pakenham and Douglas Woodruff.

[2] Gaston Palewski had just been appointed French Ambassador to Italy. He returned in 1962 to become Minister of State for Scientific Research and Atomic and Space Matters.

than when I saw her in the nursing home – and all this in the Mells of all our shouts of joy and games and kisses Ichabod – charnel-house.

Do write Reine Jeanne, Bormes-les-Mimosas, Var till 15th then c/o Reuters Rome. Back Oct – England and here – I invite you and wife or child – school spoils everything.

D

Many thanks for *Pinfold* – I'm cruelly jealous of Daphne.[1]

Evelyn to Diana

Combe Florey   *7 August [1957]*

Darling Pug

How does one sweep weed off a lake? Mine has complete blanket of soft, brilliant slime. Rather pretty but I want to grow lilies. Have sunk several plants but they disappear totally. I have a punt and set the children to work with rakes. No good. I also have numerous waterfowl. Water is not stagnant, fed by two springs and flowing out fast. What to do?

I don't find Mells 'dreadful' – such holiness and heroic patience that I find it inspiring.

Someone keeps advertising in *Times* agony colum for an antique ear-trumpet. Do you think it can be a fan of mine intending to make me a present?

We have had a lot of sweet Alice Jolliffe and of very pretty Annabel Hennessy.[2] Today Bron starts entertaining his friends as I leave for Derbyshire, first Debo then Osbert Sitwell [at Renishaw]. Bron passed his interview with Gold Stick and goes to Windsor, en route for Caterham, at the end of the month.[3] The workmen are taking a holiday leaving four candelabra unhung, no cornice in dining-room, no centre-pieces in four ceilings, but it is the quieter for their absence.

I get a lot of letters from lunies re *Pinfold* some very pathetic assuring me that their voices are undoubtedly inflicted by conspirators at the BBC.

Ann Fleming has a carbuncle. I had one once in Italy in the war. It is not a laughing matter at all – excruciating.

Meg is in a very bad mood, sulking because I will not buy her a hunter. I had to send her to her room in the middle of dinner the other evening. Contrite since, but will it last?

Come to Malta in November?

All love
Bo

[1] *The Ordeal of Gilbert Pinfold* was dedicated to Daphne Fielding.
[2] Annabel Hennessy (b. 1937), daughter of Lord Windlesham and a schoolfriend of Teresa's.
[3] He had applied to join the Royal Horse Guards (The Blues) in which his father had served for part of the Second World War. (The office of Gold Stick, an honorary appointment dating back to the reign of Charles II, was held alternately by the colonel of the Life Guards and the colonel of The Blues.)

By the way do you happen to know whether Mrs [Susan Mary] Patten got a copy of *Pinfold* I sent her at the same time as yours? Not like her not to answer. I promised to send one and should feel sad if it went astray.

You don't tell me how Nancy is taking Col. Palewski's appointment. Is it a time for friends to keep silence or condole?

Diana to Evelyn

Rome   *17 August 1957*

My only cure for weed is duck – good karki Campbell who each lay an egg daily – despise broodyism and end in the pot – to be kept shut up till 9 or 10 a.m. or they'll drop their clutch incontinently. Mrs Patten left for America about the time you sent *Pinfold* – but I am writing to ask her – doubtless the thanks have come by now.

About Mells – of course it's 'dreadful'. It fills one with dread that there is no choice to the suffering – and K. fears for his mental agony and I always favourably hope that with great faith fears diminish. I don't see the *Times* regularly – so the good man may be dead.

I've been in a state of bent mealancholly . . . in a terrestrial paradise[1] – budding with jeunes filles en fleur and young men all with flight feet and light hearts. I feel like Kay in The Snow Queen that two splinters of ugly age have got into my eyes and heart distorting vision and making me feel physically ill with pointlessness. I won't bathe except alone, I can't be sportive or pretty or helpful in any way – however it's behind me, and the listless misery shifted as I spin hundreds of miles alone in my car thinking of nothing.

I think I meet Mrs Jenny and Iris tomorrow at Foggia and explore unspoilt Calabria – then back to Rome in a week and on to Brindisi – Corfu – Peloponnese – Athens (American Express c/o) about 15th. Perhaps ship 18th to Lebanon if flying funks me too much. Back mid-October – no servants – not <u>one</u> – for Chantilly.

Love my darling Bo – write

Pug

Evelyn to Diana

Combe Florey   *20 November [?1957]*

Sweet Pug

How lovely to have a post-card. They said you were in Lebanon and Rome and hidden in Paris, that your Baby's Opera was running to three

---

[1] Paul Louis Weiller's villa, La Reine Jeanne.

volumes and that you were incommunicado until it was finished. (I say, don't take Mrs Jenny's advice on legal matters. She has landed Ian Gilmour in a hot keetle of fish. Lord Goddard says: 'You're no gentleman, sir' to him)[1]

It is a beautiful thought of yours to ask me to Chantilly. Alas, not possible this side of Christmas. Ronnie's death[2] has transformed my life. Instead of sitting about bored and idle I am busy all day long, both writing his life and managing his affairs for Trim. Ronnie's close business associates are all scrupulous dotards who write to me by every post. That part is a fiendish nuisance but I am absolutely absorbed in the biography.

Have you heard that Trim has been posted to St Lucia as a sort of suffragan Governor.[3] K. is delighted. 'Next Best Thing's' account of St L.[4] is not very encouraging except that the niggers are papists and that Trim's future house has an araucaria – is that a monkey-puzzle? – planted by Edward VIII.

I go to London from Dec 2nd–9th or 11th. Any hope of you being there then?

In February I go to Rhodesia which sounds awful but I have to grill Daphne Acton about Knox. There is so much danger of people going off their rockers these days that one has to catch them while they are still sane. Lots of insanity in Daphne's family, so I must go quick.[5]

I long to show you this house and its pictures. My children particularly poor dotty Hatty long for you. Can't you come round Christmastide. It is really quite comfortable and slightly nearer Mells (though farther from London) than Stinkers was.

My son Auberon has grown very tall and handsome, was on leave from Caterham last week, but is losing his wool.

I am afraid you will find me a great bore about Ronnie. I think and dream of nothing else.

All love
Bo

---

[1] In an article covering a Socialist conference in Venice for the *Spectator*, Jenny Nicholson wrote that Anthony Crosland, Aneurin Bevan and Morgan Phillips – all prominent members of the Labour Party – had been 'tanking themselves up' on whisky. They sued the *Spectator* and its Editor, Ian (later Sir Ian) Gilmour (b. 1926). Lord Goddard (1877–1971), then Lord Chief Justice, heard the case, and awarded each plantiff £2,500 in damages.

[2] Ronald Knox died at Mells on 24 August 1957.

[3] The Earl of Oxford and Asquith was Administrator of St Lucia, West Indies, 1958–62, and Governor and Commander-in-Chief of the Seychelles 1962–7.

[4] Patrick Leigh Fermor's travel book on the West Indies, *A Traveller's Tree*, was published in 1950.

[5] Daphne Acton became a great friend of Ronald Knox, and was instructed and received into the Catholic Church by him in 1938.

Evelyn to Diana

Combe Florey *28 December 1957*

Dearest Pug

What sort of Christmas I wonder did the Austrians give you?[1] Jolly I hope. It was very fatiguing at Combe Florey.

Thank you very much for the *Brideshead* handkerchief. It is a thing to put proudly in a cabinet – not for the nose. I am very sad not to have a present for you. What could I have sent? I am a dunce in such matters. You always so clever.

This will be a big year coming with Baby's Life and Letters. I look forward to them awfully and shall want to crib a lot I expect in my treatise on Knox.

Your Jewels sent me a pretty photograph of themselves sparkling in fancy dress.

In February I go to Rhodesia to interrogate Daphne Acton. Meanwhile it is all work and no play making Bo a dull boy.

Swans are wintering on my little lake. The peacock is growing his second tail. Bron is going bald. Meg is fat as suet. Teresa dirty. Hatty dotty. The little boys just little boys.

All send their love

Evelyn

Evelyn to Diana

Combe Florey *3 February 1958*

Sweet Pug

Where? (not whore. where WHERE)

Listen: I'm just off to Africa. My aeroplane stops at Rome. Will you be there at the beginning of March? If so, I would stop and see you. Or middle of March? No plans. But my address is c/o Lady Acton, M'BEBI, MAZOE, S. RHODESIA.

If you would like to meet me in Rome in six weeks or so please send aeroplane letter to that address.

All love
Bo

---

[1] She stayed with Raimund and Elizabeth von Hofmannsthal at Schloss Prielau, Zell-am-See, near Salzburg.

Evelyn to Diana

Combe Florey   *10 March 1958*

Darling Pug

I had breakfast at Rome aerodrome the day before yesterday and thought how lovely it would be to drive off into the town and see Baby but I hadn't heard from you and now I have so I know it would not have been any good.

I thought your obituary[1] in yesterday's *Sunday Times* very good. Who wrote it? Rupert? The Next Best Thing? Baby herself? Anyway it was top hole. Couldn't have done it better myself.

It never stopped raining in Rhodesia. I am like a pit pony in the European sun. Daphne Acton is a saint and it was most edifying staying with her – 10 children, 3 grandchildren. It is funny to hear yells of rage from a little girl struggling with a beefy little boy: 'Mummy, mummy, tell Denis he mustn't play with my Teddy', and it is an aunt complaining about her nephew. Awful discomfort. Telephone party-line ringing all day. Servants only taught to serve Mass not to press trousers. Ghastly food. All children at all meals. No semblance of a nanny. A tremendously boring ex-naval chaplain always there. Ants in the beds. All forms of physical and mental torture but Daphne radiating serene sanctity so that the horrors just did not work.

Rhodesians are very dull except the cosmopolitan displaced persons who have come in lately, but plenty of them and nice Dalhousies at Government House.[2] The black fellows are dull too. No dancing or carving or dressing up. One ancient building in the whole country called Zimbabwe but no one knows within a thousand years when it was built or by whom or why. Everything else is bungalows and scrubby trees and good roads and floods. But I got heaps of very valuable material on Ronnie from Daphne.

I have Meg living at home now. A great comfort to my old age. She is *very* fat but jolly.

All love
Bo

---

[1] An unsigned profile by Rupert Hart-Davis at the time of the publication of her first volume of autobiography, *The Rainbow Comes and Goes*. It was accompanied by a large, very dull photograph of her taken by Douglas Glass. Diana, not knowing that Rupert had written the piece, sent him a postcard from Rome saying 'Glass should be broken, and whoever wrote the praise exalted.'

[2] Simon Ramsay, 16th Earl of Dalhousie (b. 1914), Governor-General of the Federation of Rhodesia and Nyasaland 1957–63, and his wife Margaret.

Diana to Evelyn

Good ship Esperia   *20 March [1958]*
Alexandria – where Pinfold
left his ship

O! darling Bo – what a teeze you are. I was in Rome – time on my hands –
also a motor-car – and could have been on the airfield and streamlined you
to the antiquities in a trice. Who blundered? Did you change your dates – I
certainly wrote expecting to meet, and did I change mine I do not think
so.

I lived in the most delectable flat on a Tiber island – the temporary
property of Judy. I was there ten days and am to return after a week or 3
with my 'jewels'. I nearly broke all dates and did a bunk to the centre of
central Africa – in fact to Zanukville – John Huston disarmingly invited
me to be his guest – I should have seen animals as Noah saw them in much
much the same surroundings and should have lived in a little throbbing
microcosm as in *Miracle* days. My companions: The Next Best, Zannuck,
Miss Greco, that giant of Iris's [Friedrich Ledebur] whose hand you held
at the Ballon party. But – proof of age – I sensibly thought of two weeks
innoculations and travelling by air alone. (The invitation was made the
day before the great trek) and I turned the tempting scheme down.[1]

Instead I went by train for a day to Switzerland – not for a roll with
Carl[2] but to tussle with franks and dollars and wiley furriers' ways. That
night I tried to get a bed in the train to Montecarlo – no wagon-lit – no
couchette, no first-class space. I found to my surprise an empty second
with shiny narrow seats and one blazing globe of light lit from above the
door. There I set up my rest, balancing books and bags and coats into
pillow and cover. It was not long before a very tall gentleman of forty-
odd came in and took the opposite shelf, shutting the door and suggesting
that we might keep it to ourselves if he pulled down all the blinds. He
made his arrangements of comfort and we had a few travellers' words
about destination, ventilation and light. I explained that I was a bad
sleeper and relyed very much on light for reading and did he mind very
much the ceiling blaze. He said (all in French) that he didn't very much
but it would be nicer to get some sleep. I said I'd take a pill and when, if, I
fell asleep he could dous it. I woke two hours after the pill had had its hour
to act to a first idea that my spectacles had capriciously slid into – yes –

[1] John Huston (1906–87) and Darryl F. Zannuck (1902–79) were in French Equatorial Africa (now
the Cameroons), to make a film of Romain Gary's novel *The Roots of Heaven*. Zannuck was infatuated
with the French singer Juliette Greco, though she was being distinctly frosty to him. Patrick Leigh
Fermor, the scriptwriter, fell into a thorn tree while drunk and got a badly infected hand. The
overpowering heat produced sickness and lethargy in the crew, nothing went right, and finally the film
was abandoned.
[2] Carl Burckhardt (1891–1974), Swiss historian, diplomat and author. He had been Swiss Minister
in Paris during Duff and Diana's tenure of the British Embassy, and had now retired to his home near
Geneva.

hold on – my parts, and opening my eyes, I saw the huge form standing over me by the blue night-light and the huge hand searching. I heard myself saying what only an Englishwoman would say – 'Really! Really! whatever do you think you're doing?' and he jumped back to his bench like a fox hound answering the whip. Within a few minutes the compartment had filled with mothers and babies and phleghm-choked workmen – nappies and orange peel and spit flying, and my seducer-to-be fled – whether in shame or disgust I don't know. Take into count that I was wearing R[ed] R[iding] Hood's Granny's cap.

In Monte, intact, I met up with Mrs Jenny and her little car and after a quiet day and night at Daisy Fellowes with Victor Cunard and Som[erset] Maugham (memories) we drove chit-chattering to lunch at Porto Fino – and to dine in Florence with the American Rector and his disciple Dane[1] – curious it sounds, and indeed it was unusual. He [is] called Victor Stanley, and is in love with God without much proclamation – looks like a budding Orson Welles and exceedingly nice – next day a cocktail at the rectory before lunch with Berenson.[2] He dear old man has receeded a bit – not slumped – deafer and therefore less quick but still straight as a lit candle and still a bite in his warm affectionate ways.

And so to Rome where I so sadly missed you – and your letter later and the picture of me crueller than the cruel glass (mirror) and the glorious blurb by Rupert. I too had guessed Beaton – How dared you think it might be 'Baby herself' – and next Sunday came the mutilated installment like so many liquorice all sorts. I couldn't finish it – but no doubt everyone who has ever been serialised must have felt the same and worse according to the importance and their pride.

Goodbye sweet Wu – it's 9 o'clock and so sunny that I think I will go on the excursion round Alex – nothing venture – Arabic glottals and gutterals as loud as Babel come thro' the port.

Do write – your letters are the only ones that give me excited anticipation when I see the neat calligraphy.

I'll always love you –

Baby

Air to Brit. Emb. at Beirut at once – or Torre del Grillo, Piazza del Grillo, Rome.

Why not come back after Easter and bring a friend with a car (Patrick [Kinross]) and we'd all motor back. Bring Meg.

---

[1] Peter Lauritzen, the American historian and lecturer. He lived in Florence before settling in Venice in 1967, and has written a number of books on Venice, as well as UNESCO's official report on restoration work in the city. In 1975 he married Lady Rose Keppel.

[2] Bernard Berenson (1865–1959), art historian of the Italian Renaissance. He had lived for many years at the Villa I Tatti, between Settignano and Fiesole.

Evelyn to Diana

Combe Florey   *29 March 1958*

Darling Pug

What a lovely long letter – in ink too. Thanks awfully.

I am very shocked at your travelling in a foreign train without your maid. You must know what Frogs are like by this time – first, second or third class, all sexual maniacs. You are lucky to have escaped with nothing worse than an unpleasant overture. The whole band might have struck up. When he thought you drugged too – just like that disgusting book G. Greene thought so beautiful [*Lolita*].

I am not reading Baby's Opera. The gilt has been taken off too many ginger breads by snippets in newspapers so I am exercising great self restraint and holding off (unlike that Frog) until I have the book in my hands. All my family and friends are enjoying the snippets enormously.

Another great exercise in self restraint – I've given up gin (and brandy) for Lent. Goodness how I miss it. Come over quite queer regular at six in the evening. Have to take a drop of port. Not the same.

That booby Pam [Berry] will be in Rome. Not me, alas. For the first time in my life I am busy as a bank clerk and for the second time as poor. (My American fortune has at last run out.[1] I drop £6000 a year.) I live in a whirl of churchy old bachelors – Ronnie's surviving Anglican chums – and wade through letters full of unidentifiable Christian names. You can't, by any chance, tell me who 'Jack' can have been – Balliol 1910, smart, political, had Lady Randolph Churchill to luncheon? No one can place him. A few people called Edward Horner 'Jack' but never Ronald. I have come across a few references to 'those girls in Arlington Street' and a very funny description of Lady Agnes Cooper[2] by Ted Shuttleworth. Ronald kept any letter from 1909–1916 – alas those who should have kept his are all dead. The Prime Minister [Harold Macmillan] is showing a kindly interest (not unmixed with anxiety about the figure he will cut). Perhaps I can shake him down for a Life Peerage.

Meg began a novel yesterday – not *Bonjour Tristesse*.[3] I read the first line 'Minerva Chop was a blue-stocking and therefore a spinster'.

Bron has got his commission in the Blues – many sons of old Blues failed. He must have some guts. He succeeds. Scholarship at the House and now this. But he's a queer morose boy, sloping round the woods with a gun alone or playing light opera on his gramophone. Teresa has

---

[1] The royalties on *Brideshead Revisited*.

[2] Duff's mother, formerly Lady Agnes Duff, daughter of the 5th Earl Fife and sister of the 1st Duke of Fife who married Edward VII's eldest daughter, Princess Louise, the Princess Royal. Lady Agnes was disowned and disinherited by her family when she left her first husband Viscount Dupplin, son of the Earl of Kinnoull, eloping with Herbert Flower who died a few years later in 1880. Sir Alfred Cooper rescued her from destitution. They married and had four children. Duff's youngest sister, Sybil, was Rupert Hart-Davis's mother.

[3] Françoise Sagan's first novel about a young girl's sexual awakening, published in England in 1954.

had a dazzling term academically. But Meg for me anytime though she's jolly fat at the moment and eats an abnormal amount.

Katharine sounds wretched. The operation was much more painful than anyone expected and the convalescence much longer. She may get to Mells for Easter.

Ronald's complaints are all like Tom Pinch (character in M. Chuzzlewit).

What a hell of a thing they seem to have built at Lourdes.[1] Shall we go out of season and see it?

Alexandria was where Mrs Stitch betrayed Captain Crouchback. Pinfold jumped ship at Port Said.

My greetings to your poor apostate daughter-in-law.[2] My children pray for her conversion.

All love
Bo

Diana to Evelyn

Beirut   *All Fools', 1958*
Lebanon

Could 'Jack' have been Jack Churchill himself with Lady Randolph, his mother lunching? Edward Horner was never called Jack – occasionally old E. Jack Horner is Sir John – a remarkable deaf rational scholar. He allowed Edward to be prayed for in Mells church – when gravely wounded, and insisted on thanksgiving when he recovered as being 'only civil, don't you know'.[3]

Thank you for restraint showed over snippets – I wish you would show it about the book itself and hand it over to Meg and the others when it is sent you. You've seen for yourself and said 'not bad' – why not leave it at that. The whole thing is acutely embarrassing even here where I have come for jewels – also to be absent from furore or frost. The only feeling the success gives me is certainty that two flops follow.

All sympathy about restraint from gin. I can do it alright if I live like an eremite – no question otherwise. It wouldn't be fair on friends – I do admire you – no hero I can forget brandy. Here I use restraint not that

---

[1] The underground basilica of St Pius X built by Eugène Freyssinet and consecrated by Cardinal Roncalli (later Pope John XXIII) that year, the centenary of St Bernadette's visions of the Virgin.

[2] Anne Norwich used to make anti-Catholic remarks which appalled Waugh, since she had been born into an old Catholic family, the Cliffords.

[3] Sir John Horner (1843–1927), descendant of the Little Jack Horner of nursery rhyme fame. His son Edward was killed at Cambrai in 1917.

there's any lack of elixia – but John Julius though cold sober is swelling like our Randy [Churchill] – we call him Tubby. You are lucky in all your gems – they sparkle – Minerva Chop is a fine name.

Yes rather, I'll go to Lourdes with you – how would you like to motor with me and Meg earliest August. One way only alas as I have to go on with my children who I propose to meet near Toulon . . . We could 'take it schlow' as Raimund says, and stay at my expense in 'hotels isolés'.

Immediate plans are to leave this din of a town and the high, lovely place where Lady Hesta Stanhope lived and lies and the edifying collapse (oximoron?) of Balbeck's stones and the Sursok family who made a sizeable and durable fortune by cornering wheat in the great famine, and fly in a [Lockheed] super constellation (the very word is like a knell) to Rome and there to leave after 2 weeks for what I'm forced to call my home.

I suppose I'll come to England if asked to 1st night of *My Fair Lady*[1] (something of the old Diana left) but if it synchronises with May 9th (publication of Baby's *Rainbow*) I'll hesitate. Then there's that untiring Miss Foyle who's automatically asked me to lunch – I've answered that she must forgivingly understand that I can't face it – let alone say a few words or take flattery without mantling and squirming – and then I thought I was not helping Rupert – and ended (like the man who wrote pages to the senders about the handle not having arrived with the pump and added a P.S. that he had just found it) by saying 'consult with Rupert.' Anyway I shall hope to see you in the few days I'm there – and perhaps there'll be a Whitsuntide at Chantilly. My address – Reuters, Rome.

Fondest love dear Bo.

B

Evelyn to Diana

Combe Florey   *20 April 1958*

Sweet Pug

Baby's Bouquet [*The Rainbow Comes and Goes*] came yesterday, with baby on the cover looking so puzzled and eager to find out that she draws tears.

I have spent hours and hours absolutely entranced. Thank God I had the resolution to turn away from the snippets in the paper and wait for the book. How much credit, I wonder, is yours and how much young Hart-Davis's for the elegance of production? It is the best made book since the war. I am delighted to find your revival of the good habit of putting a title

[1] *My Fair Lady* opened in London on 30 April 1958.

above each right-hand page. Real chic that. All the illustrations excellent, except those taken from newspaper reproductions – Kakoo's wedding for instance.[1] Remember for future volumes only <u>actual</u> photographs can be reproduced in half-tone. Was Patrick Shaw-Stewart done from the actual drawing?[2] It doesn't look like it. He's much better (same drawing) in his *Letters*. <u>Very</u> nice to see [panels painted by Martin] Battersby on the end-papers. It's a spiffing piece of work.

So much for the look and feel of it. Now for the writing. That is top hole. I mean it isn't just a book of memoirs of someone who has had an unusually amusing and exciting life. It's a work of literary art, every sentence alive and swooping and dipping and soaring and pecking and carrying off the worm. No clichés because it's all thought and felt. Any prig who takes the trouble can write 'sloe-eyes' and then think: 'cliché' and change it to (exactly the same thing) 'bullace-eyes' and think he has said something original. But your style is yourself – rich and original and idiosyncratic. And the changes of speed are Diaghilief [*sic*]. Goodness I have enjoyed it and shall again and again. An abiding book. I long for later volumes.

The influence of Mrs Jenny seems negligible. 'Summit' as an adjective ('summit generals') is clearly hers. I suspect 'sculpt' – a beastly word, should be model – is baby's own. Also 'nostalgia' is used. Nostalgia means home-sickness – nothing else; no connexion with the past. Some-one ten years ago wrote 'nostalgia for the past' and since then Lady P. Berry etc. leave out 'past' and think nostalgia means a preference for earlier times.

I have a vicarious intimacy (through working on Ronald) with Balliol 1906–10. It's not true that Julian Grenfell[3] or Charles Lister[4] or (I think) Patrick Shaw-Stewart or (I rather think) Edward Horner had any taste for the decadent. Grenfell had at Eton, and violently shook it off.

Baby you have written a beautiful book. I knew it wasn't in you to do anything badly, but I am flabbergasted at your accomplishment.

Thanks awfully for sending it.

All love
Bo

[1] Kathleen Tennant (1894–1990), married in 1916 Diana's brother John (1886–1940), later the 9th Duke of Rutland.

[2] Patrick Shaw-Stewart (1888–1917), a Fellow of All Souls and member of the Coterie before the First World War. One of the Lost Generation. The drawing was by Diana's mother, Violet Rutland.

[3] Julian Grenfell (1888–1915), best remembered for his war poetry, and his brother Billy were both killed in the same year of the First World War. They were the children of 1st Baron Desborough and his wife Ettie, a Souls' hostess.

[4] Charles Lister (1887–1915), second son of 4th Baron Ribblesdale, and a supporter of the Independent Labour Party, mortally wounded at Gallipoli.

Evelyn to Diana

Combe Florey   *9 June 1958*

Sweet Pug

Decent of you to remember me. You are ever present in my mind and
prayers particularly now at the hour of your great literary triumph. I
don't know when I saw a book so richly and rightly praised by every kind
of reviewer and reader – not just by chums, but by the kind of people one
might have expected to be hostile. It's been a great event. I hope you have
enjoyed it all as much as I have.

'Sculpt' can't be right. The Latin is 'sculpere' not 'sculptere'. It means
to carve and shouldn't anyway be used of modelling. There is no such
word as 'sculpt' in educated use.

If you are worried about the possible extinction of Christianity in the
Lebanon, I sympathize. If about the fate of the diplomatic corps, I scoff.
The one thing still held sacred everywhere since the Boxer rising is the
welfare of diplomats. Your jewel is safe. My boy is a cornet of horse in
Cyprus. I hope he has some fighting.[1]

I wonder what made you think of me; seeing my name on a letter in *The
Times* perhaps? How bad the X-word has been lately. Why 'absconds'
why 'Levanting' on Friday?

I have been on a little Knox tour to various theological colleges, visiting
the ruins of Castle Howard and Holloway College on the way. Do you
know Holloway College – the very showy building near Windsor?[2] It has
a picture gallery with the originals of all the illustrations to our history
books – Millais' *Little Princes in the Tower*, Maclise's *Peter the Great at
Deptford Lock*. Also Frith's *Railway Station* and a superb Landseer *Man
Proposes – God Disposes*, an Arctic twilight and two polar bears finishing
off Franklin. Mr Holloway left his (pill) fortune partly to a lunatic asylum
nearby, same architect, and partly for the 'higher education of girls of the
upper middle class'. He ordained each should have two rooms. A special
act of parliament had to be passed in 1947 to deprive them of their sitting-
rooms. I said to a girl 'How disagreeable'. She said 'Oh, I think bed-
sitters much cosier'.

I am pretty bobbish but I think loose talk of euphoria must come from
my having got tight one afternoon lately in White's. It was rather sad
because I had a Monsignor dining with me that evening at St James's Club
to tell me all the scandals of St Edmund's College, where Ronnie spent

[1] The Royal Horse Guards (The Blues) alone in the British Army retained the old cavalry rank of
cornet for a Second Lieutenant. The regiment was then part of the British force fighting the EOKA
guerillas led by the extreme Greek nationalist, Colonel Grivas.

[2] Thomas Holloway (1800–83), a patent medicine vendor who discovered earlier than his competitors the advantages of heavy advertising. He founded Holloway College, at Egham in Surrey, in
1886. It is now part of the University of London and known as the Royal Holloway and Bedford New
College.

7 wretched years. Well I spent the afternoon boozing and I remember meeting the Monsignor who was about 7 feet high and a great biblical scholar, and the last thing I remember saying was 'How about some vodka with our caviar'? After that all is blackness. But next day he wrote to apologize for talking too much and keeping me up so late and blamed it on my excessive hospitality. So all one important chapter in Ronnie's life is closed to me.

I wish you would come and see this house before I start selling off the contents, which will be soon. I am jolly poor and getting poorer fast. Little Meg is very fat and rarely sober, like Maimie Lygon, and a great joy to me. Tomorrow is her sixteenth birthday. I have promised to stop slapping her and to take to pinching. Quieter except for squeals.

The house I hoped you would come and live in near here has fallen down.

Darling Baby I am so pleased about the success of your book.

All love
Bo

Evelyn to Diana

Combe Florey   *13 June [1958]*

Darling Diana

Thank you for your loving letter.

Laura is in Cyprus with Bron. His life is very precarious.[1] He seems to have had more than one bullet in lung and spleen. Details are wanting, but it sounds as though he will never completely recover. I shall go out to travel home with Laura if he dies.

One good result of the newspaper reports is that monks and nuns and priests all over the country are praying for him. Prayer is the only thing.

All love
Bo

Evelyn to Diana

Combe Florey   *[pstmk 29 June 1958]*
[postcard]

Just had the very good news that Bron is off the danger list.

E

---

[1] The machine-gun on Auberon's armoured car went off accidentally, riddling him with bullets. *The Times* of 11 June reported: 'An official statement says that Second Lieutenant Oubyn [*sic*] Waugh . . . was accidentally shot last night during anti-riot operations in the Nicosia area.' Auberon Waugh's account was that he spotted something wrong with the Browning machine-gun in the turret of his armoured car. 'Seizing hold of the end with quiet efficiency, I was wiggling it up and down when I noticed it had started firing. Six bullets later I was alarmed to observe that it was firing through my chest . . .'

Evelyn to Diana

Combe Florey   *30 June 1958*

Dearest Diana

I sent you a postcard yesterday to tell you our good news of Bron. Today your letter. The extent of his injuries is – six bullets; a lung, the spleen and two ribs removed; left hand hit with probable loss of a finger. Great heat makes his recovery slow and painful. His chest injuries make it impossible, apparently, to fly him home. Local surgeons have been very skilful. He could not have lived on a battle field being shunted from Field Dressing Station to Forward Clearing Post etc. but they were able to get him to hospital immediately.

He had the Last Sacraments and greatly impressed the doctors by his courage and resignation, quietly repeating the De Profundis in his extremity. The newspapers set people praying for him all over the world – all sorts of nuns we didn't know – and he attributes his survival to their prayers.

Laura will be returning soon. He will be very lonely and absolutely longs for letters. Do write to him. He would love it. His address is British Military Hospital, Nicosia, Cyprus.

I shall be away from July 9th–13th. Can you come any time after that with Artemis and Lebanese nanny.[1] I could bore your pants off reading *Knox* aloud. Juliet [Duff] declares that you and she and Mr Fleet[2] are to travel round the Black Sea in a liner, but I don't believe that.

Meg is taking School Certificate and is a great bore about Chaucer and Virgil. Hatty lives her own life among pet rabbits. Teresa is regarded at Oxford as a coming professional historian. If I ask her the most elementary question, she is stumped.

All love
Bo

Evelyn to Diana

Combe Florey   *[pstmk 20 July 1958]*
[postcard]

We should love to have Artemis here but I have no doubt Bognor would be more fun for her. I am glad she has cut the Yanks. Beirut must be very disagreeable now – like London in 1943 with all those putty coloured young men about the place.

---

[1] After the revolution in Iraq in 1958, and the assassination of King Faisal, US troops landed in Lebanon to prevent a similar disaster. The situation was tense for several months; John Julius and Anne decided that the five-year-old Artemis would be safer in Europe.

[2] Simon Fleet (1913–66), who was born Harry Carnes but changed his name, was Lady Juliet Duff's constant companion.

We are here always and long for your visit whenever you can come. Do bring Vol II of opus. Do stay more than one night. Poor Hatty is desolate at your postponement.

Bo

Evelyn to Diana

Combe Florey [*July/August 1958*]

Darling Diana,

It was jolly decent of you to come all this way, so far from glittering pansies, to see us and cheer us. Your visit was a huge treat.

Laura did not sell the gladioli. She professes to delight in them. They are in a great pot and she admires them. She thanks you for them heartily and tenderly.

You should have come to Castle Cary. I had 50 minutes there. The station is isolated among fields far from any habitation. There was a good train back to Frome about 5.20. I sat and read Ronald's sermons.

All authorities I consult confirm that King John is buried at Worcester.

I shall think of you and Fleet and Dame Rose[1] on the field of Inkerman.

All love
Bo

Evelyn to Diana

Combe Florey *8 October [1958]*

Darling Baby

I don't know where you are. Is there any chance of your being in England on SATURDAY OCTOBER 25th? Miss Grant is to be married that day[2] in TAUNTON and Bridget has an irrational but deep longing that Eddie's few surviving friends should be represented at the wedding. Duff was Miss Grant's Godfather. If you can come it would be a great delight to her and of course to me because you would stay here for it.

RSVP because we have to make rooms for a party.

Miss G. is very pretty. No one much likes her Mr Fraser.

Kistie Hesketh[3] will be here and Sweet Alice Jolliffe and her young man

---

[1] Dame Rose Macaulay (1881–1958), novelist, essayist and travel writer. Her best-known novels are *The World My Wilderness* (1950) and *The Towers of Trebizond* (1956). She was created a Dame of the British Empire in the year of her death.

[2] Evelyn Anne Grant (1938–84), the daughter of Edward and Bridget Grant (Laura Waugh's sister), was to marry Ian James Fraser (b. 1923), later Chairman of Rolls-Royce Motors, and Chairman of Lazard Brothers 1980–85. He was knighted in 1986.

[3] Christian, Lady Hesketh, widow of 2nd Baron Hesketh, sister of Rory McEwen.

and possibly a priest so it will be awfully overcrowded. But you aren't one to shirk a thing like that.

All love
Bo

Evelyn to Diana

Combe Florey   *14 October 1958*

Baby, that is heavenly of you. Bridget's sentimental heart will overflow when she gets the news. What's more Anne's social aspirations to keep up with the Frasers will be prodigiously boosted. And as for me, I always long for the Pug.

What you must do is forget about aeroplanes. No good in these parts and autumnal mists treacherous. You must come from London on the train specified on the card (if you won't come Fri.) and I will meet you at the church door and put you in a seat and find the place for you in the prayer book and sit by you and pinch you if you fall asleep. Then we will take you to Tetton and back from Tetton here for the night. Next day there has to be a car to near Mells (with Laura or Sweet Alice) to take my son Septimus back to school. So you see all you'll need is a taxi to Frome on Monday. No need for cars or aeroplanes.

At the edge of your card is the cryptic note 'a parcel will be sent from Kellerways for me to collect'. Not understood.

I am glad you're coming.[1]

Bo

Evelyn to Diana

Combe Florey   *[pstmk 27 October 1958]*
[postcard]

Miss Fionn[2] is giving an orgy on Wednesday at 16 Victoria Square so Annie's not dining there. You are dining with me. I don't mind where or in what company (sans Fleet) and would like Ann (sans [Lucian] Freud) but DON'T GET SHANGHAIED AGAIN. Could you, very sweetly, leave a message at White's or Hyde Park Hotel saying where when and how you would like to spend the evening.

[1] Their meeting at the wedding of Anne Grant was not so happy. Diana saw Waugh in conversation on a sofa, armed with one of his ear trumpets. 'Oh Evelyn you look ridiculous,' she said. 'Put that thing away, you don't need it' – whereupon she emptied her champagne glass into the offending object.

[2] The Hon. Fionn O'Neill (b. 1936), Ann Fleming's daughter by her first husband, Shane, 3rd Baron O'Neill (1907–44). She was married to the diplomat John Morgan 1961–75.

Diana to Evelyn

Schloss Prielau
Zell-am-See

25 December [1958]
Wherin Our Savior's
birth was celebrate
cock's begin[?]

Bo. What went wrong?

I wondered at no response to what? P cards? or hopes, expectancies, and then, lately on the telephone when I asked Katharine if you were dead she said you were alive and kicking, against me. The obstacle in my race to heaven, according to Belloc, is lack of remorse – I pray in my under-5 way to God to give me <u>remorse</u>. If I have failed you, help me to feel my lacking guilt. Nonsense, dear fool – I thought we were through with troublesome demons.

In the little time I have left to me, I need what I have long loved – please tell me what to deplore otherwise how can I be remorseful?

Anyway to Laura, Meg and Harriet true love,
    and (a better word) for greetings

Pug

Evelyn to Diana

Combe Florey

30 December 1958

Darling Pug

I don't understand international finance but I hope that Gen. de Gaulle's manipulations of the franc[1] will either enrich you or impoverish you so much that you are driven home to live among the people who love you most faithfully.

I was delighted to see that Duff's prize went to John Betjeman [for his *Collected Poems*]. There were preposterous rumours rife in Somerset that it was to go to Gen. de Gaulle.

I hope you had a happy Christmas, wherever you were. Your jewels sent us their enchanting card. Meg and I spent the three days in London keeping Bron company. I took her to *Peter Pan*; she took me to an intolerable Irish-American play about a family being drunk and rude to one another in half darkness.[2] She enjoyed both equally and drank heavily.

Sweet Alice's wedding has been postponed. We jumped to it that Mr

[1] The French government had restructured the currency with one new franc replacing a hundred old francs.
[2] The first London production of *Long Day's Journey into Night* by Eugene O'Neill (1888–1953), written in 1940.

259

[John] Chancellor had done a bunk with Fionn but it seems she is genuinely struck with jaundice.[1]

I shall be in Genoa for two nights at the end of January, embarking there for Dar es Salaam; from there wandering down Africa for six weeks and sailing home from the Cape (Pendennis Castle). Don't suppose I shall find baby on board. Jolly decent if I did.

Life of R. Knox finished. Do you know his last words? 'Awfully jolly of you to suggest it'.[2]

K. came for a night and had rather alarming spasms of the heart.

All love
Bo

Diana to Evelyn

Rome   *6 January 1959*

Darling Bo. Greatly relieved by your thistle-down letter – I wish your plans could have brought you here for 3 days – couldn't they? I think you'd be quite happy with Iris for laughs and Judy too and this after-your-heart island appartment, and all of us grovelling with fear and love and anxiety to propitiate and kowtow and love and obey. You might even bear me off to darkest white man's grave Africa – under the shadow of Lucifer (see Meredith) if this dear town looses its power to restore the spirit and spirits. It's done a Miracle this time – my Christmas, tho' I was treated at Zell–am–See as we should treat you here – quite vanquished me – children's fresh voices, easy happy Austrians – boiling stoves with seats part of them – for back-baking.

But seasonal melancholia won, and with it walks Hyperchondria with my heart murmuring in its hand. I don't give a fig for anniversaries – I miss Duff every day of the year with the same intensity – and yet as the New Year approaches all courage takes flight. Large recovery here in spite of the spartan's bed – Mrs Jenny and Iris in the snows still – Annie Flem[ing] expected for the upper room (no looking-glasses in any room – good for our vanities). My window is almost filled with the dashing muddy Tiber, above it trees and beautiful vestiges. I have a long monk's

[1] At Combe Florey one weekend, John Chancellor had gone off for an innocent but overlong walk with Fionn O'Neill and returned to find everyone furious with him for reducing Alice Jolliffe to tears of jealousy. Diana gave him a fearsome dressing-down for ungentlemanly conduct. Waugh's version of events is recounted in his letter to Ann Fleming of 3 December 1958 – see *Letters of Ann Fleming*, p. 224.

[2] 'For three days he lay in a coma, but once Lady Eldon saw a stir of consciousness and asked whether he would like her to read to him from his own New Testament. He answered very faintly but distinctly: "No"; and then after a long pause in which he seemed to have lapsed again into unconsciousness, there came from the death-bed, just audibly, in the idiom of his youth: "Awfully jolly of you to suggest it, though."' (Evelyn Waugh, *Life of Ronald Knox*, p. 333)

table and trestle – my grind stone. I'm getting down to vol III with the utmost difficulty and no one to advise. Rupert's partner [Richard] Garnett wrote encouragingly about vol II [*The Light of Common Day*] – and adds a word about writing more and using fewer letters. I'm trying but I think he's wrong. There's truth – or nearer truth in letters, and they're freshly cut and I like reading the letters of 'Life and Letters' best. *Sunday Times* said vol II is O.K. and will make a nice serial. Curtis Brown[1] on the other hand writes typically that he liked it so much that he felt guilty reading it (?) and that he'd find it v. difficult to sell. I personally find it tedeous to a degree, shapeless, with indiscretions that procure no eves droppers.

We had Willie Maugham and his catamite Searle to lunch yesterday – they both had the 'cell' treatment in Switzerland – the sells and serums of flocks of muttons and beefs and goat still pulsating with life are pumped into you – with frightening success. Willie's past mending but Searle has become a garrulous Tom Cat – right out of his bed – I heard him say while waiting for Willie's much increased impediment – to allow a word out – in a cockney-pansy voice, 'My dear you can't imagine what it's like – I wake up to find myself under a <u>tent</u>' – here an obscene gesture was made, denoting fabulous erection – 'it hasn't happened to me since I was in the scouts!' They are off to Japan by boat next autumn – I offered myself as a ship-mate. I could see they didn't like the idea – at least Willie didn't. I offered myself to the Stratford Company when they went to Russia – they wouldn't have me at any price – not even my own. Glen [Byam Shaw] wouldn't. Only you invite. I'd like to come, but we'd fall out, my love and I.

I must get Baby's gibberish set down. I might take flight to my jewels' box for a week or so – they suggest Jerusalem at Easter and Amman again. I only want them. Do ask Katharine to allow me to print a Belloc sonnet (never published). She doesn't mind, she tells Rupert – but Ronnie had kept it out, on account of it having the word 'yids' I imagine. It will be published anyway in time as there is my MS and also one in a university library. It would be in better taste for it to come where it belongs – I know Duff, the other executor, would have concurred – I'll always love you

Pug

Fond love to my 2 girls – hug them – bring them and Laura to France in the spring. Also <u>write</u> me often and with news of Bron.[2]

---

[1] Spencer Curtis Brown (1906–80), Diana's literary agent.
[2] Bron was about to undergo a further operation.

Evelyn to Diana

Combe Florey   *14 January 1959*

Darling Pug

You know this megalomania. Baby is very pretty and well thought of in the literary world nowadays, but to suppose a letter addressed to 'Baby Rome' will reach her, is too much. I once had an address for you, a tower of dragons [Torre del Grillo], but you say you now live below water-level in the Tiber, so that can't be it. I hope Miss Fay [Norah Fahie] is at Chantilly forwarding.

I am rather dreading my East African trip. It seems I have chosen the worst possible time of year – stifling heat on the coast and all roads inland washed away. It began with my idly telling my agent I'd like someone to pay my expenses somewhere warm and now I have let myself in for crossing the whole of Darkers and writing a sickening account of it when I get home. Damn.

If Mrs Jenny asks you to Porto Fino at the end of the month we could meet. I am at Genoa alone Hotel Columbia-Excelsior 28th–30th (inclusive) don't know what to do there except look at graves.

I loved the story of Mr Searle's tent. H. Macmillan was asked to luncheon to meet Maugham the other day, and called him 'Sir' throughout. Better than 'Dr'.

Meg has grown two inches and is very pretty and sunny. She was beginning to brood about her height as other girls do about weight.

Bron is probably to have his big operation next week. Laura is a little fretful about it and is going to stay several nights in London.

All love
Bo

Evelyn to Diana

Combe Florey   *24 January 1959*

Darling Pug

It is too much to hope that I can carry you off with me, nevertheless I set out my (changed) plans.

Arrive sorry [bigger writing from now on] Arrive Genoa 7.46 a.m. 29th Jan, Thursday. See Sights. Leave Genoa unspecified time Sat. 31st in RHODESIA CASTLE (Union Castle Line) said to be chock-a-block but people die. First stop Port Said Feb 4 Aden Feb 8 Mombasa 13th Zanzibar 19th Disembark 20th Dar-es-Salaam (Tanganyika). From there all is darkness until I arrive somehow at Salisbury, S. Rhodesia (c/o Lady Acton, M'Bebi, Mazoe) where I seem to be part host at coming-out ball of

Catherine Acton about 21st March in Salisbury. On Good Friday I sail from Cape Town (having got there I don't know how) in Pendennis Castle (said to be chock-a-block). Good Friday is 27th March. At Salisbury is good governor whom no doubt you know, Simon Dalhousie, and bad governor called Sir Peverel Williams Powlett (believe it or not) whose ADC is my nephew.[1] Daphne Acton would delight to put you up in frightful discomfort at M'Bebi. So Salisbury is O.K. At all or any parts or part of my trip it would be a joy godsend delight to have Pug. You could catch me by air at Dar-es-Salaam (bad season) address Club.

Katharine has taken monkish advice and says no to Belloc scurrilous poem. On the other hand I am sure she won't prosecute for piracy.

All love
Bo

Diana to Evelyn

Rome   *[January 1959]*
[postcard]

I note yr address in Genoa – write quickly and tell me exactly how long you – O bother – rereading I see you've told me so write me the hours of arrival & departure. I might make a dash for it – Also say the ship's first pause – Naples? no such luck –

all my prayers for Bron
love to my girls

D. X O X

Evelyn to Diana

From SS Rhodesia Castle   *31 January 1959*

Darling Baby

I have been had for a mug. This ship doesn't sail for hours. All I had to do was deposit my luggage and let a policeman make a mess in my passport and I could then have come back to you and seen you off and perhaps seen Mrs Jenny too. Didn't know till I got on board. Damn.

It was an absolutely glorious treat your coming to Genoa. Never really expected it. And then there you were a quick change artist in a dozen

[1] Vice-Admiral Sir Peveril Barton Reibey Wallop William-Powlett, Governor of Southern Rhodesia 1954–9. His ADC was Andrew Waugh, Alec's elder son, later captain in the Royal Navy.

different smart sets of clothes and strong as a horse striding over the cobbles. It was heavenly of you. Thank you, thank you.

This is a very English ship. Well you wouldn't mind that. The loud-speaker announces test match scores every half-hour. No Captain's table trouble – on my own in a corner. But prep school rules – breakfast is served <u>at</u> (not <u>from</u>) 8 <u>or</u> 9. You must make up your mind in advance. Well you wouldn't mind that, would you?

I have sneezed a dozen times. Sad if I take a cold to the tropics – they are incurable there.

All love
Bo

Evelyn to Diana

From SS Rhodesia Castle   *9 February 1959*

Darling Pug

I am very much thinner than when we parted. Could it have been the food, sir? Yes, by Jove, it could. Everything has been kept for glacial ages and has no taste or form. So I live on cold ham and grape fruit and as I have no crony to drink with I go slow on 'the liquids'. My aches and pains have almost ceased and I can stoop and turn without anguish. So it is all beneficial but boring. There are three priests on board and some nuns and some protestant nuns who look like spinsters and lack that placid half-baked joy that real nuns have.

The ship is very full mostly of the aged and of young married couples with hosts of children. They were very euphoric yesterday at Aden haggling over Japanese binoculars and watches. There are some rather succulent 12 year old girls but I don't mix with them. Just leer as they gambol round the swimming-bath. It is not at all hot but the young men play cards bare to the waist and sweat on the chairs. Not nice.

I think a great deal about why you lack the Faith. It isn't only absence of remorse. It is the inability to interest yourself in <u>general</u> ideas – moral or philosophical. You think one can live by taste alone, without intellect. A jolly hard case.

I have read Maurice [Baring]'s *C* for the first time.[1] How frightfully careless he was. A house is six miles from Oxford on one page and nine on the next. Worse, a woman is an elderly widow in one chapter, a dim married woman in another and a femme fatale with a lover at the end of the book – smart and sinister and 'the essence of London'. Does that sort

---

[1] *C*, a novel by Maurice Baring, was first published in 1924.

264

of discrepancy worry you? It does me. But what Maurice had was a haunting love of failure and a sense of the inextricable intercalation of human lives which is impressive. But how badly he wrote – cliché after cliché – 'dancing blue eyes' etc. The curse of the polyglot. Why do I write you Literary Notes like this? Well there's been nothing to think about except Baby's soul and Maurice's style. I wish both were brisker.

How can you, living in Rome, not detest Garibaldi? No general ideas again. You just see a flamboyant beacon with no implications. Does Miss Judy revere the 1870 Jewish Mayor of Rome and frequent the synagogue he built to insult Pius IX. Give her my love, please, and my warm respects to Mrs Jenny and Countess Iris.

The English of Kenya who are all high born have developed a cockney accent in one generation.

I really am worried about Maurice's bad writing. Think of him and Ronnie in opposite corners of the library at Beaufort typing away all day long such very different works.

Spontaneity is the enemy of Art. Ronnie always longed vainly for it.

I have reported to my children how you showered your food with tooth picks.

All love
Bo

Evelyn to Diana

Combe Florey   *21 April 1959*

Darling Pug

Just home, greatly rejuvenated by trundling round Africa and meeting scores of people I never want to see again and seeing no works of art and reading antiquated best sellers.

Auberon [Herbert] told his sisters that he had telephoned to us from Porto Fino but had not been able to get to Genoa. Odd.

I long for your book. It hasn't come yet. I won't read it in *Sunday Times*, that spoils all.[1]

I went to Oxford to unveil Ronnie's portrait and drew many tears from his assembled friends. Katharine was there as spry as if she had been in Tanganyika. Also, with great effrontery, the Hyltons who haven't contributed sixpence to the fund.

Miss Acton's coming out dinner party was a wow. Very cosmopolitan – Frogs, huns, hungarians, greeks and a few exiled English noblemen.

---

[1] This is *The Light of Common Day*, the second volume of Diana's autobiography.

There was even a pansy who is introducing the interior decoration of 1925 to the boers.

I went to dinner with the Paramount Chief of the Chagga tribe. He said: 'Don't dress. Come in your tatters and rags'.

It is all balls about the blacks massacring the whites.

I have the builders in, or rather out, pulling down that porch. I brooded about it a lot in Africa.

The captain of my ship said à propos of *Pinfold*: 'Funny thing this is the first voyage I've had without one of the passengers going mad. Coming out I had two stewards sitting on a man all the way to stop him going over board.'

Did you know Ronald Graham?[1] Well Meg looks just like him now. I think it must be the drink.

A highly placed official in Tanganyika told me in strict confidence that the Queen's marriage was 'on the rocks' because of the Duke of Edinburgh's infatuation with Judy Montagu.

There was a great feast in Trinity on Saturday – not on account of Ronnie but I was asked because of him. Dozens of delicious wines. I had my deaf ear to a Jew called, literally, Professor Wind[2] whose lectures on Picasso are so popular that he has to give each twice over. My good ear was with a fiendish bore called Sir Somebody Luke.[3] Hadn't brought my trumpet so was wretched.

Bron has made a great recovery and is hardly an invalid at all now, but his long life in hospital has given him an unhealthy interest in medicine and surgery.

Are you coming to England with Jewels? If so can't you bring them here for a night?

All love
Bo

Diana to Evelyn

Château de St Firmin   *[pstmk May 1959]*

Darling Wu

I'm so really happy to hear of Bron's recovery.

When I come to London with my jewells I shall do a western tour and hope to call upon you – with luck I'll see you before that distant date in earliest July. I come for two nights about 25th May to sign poor *Common*

---

[1] The Rt. Hon. Sir Ronald Graham (1870–1949), diplomat and Trustee of the British Museum.
[2] Professor Edgar Wind (1900–71), art historian.
[3] Sir Harry Luke (1884–1969). He held a number of posts in the Colonial Service, and wrote history and travel books.

Day at Hatchards, then again for the Hoff ball 25th June when I shall hope for life bouys from you.

I wish I thought something would bring you here in June – if I live. I don't feel that I shall – It's either heart or fatigue that's reached a disease category. Hope you got *Common Day* – I told Rupert to send it. Be lenient – the matter is so trivial.

D.

Evelyn to Diana

Combe Florey   *[pstmk 5 May 1959]*
[postcard]

No copy of *Common Day* yet. I won't read it in *Sunday Times* but yesterday I saw a very pretty photograph of myself and read that you picked me up in Manchester. I think we met at Hazel Lavery's in London. I pursued you through the provinces later. Never mind, I will come to Hatchards and buy a copy and get it signed by Baby herself if you'll tell me the right date. I suppose you are booked to lunch with your publisher that day? Yes? No? Soon I will send you a photograph of my jewels and a speech at Trinity about Ronald to bring tears to the eyes. Didn't like being put in same galère as S[imon] Fleet.[1]

Diana to Evelyn

Château de St Firmin   *[pstmk 11 May 1959]*
[postcard]

My publisher [Rupert Hart-Davis] has the jaundice – I'd love to lunch with you – but I have to be at Hatchards (a silly racket) at 2 which would mean Wilton's (so close) at 1. May 28th.

You don't allow for *S. Times* hash – I say the *Miracle* brought you to me because I was in the *Miracle* and we went to the kill of the treasure hunt. Manchester I well remember came after. True the *Miracle* also brought me Simon and the man who spoke of 'Mr and Mrs Wood in front' – name escapes me. It's a glorious snap of you – sort of Boni de Castellane.[2]

O X O B.

---

[1] The list of those she had met thanks to her performance in *The Miracle*.

[2] The Marquis Boniface de Castellane (1867–1932), one of the great dandies of the Belle Epoque, married the extremely rich but unattractive heiress Anna Jay Gould of whom he made the doubly disobliging pun: 'Vue de dot, elle n'est pas mal'.

Evelyn to Diana

Combe Florey   *14 May 1959*

Darling Pug

Your jaundiced nephew has sent me the long-watched-for book. I wish it had come in time for me to join the scramble to extol it in print. But you will get enough honey to drown in without me and anyway you don't need praise from anyone. You are an Established Writer now Baby. But you'll be pleased to know what delight it has brought to one sequestered old chum. It comes on the morning – Friday – which is usually soured for me by the arrival of the *New Statesman* and the *Spectator*.[1] I throw them in the rack unopened and begin on Pug. Haven't finished it yet. All I have read in an exulting morning is every bit as good as Vol 1. Nothing common or mean about the light of your day. Just glanced at *Daily Express* before settling down to Pug and saw middle page full of unstinted applause (by some Cambridge man who says you lived at Goodwood. Surely that was another actress?)

Not much about me. There'll be <u>much</u> more about <u>you</u> in <u>my</u> memoirs. I can't really enjoy being away from the book. I've not had ½ of it yet. The jaundiced boy hasn't done very well with his Index.

I am coming to London night of 27th (St James' Club) only to see you next day so if you have any other times bugger-free before 1 p.m. Corpus Christi, please spare some for me.

Hoops of steel are stainless and unbreakable.[2]

                                                                      WU

You gave so handsomely to Ronald's memorial, perhaps you'd like to see a speech which drew tears from many old eyes.

Evelyn to Diana

Combe Florey   *[May 1959]*

Darling Hoopers

I have finished reading Tome II with unwavering delight. I hope you haven't let yourself take notice of Cyril's disreputable review in the

[1] According to Frances Donaldson, 'The day of the week on which he received the *New Statesman* became known as Black Friday because it always provoked him so much. Once he could endure it no more and he cancelled it, but Friday became so much blacker without it that he had to order it again.' (Donaldson, *op.cit.*, p. 24)

[2] Describing her first meeting with Evelyn Waugh in *The Light of Common Day*, Diana wrote: 'I knew then that I wanted to bind Evelyn to my heart with hoops of steel, should he let me.'

Sunday Times.[1] It is one of the worst professional vices for a critic to complain that the book he is reviewing is not an entirely different book by an entirely different writer. I had pen in hand to chastize him and then thought what the Hell. A man who can call Maurice and Belloc 'tame' and Conrad 'pawky' simply doesn't know the meaning of words. (A propos Baby you can't 'decapitate a head'). And what's more Pug can look after herself. I can't see you as the pathetic waif. I have always seen you as a ruthless go-getter, enormously accomplished, dauntless, devoid of conscience or delicacy, Renaissance Italian, a beautiful and sweet tempered Venetian but more frivolous. Perhaps that's why I have never, that I can remember, given you a present. All your other friends were always giving you things. I never. I always see you as having everything you want. But Andrew Devonshire says I am a sponge. Perhaps that's the real reason.

I was appalled at the revelation that you were so frightened of the Germans you thought of killing yourself. The yellow streak of bastardy? The descriptions of the Duke of Windsor are brilliant – the remark that the librarian at Windsor would let him in whenever he liked brought tears. I think Tome II is a much finer achievement than Tome I because almost everyone (not I) can make a story of enchanted childhood but to carry it into maturity is altogether different.

I suppose Conrad and Ronald Knox must have met quite often. It is sad they never knew one another.

Is the Turkish ambassador's comment on *Lolita* a chestnut: 'I don't like reading about things like that. I prefer to see them'? The best joke I've heard for years, but jokes reach me late.[2]

When you wrote about your fear of the Germans I was reminded of the time you tried to play the wireless news at Stinkers.

Would you like me to kick Connolly's bottom next time I see him? More dignified than writing to *Sunday Times* about him.

Delicious Spring smells here. A joy to stick one's head out of the window at dawn before the second swig of paraldehyde.

All love
Bo

---

[1] It is hard to see why Diana's supporters – Waugh was not alone – should have reacted so strongly. Connolly gives *The Light of Common Day* due praise, and simply regrets that she does not describe the remarkable people she knew well: people like Rex Whistler, Maurice Baring, Hilaire Belloc, and Waugh himself. 'Lady Diana takes them too much for granted. One would like to hear what she thought of them and their books, what she thought they were *like.*' (*Sunday Times*, 17 May 1959)

[2] The joke may not have been that old. According to Ann Fleming in her letter to Waugh of 1 May, Nuri Birgi (b. 1908), the Turkish Ambassador in London, 1957–60, made this remark at one of her lunch parties. He became flustered when she announced it to the table at large. (*Letters of Ann Fleming*, p. 229)

Evelyn to Diana

Combe Florey   *[pstmk 19 May 1959]*

I mean elbowing the viscounts out of the way at the Abbey. That is of the
essence.[1]

Evelyn to Diana

Combe Florey   *[?May 1959]*

Did you know May 28th was Corpus Christi? Well, it will be a great
celebration to lunch with you. Are you sure Wiltons still exists. I haven't
been there for many years and I heard Marko had had a stroke. No oysters
in May. But if that is what Baby wants she shall not cry for it in vain. King
Street is a long way from Hatchards. You are thinking of Jermyn Street.
Sorry young Hart-Davis has the jaundice – may be cancer of the liver. I
bet you don't sell 200 copies of your book by signing them, but I hope
you do. Say 250 @ 10% of 30/- = £37. Journey from Paris costs as much
but can be put down against B's income tax. Worth it? Just. Don't know
anything of 'Hof Ball' but, if asked, wouldn't go. Too deaf. Even when I
knew it, Wiltons was full of criminals. Don't wear your sparklers there.
Why not just sit and booze at the Ritz 12.30–1.55 on Corpus Christi.
They sell sandwiches at Fortnum & Mason. Send Hatry out for one while
you wait for customers.[2] Does Hatry still own Hatchards or has he had a
stroke too? Today is Hatty's 15th birthday. She is very backward and
Meg is ugly as hell.

All love
Bo

Don't worry about my complaints. I'll be at Wiltons at 1 on 28th.

---

[1] Diana, who saw herself as frail and vulnerable and a prey to constant anxieties both real and
imaginary, must have protested against Waugh's description of her as a ruthless, accomplished and
dauntless go-getter. Waugh's reply refers to her description, in *The Light of Common Day*, of how she
persuaded Duff to worm his way up to the exit so that they should get out ahead of all the other
Viscounts after the Coronation. 'It was a moment after my own heart,' she wrote.

[2] Clarence Hatry, after his release from prison for fraud, was set up as a bookseller in 1938 by Sir
Thomas Moore MP who purchased Hatchards, then reputedly in a filthy state. But at the time of
Diana's signing session, Hatchards belonged to William Collins, the publishers.

Evelyn to Diana

Combe Florey   *25 June 1959*

Darling Pug

Listen. Will you do something very kind? My artichokes won't bear decent heads – fine foliage and then wretched little nobs of spikes. Everything has been tried. Can't be the weather this year. We have decided they must be botanically wrong. Will you go to Vilmorin and get me some seeds of the big frog kind? You will have to smuggle them as there is some law against importing plants. Bring them when you come back 29th?

Katharine has been ill again – 'flu' – still laid up.

My younger peacock committed suicide last Friday to my great grief. No one else minds least of all his father and mother.

I say, Baby's buggers didn't rally round much at Hatchard's, did they?[1]

Hoops of steel

                                                 Bo

Evelyn to Diana

Combe Florey   *30 June 1959*

Dearest Pug

We grow the Jerusalem artichoke successfully. It is only the genuine plant that worries us. Is it *Gryll Grange* that has the dissertation on Zion soup?

Can't understand Baby's movements at all. Last word I had was a card saying 'Here I am in London. Returning Chantilly Friday to pack'. Now another card posted S.W.1. saying an answer required to 1st P.C. But that P.C. was about previous visit to London. Head is in a whirl. Don't know where to write or what to say. I am having my hair cut tomorrow in London, after that shan't be there at all. Am hoping you will come and visit me <u>anytime</u> any length. But don't let on to Auberon Herbert. I have greatest difficulty keeping him from the door as it is.

What are your winter plans? Must leave England Jan.

Randolph's book on Jerk contemptible.[2]

---

[1] But Waugh did in his inimitable way. Rupert Hart-Davis wrote to George Lyttelton on 29 May: 'Yesterday Diana Cooper signed copies of her book at Hatchards, and five hundred copies were sold! Apparently Evelyn Waugh escorted her there, extremely tipsy, and bullied everyone who came into the shop to buy a copy and get it signed.'

[2] *The Rise and Fall of Anthony Eden* (1959).

Read life of fascinating Edward Johnston by his daughter.[1]
Invitation to visit of course includes jewelry.

All love
Bo

Turning the problem over and over have decided to send this to Lady Hulton's. Mad?

Evelyn to Diana

Combe Florey   *[pstmk 30 July 1959]*
[postcard]

Thanks for pretty P.C. Sorry you didn't visit me. Cool and ascetic here but warm and rich with love. Have pulled down porch revealing doorway that reminds me of Genoa. Have written description of Mrs Stitch collecting gruesome coat in station there, in book of ineffable tedium and triviality.[2] Hope jewels' little jewel proves male and (more important) Christian.

Diana to Evelyn

5 Belgrave Square   *[October 1959]*

Darling Bo. Thank you for the book [*Ronald Knox*] – I take it with me to France and shall read it slowly in bed and doubtless admire you and Ronnie more than ever. I'm flattered to have so limited a copy – any hope of you in France for a beano of rest? What are your winter plans – can I share them in part? I'm told you are India bound – you might have a few days in Rome en route. I leave for Chantilly the damned tonight on ferry – to put my poor once snub nose on the grindstone and write the story of my finished life – a tale of tideum if ever there was one. The election[3] I've enjoyed thanks to ten days of total abstinence and feeling WELL – yes, chipper even.

Do write – the smart establishment cheered when they heard Mark B[onham] Carter was defeated. Ugly of them.[4]

I love you

Baby

[1] Edward Johnston, the calligrapher, typographer and illuminator, who designed London Transport's sans-serif typeface.

[2] Presumably a scene written for but never used in *Unconditional Surrender* (called *The End of the Battle* in the USA) published in 1961.

[3] The Conservative Party under Harold Macmillan won the general election.

[4] Mark Bonham-Carter (b. 1922), a grandson of the Prime Minister H. H. Asquith and a nephew of Katharine's husband Raymond Asquith, had won Torrington, North Devon, for the Liberals in a by-election the previous year. This was the first sign of a Liberal revival since the war, but their victory was short-lived. The general election of 1959 was a triumph for Harold Macmillan and the Tories, and Mark Bonham-Carter lost his seat.

Evelyn to Diana

[comic postcard]   *[October 1959]*

Lovely to hear from you. You are never out of my thoughts. I long for the third volume of *Opera*. No news of me is good news. I plod away at a pot-boiler about Africa. Family all well. Page 78 of *Knox* is slow-going. I hope this means you are having plenty of sleep. I hope all your buggers are well. No plans made yet for Feb. Will you be bugger-free then, and where? India? No drink but fine buildings and likely soon to be inaccessible. Shall we go while going is good.

Bo

Diana to Evelyn

Château de St Firmin   *6 November 1959*

Delighted to hear that I've not quarrelled with you – I shall be in London for one night 12 November because of a 'do' to do with Rex Whistler and my murals (that's a vile word) given at the Dorchester Pent-house at 6 that day.[1] If you were in London do come or better we could perhaps have a meal with Annie who I've warned of my arrival. p75 was alright because Papist Norah had first 'couldn't put it down' – ½ way now and still I'm engrossed – he's poped.[2]

What a really filthy post-card [of the seaside variety] no wonder you enveloped it. Fie!

Re India – the Peninsula's enormous – can you give me precisions – air or sea or Puff Puff. Could I get back by Persia – meet my jewels there in March? I'd wait for you in Rome – Christmas in bugger-ridden Bulbridge [the house of Juliet Duff] – but should be B[ugger] free immediately after.

Love to the 2 children I love, and Laura. Auberon [Herbert] was here for a night – Fatted danger – 16 stone – he must untrench.

O X O

B

---

[1] The Rex Whistler decorations done for Duff and Diana's house in Gower Street were exhibited when the Dorchester penthouse, designed by Oliver Messel, was opened. They were given to London University.

[2] Although Ronald Knox designated Christmas Day 1903 (p. 69) as the day he accepted Catholicism, he did not become officially 'poped' until 1917 (Evelyn Waugh, *Life of Ronald Knox*, p. 158).

273

Evelyn to Diana

Combe Florey   *[pstmk 8 November 1959]*

[newspaper clipping pasted on card:]

CHINESE MARRIAGE DECLARED
VALID
WOU V. WOU (WOU OTHERWISE
COLLINGWOOD INTERVENING)
WOU (OTHERWISE COLLING-
WOOD) V. WOU

Love from Collingwood

Diana to Evelyn

Bulbridge House   *25 December 1959*
Wilton
Salisbury

Darling Bo. I've had a good laugh at *Kaplan*[1] – but I'm 'taking it schlow' as Raimund says. You are very good to me as Faithful was to Christian. I should like to have travelled with you thro' a winter of discontent. Despairing I settled for America in gratitude to those who made me out a redeeming plan ('she can't go on like that'). This morning after talking to a jewell I have burnt the Q Elizabeth and have chosen Assuan as my rendezvous with Change.

Jewells and I will look our last on doomed temples and drift down old Nile in what I thought till adulcy was a diarrhoea (public I presume) – I shall leave about the 20th. Jan pause in Rome (you with me?) and then take my familiar Adriatica boat to Alex from Naples . . .

Darling Evelyn – I love you as always – Laura too Meg and Hatty Love to them all

Diana
Pug
B

---

[1] *The Return of Hyman Kaplan* by 'Leonard Q. Ross' (Leo Calvin Rosten), 1959.

PART IV

1960–66

IN THE MONTHS AFTER DUFF'S DEATH, DIANA HAD DREADED *going back to Chantilly. Yet when the Institut de France announced that their plans for Château de St Firmin no longer included having her as a tenant, she could hardly bear to leave.*

However sad she was at packing up the house where she and Duff had spent their last years together, she looked forward to moving back to London. John Julius had found a large house in Paddington, looking on to the Regent's Canal. Many old friends lived in the neighbourhood, which was called Little Venice; and Diana took a long lease on 10 Warwick Avenue, a terraced house overlooking the Paddington Basin. Moving from a large country house in France to a small town house took a long time, and she did not settle into her new home until March 1961.

Once installed, however, Diana looked at life with fresh eyes. She took a renewed delight in her grandchildren, and a series of lunch parties drew a whole new set of friends into her orbit.

Both Diana and Waugh hoped to see more of each other now that she was back in England – but the opportunity seldom arose, since each wanted the other to do the travelling.

Waugh came up to London less and less. In the early 1960s he produced three books – Unconditional Surrender, Basil Seal Rides Again *and the first volume of his autobiography,* A Little Learning. *As his sixtieth birthday approached, he tried to do something about his health and his appearance by taking a cure at the Forest Mere Hydro – 'I shall then have less difficulty in making and changing my soul before appearing at the Judgement Seat,' he confided to Christopher Sykes. But he was soon drinking as heavily as ever, and seldom went out of doors.*

In the winter of 1964 and 1965, he had his teeth removed – and refused to take any anaesthetic. This painful operation did little to improve his health, or his appetite; on the occasions that Christopher Sykes saw him in 1965, Waugh hardly ate or drank at all.

Evelyn to Diana

[postcard]   *[March 1960]*

No, alas, I shall not be in London next week. Don't like the place. Wish you would come here. I had a fine spree at the expense of the *Daily Mail*. Met Esmond [Rothermere] and Boofy[1] living very plain in Monte Carlo. I was living pretty high. E. said: 'What are you doing here?' I said: 'Spending your money'. Boofy v. shocked. Now I have to write dreary articles to pay for it. I wrote a treatise on the history and architecture of Rome and they cut it down to a paragraph about a cinema film. I love Miss Judy. Meg met her first real drunk in Athens and liked him. Bad sign. Was Nile O.K.? I despise Egypt.

Evelyn to Diana

Combe Florey   *[early April 1960]*

Darling Pug

Thanks awfully for giving me the right note for condolence. Will you be very kind and address this to Susan Mary.[2] I don't know where she is.

How rum of you to go to London for Frog week [state visit of General de Gaulle]. Please explain why Mr Lehmann dined with you and the Queen.[3]

What a lot of deaths lately – Cynthia,[4] Christopher Holland-Martin.[5] Gaston told me Momo[6] was dying.

Meg looks like a toad. She has failed to get into Oxford so I am setting her to work with the Jesuits in Mount Street. She is to help canonize Campion.

---

[1] 8th Earl of Arran (1910–84). Broadcaster and journalist. Described as 'a poor man's Duke of Bedford and a rich man's Godfrey Winn', he played a prominent part in the campaign to reform the laws against homosexuality and introduced the Badger Protection Bill. He had a very charming pet badger called Rosie.

[2] Bill Patten died on 26 March, having suffered from chronic asthma and emphysema for many years.

[3] John Lehmann (1907–87), editor and publisher with strong leanings towards France, brother of the novelist Rosamond Lehmann. President of the Alliance Française in Britain 1955–63. The climax of the state banquet on 5 April was *Glace de Gaulle* made in the shape of a huge cross of Lorraine.

[4] Lady Cynthia Asquith (1887–1960), daughter of 11th Earl of Wemyss, sister of Diana's brother-in-law Ego Charteris killed in the First World War. In 1910 married the Hon. Herbert Asquith, son of the Prime Minister. Writer of fiction and books for children. Lord David Cecil, in an addendum on 5 April to a *Times* obituary, described her as 'a pre-Raphaelite princess'.

[5] Christopher Holland-Martin (1910–60), Conservative MP for Ludlow, married Lady Anne Cavendish, daughter of 9th Duke of Devonshire and sister of Lady Dorothy Macmillan, wife of the Prime Minister.

[6] Momo (Maud) Marriott, heiress of the financier Otto Kahn, an influential hostess in wartime Cairo, and wife of Major General Sir John Marriott, an authority on big game. She died in October, after a very painful illness.

277

I hope you didn't see my articles in the *Daily Mail*. They were pretty bad as I wrote them. As the editor cut and titled them they were pitiable. It is the hell of the popular press. They pay exactly 20 times as much as respectable papers but they always make a booby of one. Mustn't quarrel with bread and butter though not at my age.

My poor son Auberon lives in a lethargy. So do I most of the time. Holy Week at Downside, Easter at Mells.

Magdalen [Eldon] declares she is dying.

I have a ripping photograph from Genoa Campo Santo to illustrate Pot-boiler [*A Tourist in Africa*].

All love
Bo

Evelyn to Diana

Combe Florey   *14 July 1960*

Darling Stitch,

What a Will o the Whisp you have become?

I long to see you but it won't be in London for I don't live there. I live here, remember?

A good train leaves Paddington at 9.30; also at 3.30 and 5.30. Take any of these and I will be on Taunton platform with open arms. I am nowhere near the Stratford Theatre. The only entertainment I can offer is wine and my own company. Margaret alas lives in London canonizing 40 martyrs.

Everyone assures me you have moved to the vieux port of Paddington. Clearly not true.

Look at tomorrow's *Spectator* and read about Genoa.

All love
Bo

Diana to Evelyn

Cleeve Lodge   *[July 1960]*
42 Hyde Park Gate
[the house of Sir Edward and Lady Hulton]

Darling Bo (not peep) I was saddened by your letter. You ask a lot of the old – and to make your lack-love more wounding Annie tells me you come once a week – Fridays I think – to London. I should like to have gone to the pictures (stills or moving) or a matinée with a tray of tea between us, or even born for your sweet sake the Hyde Park Hotel. But no I must fettle my fine joints and go to the mountain – and I can't, not this time. It was easier to go to Genoa.

I am leaving on Sunday for Salzburg out of loyalty to most faithful Raimund who has pressed everyone from the Prime Minister downward to be present at the inauguration of the new Festspielhaus and no one will yield but me (bang goes 50 quid). On my return July 30th I go straight to my retreat at Send there to fast and pray, and pray too for the reumaticks to be exorsized from my fine joints – this will last 14 days when I take wing or wheel to the isle of Greece called Spetzie [*sic*] where Michael and Anne Tree have a house.

I'll come back via Italy or Corsica and perhaps at long last find you in mid-Sept before settling down to my last six months in Chantilly. You and Meg would be welcomed for autumn picnics or expeditions to archiological or litterary pilgrimages.

I was so glad good Stitch still lives. Keep clear of vol 3 of Baby's Life and Letters[1] – it stinks. I'll always love you –

B

Evelyn to Diana

Combe Florey   *[July/August 1960]*
[on Ethiopian writing paper]

Darling Stitch

There is no truth whatever in Mrs Fleming's statement that I come regularly to London on Fridays or any other day. I went once to submit to a television interview.[2] The distance from Combe Florey to Hyde Park Gate is precisely the same as that from Hyde Park Gate to Combe Florey. You are much more spry than I am. I never leave home. You flit anywhere except here.

Do you remember this writing-paper? I had it made for the war of 1935 by the job printer in Addis Ababa. Jolly pretty, wasn't it?

It is sad we don't meet. I am always on tap here and always loving. My idea of a meeting is some days together in converse – not a shared half hour at the Picassos. I abominate London and parties.

I hope you have a lovely time in Salzburg without too many Americans. It's a bad time for them everywhere but here.

Your idea of friendship is to do things together; mine simply to be together.

I am writing the description of a funeral. Very rusty on points of etiquette.

---

[1] *Trumpets from the Steep*, her third and final volume of autobiography.
[2] On 26 June 1960, Waugh was interviewed on the programme *Face to Face* by John Freeman (who later served as British Ambassador in Washington 1969–71). Freeman's final question was why, given Waugh's strong views on the right of privacy, he had consented to be interviewed. Waugh smiled and said, 'For the same reason that you do. I need the money.'

It looks as though we shall be at war in September. Come and take refuge here from the bombs.[1]

All love
Bo

Evelyn to Diana

Combe Florey   [pstmk 25 September 1960]
[postcard]

What do you mean 'Vol III Pug stinks'? Have just read extract in *Sunday Times*. Always hate 'extracts', but this is jolly good.

Hoops of steel hold fast.

Bo

Diana to Evelyn

Château de St Firmin   [September/October 1960]

My beloved Bo. Thank you for sending me your book [*A Tourist in Africa*] – you will receive mine bearing the silliest possible tittle. Rupert [Hart-Davis]'s insistence most unsuited to the cover picture all backgrounded by an embarrassing shade of the fashionable African Violet. I wanted 'Noisy Years' but he wouldn't hear of it, and he's cut out (perforce the cutting) all my favourite bits.

I miss you very very much but within a year I'll be in Little Venice next door to John Julius and Kitty Giles and Ld Birdwood[2] and Ld Kinross and Kitty Farrell[3] and June [Osborn] and Lennox Berkeley[4] – and there will be a spare room and bath for you, but I imagine you'll always prefer deft service in greater hotels. I'm coming October 25th and will not give up hope of seeing you.

love
Pug

Haven't opened the book – yours – shan't till I get a char.

[1] On 10 July, Khrushchev threatened to use rockets against the United States if she intervened in Cuba.

[2] Christopher, 2nd Baron Birdwood (1899–1962).

[3] Lady Katherine Farrell (b. 1922), Diana's niece, daughter of the 6th Marquess of Anglesey. She married first, Lt. Col. Jocelyn Gurney; and second, Charles Farrell.

[4] Lennox Berkeley (1903–89), composer. He was knighted in 1974.

Evelyn to Diana

Combe Florey   *6 October 1960*

Darling Stitch

Trumpets arrived from the steep 'with the author's compliments'.
Thanks no end for the comps. Same to you with nobs on. This morning a
letter from you, for which more thanks.

Trumpets is absolutely ripping. Dismiss all doubts. I agree with you
that the title is not very apt but that won't matter at all. All that your
readers ask is more and you have given them more than dared hope for.
The first volume was delicious, but others have written charmingly of
childhood; the second volume was cram full of extraneous delights, but
there was less of you in it. Vol III is all you and therefore entirely
entrancing. Taken together the three books are a single work of art, one
of the great autobiographies of the century. I am sorry you let Hart-Davis
overrule you into curtailing it. The artist is the sole judge of his own
scope. If he was shy of expense he should have cut the press-photographs
of politicians. I should have liked a full 100 pages more about the
Embassy, particularly an analysis of the sinister rites of the cult of Palfi. I
should have liked your mermaid journey from the north. More of your
adventures scrounging rations from your successors. But it's churlish to
complain. The whole book is so rich and idiosyncratic and the golden
voice from Mells [Conrad Russell's] insinuated with such exquisite
precision. The last chapter is not sob stuff – real classic grief, and the last
aspiration a joy to all who love you. Faith doesn't just arrive on the
breakfast tray like a Valentine, you know. It has to be sought bare foot.

I barely knew Rex Whistler. How I love him for asking 'What has
victory to do with it?' It was the question one longed to hear asked in the
last years of the war and not hearing it made me morose. It is the theme of
my own little trilogy.

No umbrage taken by your beastly references to me. What you (and, a
fortiori, Randolph) never understood was that very junior officers do not
shout down their superiors at table and that no soldier of any rank talks to
journalists. Your guests were all either generals, journalists or communist
agents.

I plan a tour of India (avoiding the royal progress) in January. Coming
too? So much to be seen before the Chinks move in.

Don't, please, attempt to read my African pot-boiler.

You need no puff from me but I've sent one to Hart-Davis in case his
commercial travellers like to have something to show booksellers who
idiotically always maintain that sequels never succeed.

You will be nice and near Paddington station. We can meet at the Great
Western Hotel where Bloggs always stays.

All the trumpets will be sound for you on this side.

                                                                    Bo

Evelyn to Diana

Combe Florey   *24 December 1960*

Darling Pug

It was nice of you to think of your faithful old friend amid all your worries of moving house. You are never long from my mind and never for a moment from my heart. I sometimes hear strange travellers tales such as that your butler has been assassinated by Algerian terrorists and that you have given your literary prize to an octogenarian clergyman.[1]

I have been indoors all the summer writing the final volume of war novels. Nothing to tempt me into the rain. As soon as the book is finished I shall make tracks for foreign parts – but where? The Queen is opening up India as a tourist resort and everywhere else is being shut down by politicians.

My daughter Teresa is to marry a studious, penniless American.[2] My son, Bron, has had an undeserved but gratifying success with a novel [*The Foxglove Saga*] and is a dandy with rooms in Clarges Street and a thousand cards of invitation and is enjoying himself top hole. Margaret is my darling still – much prettier again after a time of looking like a toad. Laura has at last had to give up her herd of cows and mourns them. They cost as much to keep as a troupe of ballet girls and the horrible politicians made a law that one can no longer charge them against income tax.

Do you see the English papers and did you see all the excitement of Dr Fisher of Canterbury calling on the Pope? Archbishop Roberts (Catholic) had an audience a few days later and the Pope said: 'There was another English Archbishop here the other day. Who was he?'

Mrs Fleming's health gives cause for alarm.

All love
Bo

Diana to Evelyn

Paris   *[pstmk 4 January 1961]*
[postcard]

[Rubber stamp reads INSUFFICIENTLY PAID. 1d. TO PAY]

I love you and miss you.
Please tell me what [you] think about Graham Greene's book.[3]

---

[1] The Duff Cooper Memorial Prize was awarded to the Revd Canon Andrew Young (1885–1971) for his *Collected Poems*.
[2] John D'Arms (b. 1934), whom Teresa met at Oxford. Later Professor of Classics at the University of Michigan, then in 1977 Director of the American School of Archaeology in Rome.
[3] *A Visit to Morin*, privately printed in 1959.

Is Morin himself? Come before Epiphany and see the crêche I made with my hands and invention. It's a gem –

love H.N.Y[1]

Baby

Diana to Evelyn

Château de St Firmin   *[January 1961]*

Darling Wu – I've lost your last book after reading only so far as I ran – when I say lost, it's clearly been pinched by my rough-shod hairy-heeled guests – but now when the awful change begins I shall perhaps find it while buffetting the books – if I don't I'll send you one to re-dedicate. I must have my Waugh total.

Your reference to Mrs Fleming's health worried me a lot so when I got to London the other day I got on to Mrs Crickmere (cook) a regular Cassandra – who said in her days of Annie's illnesses 'I think she's going' – she was full of good auguries. 'You know what she is – my lady – overdoes it and has to pay for it. She's in Switzerland and going off to Jamaica, she's alright.' Then I got a letter from Pontresina whining and wailing at the snow and tedium of hotel life but chippo as a bird and not mentioning health. I love her so much, and your grave line froze my old blood.

S. Mary is to marry Joe Alsop[2] – a splendid solution to fatherless children – a lonely rich man thirsty for love which he has always felt was not owed to any monster – and he was one – an 18 stone one – and can never believe that he is now as all men. She will be very happy . . .

I'll miss her. Our 'bande' in Paris is broken up . . . God knows I need help. How can I cope with the 'Fisk' (or is it fisque?) and the Percepteur and all these fearful technicalities and obstructions in a change of residence. If I had more space I should be calmer – in Little Venice there's not room for any spare parts or jokes or books laces or furs. Still I'll see more of you perhaps, and the Telly's a companion to me.

God bless you – give my felicitations to Teresa and my hopes that she'll love her American till death – and love to Laura and my dear girls.

Pug

---

[1] Happy New Year.
[2] Joseph Wright Alsop Jr. (1910–89), the American political writer and columnist.

Evelyn to Diana

Combe Florey   *21 January 1961*

Darling Pug

It was exhilarating to get a letter from you after how many years of post-cards. Of course I will proudly give you another Pot-Boiler to replace stolen copy, but I imagine you don't want to accumulate any more possessions in France. I will bring it to the Red Light District when you are settled there.

I heard rumours of Susan Mary's engagement. Was there not an American journalist named Alsop whom Miss Judy pursued hotly. Is it the same? I heard of the engagement because a reporter rang up, of all people, little Meg to ask what S.M. was like. Meg drawing on childhood memories said her main interest was acting charades.

The death of Mrs Fleming seems to have been postponed. She dined with me and ate voraciously, drank moderately and talked lucidly.

You may well ask, what about Graham Greene's Christmas story? Is he Morin? He has now produced a novel[1] with a precisely similar character – distinguished Papist who has lost his Faith and is disgusted with those who still look to him as a leader. I have had a sharp little Claudel-Gide correspondence with him which ended by my saying 'Mud in your mild and magnificent eye'. His alienist Dr Strauss kicked the bucket last week.[2] No one to keep an eye on him now.

I long for India but am chained to my desk till I have finished novel.

All love
Wu

Evelyn to Diana

Combe Florey   *15 March 1961*

Darling Mrs Stitch

How I envy you in Rome. I am stuck at my desk finishing a sad novel [*Unconditional Surrender*] which if I once put down I know I shan't have the strength to pick up. And for that same drab reason I can't come to Chantilly on 20th as you so kindly suggest. I would go anywhere to see you if I were free. I am much surprised to hear of you still in Chantilly. Supposed you were in passage to Paddington. When do you reach London? Perhaps it is not an occasion for house warming presents – you must be disposing of mountains of beautiful furniture.

Is Artemis really turning into a Meg? I am so glad. Keep her soberer than I have kept Meg. She shows signs of becoming dypso.

My danger is to become like Belloc bewailing overwork and poverty.

[1] *A Burnt-Out Case* (1961).
[2] Eric Benjamin Strauss (1894–1961), psychiatrist, author of *Sexual Disorders in the Male* (1949).

My love to Miss Judy if she is with you. And to Mrs Fleming. Thunderbird shows great good taste in not naming his 'publications' in *Who's Who*.

We have no servants. It is a great pleasure to be able to throw away all the presents they gave us. I have given up eating so I suffer no inconvenience.

Don't read beyond Genoa in Pot Boiler.

What do you mean 'lost to' you? I'm always here as stable as Gibraltar and always full of love.

Evelyn to Diana

[Combe Florey]   *[?May 1961]*

[Written on back of invitation to a party at Quaglino's to celebrate Teresa Waugh's forthcoming marriage to Mr John D'Arms on Thursday, 1 June. The ceremony took place on 3 June in Taunton. Evelyn had envisaged a double wedding with his son Auberon's marriage to Lady Teresa Onslow, daughter of the 6th Earl of Onslow, but she refused to become a Catholic.]

Darling Pug,

This will be a gruesome party. Don't dream of coming or sending a present or of paying any attention except to me whom you haven't written to and who don't know where you are living. I send this card just to show what is going on. The boredom and expense of two weddings in a month is breaking my great spirit.

Where are you? I was in London for the day and asked and no one knew. Someone said all the radiators had been stolen from your house and your cook killed by *plastiqueurs*. True?

I had supper with Raimund. He seemed deeply sad.

Little Meg is O.K. Just. I have finished a good novel, also a dissertation on Sloth and am now writing a panegyric of P. G. Wodehouse for the 20th anniversary of Duff's attack on him. Peahen is sitting. No servants. No cows. No money. Would you consider Salt Lake City in August?

All love
Bo

Diana to Evelyn

2A Nugent Terrace   *[?May 1961]*

Darling Bo – what a joy to hear of you – I have eaten no bite or sip for 5 days to try and raise morale which has only once been lower – so it made the card more satisfying.

I shall certainly be there June 1st in order to see you – and would there be any other meeting possible? With Annie or alone or with June Osborn – I live in her garden studio in utter dejection – by the waters of Babylon is where I sit in spirit. No heart for the new house which for a nutshell has infinite space – the workmanship makes me mad with rage – my goods and chattels are lost – I assume they were packed in Pantechnicons 4 weeks ago, and there's no sign of their arrival. I am lost in Limbo like them. The radiators went six weeks ago – once the paraphanalia comes I shall certainly give both your children a wedding present. How old is Meg? Would you like to bring her to what should be a very <u>pretty</u> ball at Zion [Syon Park] – given by a great friend of mine called Miki Seckers[1] – patron of arts and silk weaver – a Medici – 19th June.

Salt Lake City in August? I've been there – it's like a free mason picture of a hilly desert with a cyclops eye – arid and baked – not attractive in summer's heat – but anywhere you say.

Diana – Pug Baby

Evelyn to Diana

Darling Pug,

Your presence on June 1st would add great lustre to the celebrations. It would be agony for you. I have ordered a military band to make conversation impossible. They are to play very loudly in a small room. If you are really brave enough to come do bring Mrs June too.

It is very kind of you to ask me to Mr Secker's pretty ball. Not for me. I have no doubt little Meg would like it if someone were to ask her to dinner first and take her there in a motor. Or does 'pretty' mean fancy dress? She can't afford that poor child on her £10 a week from the Jesuits.

I come to London on 31st for two nights. Believe it or not I dine at the Mansion House on 31st but shall be free all the afternoon and all the next day until dinner time. Holman Hunt's *Lady of Shallott* is at Christie's. I want to go and see it though I fear it will make much more than the few hundred I have to spare. 25 years ago it would have gone for nothing. I've never seen it but it looks lovely in the books.

Has Mrs June still got a nigger-sculptor in her studio? He should be nice company.

Now how are you fixed for 31st, 1st and come to think of it the

---

[1] Nicholas ('Miki') Sekers (1910–72), textile magnate of Hungarian origin, on the board of several orchestras, knighted in 1965.

morning of 2nd? I am all yours. You will find me in a highly nervous condition half destroyed by this wedding.

Laura sends her love. Me too

Bo

I hear Mrs June has had her warts removed by a trumpeter. She tried him out on my former neighbour Col. Donaldson[1] who is now pretty enough for Seckers pavilion.

Evelyn to Diana

Combe Florey   *9 June 1961*

Darling Pug

Are you irrevocably committed to letting your lower parts to [Alastair] Forbes? If not would you consider me as a tenant? I am anxious to find rooms in London which my daughters Meg and Hatty could share this autumn, where a trusted friend could keep an eye on them. They could, when required, do devoted duty as ladies in waiting.

Any hope?

Bo

Diana to Evelyn

2A Nugent Terrace   *15 June 1961*

Darling Bo – It's a delightful suggestion – but I don't yet see light in 10 Warwick Avenue.

I do not see myself getting into the house this side of the holidays – and even when I am 'in' the room that would suit them will be still stacked with cases containing the library – which I cannot unpack until by order in the rest of the house I can have space and more shelves for the operation.

You don't give me enough detail – when you do want them to come and for what term – not terms because of course they'd be my guests so as to get more slavery out of them. I have to leave middle of July or 22nd – and I shall not come back till middle or beginning of Sept. I should leave a servant if I can get one – as they cannot be alone in the house. She would cook and clean and they could keep their own accounts. They could have the run of the drawing room (huge) as I never leave my bedroom except for when people come.

---

[1] John George Stuart Donaldson (b. 1907), husband of the writer Frances Donaldson. He became 1st Baron Donaldson of Kingsbridge in 1967 and was Minister for the Arts in the Labour Government of 1976–9.

Can they sleep in one room – Ali's room where the unpacked books are – is untenable: I have the spare room on the first floor but it's small for two. They'd have to go upstairs to their baths – I fear they'd be too uncomfortable without Ali's room in commission – it has its own bath. Don't let's forsake the idea – if now it looks a little foggy – but give me please more detail of time – as rent you might install a tellyphone in the garden room.

I'm stuck in the bog of the canal.

love
Pug

Evelyn to Diana

Combe Florey   *22 June 1961*

Darling Pug

Your letter was here when I got home. Thank you very much for considering my suggestion. Here are the essential data about the little girls.

Harriet. Aged 17. Low mentality, high character. She has inherited her father's deep love of you. She regards you as a lady of the theatre rather than of fashion or letters or high politics. She is pretty when she smiles which is often; sometimes she lapses into blank sullenness. She has no pleasure in rural life and no knowledge of the town. Strong theatrical interests. Strong sense of humour. Chaste, sober, wants to get married but has exaggerated ideas of her market value thinking only elder sons of old nobility suitable. Clean and economical. She leaves school this term without learning one word of any foreign language and is therefore unsuitable for finishing abroad. She goes with a school-friend whose father is on post there at our embassy, to Beirut for August and first three weeks of September. After that she will be a problem. I believe you might find her quite amusing and useful as understrapper. Can't spell at all. No secretarial qualities.

Meg aged 19 'works' all day with Jesuits at Farm Street. Drinks all night with impecunious young men. Expensive tastes. Snob. Chaste but self-indulgent. Smokes when I am not near. Loving but grasping. Has also inherited her father's love of you. Filthy in habits. Always in debt. At present she lives with her cousin Anne Fraser (60 Drayton Gardens, S.W.10. Freemantle 9000) who now has two babies and wants to be rid of her. I will not let her live alone. She can't find any suitable friend to share with. It would be no good setting her up with Hatty. She would not look after Hatty and Hatty would have nothing to do all day. Meg would enter with enthusiasm into all your undertakings of house arrangement, talk engagingly while others toiled and do nothing herself. I find her company so bright that it compensates for her deplorable failings.

Anne Fraser does not threaten immediate eviction but would be glad to get her out by end of September.

I wish you wouldn't hide behind smoked glasses. I have given up using ear trumpet in your presence.

All love
Bo

Evelyn to Diana

Combe Florey   *[early July 1961]*
[on Ethiopian writing paper]

Darling Pug

Do you remember this writing paper on which I used to write to you when you stitched me up as a war-correspondent in 1936.

What has become of you? What is going to become of you? What is the future of my two daughters?

I came to London for the day for my son's wedding.[1] The heat was stupifying. I met pauper Kinross who told me you had moved into your mansion. Next day there was a photograph of me taken at that wedding, which was a ghastly shock. Since then I have eaten and drunk nothing and look like Dr Maugham. I should like you to see me before I put it all on again. Any chance of beguiling you here? If not, do write a long letter to faithful old

Bo

Diana to Evelyn

10 Warwick Avenue   *[October 1961]*

Dear Darling Bo. Thank you with a full heart for sending me your book.[2] I swallowed it all down in one curious gulp at St John & St Elizabeth's. I went in (no nuns left, just nice common hoydens – 42 guineas a week and a towel kept in the basin) to have most of my back teeth out – how can I have become so senily unattractive? All I read the night before I revelled in – the computer – R. Victorian institute – the old caste – but next afternoon and evening still gulping avidly I finished it, and not a wrack [?] remains in my memory so I'm off again, clear of numbing drugs.

I know if it keeps up to the beginning high order it will be hilarious and moving.

---

[1] Auberon Waugh married Lady Teresa Onslow on 1 July 1961.
[2] *Unconditional Surrender*, the final volume of his war trilogy.

Thank you again. Please don't visit White's without telling me – I'm jealous of Annie who seems to get more petits soins not to say love – I'm more reliable tho'.

Kisses hugs and more

Pug

House gone <u>back</u> – drawing [room] once all but finished now has carpet up again.

Evelyn to Diana

Combe Florey   *30 March 1962*

Sweet Pug

Your letters are not as frequent, full and fond as those which Conrad sent you. Nevertheless I thank you for your picture postcard and rejoice that you are home. Swapping yarns is best done in writing. Who knows who might interrupt us in Paddington – Forbes, the widow Hemingway [Martha Gellhorn], A. Herbert or worse. I went to London last week and did not enjoy it at all. I was sitting in my club at 7 p.m. 'doing no harm to anyone' when I was accosted by a man known to me by sight but not by name, older than me, better dressed, far more common, who said: 'Why are you alone?' 'Because no one wishes to speak to me, I suppose'. 'And I can tell you exactly why. It's because you sit there on your arse looking like a stuck pig'. Hard words. Another thing. In Trinidad I was asked to stay by a man I used to know very slightly called Patrick Buchan-Hepburn, now a lord,[1] and I was convinced that I delighted him and his wife. A letter from Clarissa to Mrs Fleming says: 'the Haileses (P.B.H) found Evelyn a great bore'. Well, I mean to say. Then Debo tells Nancy that I am her 'enemy'. You see there is a conspiracy and I daren't show my face.

Another thing: I went to B. Guiana at the *Daily Mail*'s (generous) expense to write travel articles. I came back to find that the editor had changed. New one said: Why do you want to write about Guiana? Well I had made myself a great nuisance to everyone there and said I was a foreign correspondent and been given private aeroplanes etc. to get about and had interviews with politicians of all colours. Now *Daily Mail* says: 'write us instead some hard-hitting articles about modern social usage'. What does a man of honour do? Repay £2,000 already spent (tax free)? The truth is never never to have any truck with popular press. Too late to learn. I am caught every time. Damn. So you see my pecker is down too. Sorry about your pecker all the same.

---

[1] The Rt. Hon. Patrick Buchan-Hepburn (1901–74), former Conservative Chief Whip, created 1st Baron Hailes in 1957. Governor-General and Commander-in-Chief of the West Indies 1958–62.

Well, little Meg proved a good travelling companion, never sea sick in the smallest ships in the worst storms, never complaining of discomfort but jolly appreciative of occasional bits of luxury. We came back in a lovely frog steamer full of decaying literary gents. Now her pecker is down and she wants to circumnavigate the globe.

Poor little (fat) Hatty comes out soon. Mary [Herbert] is giving a ball for her at Pixton. Telephone never stops. This ball is June 23rd. I must leave the country for it. Where shall we go?

Lady Norwich wrote to congratulate me on an essay on Sloth.[1] Pulling my leg? I met someone really called Jewel on the ship home – Lady Sebag-Montefiore-Magnus-Allcroft.[2] Meg taught her canasta.

I shall be at Downside (next door to Mells) for triduum of Maundy Thursday–Easter. The new liturgy leaves endless blank periods, particularly Holy Saturday. Why don't you go to Katharine then? You know she has let the Manor? Providential.

All love and xxxxx
Bo

Evelyn to Diana

Downside Abbey　　　　　　　　　　　*Good Friday [20 April] 1962*
as from Combe Florey

Dearest Pug,

A very happy Easter to you in your new house or wherever you are. You are constantly in my prayers here where, as usual, I am spending the triduum. It gets lovelier every year – fewer friends. Once Simon Elwes used to make a house-party of it. Now I am alone with the new, impoverished liturgy. I see Katharine and Per [Hylton] in the distance. No chums in the monastery.

Can give you good luncheon and dinner at the St James' Club – open to Ladies on Sundays. Please send P.C. to Combe Florey saying Yes or No.

All love
Bo

---

[1] Waugh had contributed this essay to the *Sunday Times* as one of a series, by different contributors, on the Seven Deadly Sins.

[2] Jewel Magnus-Allcroft. In 1943 she married Sir Philip Montefiore Magnus, 2nd Bt., the historian, who added her name of Allcroft to his own in 1951. Sir Philip was a great-grandson of Sir Joseph Sebag-Montefiore.

Evelyn to Diana

Combe Florey   *[pstmk ?25 April 1962]*
[postcard]

Of course don't alter plans for Sunday. I am fully occupied Monday but
free all day until evening Thursday, ditto Wednesday. I greatly want to
visit your new palace but can I be sure I shan't see the Widow Hemingway
there? Saw K on Sat. She said you did not write full, fond, frequent letters
to her either. Meg is a heavy drinker. Not so Hatty. Bad brandy is Meg's
favourite tipple – 'Stock' if procurable. If not put off I will call at Warwick
Avenue at 11 on Tuesday hoping for many hours with you. Keep
Auberon out.

Evelyn to Diana

Combe Florey   *16 August [?1962]*

Darling Lady Ismay,[1]
    You are in Venice and I don't know where. I hope someone will
forward this letter for it is the announcement of our Meg's engagement.
She has fallen head over heels for an Irishman, 27 years old, short, rather
oriental in face, raffish, penniless, a stock-brokers clerk of ten days'
experience, but a gentleman and a Catholic – name Giles FitzHerbert.[2] I
have not the heart to keep them apart. They will soon be spliced. I told
Meg I consented to a marriage not to a wedding. She said: 'But I must
have Lady Diana there'. FitzHerbert, before meeting me to ask for her
hand <u>bought</u> baby's book to see how Duff tackled the Duke of Rutland
and was greatly discouraged. You should find these two episodes sympathetic. Meg is bird happy about her affair. Let her enjoy it quick before
the Light of Common Day.
    Who should turn up to breakfast on Monday but Bloggs [Baldwin].
Said he and Elspeth had been 'bickering' and he needed male company.
Stayed an hour. Then off with Elspeth to Amsterdam. Stone deaf.
    Venice means so many things to you. To me it means you and Hubert
[Duggan] and Maimie and [Sir Richard] Sykes branding the yankee
[Doris Duke] and [Michael] Rosse deafening Tug boat Annie
[Armstrong-Jones] and [Edward] James marooning Tilly [Losch] – how
long ago? Twenty years? No damn it nearer 30.

All love
Bo

[1] General Lord Ismay was known as 'Pug'.
[2] Giles FitzHerbert (b. 1935). From 1962–6 he worked for Vickers de Costa & Co, and then became a
diplomat. Ambassador to Venezuela since 1988.

Diana to Evelyn

Ca' Leone Giudecca   *[25 August 1962]*
Venice

My darling Bo – my heart shakes for you. Comes the time that I have so often dreaded for you – a time that I have known myself when one must deliver one's treasure to another with a show of generous approval. I minded dreadfully – John Julius was 21.[1] You seem to be full of grace about the sacrifice – but I know it must give you cruel pain. Your letter has been over a week coming – the darling Meg may be married by now. I hope they will settle in Little Venice – handy for stockbrokerdom.

You might be rather happy on this old Giudecca – because it does not harbour any foreigner on account of the difficulty of boarding it.

Age overpowers – my legs hurt wickedly from the trudging – I'm too ugly to strip for bathing – I <u>cannot</u> understand the language of the six Lambton children and 2 Freuds, and find cheerfulness rarely.[2]

O! Bo, O! Bo – Give Meg my fond love and kisses for wishes – I should be back the 7th or so.

That pretty Catholic Sukie Phipps that was knows about Little Venice flats.

Love and more love

Pug

Evelyn to Diana

Combe Florey   *28 August [1962]*

Darling Stitch Pug Baby

Your letter full of understanding. It is, to me, a bitter pill and ungilded. I would forbid the marriage if I had any other cause than jealousy and snobbery. As it is, I pretend to be complaisant. Little Meg is ripe for the kind of love I can't give her. So I am surrendering with the honours of war – without war indeed. The wedding will be at the end of October. I think in London. They will make all arrangements. I have given them a meagre sum of money and said spend it on trousseau or linen or festifications with bad champagne and photographers, just as you please. I will, of course, go to the church – not, I think, to any subsequent party. I haven't met FitzHerbert's widowed ma.

Your Venice sounds sad. What does 'two Freuds' mean? One is ghastly. I thought his pretty wife escaped to America.[3]

---

[1] John Julius married a month before his 23rd birthday.

[2] Ladies Lucinda, Beatrix, Rose, Mary and Isabella Lambton, and Edward (Viscount Lambton), and the painter Lucian Freud (b. 1922) and one of his daughters.

[3] Lucian Freud married the novelist Lady Caroline Blackwood, daughter of 4th Marquess of Dufferin and Ava, in 1953. She left him in 1957, obtained a divorce in Juarez, Mexico, and married Israel Citkovitz in New York in 1959. In 1973 she married the American poet Robert Lowell.

Listen. London. Do you ever spend Sunday there? I am being driven from home Sept 14th–16th by a young people's house-party. I would take refuge in Hyde Park Hotel if you were in Paddington and would give me your company. Let me know.

Winter plans? Any? Shall we sail to Madagascar with Mrs Rodd and Raymond Mortimer?[1] I don't care about sun. Just to escape Christmas.

Do you remember books I wrote about a character called 'Basil Seal' – a mixture of Basil Murray and Peter Rodd. I suddenly yesterday began a story about Basil Seal at 60.[2] Jolly good so far.

How long since you read Max Beerbohm's essay on Venice? His best. and, did you know?, commissioned by Northcliffe for *Daily Mail*. Rum.

You see I feel that with Meg I have exhausted my capacity for finding objects of love. How does one exist without them? I haven't got the Gaiety euphoria that makes old men chase tarts. My ghastly brother calls them 'pipe lines' through which he is refuelled with youth. Not for me. Did I tell you my brother has written an autobiography in which he says: 'Venus has been kind to me'?

Meg and FitzHerbert have found a lodging in Westbourne Grove, not very far from the canal zone. I suspect him of being a crook. I cannot doubt the sincerity of his love for Meg – nothing to be got from her or me. When I said 'gentleman', I meant of respectable ancestry. He has rather a common way with him.

Please tell me about week-end 15th September. Oysters and grouse. We might have fun of a subdued sort.

Last time we met – at least not last time, that was when the spectre Auberon buggered everything – we talked of books in which you appeared as character.[3] I forgot one by a man who was shot in Mexico – can't remember his name. Title something like 'Way of Contrition – Revelation'? Does that suggest anything?

Pray for me at the tombs of St Mark and Giustiniani.

All love
Bo

---

[1] Raymond Mortimer (1895–1980). Writer and critic, and sometime literary editor of the *New Statesman*. Biographer of Duncan Grant.

[2] *Basil Seal Rides Again, or The Rake's Progress* (1963).

[3] The books included novels by Arnold Bennett (*The Pretty Lady*), D. H. Lawrence (*Aaron's Rod*), Maurice Baring, Nancy Mitford (*Don't Tell Alfred*), Enid Bagnold (*The Loved and Envied*) and, of course, by Waugh himself.

Evelyn to Diana

Combe Florey   *10 September 1962*

Darling

Has it caught your eye that there is a congress now sitting called PUGWASH.[1] Look out.

I shall be at Hyde Park Hotel all Saturday 15th and Sunday 16th. On Saturday evening a dear gentle Jesuit (who is in love with Meg) called Fr. Caraman dines with me.[2] I'd like you to meet him. At all other times I am free as air and avid for your company.

I say I don't like to think of my last letter to you lying about. It had confidences for your eyes only. Do please burn it when it turns up.

Longing for Saturday and Sunday.

Bo

Evelyn to Diana

Combe Florey   *15 October [1962]*

Darling Pug

We meet on Thursday evening. I will then arrange for a guide to take you to Meg's marriage. The ceremonies will be long and unintelligible to Baby. Why not come straight to the party at Sweet Alice [Jolliffe]'s at noon?

All except tough old me are ill. Meg has the undulating fever – but I will drag her to the church on wheels if necessary. Congress may be postponed a day or two. Laura has been struck down by some kind of flu. FitzHerbert has the common cold.

(N.B. Route on back of wedding invitation not adequate.)

All love
Bo

---

[1] This was the 10th Pugwash Conference on Science and World Affairs – the name came from the town of Pugwash, Nova Scotia, where the first took place – attended in London by 200 delegates from 38 countries.

[2] Father Philip Caraman (b. 1911), Jesuit and writer, who became a close friend of Waugh's.

Evelyn to Diana

Combe Florey *[October 1962]*

Darling Pug

Oxford Dictionary gives the following quotations:[1]

1589 'It is two strange serpents entangled in their amorous congress'
1737 'They had each of them a son from that incestuous congress'
1767 'People expect the issue of such a marriage to be tawny; which indeed is the usual effect produced by the congress of black and white persons'
1870 'In all higher Vertebrata the ova are impregnated by sexual congress'

So you see the Diabolic Doctor[2] has four centuries of precedent for the phrase which struck you as odd.

Little Meg's condition has been diagnosed as Maltese Fever.

She is throwing out the electric clock but when I gave her the alternatives you offered as a present she said that the dressing-table mirror would be even more desirable than the clock.

She doesn't like the idea of whitewashing her oak. They paid £300 for 'fixtures'; rent is £450. I think they have a bargain.

All love
Bo

Diana to Evelyn

[10 Warwick Avenue] *15 March [1963]*

[letter written on the relevant pages torn from Christie's catalogue of pictures to be sold on 22 March:]

Darling Bo – Imagine my joyous evocations when dear Simon (buggaredface) Fleet[3] (once Harry Carnes) took me to Christie's saying 'I've got a lovely surprise for you'.

Christie's sale – March 22nd

[under lot 109:
Charles Spencelayh, R.A.
SHE STOOPS TO CONQUER]

not dated – I would opine past peak period.

---

[1] Diana was evidently puzzled by his use of the word 'congress' in the letter of 15 October.
[2] Dr Charles Talbut Onions (1873–1965), philologist and co-editor of the *Oxford English Dictionary* 1914–33.
[3] Simon Fleet had recently had a facelift.

[between lots 110 and 111:
Charles Spencelayh, R.A.
GRANDMOTHER WITH HER KITTENS and
GRANDFATHER READING]

Baby's poor blind eyes did not spot these two well-titled canvases.

But silly Simon showed me only *She Stoops to Conquer* – a very 'risqué' work of the master not to say vulgar – Manchester regained for me.

I'm back from the States – full of stories about the court of King Jack at Washington.[1] Any hope of seeing you?

Might you consider Rome for ten days end of the month? Mrs Jenny won't be there but Miss Judy, who has been so long in love with you, will and the Countess Iris . . .

U.S.A. has been a moral booster – the great thing is, not getting new blood, but being new blood. Susan Mary sends you 'her greetings' as Kaetchen [Kommer] used to say. I've always loved you.

Pug

Evelyn to Diana

Combe Florey   *18 March 1963*

Darling Pug

Welcome home. I was asked by Liz [von Hofmannsthal] to greet you at dinner but my house was full of senile aunts and neurotic clergymen.

We had a pleasant English invalid winter at Mentone but returned too soon.

Very interesting about the Master's erotic *She Stoops to Conquer*. My imagination very unhealthily active on the subject. I can only suppose something like those Hindu friezes with Lady Chatterley doing what John Sparrow proved she did.[2]

I love Mother Judy but I don't think Holy Week a good time to spend with infidels although Pope John has made us stop praying for them as 'perfidious'. Countess Iris is, I think a theosophist. These are not

---

[1] The glamorous style of the Kennedys in the White House gave rise to the nickname of Camelot. Diana had been staying in Washington with Joe and Susan Mary Alsop where she enjoyed a great success. They gave a dinner in her honour to which President Kennedy came. He left shaking his head, saying, 'What a woman!'

[2] After the famous trial against Penguin Books for publishing *Lady Chatterley's Lover*, John Sparrow demonstrated in an article in *Encounter* that Mellors had buggered Lady Chatterley. This revelation appealed greatly to Waugh because an Anglican bishop had said, in evidence for the defence, that there was nothing in the book which he had not done to his own wife.

the people for baby to spend Passiontide with. You'll never become Christian unless you <u>try</u>.

Meg and her bridegroom are back in the Paddington purlieus. He was jolly ill and she has had to give up working at Farm Street to cosset him.

I read some alarming headlines about Norwich in yesterday's paper and then found they referred to a football team not to your jewel.

It is Freedom from Hunger week so remember your three meals a day.

I am very lame. Rheumatic limbs can't carry the weight. Can't reduce weight by healthy exercise on account of lameness. Vicious circle.

If you see Belloc's leprechaun[1] please tell him I got back the sheet of manuscript. I don't know where he lives.

Too many people getting married. A wedding present a week. Ruinous.

I shall never learn Mother Judy's new name.[2] Why doesn't she revert to the ancestral Samuel?

Delighted that you enjoyed the Americans. They are better in their own country. They should be kept at home like the Russians.

The last time I was in London I got tight and where should I find myself ending up but in the American ambassador's car again – the one you think lives in Paddington.[3]

I never knew about Lady Wemyss and Arthur Balfour.[4] I thought her lover was an Egyptian.

Rosebery is very good.[5]

Have you seen Betjeman's 25 guinea joke?[6]

I had ten awful days alone at Mentone when Laura was in Italy. I don't mind solitude. I can't bear hearing other people talk. Sometimes *The Times* arrived in the evening. Sometimes next morning. I used to be glad when it was late because it gave me something to look forward to. When Laura came the sun came out and we gambled and drove to restaurants. I took her to Venice. When we were there we didn't lunch, did we? Good restaurant.

---

[1] Julian Jebb, son of Reginald and Eleanor Jebb (Belloc's daughter). A BBC producer, he died in 1984.

[2] Mrs Milton Gendel. Their only child, Anna, was born in 1963.

[3] David Bruce (1898–1977), US Ambassador to the Court of St James 1961–9. Diana's idea of Paddington evidently included Winfield House, the US Ambassador's residence in Regent's Park.

[4] Kenneth Young's biography published that year revealed that the Countess of Wemyss, the mother of Cynthia Asquith and Diana's brother-in-law, Ego Charteris, had a long and influential liaison with Arthur James Balfour (1848–1930), Prime Minister 1902–6 and author of the Balfour Declaration of 1917.

[5] Robert Rhodes James's biography published that year.

[6] *Some Immortal Hours – A Rhapsody of the Celtic Twilight Wrought in Word and Watercolour* by Deirdre O'Betjeman. This spoof, published by John Murray in 1962, was a very limited edition of twenty books, priced at £25, a large sum then. Each copy had seven pages of block-printed drawings by John Piper hand-coloured by Piper and Betjeman. Betjeman designed the illuminated mock-Celtic typeface.

How happy all the buggers must be at your return. I wish you could shake them off for one day and come and visit us but you won't, I know.

All love
Bo

Evelyn to Diana

Combe Florey   *Feast of Annunciation*
[25 March, 1963]

Darling

English bankers keep holiday on both Good Friday (12th April) and Easter Monday (15th). Which bank holiday do you mean?

Can't you make your Roman holiday a day or two later? I want to come on Saturday 13th and stay a week. I shall be entirely at your beck and call and long for it. Last time we were in Rome together it was with Bloggs and Randolph and frightfully hot and I was only part recovered from air smash.[1]

Rome will be very full at Easter. Tourists like me must make reservations early. So please send telegram (not yet 5d a word. Last chance to get in on the old rates) saying 'Will stay till 20th'.

Can't understand all the obscure references to the Minister for War shooting a nigger at Cliveden.[2]

All love
Bo

Evelyn to Diana

Combe Florey   *[pstmk 5 April 1963]*
[postcard]

I arrive on Spy Wednesday at Leonardo da Vinci aerodrome at 12.10. It would be jolly nice if you met me and came to luncheon with me. If I don't see you I will go on to Grand Hotel. All afternoon and evening free. I should <u>very</u> much like you and Judy to spend the time with me. Big dinner Ranieri? Please chuck whatever you have to do on 16th and stay on in Eternellers.

[1] The ill-fated start to Waugh and Randolph Churchill's war-time mission in Topusko, Tito's Partisan Headquarters in Croatia. They took off from Bari on 16 July 1944, the plane crash-landed, and Waugh and Churchill were flown back to Italy to recuperate. They returned to Yugoslavia in September.

[2] John Profumo (b. 1915), Conservative MP and Secretary of State for War, met a call girl, Christine Keeler, at Cliveden, home of Lord Astor. She was later shot at in London by a jealous former lover of West Indian origin.

Evelyn to Diana

Combe Florey [*April 1963*]

I don't suppose poor pagan Pug knows when Spy Wednesday[1] is. This year it is 10th April. On that day I shall descend on Rome. I have spent a fortune in cables in getting rooms at the Grand Hotel. The Eternal City is going to be chock-a-block.

Now look at the pouch in front of you in the aeroplane. You will find paper and envelopes. Please write, and give to stewardess to post, the name (Mendl? Wendall?) of Mother Judy and her new address – I take it she isn't installing nursery and inglorious Milton in her island mortuary.[2] I <u>love</u> Mother Judy. Also name and address of Iris Tree, if you are to be there. And leave messages at Grand Hotel where you will be all hours of Spy Wednesday.

Longing for our treat

Bo

Evelyn to Diana

Combe Florey *25 April 1963*

Darling Pug

Here is a little picture to remind you of our happy days in Rome. How happy you made them. It was years since I saw so much of you. Time fell away and I was back on tour with *The Miracle*.

My Florentine excursion was very different – all palaces full of white gloved footmen and colossal statuary. At Harold's[3] I had a bed-room as big as the throne room at the Vatican and not unlike it. Light switches indistinguishable from bells concealed behind tapestries. Whenever I woke in the night to take my poison I rang by mistake and troups of servants of all ages and sexes charged in crying 'Il bagno adesso?' We visited many American millionaires in neighbouring palaces and I pined for Piazza S. Bartolomeo and even the rough grass of Pogson's park. The grass here, by the way, is very brilliant and succulent and offers rich grazing for you all the summer. Do come and browse.

Admiralty House has gone down hill since baby's time.[4] The fine dining room is transformed into offices, the dolphin furniture banished with the Capt. Cook paintings. White paint everywhere. Baby's bed-room is the drawing-room, but the luncheon party was very cosy. I think

---

[1] The Wednesday before Good Friday.
[2] She lived on Piazza San Bartolomeo in Isola, an island in the Tiber.
[3] Harold Acton's villa, La Pietra, outside Florence.
[4] 10 Downing Street was found to be suffering from dry rot; and while it was being dealt with, the Prime Minister, Harold Macmillan, moved into Admiralty House.

the Prime Minister wanted to escape the cares of state by recreating Balliol 1912.[1] The only discordant voice was that of Thomson the Canadian newspaper-owner, a pathetic oaf.[2] I said to him: 'We met at the first night of *Dr No*. I couldn't understand it, could you?' Thomson: 'There were girls without much clothing. I liked that'. E.W. 'You must be very over-excitable sexually'. That made the wop ambassador split his sides.

Home to find piles of letters to answer and Lady Onslow in residence.[3]

I shan't come to London for a long time. If you come here (not in easy reach of Stratford or Bath) I promise you shall never enter the dining-room but have all meals on the grass wet or fine.

All love
Bo

Evelyn to Diana

Combe Florey   *[?May 1963]*

Darling

I don't send invitations to my skinning. The Royal Literary Society [the Royal Society of Literature] is a thing like the Zoo or the R. Geographical S. which anyone (not I) belongs to by paying a guinea or two a year. This ghastly dinner on Tuesday is for members of R.L.S. who care to buy tickets.

For some curious reason Mrs Fleming and Fr Caraman are members. They have taken tickets and guests. I don't know any other members. Perhaps Quennell?

The whole idea of Companions of Literature is a little joke of Freddy Birkenhead's.[4]

All love
Bo

[1] Harold Macmillan had been at Balliol when its guiding spirit was the historian F. F. 'Sligger' Urquhart (1863–1934).

[2] Roy Thomson (1894–1976), created 1st Baron Thomson of Fleet the following year (after he had become a British citizen). At that time he owned *The Scotsman* and the *Sunday Times*, and he went on to acquire *The Times*.

[3] His son Auberon's mother-in-law. Born the Hon. Pamela Dillon, she had divorced her husband, the 6th Earl of Onslow, in 1962.

[4] It was also a way of getting active writers into the Royal Society of Literature.

Evelyn to Diana

[newspaper cutting   *[pstmk 13 May 1963]*
stuck on Combe Florey postcard:]

TITLED LADIES required at Writers' Weekend School in Elizabethan Manor House in Norfolk. Exciting residential posts available – Write Box X1747

Here's a chance for Pug. What can it mean?

Evelyn to Diana

Combe Florey   *[?June 1963]*

Darling

No I mustn't say that. It is now regarded as proof of 'impropriety'.[1]
My dear Diana

No I mustn't say that either. It was held to imply buggery in the Vassal case.[2]

Dear Lady Diana

That must pass.

You asked me once (I expect you have forgotten) to send you proofs of last story.[3] Well here they are – here it is – not bad for an old buffer and BIG PRINT FOR BLIND BABY especially.

Do come and visit us. Well I know you won't. No Festival, no buggers.

Living as I do, reading the papers, I think Londoners must all be mad – entangled in Pamberry's great moustaches. Ever since I knew the meaning of 'adultery' I have associated it with ministers of the Crown.

As for lies think of Rufus Isaacs in H. of C. and A. Bevan perjuring himself against your schoolfellow Mrs Jenny.[4]

All Love no damn it I mustn't say that the papers will impute adultery.

OXO that's the word

Bo

---

[1] On 22 March 1963, John Profumo, then Secretary of State for War, publicly denied his liaison with Christine Keeler. On 5 June he was forced to acknowledge it, and he resigned the same day.

[2] John Vassall, an Admiralty clerk who had been in the British Embassy in Moscow, fell into a homosexual blackmail trap and spied for the Soviet regime until caught. He was sentenced to eighteen years' imprisonment.

[3] *Basil Seal Rides Again.*

[4] See Waugh's letter of 20 November 1957, p. 245.

Evelyn to Diana

Combe Florey   *3 September 1963*

Darling Pug

Thank you for your pretty postcard.

I have had a dull, damp, idle summer. Can't leave home between Easter and Michaelmas for fear of the crowds. Soon I shall be on the move again. First stop Enton Hall. I must spend at least a fortnight preparing for my sixtieth birthday [on 28 October]. The 50s I think are a deadly decade. Life I hope begins at 60 but I must lose 2 stone. The difficulty is to find a time when the fiend Auberon [Herbert] is not in residence. He has made it his London headquarters.

I go on sentence by sentence writing my autobiography.[1] Still at Oxford.

Little Meg is taking her pregnancy rather peevishly.

My younger sons have been in France. They return tonight. I dread it.

When is your starving season? It would be jolly decent if you came buggerless to Enton Hall.

All love
Bo

Evelyn to Diana

Combe Florey   *18 November 1963*

Darling Pug

O Dear. I never hoped that you really meant to be up and about in the early morning. I weep for the lost hours I might have spent with you.

That was a very jolly luncheon party on Thursday. Jollier than the sexagenarian jaunt that evening.

Meg was safely delivered of a daughter on Friday. She is very discontented in her paupers' ward and threatens to arrive here at once.

All love
Bo

Evelyn to Diana

Combe Florey   *[?December 1963]*

Oh I am sorry about the balls up at the week-end. I forgot that the posts take twice their normal time in December when all the heathen send one

---

[1] *A Little Learning*, published in 1964.

another Christmas greetings. When I did not hear from you I assumed you were away. Then late on Friday night my son-in-law arrived here and said you had telephoned to him. By then it was too late. Misery and vexation and shame.

The baptismal celebrations were ghastly. Meg has cleverly named her daughter Emily-Albert. All else was tedious.

Just rid of her in-laws. Today Pamela Onslow comes crashing in. And the fires smoke and it is bitter cold and I already sicken with dread of Christmas

Very sorry Cooper's prize should go to a Yank.[1]

All love
Bo

Evelyn to Diana

Combe Florey   *22 February 1964*

Darling Pug

I read in Mentone the sad news of Mrs Jenny's death. I know she will be a great loss to you and my heart goes out. I telephoned you on my way through London but you were away.

The Mentone trip was a great flop. I was struck ill and no good for anything and Laura's annual holiday curtailed and quite spoiled. Now I am well again but that does not make up for Laura's lost treat. In the middle of next month I go into Sister Agnes's[2] to be examined for the cause of my illness. I saw a doctor in London and he asked me my habits. I said: 'about 7 bottles of wine a week and 3 of spirits, 30 cigars, 20 grains of Sodium Amital, a bottle of paraldehyde.' 'Paraldehyde,' he said, 'Now that is <u>very</u> good for you.'

Grandchildren come thick and fast. Little Meg is your neighbour at 15 Westbourne Terrace. Do pop in and see her.

Did you see that Captain Hance kicked the bucket? He had trumpeters at his funeral. I had a moving letter from Jackie, now a grandmother and horseless. The Captain's legs fell off and his last years were very painful. Bloggs broke the news to me.

Where are you keeping Easter? If in Rome I could join you. I missed Mrs Gendle] when she was in blighty.
    Gendel]

Tout à toi
Bo

---

[1] Aileen Ward for *John Keats – The Making of a Poet*. The prize was presented by David Bruce, the American Ambassador.
[2] King Edward VII's Hospital for Officers, Beaumont Street, London W1.

Diana to Evelyn

10 Warwick Avenue   *[late February 1964]*

Darling Bo. Sad about the horsey captain – it's a wonder tho' that he lasted so long. Dreadfully upset about your health – I had heard about the return from Mentone and rang up H[yde] P[ark] H[otel], then your Bright Meg – who told me with youthful unconcern that you were waiting for a bed at Sister Agnes's (I knew her well Boratio).[1] My blood froze but your letter has reassured me.

Please meet me in Rome. I think of starting about 24th and must step off in Paris but only for the day. I minded very much the sudden death of Mrs Jenny – I battened on her vitality and really loved and admired her – many did not – she gave too much. Rome will be sadder for our group – and the flat is to be liquidated.

I loved you on the telly. I thought your interviewer who I well know totally miscast – humourless and on the screen not beautiful.[2]

Tell me exact date of Sister Agnes – Annie returns 14th. We might all lunch 15th or 16th. I'd get the FitzHerberts – Tried to get Meg the other night to give her Margot Fonteyn ballet tickets – alas! No reply –

Write again dear Bo

Pug

Evelyn to Diana

Combe Florey   *3 March 1964*

Darling Pug

My newspaper announced that Randolph had taken up residence at Sister Agnes so I have cancelled my reservation there. I have been a fellow patient of his before. Anyway I have quite recovered from my indisposition.

I will come to Rome for Easter, arriving at Grand Hotel Spy Wednesday (March 25) and staying a week. Please keep all your time for me. Will you be on Miss Judy's Island? Please inform.

All love
Bo

---

[1] Sister Agnes, the founder of the King Edward VII Hospital for Officers, was a close friend of the King and persuaded him to help finance it.

[2] Elizabeth Jane Howard (b. 1923), playwright and novelist. On 16 February she had interviewed Waugh for the BBC's *Monitor* series.

Diana to Evelyn

10 Warwick Avenue *[March 1964]*

Darling Bo

Poor Randy – he may be iller than we think – I spoke to his Mama yesterday. He's had a broncoscopiy and they are not satisfied so he's going back and keeping you out – Give him a prayer. My plans for Rome are to leave 24th for Paris at dawn, to pause in Paris and take the night train to Rome arriving Spy Wed[nesday]. I shall be staying not with Mrs Judy but at her husband's three minutes away and up 96 steps – an old heart cease from overbeat – but on the Monday I hope to move in and stay another week or ten days.

I'll inform Miss Judy of your visit so we'll hope to meet Spy Wed. at dinner.

No food has passed my lips for nearly six days – I feel like a bird on the wing with heightened morale.

All love
Pug

Diana to Evelyn

10 Warwick Avenue *April 1964*

'Mishate me not for my complexion' in Rome this Easter. I did feel so ill and you were as mellow as a Ripston Pippin and Lady McEwen[1] was the gentlest of fair ladies, and Tom Jones Judy ever so loving and giving – Well there it is – I'm sorry. I had a purgatorial journey home flying alone at dawn overloaded with baskets and sticks and fears – at Geneva by nine I hired a room where I laid on the floor till twelve when I had an appointment, and then boarded an Arabian plain 'Mahamet Ali and his crew welcome you aboard' in glottal stop, untranslated Arabic, got to Taxi-less Paris, walked my phlebitis all the bloody way to dead Hoytie Wyborg's, to condole with her heartbroken maid for two hours, who spared me no detail of 'la toilette de Mademoiselle (morte, bien entendu) j'avais surtout beaucoup de difficulté avec sa bouche' (do it yourself Forest Lawn). Hired another room and lay on the floor like a floundered balloon till ten thirty p.m. then to London airport at 0.30.

You were most universally loved in Rome – and I am not one to say nice things. What about you and the Megs lunch with me next time you come to town? Susan Mary comes for three days April 15th.

X Baby X

[1] Bridget, Lady McEwen, widow of Sir John McEwen, 1st Bt. (1894–1962), writer and Parliamentary Under-Secretary of State for Scotland 1939–40. She was the mother of the artist Rory McEwen.

Evelyn to Diana

Combe Florey   *[April 1964]*

Darling Pug

I cannot and will not attempt to say that your illness in Rome was anything but a deep sorrow – perhaps deeper to me than to you as you were asleep so much of the time. I rejoice that you are safe home – but <u>are</u> you safe? Have you seen an English physician? You don't cosset yourself. You were in no condition for that awful return journey which would have killed me, tough old soldier as I am. You should hire a pansy as permanent guard and guide. Why don't you marry Belloc's leprechaun? <u>Much</u> better than Beaton.

Alfred Duggan kicked the bucket [on 4 April] and Laura and I have to go to the Welsh Marches for his requiem.

Daphne's book on Rosa Lewis very amusing but frightfully common title.[1] Did you ever hear her referred to as 'the Duchess of Jermyn Street?' I certainly did not.

Take care of yourself, Pug. Don't go in for wild austerities like sleeping in cellars and fasting and flying in crowded night aeroplanes.

All love
Bo

I have become reconciled with Randolph. He looked so pathetically thin and feeble and when he tried to shout a whisper came. So 12 years enmity are expunged.

Evelyn to Diana

Combe Florey   *21 August 1964*

Darling Pug

Thanks awfully for asking me [to] stay. If it were in Tierra del Fuego or even Inverness I would come like an arrow from t[he] b[ow] but the South of France in August is more than my decaying flesh and crumbling bones could survive. I go to Spain for the first 3 weeks of October to avoid democracy. Any chance of your joining us (Laura and me) there?

I have a book for you.[2] I'll send it 'please do not forward' to Paddington. Do you know the (true) story of C. Connolly at Le Canadel? He took a villa and got no letters for weeks so he went to the post-office to enquire. A female mutilée de la guerre said Yes we have many letters and

---

[1] *The Duchess of Jermyn Street* appeared that year. Twelve years later it was made into a television series.

[2] *A Little Learning*, recently published by Chapman & Hall.

parcels for M. Connolly but they are addressed au Canadel. The boundary runs between your house and us. You do not live in Le Canadel so we are sending them back marked 'unknown'.

Not a week passes but some friend, acquaintance or notable falls downstairs, usually fatally. 1964 will be for me The Year of the Stroke. Keep close to the bannisters.

All love
Bo

Diana to Evelyn

Le Reine Jeanne   *[?August 1964]*
Bormes-les-Mimosas

My darling Bo. I've just read three reviews of your book – the Gutter Press (i.e. *Mail, Express*) can't say anything more lauditory, *The Times* wearisome and derogatory with their Woodhouses Mitfords Powells comparisons. Anyway I do love you to have praise and I hope it pleases you – 'Nothing pleases me, or this would; everything annoys me, or this wouldn't' Harry Cust[1] used always to try with muddle to quote, I think, Byron (the worst muddle was made by the orators of the world in the Albert Hall with the letters of fire behind their backs trying to get right the 'Many and so few')

I never write a letter, nor anything at this moment. As a creature of God's – who prays nightly – I'm a prey of near despair – my old children and young grandchildren encircle me, the skies and sea are limpid – we live free on Poor Louis's bounty – and I could howl – What shall I do to be saved?

Duty calls – yesterday I had to go to lunch with a dreadable octogenarian Tony Gandarillas.[2] The anguish did me good – Don't leave me.

Diana, Pug, Baby

you might well think drunk but cold sober, alas!

---

[1] Henry John Cust (1861–1917), politician, poet, and editor of the *Pall Mall Gazette* 1892–6. In 1893 he married Emmeline Welbey-Gregory.

[2] Baron Antonio ('Tony') de Gandarillas, Chilean diplomat.

Evelyn to Diana

Combe Florey   *17 September 1964*

Darling Diana

That was a sorrowful letter.

I sent a copy of my autobiography to Warwick Avenue where I hope you will find it waiting your return. I am sending this letter there too as I don't know how long you are spending at Le Lavandou. I go off to Spain at the end of the month to escape the elections.

Prayer is not asking but giving. Giving your love to God asking for nothing in return. Accepting whatever he sends as his will for you. Not 'Please God give me a happy day' but 'Please God accept all my sufferings today in your honour'. He doesn't want sugar-babies. Have you ever experienced penitence? I doubt it. No wonder you are in the dumps. Do you believe in the Incarnation and Redemption in the full historical sense in which you believe in the battle of el Alamein? That's important. Faith is not a mood.

I got such a wigging from Katharine for the smutty bit in *A Little Learning*. I don't care about reviewers. You and she are the people whose opinion I value.

All love
Bo

Diana to Evelyn

10 Warwick Avenue   *[September 1964]*

O! beastly Bo, you are very severe that's not the way to answer those in pain. You Papists are not consistent; tho' you think you are; Maurice told me to pray for everything – Everything – and he was more Christian than you are; more charitable, less Calvinistic.

I've always told you that I don't know penitence – but I pray for it; I do not believe as you do in the historical certainty of the Redemtion but I have a mustard seed of faith which causes me to pray on my knees asking for that seed to be watered and graced. I give nightly thanks for benefits, and accuse my nature as a beast inherited that I try and have so far failed to daunt – all right? I pray at length for the souls of the dead – a special one not unnaturally for Duff's and for reunion.

I don't pray for myself except in extremis – I do pray for John Julius which is all I have really to love, I pray for his soul, his honour and his safety – if I did not pray for his safety it would be against nature, instinct, and Christ's human links –

<u>Do</u> be more tender

Pug

P.S. I forgot. Thank you for sending me your book – I'm in Hampstead and entranced. Have I come to Katharine's dirty piece that she socks you for? is it the little girl showing you her parts? Or is there worse to come – I'm so afraid I've lost recognition of dirt.

Evelyn to Diana

Combe Florey   *[? September 1964]*

Darling Pug

Re K's smut: far worse to come, right at the end.[1]

Re prayer: I am not expert or model. I was once taught a useful mnemonic ACTS = Adoration, Contrition, Thanks, Supplication, for the order of precedence.

I think what you need is a straight catechism. Who made you? Why did he make you? Whom are you addressing in prayer? Christ said: 'Ask in my name'. Who was he? Christianity is a historical religion based on certain events in time and space. Without that certainty (or as Pascal thought probability) prayer becomes merely a mood. You, presumably, unlike the Calvinists, believe in purgatory else you would not pray for the souls of the dead. How can they be redeemed except by Christ's sacrifice? You must get the basic grammar of the Faith. You don't need tenderness – you have been surrounded by that all your life – but instruction.

We live in a dark age of the Church but many have thought that in earlier times and the Church has survived.

Just off to Spain, where I wish they still burned heretics.

All <u>tenderest</u> love

Bo

---

[1] The incident involved 'Captain Grimes', whom Waugh used in his novel *Decline and Fall*, and took place during his time in North Wales as assistant master at a prep school. In honour of the birthday of the headmaster, the school was packed off with a picnic to the slopes of Mount Snowdon:

'When it was all over and the boys in bed we sat in the common-room deploring the miseries of the day. Grimes alone sat with the complacent smile of an Etruscan funerary effigy.

'I confess *I* enjoyed myself greatly,' he said as we groused.

We regarded him incredulously. '*Enjoyed* yourself, Grimes? What did you find to enjoy?'

'Knox minor,' he said with radiant simplicity. 'I felt the games a little too boisterous, so I took Knox minor away behind some rocks. I removed his boot and stocking, opened my trousers, put his dear little foot there and experienced a most satisfying emission.' (*A Little Learning*, pp. 227–8)

Evelyn to Diana

Combe Florey   *24 October [1964]*

Darling Pug

I am very sorry to hear you have been in hospital. I have few teeth left, no false ones yet. When the last go I shall harden my gums with salt and eat soft foods. I don't like the prospect of false teeth at all.

I too have lost my memory for what I read. It is a great convenience as I need no new books. I can assure you that my last book has no offensive caricature of Miss Judy.

Haven't seen Mrs Fleming for ages. She writes me long letters of gossip which I value. I never go to her house. Don't like her chums. Her daughter, Mrs Morgan, says I should write about her (Mrs F) because she is courageous. She can't know the damning story of Lord Brownlow's hat.[1]

Meg is gallivanting in Rome. I have given Hatty a full set of bound <u>Strand</u> Magazines. They keep her silent.

The newspaper says the only way to see you is to get jugged in Holloway but I refuse to squat in the streets even for that joy. If you came here I would give you pink champagne.

I may have to go to London before I sail. If so I will rush to Warwick Avenue, Hyde Park Gate, Holloway Gaol and all other possible places of finding you.

Why was 'prima donna' 'straight laced' – yesterday's X-word?

All love
Bo

Evelyn to Diana

Combe Florey   *All Saints 1964*
[1 November]

Darling Pug

What are the news on the Little Rialto? Laura and I telephoned to you on our way through London – 22nd and 23rd – but were told you were away. I long to see you but I know I never shall so do send blind scrawl.

I never want to travel again. I am too old for adventures with canoes and camels and all the civilized places are infested with tourists (even the French are on the move) and being reduced to crowded uniformity. I thought October might be safe – not a bit of it. Hotels packed and

[1] Evelyn was rowing Ann Fleming in a rubber dinghy off a beach in Jamaica in February 1955 when his panama hat, borrowed from Lord Brownlow, blew off and started floating towards the coral reef. Ann begged Waugh to turn back and leave the hat rather than wreck the dinghy, but Waugh rowed on regardless. Promising to fetch the hat, Ann dived into the water – and swam briskly to shore.

311

unwelcoming. But the object of the expedition was to give Laura a month away from the kitchen sink. She has returned rejuvenated; I much fatigued and now I must sit down and pay for it all with an article on Spain. What can one say nowadays after twenty first-class writers have studied the country and expatiated? Ever been to Corunna? We visited Sir J. Moore's grave – very well kept. And the air was bracing as Skegness. I can't speak the lingo so we had no native life. No comfortable, well-lighted chairs even in the most expensive hotels. Food no longer poisonous but reduced to tasteless, hygienic aeroplane standards. In fact I didn't enjoy myself at all but rejoiced to watch Laura casting cares.

The Vatican Council weighs heavy on my spirits. Truth will prevail I have no doubt but a great deal of balls is being talked.

Was Max Beerbohm impotent? I have read David Cecil's very ill written book without learning.[1] I suspect he was.

Who told Jenkins about Mr Asquith's letters to Venetia?[2]

Meg has a pleasant house on Blackheath empty of furniture and full of guests. She will have another baby soon. She was stoned in Co. Fermanagh where her husband forfeited his deposit as Liberal candidate. Her husband had a suit of clothes literally torn to shreds off his body by an enraged Protestant lady.

Bloggs is going to build a Moorish villa near Tewkesbury for his declining years.

John de Bendern[3] says Vitamin B is the thing. I bought a bottle but notice no change.

All love
Bo

Diana to Evelyn

10 Warwick Avenue *[November 1964]*

Darling Mr Wu – I wish I could woo you more successfully. You write me a delightful letter about your care-free wife, your own fatigue – Bloggs's Moroccan folly and I do not answer it for days and days and allow paralysis to settle on my pencil – dearth of correspondents, no Duff, no Conrad, no admirers is the cause of the atrophy.

Talking of Bloggs – what about his nervous son[4] who I heard from

---

[1] *Max*, 1964.

[2] Roy Jenkins's biography *Asquith*, 1964. The correspondence between the Prime Minister and Venetia Stanley was published in 1982.

[3] John de Forrest (b. 1907) inherited the Liechtenstein title of Count de Bendern. He was Duff's private secretary in Paris 1946–7.

[4] Edward, Viscount Corvedale (b. 1938), Lord Baldwin of Bewdley's only son. He became an American citizen for a time when working in San Francisco in 1964.

someone was breaking his mother's heart. Is it true that he is to become a citizen of the U.S. – and shake the dust of this country from his melancholic feet? Has Meg left this quarter? Nothing but questions

No news from the little Rialto It's teeming with Venetian friends – Lord Kinross, the Lennox Berkeleys, Mr John Huston, Norwichs, two Lady Kittys – Giles and Farrell, Sir Martin Wilson, Christopher Frys, Barbara Rothschild Ghika, Elizabeth Jane Howard your interloquutor. And Adrian Daintree – Lanning Roper and quite a few more.[1] No niggywigs except one – a nurse in snow white who comes to inject me with Vitamins – the kind you say do you no good – I think rather highly of them. They make me quite prone to walking the streets.

What I should love of all things would be to see you for lunch alone or with Annie or Patrick K[inross] or both. Do warn me of a day before Christmas – Annie needs help, the diversion of friends – Ian's will is a bugger, all the millions will accrue for that delinquent old Caspar.[2] He detests his mother and tells her so. He said he wished he was dead so that he could be with his father and not his mother – he was awful to his father when he lived.

Lady Longford's Queen Vic. is a treat.[3] I lost *A Little Learning* and paniced – I accused Miss Judy and many another of theft – I was on the point of ordering another for you to write in when the dear thing came out of hiding in a motor-car pocket.

Miss Judy went to Aspenal's gambling Hell, foolishly went 'in' with Lord Derby and lost £1700. I met her coming in at 7.30 a.m. as I was going out to catch an early bird's flight and she was all smiles and whisky and feeling sure her partner wouldn't cash her cheque. When I came back two days later she was laid low as a corpse with internal spasms – tears pouring down gaunt cheeks with contrition and shame – 'I've robbed Anna[4] of £1700' was the cry – 'stiffen up you wreck' was mine, telling her that with investment and taxation it represents £12-10-0 roughly – but she would not be comforted and went back to Rome immediately seeking her husband and child. <u>She is most happily married.</u>

O do come and see me

Pug X X

[1] Sir Martin Wilson, 5th Bt. (b. 1906); Christopher Fry (b. 1907), the playwright, and his wife Phyllis; Barbara Ghika, wife of the painter Niko Ghika, formerly married to Victor, 3rd Baron Rothschild; Adrian Daintrey, the painter; and Lanning Roper, the gardening correspondent of the *Sunday Times*.

[2] Ian Fleming's estate amounted to £289,170, of which the bulk went to his wife. All the royalties from the James Bond books were left to Caspar, who committed suicide in 1975.

[3] Elizabeth Longford's biography, *Victoria R.I.* (1964).

[4] Her daughter, Anna Gendel.

Evelyn to Diana

Combe Florey   *28 November 1964*

Darling Pug

What do you mean: 'no admirers'. My admiration is undeviating and increasing.

Now how about the evening of Sunday Dec 13th? I shall be at Hyde Park Hotel but you would not be subject to the vulgar glare in the public dining-room; have private parlour. Do dine alone or are you staying with buggers? Failing that there is the next evening but I have suggested Annie for that and I would prefer you tête-à-tête. Also I shall be crapulous on the Monday as the result of Brian Franks's[1] orgy-luncheon.

It is very sad about Annie. She has always been one for the fashion and we shall all be dirt poor very soon. You rode out the storm of the Cripps-Attlee terror without knowing how we under-privileged people suffered. So did she. Now it will be 1964 again with knobs on.[2]

I fear it may be true about Lord Corvedale's defection. It was published in the papers and not denied. Bloggs has always seemed to me the backbone of the old country. Betjeman's son has become a Mormon. Ghastly but B is Dutch. But think of Lord Chetwode turning and turning in his grave.

Should a loyal friend and cousin dispose of Old Kaspar? It should be easy in that Swindon swamp.[3]

I knew no good would come of Mrs Judy's joining that place in Berkeley Square.[4] She was altogether too cop a hoop [sic] about it.

Now please send me a post-card saying you will dine on Sunday 13th.

14th is rather a gloomy day. It is an annual luncheon which was a huge treat when instituted in 1946 when there was no food or wine in England. Now we are all old, deaf and on regimes.

All love
Bo Wu etc.

What peculiar people win Cooper's prize these days.[5]

---

[1] Brian Franks, Managing Director of the Hyde Park Hotel, gave an annual lunch for his friends.

[2] Presumably Waugh meant to write 1946. 1964 saw the end of thirteen years of Conservative rule when Harold Wilson became Prime Minister at the head of a Labour government.

[3] In 1959, Ann and Ian Fleming bought Sevenhampton Manor, near Swindon, Wiltshire. It had an overgrown lake, and according to Patrick Leigh Fermor, 'trees and water seemed to vanish into misty distances, giving an illusion of vast extent'.

[4] John Aspinall's gambling club.

[5] Ivan Morris won that year with *The World of the Shining Prince*. Harold Macmillan presented the prize.

Diana to Evelyn

10 Warwick Avenue   *[?December 1964]*

My darling Bo. I <u>am</u> exercised about your condition. Boring God as I so often do about my prayers, you now have got onto that list of Ss (supplication) that I try and keep so spare. You force yourself in willy, nilly because I'm fearful for you – having loved you for years. Let's not forget Pinfold – with your laudenum and creme de menthe, or whatever that dread concoction was you did not know you were Wrong (capital) till madness claimed you.

You will tell me that your present symptoms are totally different – but drink-drug-escape addiction can bring you by different streams to the same Slough of Despond. Find a way to feel better than you do – and I am almost sure that a disagreeable restraint – little grains – ⅛th grains – more reading, less calmatives would slowly restore your appetite – appetite brings home your zest.

I'm ten or twelve years older than you and cannot afford your doldrums or your death – it makes me too unhappy. Don't resent this appeal, it is written in love.

Pug

Zest or no zest I did enjoy my dinner

Evelyn to Diana

Combe Florey   *20 December 1964*

Darling Pug

Posts are slow and haphazard. I hope this reaches you in time to give you my full Christmas love.

Ill as I felt I deeply enjoyed our Hyde Park evening. Did I, I wonder, show my deep gratitude for the beautiful *Don Quixote* you gave me. It is a delight. I have nothing for you. My shopping was curtailed by illness – not the mind, but the stomach. I slunk home in bad shape and was seedy all the week – what is called 'an infection'. Cured now and facing Christmas with fortitude.

I am greatly touched by your solicitude. Of course I don't resent it. Who, if not you, has the right to haul me over the coals? But I believe your diagnosis and prognosis are both in error. I may buy a lot of new teeth in the new year and see if they help. Most of my lack of appetite comes from the boredom of chewing with my few, loose teeth. Not eating drives me to the bottle – both spirits and drugs. One can't sleep hungry.

All love
Bo

Evelyn to Diana

Combe Florey   *7 February 1965*

Darling

I go to have snappers examined this week. I don't know how long the process takes. The expense is damnable, the posture absurd. When I have teeth I will come and flash them at you. 'Pecker' is all I have now; I pop beak into beaker rather than plate.

This is the first February for many years I have spent in England. I don't like it at all but there is nowhere else I want to go.

I suppose you mourn Sir Winston.[1] I never had any esteem for him. Interesting how all his crook associates began with B – Birkenhead, Baruch,[2] Beaverbrook, Bracken, Boothby.[3] The Sutherland caricature caught the Tammany Hall aspect very well.[4]

How did they find a 'family banner' for him – Mindelheim?[5] As son of a younger son he can have had no claim. My dotty daughter Harriet works at the College of Arms. I suppose she invented it.

Nice to go to Rome. They are destroying all that was superficially attractive about my Church. It is a great sorrow to me and for once undeserved.

If you see Cardinal Bea[6] spit in his eye.

All love
Bo

Diana to Evelyn

Rome   *[pstmk 18 February 1965]*
[postcard]

Not a bit surprised by your bit about Winston. Arrived here this morning – Mrs Judy been metamorphosed by a shot of LSD (Lysurgic acid . . .) Blue skies brisk frosty air – come quickly for a week and walk the streets and churches and temples.

Pug

[1] Churchill died on 24 January.

[2] Bernard Baruch (1880–1965), the American financier.

[3] Robert Boothby (1900–86). Conservative MP 1924–58, when he was created a life peer. He was also a radio and television personality.

[4] This unsettling portrait of Churchill in old age was burned by his widow, Baroness Spencer-Churchill.

[5] John Churchill, 1st Duke of Marlborough, was made Prince of Mindelheim in Swabia by the Emperor Joseph. The title was inherited by the Duke of Marlborough of the day, but not, of course, by Winston Churchill.

[6] Cardinal Augustine Bea SJ used Pope John XXIII's encyclical *Pacem in Terris* to develop his liberal ideas in his paper 'The Importance of Religious Liberty' (1963). Waugh, appalled by the reforms of Vatican Council II, loathed all cardinals who supported the abolition of the Tridentine Mass in Latin.

Diana to Evelyn

10 Warwick Avenue　　　　　　　　　　*[pstmk 7 March 1965]*
[postcard]

Can you imagine the luck – I went up in a tiny lift with Cardinal Bea in full canonicals preceded by two candles – so with a spluttered greeting I was able to spit in his eye for you.

I'm home thank God and waiting for a visit or a word – I hear *Scoop* is to be filmed?

You'll be glad to hear the Maison Dixon = British Emb. Paris[1] did not lower its flag for Churchill's funeral – tho' de Gaulle did.

　　　　　　　　　　　　　　　　　　　　　　　Pug

Evelyn to Diana

Combe Florey　　　　　　　　　　*Ides of March [1965]*

Darling Pug

Thanks awfully for your two postcards. I didn't feel up to Rome though I longed to be with you and just as I began to strengthen I hear you are back.

I have had a lot of teeth out and new false snappers substituted. Humiliating and costly.

Snow has given place to rain. I never leave the house. Little Meg (very gravid) cosseted me in London during the teething and consumed great quantities of caviar.

Ten days post to answer. I ought to engage a secretary. Then I could devote all my feeble energy to writing to those I love.

　　　　　　　　　　　　　　　　　　　　　　X X X X X
　　　　　　　　　　　　　　　　　　　　　　Bo

Evelyn to Diana

Combe Florey　　　　　　　　　　*20 May 1965*

Darling Pug

It is very good news that you will be in London and free to cosset me during my teething troubles.

I arrive on Tuesday June 1 at Hyde Park Hotel and stay till Wednesday afternoon. I go to my snapper-jack early on Wednesday morning and late on Wednesday afternoon.

---

[1] Sir Pierson Dixon (1904–65), classicist, archaeologist, and diplomat. British Ambassador to Paris 1960–65, and Permanent Representative of the UK to the UN 1954–60.

Now why don't we go to the play on Tuesday evening? I should like to see *Who's Afraid of Virginia Woolf.* Can you get tickets and I will recompense you.

Then why not egg and chive pap at your house and luncheon with Ld Kinross on Wednesday? That would be a huge treat for me. Though toothless I can speak fairly coherently.

Or should I come to you for pap before the theatre on Tuesday <u>as well</u>. I want to see as much as you can bear of me.

The FitzHerberts have gone to foreign parts leaving this house full of my granddaughters.

All love
Bo

Evelyn to Diana

Combe Florey   *Whit Monday [7 June] 1965*

Dearest Mrs Stitch

It was a rare treat seeing you last week. I am sorry my strength failed at luncheon. I am no longer sortable. My deafness is such a strain when more than one person is talking that a party of five knocks all the stuffing out of me. But I loved our tête-à-tête and the play.

You were right about the Hallams of Wimpole Street. I also looked up the Cazalet pedigree. They bought Fairlawne in 1882 – before that merchants in city of London and St Petersburg.

I hope you have a lovely time in Ireland.

One of my earliest memories of you is your lament at having to go out to luncheon with Alan Parsons (whom I knew by repute as a wit, scholar and charmer)[1] because you said he was so decayed. That's me. I first realized I had become a bore when the Haileses remarked on it to Clarissa. I had thought I was particularly bright with the Haileses. Traumatic.

Randolph is toothless too.

All love
Bo

Evelyn to Diana

Combe Florey   *[?September 1965]*
[postcard]

While you are desporting yourself there is a beaver escaped from Regent's Park in your canal. Pray cherish it if it is there to greet your return.

---

[1] Alan Parsons (d. 1933), theatre critic and columnist for the *Daily Sketch* 1925–9 and the *Daily Mail* 1929–33. His asthma kept him from fighting in the Great War, and hastened his early death.

The last 12 months have been awful – dentists and funerals, sloth and melancholy. But I think my condition has slightly improved.

I can't decipher 'he's my eldest mate'.

Not much flicker of life in this old dog but abiding love. If you miss the road and find yourself in Oslo call on Fr. Caraman, Akersvejan[?] 5.

Diana to Evelyn

10 Warwick Avenue   *22 September 1965*

Darling B. I never got to Norway, so never saw the good Father – I got to Travermünde tho' and that's the north tip of the Germanies, having been driven by Iris in a Volks Wagen from Switzerland. She, without a roof or a tosser [penny], or a colon left, is in much better form and vigour than we are. We had with us her familiar – a great black ½ human dog and were bound for to see how her second son – a new doctor of six foot six – fared in his clynic, catering for a provincial Swedish town. As we tumbled broken out of the car and onto the boat we were told that dogs go into six months quarantine in all the Scandinavias. Consternation! No going back as nowhere to go – she was going to live with her doctor for two months and leave the dog for another month while she visited England. So into a 4' by 4' barred cage went the poor brute and left Iris in tears, and of course she won't leave him there and will move on in a week, but to where? It's a desperate situation.

And now St Martin throws a summer in for good value[1] and it's too late and I don't know what to do with it. Go to Annie [Fleming]'s? Gasper having gone to Eton – or to old Juliet [Duff]'s? who lost her balance yesterday as she got out of her bath, fell back into the suds, lay there for an hour while the water chilled and had to be <u>lifted out naked</u> by the butler.

I'm glad, you'd be surprised how glad, I am that you admit improvement – do come and see me. I'd get your pretty daughter or who you liked –

I hope the struggle availeth – I'm lonely and listless

> 'Is there any reward?
> I'm beginning to doubt it.
> I am broken and bored –
> Is there any reward?
> Reassure me, Good Lord
> And inform me about it:

[1] A St Martin's summer is roughly the equivalent of an Indian summer.

Is there any reward?
I'm beginning to doubt it.'
H.B.[1]

Ever loving
Pug

Evelyn to Diana

Combe Florey   *23 September 1965*

Darling Pug

My peacock died last night. He was in fine feather and voice all the summer, ailed for two days (it is thought from a surfeit of melon seeds) lost the use of his legs and then turned up his toes. The latest of a 12-month long series of bereavements. Fortunately he leaves progeny. He was 11 years of age – early middle-age for his breed.

Thank you for your letter of yesterday. What a powerful butler Juliet must have. It can't still be old Fish? Or had he a sodomite to help lift her?

If you are really at a loose end for somewhere to go, do come here. It would be a joy to Laura and me. But would you like it? We can offer love, constant hot water, clean beds, but we keep no company and live off boiled eggs and tinned turtle soup. Lots of good wine. Do come but if you do, don't tell Auberon Herbert. He's always trying to get in.

I have bust my snappers and the dentist can't mend them until October 14th. I come to London for the night of 13th and shall be toothless at liberty after 3 p.m. Hyde Park Hotel. No good meeting at your house – telephone and hangers-on. No fun for you sitting in marble halls.

Ref H.B. No, there's no 'reward' in this world. Perhaps retribution hereafter. A propos, can you give me the text and provenance of

La vie est brêve (wish it were)
Un peu d'espoir
Un peu de rêve
Et puis bonsoir

I have read a new good book about Swift by a man called Nigel Dennis [*Jonathan Swift: a Short Character*]. I found many affinities with the temperament (not of course the talent) of the master. Except his bossiness. That doesn't trouble me, thank God.

Little Meg has grown peevish. Not up to the struggle of life.

All love always
Bo

---

[1] Epigram LXI, in Hilaire Belloc's *Sonnets and Verses* (1954). Diana's slight misquotations of the poem have been corrected.

Evelyn to Diana

Combe Florey   *25 September 1965*

Darling Pug

If I had known Juliet was in extremis I should not have written so flippantly of her. I know you were fond of her and will miss her. I did not like her much but as a bachelor accepted much hospitality from her. I think this is normal and permissible in a bachelor. I remember your once sharply rebuking me for mocking her at your table in Gower Street. Forgive me for mocking her while she was at the time of writing dead.

All love
Bo

Diana to Evelyn

10 Warwick Avenue   *28 September 1965*

Don't worry darling Bo I'm used to your mockery – I'd written you a jaunty account and therefore asked for a jaunty reply. Neither of us knew Juliet was on the brink. Fulco,[1] the Sicilian duke who made good looking at the visitors book on the day of the funeral found it began on the date of her death 32 years ago and only you of the party and he have survived.

She was my friend faithful and good to me, but I never loved her much – I love the bugger Simon [Fleet] who has succoured her these 30 years. What is to become of him and his total indigence? It's a long story – I'll tell it you in a nutshell when I see you. There's a catch as catch can going on with her possessions – winner son will take all.

I've marked your snapper-date in my diary – say what would give you least discomforture. Dinner? Lunch, here? Play? – Annie – Patrick Balfour – Megs?

Xan [Fielding]'s inheritance has risen to one million £s. 11 million was the sum of which ⅔rd have gone in bribery and a 100,000 on costs over 32 years – now if de Gaulle dies or the government changes the bribes will have to be repeated to the new gang.[2] Meanwhile poor Dives (potential) Fielding can't sleep or work. He lunched here three days ago re that horse's mouth stuff. I stayed with Annie who told me you'd offered her

---

[1] Fulco Santostefano della Cerda, Duke of Verdura (1898–1978), designer of jewellery. He was discovered by Coco Chanel, and was one of the most fashionable jewellers in New York in the 1950s.

[2] Xan Fielding's grandmother, Mary Fielding (née Yackjee), owned a large villa and some land in Nice. She let a strip of her land to the municipal authorities, for the purpose of building a boulevard; but the road was never built, and the land should have reverted to her heirs. The heirs (including Xan) took it to court, and won after years of litigation; but the case had been so badly handled by Xan's brother-in-law that almost all the millions won were eaten up in legal fees.

Gasper, the matricide's (potential) ticket free to N.Y. for a vile purpose –
Bad Bo.[3]

I do so hope to see you soon – I'll come because I love you and I'd be
most happy in seeing Laura.

Baby

Evelyn to Diana

Combe Florey   *[pstmk 10 October 1965]*
[postcard]

Thanks awfully for your telegram. It is very kind of you to let me inflict
an Alan Parsons on you on Wednesday. I look to you for any comfort and
amusement you can devise on Wednesday night and afternoon. No
Society. No telephones. I shall be travel-worn, toothless and weary from
the attentions of my dentist. My appointment is in Harley Street at 2.45
and I shall go direct to White's in the hope of finding a message from you.
Cinema or play in the evening. Tête à tête gossip in afternoon. I shall be
very poor company.

Bo

> On the evening of 2 February, Diana was in her room with her
> secretary, Daphne Wakefield. Iris Tree, who was staying with
> Diana at the time, was in the room next door. The doorbell rang, and
> it was answered by the Italian maid. Then there was a thump.
> Daphne went down to investigate, and found two intruders in the
> house. They knocked out the maid and her husband (Diana's cook),
> and Daphne was thrown aside on the stairs as one of the men raced up
> and went into Diana's bedroom. Daphne went to Diana's rescue, and
> was also knocked unconscious. Diana and Iris were tied up and left on
> their beds, while the men burgled the house.

---

[3] On 14 September Ann Fleming lamented in a letter to Evelyn: 'Two months driving Caspar on
Scottish visits have proved exhausting. Caspar hates me and talks of little but matricide. What shall I
do? He is too old and strong to hit.' Waugh replied, 'It is very wrong of Caspar to plot your murder . . .
I suffer far more than you can understand by the present degradation of the Church. I will pay Caspar's
single fare (first class) if he will go to New York to assassinate the Pope [John XXIII].' (*Letters of Ann
Fleming*, p. 370)

Evelyn to Diana

Combe Florey — — — — — — — — — — — — — — — *3 February 1966*

Darling Diana

I was aghast to read in this morning's paper of the dastardly attack on you. I get an early edition so the information was meagre but whatever the details it must have been a beastly experience. I wish I had been there to chastize the robbers. I hope they are soon caught and given condign punishment and that all your friends are rallying for your consolation and future protection. The outrage could not have happened in our youth. I am miserable to think of it happening to you now.

All my love
Bo

Diana to Evelyn

10 Warwick Avenue — — — — — — — — — — — *[?February ?March 1966]*

Darling Bo It always gives me excited pleasure to see your handwriting address to me even, perhaps more especially when it arrives in litterally piles of kind sympathies from the 4 corners – but one answers Australian strangers before buddies – they are easily fobbed off with an inimitable postcard and your words of loving condolence confront me with an innate lack of confidence in my letter ('Baby's Life and Letters' title used since coined by Judy and me). It was as horrid as you can imagine – no faces and ladders in the nylons – gloves cockney voices – laconic and exceedingly strong – I was less frightened than I am in aeroplanes and when anxiety grips me, or in a storm at sea or being driven in a car by drunk – But the fact of feeling ridiculously theatrical shows I wasn't too far gone. The funniest moment was stooping to pick up a leather belt for them to hand-cuff me with, and the thugs saying 'thank you' – I suppose I wanted to get the whole thing over – and be left trussed behind locked doors – Iris and I bound for the guillotine or oven laid across the bed with the faithful Italian gagged and fettered and out of sight at our feet you might illustrate.

Beloved Bo – How are you in flesh and mood – do write again – I think of you such a lot – and worry over your mealancholly – What about deep sedation for Lent? or spending it in London for the greatest of ordeals?

What did you think of G. Greene's book[1] – I read it at one go – half listening for padded feet – it helped a lot.

Fond love now this minute and till I die

Diana

---

[1] *The Comedians*, published that year.

Evelyn to Diana

Combe Florey *[February 1966]*

Darling

Lovely to get a letter. I was worried about the possible effects of the intrusion and by Iris's mad invitation to the ruffians to return. When I was raided in Gloucestershire by Lord Noel-Buxton and Miss Spain I at once put the house up for sale. I felt it polluted. I hope you have not the same feeling. I am not sorry that the brutes got away with your coat of shame – heavily insured I have no doubt. Most of your other possessions, as I remember them, are highly individual. The fences will give them little. But the shock and indignity must have been incalculable. You need baby watchers – not beatnik Iris but a 24 hour a day guard. Buggers are jolly brave, as I saw in the war. Can't you organize a standing picket of them? Or have a 'hot line' to all your neighbours?

Your handing the belt to the blackguard recalls that film you took me to when last we met – the only erotic moment when the girl put her hands out to the lunatic.

I hope Ann [Fleming] explained, as I asked her to do, why I left you so abruptly and impolitely that evening. I am healthier and stronger than then – eating and sleeping. I get earnest enquiries from remote friends who think I am going dotty.

I greatly enjoyed G. Greene's book and admire his stamina. It might have been written 30 years ago.

I thirst for the blood of your assailants. Iris's interview shocked me to the core.

Snappers a bit more effective.

All love
Bo

Diana to Evelyn

10 Warwick Avenue *28 February 1966*

My darling Bo – your last letter sounded brighter – and now I think I've answered it, and now I think I haven't: my mind is fading fast. Iris has deserted this polluted house, and taken refuge in her son's office under which sleeps a protective servant. Last night my Italian man left the house before my return at 7 without mentioning it. His wife (and baby) realizing that I was going to bed and would be alone asked if she could go round to other Italians at John Julius's – I had to say 'yes' a little sourly – and I sweated the long evening out listening for padded footfalls and featureless faces – not that those foolish wops would have helped had the Inhumans come – except for dialling 999. This late-in-time jumpiness punishes me for bragging thro' life about not minding sleeping in empty houses scoffing at servants' fears – and also for being smug about this little house. I'm unaccustomed to smugness and was surprised to feel it when I thought about this pretty little house – I don't care for it now – and serenity of solitude has gone. I pray it comes back.

I've been trying – before the visitation – to find a ship from London to Gibraltar the first fortnight of March – not one going from any country! At last a cargo ship of MacAndrew Line (Kipling?)[1] I discover takes fourteen passengers (J. Conrad) Good-O, I thought, I'll read the entire war book of Bo's[2] and George Paynter's Proust[3] – Bad-O – not a bunk unoccupied.

I had a letter from Daphne – a draught of vintage as always, saying she had lost a stone and a half – I'm so glad; but alas they can't touch that lolly – I so fear they never will – meanwhile Xan is obsessed, can't eat or sleep or work.

I so loved Graham Greene's book. Started rereading when I'd finished it and knew the people so well – I don't think I've done that since I was 7 and read and reread *Stumps* – a lovely book where 'Stumps' in her six year old naughty pride causes a mere groom to break his back, resulting in total paralysis for life.

Annie is very low with tubes in her nose.

Judy is very low – health 'as bloody as usual' and friendless in Rome. She's down to Paul Getty[4] as a companion – you can't go lower. My friends the Trees are forced to sell Mereworth, my favourite 'get away'.

Poor Louis is replacing the coat of shame. Nancy M. says I planned the burglary, because a new one was needed.

If you are better, I am better.

Love to Laura
Baby

Evelyn to Diana

Combe Florey   *28 February 1966*

Darling

Do you know a florid fellow in White's named Bill Levita? He owns a travel agency named 'Rufford'. I have always found him efficient in getting berths on ships when his competitors said: impossible.

---

[1] From Kipling's epic poem *The Mary Gloster*.
[2] *The Sword of Honour* trilogy had been revised and reprinted in one volume.
[3] George Painter's *Marcel Proust* won the Duff Cooper prize for 1965.
[4] J. Paul Getty (1892–1976), oil magnate, who was for many years the richest man in the world. Although notoriously mean, Diana managed to get him to pay for a new front door for 10 Warwick Avenue.

You speak of reading my war novels. Did I ever send you the single volume recension? They are best so read, both on board ship and in the parlour.

How deeply I sympathize with your distress at the invasion of your lovely little house and the desertion of friends and servants. You must, as I suggested before, recruit a Praetorian Guard of buggers to watch night and day. The police are no protection nowadays. Buggers are the thing.

Mereworth is a splendid work of art but for me it means that last ghastly week-end before Peter [Beatty]'s suicide.[1] It is a cursed place from long ago. I would not accept it as an endowed benefaction.

All love
Bo

This was the last letter he wrote to Diana. He died on 10 April, Easter Day. 'Don't be too upset about Papa,' wrote his favourite daughter Margaret to Diana. 'You know how he longed to die and dying as he did on Easter Sunday, when all the liturgy is about death and resurrection, after a Latin Mass and holy communion, would be exactly what he wanted. I am sure he had prayed for death at Mass. I am very, very happy for him.'

Laura Waugh to Diana Cooper

Combe Florey   [April 1966]

Darling Diana

Thank you so much for your letter. You meant so much to Evelyn and you do understand so well – I think he had been praying for death for a long time and it could not have happened more beautifully or happily for him – and without any physical suffering or illness. So I can only thank God for his mercy to Evelyn. But life will never be the same for any of us without him.

There is a memorial mass for him on Thursday at Westminster Cathedral but I shouldn't come as I know you have always hated the trappings of death – But do please say a prayer for him and for me –

all my love
Laura

[1] See exchange of letters in November 1952, pp. 148–9.

BIBLIOGRAPHY

INDEX

Bibliography

Susan Mary Alsop, *To Marietta from Paris* (Doubleday, 1975)

Mark Amory (ed.), *The Letters of Evelyn Waugh* (Weidenfeld & Nicolson, 1980)

—— *The Letters of Ann Fleming* (Collins Harvill, 1985)

John Charmley, *Duff Cooper* (Weidenfeld & Nicolson, 1986)

John Colville, *The Fringes of Power: Downing Street Diaries 1939–1955* (Hodder & Stoughton, 1985)

Artemis Cooper (ed.), *A Durable Fire: The Letters of Duff and Diana Cooper 1913–1950* (Collins, 1983)

Diana Cooper, *The Rainbow Comes and Goes* (Rupert Hart-Davis, 1958)

—— *The Light of Common Day* (Rupert Hart-Davis, 1959)

—— *Trumpets from the Steep* (Rupert Hart-Davis, 1960)

Duff Cooper, *Old Men Forget* (Rupert Hart-Davis, 1953)

Michael Davie (ed.), *The Diaries of Evelyn Waugh* (Weidenfeld & Nicolson, 1976)

Frances Donaldson, *Evelyn Waugh: Portrait of a Country Neighbour* (Weidenfeld & Nicolson, 1967)

Donat Gallagher (ed.), *The Essays, Articles and Reviews of Evelyn Waugh* (Methuen, 1983)

Selina Hastings, *Nancy Mitford* (Hamish Hamilton, 1985)

Diana Mosley, *Loved Ones* (Sidgwick & Jackson, 1985)

David Pryce-Jones (ed.), *Evelyn Waugh and his World* (Weidenfeld & Nicolson, 1973)

Martin Stannard, *Evelyn Waugh: The Early Years, 1903–1939* (J. M. Dent, 1986)

Christopher Sykes, *Evelyn Waugh: A Biography* (Collins, 1975)

Nicholas Wapshott, *The Man Between: A Biography of Carol Reed* (Chatto & Windus, 1990)

Evelyn Waugh, *The Life of Ronald Knox* (Chapman & Hall, 1959)

A. N. Wilson, *Hilaire Belloc* (Hamish Hamilton, 1984)

Philip Ziegler, *Diana Cooper* (Hamish Hamilton, 1981)

Index

Aaron's Rod (Lawrence) 294n
Abdy, Lady Diana 46n, 220, 226
Abdy, Sir Robert, 5th Bt ('Bertie') 46n, 220, 226, 227
Abdy, Sir Valentine, 6th Bt 220
Abetz, Otto 159
Acton, Catherine 263, 265
Acton, Daphne, Baroness 59, 245, 246, 247, 262, 263
Acton, Sir Harold 5, 71, 96, 132, 134, 135, 300
Acton, John, 3rd Baron 35n, 59n
Acton, Peter 35, 37
Acton, Richard, 2nd Baron 96
Agate, James 16
Agnes, Sister 304, 305
Alba, Fernando Alvarez de Toledo, 3rd Duke of 70
Aldrich, Winthrop Williams 211
Alexandra, Queen 144n
Alfonso XIII, King of Spain 32n
Alsop, Joseph Wright 136n, 283, 297n
Alsop, Susan Mary *see* Patten
Amery, Julian, 85n
Amery, Leo 85
Amory, Mark, 1, 2, 210n
Ancaster, 2nd Earl of 17n
Ancaster, Eloise, Countess of 17
Anglesey, Charles, 6th Marquess of 85n, 280
Anglesey, Henry, 7th Marquess of 199n
Anglesey, Marjorie, Marchioness of (née Manners) 85, 91, 97n, 153
Anglesey, Shirley, Marchioness of (née Morgan) 199n
Anstey, F. 79n, 179n

Antrim, Angela, Countess of (née Sykes) 137n, 226
Antrim, Randal, 13th Earl of 137, 226n
Aragon, Louis 162
Arden, Elizabeth 162n
Aribert, Prince, of Anhalt 32n
Arlen, Michael 39, 129
Armstrong-Jones, Anne (née Messel; later Countess of Rosse) 14n, 292
Armstrong-Jones, Antony (later 1st Earl of Snowdon) 14n, 210n
Arran, 8th Earl of ('Boofy') 277
Ashley, Anthony, Lord 204n
Ashley, Sylvia, Lady 48n, 204
Asquith (Jenkins) 312n
Asquith, Lady Cynthia 14n, 277, 298n
Asquith, Lady Helen 31, 32, 33, 37, 48, 49, 89
Asquith, Herbert ('Beb') 277n
Asquith, Herbert Henry, 1st Earl of Oxford and Asquith 77n, 111, 272n, 277n, 312
Asquith, Julian, *see* Oxford and Asquith
Asquith, Katharine 30–33, 37, 43, 44, 46, 48, 50, 51, 53n, 60, 61n, 68, 79, 89, 95, 98, 109, 110, 118, 140, 184, 191, 193, 196, 197, 201, 205, 206, 207, 214, 216, 228, 229, 231, 234, 236, 238, 239, 242–3, 251, 259, 260, 261, 263, 265, 271, 272n, 291, 309, 310
Asquith, Lady Katharine Rose 146n
Asquith, Lady Mary Annunziata 146n
Asquith, Lady Perdita *see* Hylton
Asquith, Raymond 31, 32n, 110n, 272n
Asquith, Raymond, Viscount 146n
Astor, Alice *see* Pleydell-Bouverie

Astor, Nancy, Viscountess 146
Astor, William Waldorf, 2nd Viscount 146
Astor, William Waldorf, 3rd Viscount 299n
Atatürk, Mustapha Kemal Pasha, 19n
Atkinson, W.A. 111n
Attlee, Clement, 1st Earl 86n, 191n, 314
Attlee, Felicity 191
Austen, Jane 48n, 120, 168

Bacon, Virginia 162n
Baddeley, Angela 228n
Bagnold, Enid see Jones
Bailey, John Miller 14n
Baldwin, Arthur, 3rd Earl Baldwin of Bewdley ('Bloggs') 64n, 66, 83, 87, 109, 111, 218, 219, 221, 281, 292, 299, 304, 312, 314
Baldwin of Bewdley, Elspeth, Countess 221, 292
Baldwin of Bewdley, Lucy, Countess 64n, 83
Baldwin, Oliver 229
Baldwin of Bewdley, Stanley, 1st Earl 7, 58n, 83
Balfour, Arthur James 298
Balfour, Patrick, see Kinross
Balfour, Ronald 191n
Balfour, Susan 191n
Baring, Maurice 9, 30, 41, 48n, 68, 83, 100n, 109, 124, 125, 142, 229, 264–5, 269n, 294n, 309
Barnardo, Syrie see Maugham
Barthélemy, Abbé 155n
Bartleet, Robert 12, 16, 18, 19, 61
Barton, Marion (later Falconi) 53n
Barton, Sir Sidney 52n, 53n
Baruch, Bernard 316
Basil Seal Rides Again, or The Rake's Progress (Waugh) 276, 294, 302
Bath, Henry, 6th Marquess of 102n
Bath, Daphne, Marchioness of, see Fielding
Battersby, Martin 116, 118, 127, 142, 253
Bea, Cardinal Augustine 316, 317
Beaton, Cecil 8, 12, 41, 42, 44, 94, 116n, 117, 135n, 205, 216, 249, 307
Beatrix, Infanta 32, 33, 35
Beatty, David, Admiral of the Fleet, 1st Earl 148n
Beatty, David, 2nd Earl 204n

Beatty, Peter 148n, 149, 150, 326
Beauchamp, 7th Earl 6
Beauchamp, Lettice, Countess (née Grosvenor), 6
Beaufort, Henry, 10th Duke of 111
Beaverbrook, William Maxwell Aitken, 1st Baron 13, 41, 97n, 144n, 150, 161n, 173, 218, 223, 224, 227, 234, 237, 316
Beaverbrook: A Study in Power and Frustration (Driberg) 218n
Bedford, Sybille 223n
Beerbohm, Sir Max 96, 163, 180n, 197, 225, 227, 294, 312
Behrman, S.N. 139
Beistegui, Charles de 119n
Belleville, Rupert 31
Belloc, Eleanor (Mrs Reginald Jebb) 146n
Belloc, Elizabeth 146n
Belloc, Hilaire 9, 30, 48n, 101n, 112, 130, 145, 146, 174, 176, 177, 178, 180, 181, 193, 194, 195, 234, 259, 261, 263, 269, 284, 298, 307, 320
Bendern, Count John de (formerly Forrest) 312
Bennett, Arnold 294n
Benson, Guy 170n
Benson, Lady Violet (née Manners, 'Letty') 170, 173
Berenson, Bernard 116n, 249
Berkeley, Sir Lennox 280, 313
Berkeley, Mary, Countess of (née Lowell) 213n
Berkeley, Randal, 8th Earl of 213n
Berlin, Sir Isaiah 134
Bernadette, Saint 251n
Berners, Gerald, 14th Baron 49n, 113n
Berrier, Count du, 55
Berry, Michael 117n, 127
Berry, Lady Pamela (née Smith) 117, 123, 127, 128, 136, 137, 147, 156, 220, 221, 223, 230, 250, 253, 302
Bertier, Mme 134
Betjeman, John 47n, 67, 101n, 113, 121, 209n, 259, 298, 314
Betjeman, Penelope (née Chetwode) 47, 83, 167, 168, 202n
Bevan, Rt Hon. Aneurin 191, 245n, 302
Bevin, Rt. Hon. Ernest 86, 130n
Bibesco, Princess Marthe 100n
Big Parade, The (film) 56
Bigelow, Josephine 210n

Birdwood, Lord 280
Birgi, Nuri 269n
Birkenhead, Frederick Edward, 1st Earl of 171, 316
Birkenhead, Frederick, 2nd Earl of 83, 171, 229, 301
Birkenhead, Sheila, Countess of (née Berry) 201
Birkett, Sir Norman (later Lord) 84n
Birley, Mark 225n
Birley, Oswald 225n
Birley, Lady Rhoda 225
Black Mischief (Waugh) 5, 15, 16n, 28n, 43, 44n, 52n
Blackton, J. Stuart 7
Blackwood, Lady Caroline 293n
Blake, Robert (later Baron) 218, 219
Blundell, Mrs Violet 35
Bonham-Carter, Mark (later Baron) 272
Bonham-Carter, Lady Violet (later Baroness Asquith), 46, 163
Bonjour Tristesse (Sagan) 250
Boothby, Robert (later Baron) 316
Borghese, Pauline 80
Bossuet, Jacques 26
Boulby, Mr 12, 18, 23, 31, 139
Bowles, Jane 211
Bowles, Paul 211
Bowra, Sir Maurice 47, 197n, 231
Boyle, Stuart 100, 103n
Bracken, Brendan, later 1st Viscount 69, 97, 155, 316
Bradford, 5th Earl of 46n
Brains Trust, The (radio programme) 87
Brazilian Adventure (Fleming) 38
Brideshead Revisited (Waugh) 60n, 80, 81n, 82–3, 85, 90n, 246, 250n
Brissac, Pierre de Cossé, Duc de 119
Broglie, Prince Jean de 79
Broome, Mrs (caretaker) 38, 39
Broome, Teddy 40
Browning, Robert 104n, 163
Brownlow, Dorothy, Baroness (previously Countess Beatty) 204n
Brownlow, Edward, 7th Baron 204
Brownlow, Katherine, ('Kitty') Baroness (née Kinloch) 14, 43, 90n, 173, 204n
Brownlow, Peregrine, 6th Baron ('Perry') 13, 14n, 43, 59, 60, 90n, 173, 186, 198, 199, 204, 311n
Bruce, David 298n, 304n

Buckingham, George Villiers, Duke of 163
Bullock, Captain Malcolm 29
Bullock, Lady Victoria (née Stanley) 29n
Burckhardt, Carl 248
Burgess, Guy 161n
Burnt-Out Case, A (Greene) 284n
Butler, Dame Georgina 33, 36
Butler, R.A.B. 210, 224
Butler, Reginald 161n, 165
Butlin, Billy (later Sir William) 90
Byrne, John 4
Byron, George Gordon, 6th Baron 308
Byron, Robert 71, 91
Bystander 31n

C (Baring) 264–5
Cameron of Lochiel, Colonel Sir Donald, 78
Camoys, Ralph, 5th Baron 205n
Campbell, Commander A.B. 87
Campbell, Robin 82n
Camrose, Mary, Viscountess 137
Camrose, 2nd Viscount 45n
Canova, Antonio 157n, 164
Capel, Captain Arthur ('Boy') 135n
Caraman, Father Philip 295, 301, 319
Cardenas, General Lazaro 67n
Carlsen, Captain Kurt 125
Carnarvon, 4th Earl of 51n
Carnarvon, 5th Earl of 37n
Carnes, Harry *see* Fleet, Simon
Carr, Robert (later Baron Carr of Hadley) 161, 163
Carter, Howard 37n
Casati, Marchese 47n
Cassel, Sir Ernest 197
Castellane, marquis Boniface de 267
Castlerosse, Valentine, Viscount 43n
Cautionary Tales for Children (Belloc) 176n
Cecil, Algernon 61, 71
Cecil, Lord David 15, 69, 199, 277n, 312
Cecil, Lady David (Rachel, née McCarthy) 15, 69
Cecil, Lord Edward ('Nigs') 157n
Cecil, Michael 37
Cecil, Robert (later 6th Marquess of Salisbury) 37
Ceram, Kurt Marek 164n
Chalk Garden, The 96n, 239n

Chamberlain, Neville 69
Chancellor, John 238n, 260
Chanel, Coco 321n
Channon, Sir Henry ('Chips') 12, 34, 233
Chaplin, Charlie 95, 129
Charteris, Hugo (novelist) 191
Charteris, Hon. Guy 124n
Charteris, Laura *see* Marlborough
Charteris, Mrs Hugo (Virginia) 191n
Chesterfield, Philip Stanhope, Lord 103n
Chetwode, Field Marshal, 1st Baron 47n, 314
Chetwynd-Talbot, Lady Victoria 48n
Chiang Kai-shek 85n
Chirnside, Joan 44n
Chitto, Pierino 119
Choiseul, Duc and Duchesse de 155
Christian, Prince, of Schleswig-Holstein 32n
Churchill, Clarissa *see* Eden, Clarissa
Churchill, Clementine, Baroness Spencer, 208, 316n
Churchill, Diana (later Duncan-Sandys) 14
Churchill, John ('Jack') 86n, 251
Churchill, Lady Randolph ('Jennie') 250, 251
Churchill, John, 1st Duke of Marlborough 316n
Churchill, June (Mrs Randolph Churchill, née Osborne), 103, 175, 214–15
Churchill, Pamela (née Digby) 103n, 200
Churchill, Randolph Spencer 12, 13, 14, 74, 80, 87, 103, 113, 161n, 163, 174, 175, 177–80, 183, 190, 206, 207n, 214, 222, 226, 229, 234, 252, 271, 281, 299, 306, 307, 318
Churchill, Sarah 222
Churchill, Sir Winston 13, 14n, 41n, 69, 70, 74, 75, 85n, 86n, 89n, 100, 129, 136n, 143, 151n, 152, 169n, 206n, 207n, 232, 316, 317
Citkovitz, Israel 293n
Clark-Kerr, Sir Archibald and Lady 58
Claudel, Paul 142
Clifford, Alexander 132
Clifford, Lady (Alice) 119
Clifford, Anne *see* Norwich
Clifford, Atalanta 119n
Clifford, Sir Bede 119n
Clifford, Pandora (Mrs Timothy Jones) 117, 119n

Coat Without Seam, The (Baring) 83
Cobb, Mrs Postlethwaite 5
Cochran, C.B. 7–8, 13
Cochrane, Thomas (later 13th Earl of Dundonald) 33, 36
Cocteau, Jean 125, 162
Coglan, Mr 35, 36
Colefax, Sybil 157
Colette 198
Collens, Rupert *see* Mackeson
Colville, Sir John 136n
Comedians, The (Greene) 232n
Connolly, Cyril 81, 83, 91, 92, 99, 113, 191, 215, 217, 268–9, 307–8
Connor, William ('Cassandra') 105n
Conrad, Joseph 325
Continental Daily Mail 160n
Cooksley, Rev. G.A.H. 141
Cooper, Lady Agnes (née Duff) 250
Cooper, Sir Alfred Duff, 1st Viscount Norwich 6, 7, 8, 14, 18, 23, 26n, 30n, 31n, 44, 47, 49, 50, 51, 58, 63, 64, 69–70, 74, 75, 77–80, 83, 85, 86n, 88, 90, 97n, 98, 100, 103–4, 105, 108, 109, 112, 116, 117, 124, 128, 137, 138, 139, 144, 151, 153, 155, 159, 160, 162, 163, 167, 169–72, 175, 176, 178, 179, 180, 182, 183, 185, 186, 189n, 192, 193, 194, 202, 218, 219, 228n, 232, 235–6, 242, 248n, 257, 259, 260, 261, 270n, 276, 285, 292, 304, 309, 312n, 314, 325n
Cooper, Artemis 167, 205, 206, 207, 219, 222, 225, 235, 240, 256, 284
Cooper, Sybil 180n, 250n
Cornhill Magazine 85n
Corrigan, Laura 12, 31n
Corvedale, Edward, Viscount (later 4th Earl Baldwin of Bewdley) 312–13, 314
Coward, Noël 29n, 41n, 108, 110, 112
Cowles, Fleur 162
Cowles, Virginia (later Crawley) 162
Cranborne, Viscountess (née Vere; later Marchioness of Salisbury; 'Betty') 30, 31, 33, 37, 152, 200
Cranborne, Robert, Viscount (later 5th Marquess of Salisbury; 'Bobbity') 30, 31, 33, 37, 43, 155
Crawley, Aidan 162n
Crewe, Marchioness of 64
Crickmere, Mrs 283
Cripps, Sir Stafford 314
Cronin, Fr. 141

Cronin, Vincent 230, 231
Crosby, Caresse 210
Crosby, Harry 210n
Crosse, Jenny *see* Nicholson
Crosse, Patrick 132n, 188n
Cruddas, Captain Hugh 113n
Cudlipp, Hugh 183n
Cunard, Sir Bache, 3rd Bt 14n
Cunard, Lady (Emerald; née Burke) 4, 12, 14, 17, 94, 102n
Cunard, Nancy, 102n
Cunard, Victor 249
Curtis Brown, Spencer 261
Curzon of Kedleston, Grace, Marchioness, (formerly Mrs Alfred Duggan) 71, 157
Curzon of Kedleston, George, 1st Marquess 19n, 71n
Cust, Henry John 6, 308
Cuthbertson, Graham 110n
Cuthbertson, Penelope (Mrs Desmond Guinness) 110n
Cuthbertson, Richard 110n
Cuthbertson, Teresa *see* Jungman

d'Abernon, Edgar, 1st Viscount 31
d'Abernon, Viscountess 35
Daily Express 13, 20n, 41n, 59, 208n, 223n, 227n, 234n, 236, 268, 308
Daily Herald 13
Daily Mail 28, 49, 51, 52n, 53, 54, 100, 124n, 132n, 170, 185n, 234, 277, 278, 290, 294, 308, 318n
Daily Mirror 105n, 183n, 185n
Daily Sketch 19n, 318n
Daily Telegraph 117n, 234n
Daintree, Adrian 313
Dalhousie, Margaret, Countess of 247
Dalhousie, Simon, 16th Earl of 247, 263
d'Arcy, Father Martin, SJ 30, 33–6, 70, 88
D'Arms, John 282n, 285
Dashwood, Lady 29
David (Cooper) 83
Davie, Michael 62n
De La Warr, 9th Earl 130n
Deakin, F.W. (later Sir William) 89
Dean Paul, Brenda 71
Dear Animated Bust (Baring) 48n
Decazes, Duc de 79n
Decline and Fall (Waugh), 4, 42, 91, 190n, 310
Deedes, William (later Lord) 57n

Deffand, Marie, Marquise du 155
Delavigne, Doris (later Viscountess Castlerosse) 43
Denham, Sir Edward 22n
Dennis, Nigel 320
Derby, Edward, 18th Earl of 149n, 313
Derby, Isabel, Countess of 149
Desborough, 1st Baron 253n
Desborough, Etty, Baroness 253n
Devonport, Lord 193
Devonshire, Andrew, Duke of 117n, 149n, 242n, 269 277n
Devonshire, Deborah ('Debo') Duchess of 172n
Diana Cooper (Ziegler) 144n
Diary of a Nobody (Grossmith) 93
Dietz, Howard 103n
Dixon, Sir Pierson 317
Dr No (film) 301
Don Quixote (Cervantes) 315
Donaldson, Frances 8, 184n, 197n, 268n, 287n
Donaldson, John George Stuart 287
Donaldson, Rose 197
Donegall, Edward, 6th Marquess of 15
Dorment, Richard 215n
Doughty-Tichborne, Sir Alfred Joseph, 11th Bt 240n
Douglas, Norman 87
Driberg, Tom 161, 218n, 241
Drinkwater, Fr. 141
Dru, Alexander ('Alick') 37n
Duchess of Jermyn Street (Fielding) 307
Dudley, Eric Ward, 3rd Earl of 19
Duff, Lady Caroline, (née Paget) 112n
Duff, Lady Juliet 48, 112n, 145, 189, 199, 225, 241, 256, 273, 319, 320, 321
Duff, Sir Michael, 3rd Bt 112n
Duff, Sir Robin 48n
Dufferin and Ava, 4th Marquess of 293n
Duggan, Alfred (Sr) 71
Duggan, Alfred 19n, 30–33, 35, 37, 150, 152, 154, 157, 307
Duggan, Hubert 19, 56, 111, 292
Duke, Doris 12, 15, 292
Duncan-Sandys, Rt. Hon. (later Lord) Edwin 14n
Dunn, Lady Mary, 60n
Dunn, Philip, 2nd Bt 40, 60
Dunsany, Beatrice, Baroness (née Child-Villiers) 36
Dupplin, Viscount 250n

Duveen, Joseph, 1st Baron 139

Eden, Anthony (later 1st Earl of Avon) 51, 68n, 86n, 100, 150, 151, 160, 161n, 163, 164, 206, 234, 271
Eden, Clarissa (née Churchill, later Countess of Avon) 151, 161, 163, 164, 290, 318
Edinburgh, Prince Philip, Duke of 151n, 266
Edmund Campion (Waugh) 47, 52, 56, 61n, 277
Edward VII, King 250n, 305n
Edward VIII, King (later Duke of Windsor), 14n, 62n, 245, 269
Egg, Augustus, R.A. 161, 163, 164, 224
Eisenhower, President Dwight D. 162n
Elcho, Hugo ('Ego') Charteris, Lord 170n, 277n, 298n
Eldon, 4th Earl of 33n
Eldon, Magdalen, Countess (née Fraser), 33, 35, 110, 112, 190, 234, 278, 321
Eliot, T.S. 45, 71n, 222n
Elizabeth, Queen, the Queen Mother 14n
Elizabeth I, Queen 128n, 129, 130
Elizabeth II, Queen 128, 129n, 151n, 156, 266, 277, 282
Elmsley, Lord see Lygon, William
Elwes, Simon 48n, 291
Emeny, Stewart 51n, 57n
Encounter 209n, 214, 297n
End of the Battle, The (Waugh) 272n
Enthusiasm (Knox) 111
Erroll, 17th Earl of 235n
Eurich, Richard 118
Evelyn Waugh: A Biography (Sykes) 69
Evelyn Waugh: Portrait of a Country Neighbour (Donaldson) 197n
Evelyn Waugh: The Early Years 1903–1939 (Stannard) 52n
Evening Standard 232

Face to Face (TV series) 279n
Fahie, Norah 180, 194, 198, 262, 273
Fairbanks, Douglas, Jr 167, 168
Fairbanks, Douglas, Snr 48n, 204n
Faisal, King of Iraq 256n
Falconi, Muzio 53n
Farouk, King of Egypt 113, 229n
Farrell, Charles 280n, 313
Farrell, Lady Katherine ('Kitty') 280, 313

Fellowes, Marguerite ('Daisy') 79, 135, 153, 205, 249
Fellowes, Reginald 79n, 153
Fermor, Patrick Leigh ('Paddy') 9, 108, 136, 147, 148n, 149n, 156n, 163, 197, 198, 211, 236, 239, 245, 248, 314n
Février, Jacques 120
Fielding, Major Alexander ('Xan') 102n, 170n, 192, 217, 219, 220, 321, 325
Fielding, Daphne (née Vivian, then Marchioness of Bath) 102, 170, 192, 201, 217, 219, 220, 239, 240, 243, 307, 325
Fielding, Mary (née Yackjee) 321n
Fife, Agnes (née Hay), Countess of 235n
Fife, 1st Duke of 250n
Fife, 5th Earl of 250n
Figaro Littéraire 198
Fisher, Dr Geoffrey 282
Fitzclarence, Lady Elizabeth 235n
Fitzgerald, F. Scott 13n
FitzHerbert, Emily-Albert 304
FitzHerbert, Giles 191n, 292–5, 305, 318
FitzHerbert, Margaret see Waugh, Margaret
Fleet, Simon (Harry Carnes) 256, 257, 258, 267, 296, 297, 321
Fleming, Ann (née Charteris, previously O'Neill; Rothermere) 123, 124, 129n, 130, 142, 146, 170, 184, 191, 199, 203, 205, 207, 208, 209, 210n, 226, 234, 241, 243, 258n, 260, 269n, 273, 278, 279, 282–5, 290, 301, 311, 313, 314, 319, 321, 322n, 324, 325
Fleming, Caspar 142n, 146n, 313, 314, 319, 322
Fleming, Ian 129n, 150, 154, 155, 205, 313
Fleming, Peter 38, 85n, 209n
Flower, Herbert 250n
Fonteyn, Margot 305
Forbes, Alastair ('Ali') 105, 186, 205, 221, 239, 241, 287, 288, 290
Ford, Ford Madox 127
Foucauld, Father Charles de 193n
Four Studies in Loyalty (Sykes) 91n
Foxglove Saga, The (A. Waugh) 282
Foyle, Christina 241, 252
Francis Xavier, St 150, 151, 152, 154
Frankau, Pamela 163
Franks, Brian 314

Fraser, Lady Antonia (née Pakenham) 14, 29, 33n
Fraser, Evelyn Anne (née Grant) 257, 258, 288, 289
Fraser, Sir Hugh 33
Fraser, Sir Ian James 257, 258
Fraser, Magdalen *see* Eldon, Lady
Fraser, Veronica 83n
Freeman, John 279n
Fremantle, Anne (née Huth-Jackson) 193
Fremantle, Christopher 193n
Freud, Lucian 123, 258, 293
Freyssinet, Eugène 251n
Frith, W.P. 254
Frog, The (Wallace) 151n
Fry, Christopher and Phyllis 313

Gable, Clark 48n, 204
Gage, Henry, 6th Viscount 172, 225
Gage, Imogen Viscountess ('Mogs') 172, 226
Gallipoli (Moorehead) 230, 231
Gandarillas, Antonio ('Tony') de, Baron 308
Gange, Christopher 2, 3, 4
Garbo, Greta 41n
Gardiner, Gerald (Baron Gardiner) 227n
Gardner, Evelyn, (Mrs Evelyn Waugh) 5, 17n, 58n
Gargoyle Club 71n
Garibaldi, Giuseppe 265
Garland, Rodney 185n
Garnett, Richard 261
Gary, Romain 248n
Gaulle, Charles de 74, 242n, 259, 277, 317, 321
Gellhorn, Martha 9, 185, 290, 292
Gendel, Anna 298n, 313
Gendel, Judy 108, 111, 137, 211, 235, 241, 248, 260, 265, 266, 277, 284, 285, 297, 300, 304, 305, 306, 311, 313, 314, 316, 323, 325
Gendel, Milton, 235n, 298n, 300
Gentlemen Prefer Blondes (Loos) 139
Geoffroy, Georges 83n
George V. King 43n
George VI, King 14n, 62n, 128, 129
Getty, J. Paul 325
Ghika, Barbara (formerly Rothschild) 313
Ghika, Nico 197n, 313n
Giles, Frank 130, 209, 224

Giles, Lady Katharine ('Kitty') 130n, 209n, 224, 280, 313
Gilmour, Sir Ian, 3rd Bt 245
Glasgow, Miss Marjorie 34
Glass, Douglas 247n, 249
Glen, Sir Alexander 45n
Glenconner, Christopher, 2nd Baron 21n
Glover, Dr 36
God and the Atom (Knox) 89
God, Graves and Scholars (Ceram) 164
Goddard, Rayner, Lord Chief Justice 245
Goffin, Magdalen 222n
Goller, Dr 118
Goodman, Arnold, Baron 2
Gordon-Lennox, Victor 234
Gormanston, Jenico, 17th Viscount 218
Gould, Anna Jay, (marquise de Castellane) 267n
Graham, Alastair 60
Graham, Sir Ronald 266
Grandi, Count Dino 53, 219
Grant, Major Allister Edward 71, 98, 257n
Grant, Bridget (née Herbert) 31, 71n, 98, 124n, 165, 229, 257n, 258
Grant, Duncan 294n
Grant, Polly 124
Graphic, The 5
Graves, Robert 132n
Greco, Juliette 248
Green, Henry *see* Yorke, Henry
Greene, Graham 137n, 138, 142n, 164, 165, 166, 191, 198, 199, 218, 250, 282–3, 284, 323, 324, 325
Grenfell, Julian 253
Greville, Mrs Ronald 14
Griffith, D.W. 7
Grimond, Joseph (later Baron Grimond) 161, 163
Groom, Archie 161
Grünne, Willy de 184
Gryll Grange (Peacock) 271
Guinness, Alec 242n
Guinness, Beatrice (previously Jungman; 'Gloomy') 29
Guinness, Bryan (later 2nd Baron Moyne) 5, 14n, 90n
Guinness, Desmond 110n
Guinness, Diana (née Mitford; later Lady Mosley) 5, 6, 14, 90n
Guinness, Lady Honor 34
Guinness, Joan (née Yarde-Buller) 45

Guinness, Jonathan 5, 90
Guinness, Group Captain Thomas Loel 45n, 140
Guinness, Richard 29n
Guinness, Tanis 103, 226, 227
Guinness, Walter *see* Moyne, 1st Baron

Haig, Field Marshall Lord 105n, 218, 219
Haig, Lady 219
Haile Selassie, Emperor 5, 49
Hailes, Patrick Buchanan-Hepburn, 1st Baron 290, 318
Halifax, Edward, 3rd Viscount 68
Hamilton, Hamish 218
Hance, Captain J.H. 15, 16, 304, 305
Hance, Jackie 16, 19, 61, 304
Handful of Dust, A (Waugh) 38, 40n, 41, 45
Harding, Philip 104
Hardinge, George (later 3rd Baron Hardinge of Penshurst) 157n
Harriman, Averell 103n
Harris, Henry ('Bogey') 14
Hart-Davis, Deirdre (Mrs Ronald Balfour) 191
Hart-Davis, Richard 180n
Hart-Davis, Sir Rupert 180, 231, 247, 249, 250n, 252, 261, 265n, 267, 268, 270, 271n, 280, 281
Hartin, W.F. 53n
Harton, F.P., Dean of Wells 168
Hastings, Cristina, Viscountess (later Baroness Milford) 47
Hastings, John, Viscount (later 15th Earl of Huntingdon) 47n
Hatchards 267, 270, 271
Hatry, Clarence 170
Hay, Ian, (Major-General John Hay Beith) 122
Haynes, Mr (commissioner in British Guiana) 23–4
Hayward, John 222
Head, Antony, (later 1st Viscount) 113, 142
Head, Lady Dorothea, (later Viscountess, née Ashley-Cooper) 13, 117, 225, 226
Hearst, W.R. 40, 54
Heart in Exile (Garland) 185
Heber-Percy, Robert 113n
Helena (Waugh) 83, 105, 109, 110, 112n, 202, 203
Helena, Princess of Schleswig-Holstein 32n

Hemingway, Ernest 54, 143, 185n
Hennessy, Annabel 243
Henriques, Colonel Robert 218, 219, 221
Herbert, Auberon 87, 88, 93, 109, 112, 117, 206, 222, 231n, 271, 273, 290, 294, 303, 320
Herbert, Aubrey, MP 37n, 51n, 191n
Herbert, Bridget *see* Grant
Herbert, David 41
Herbert, Gabriel 31, 37
Herbert, Laura *see* Waugh
Herbert, Mary (née Vesey) 37n, 51, 60, 63, 70, 197, 222, 230, 231
Herbert, Mervyn 231
Hesketh, Christian ('Kistie') Baroness 257
Hesketh, 2nd Baron 257n
Heygate, John 58n
Hill, Derek 219
Hitler, Adolf 59, 69, 78n, 215
Hoare, Sir Samuel, 2nd Bt, (later 1st Viscount Templewood) 51n
Hofmannsthal, Lady Elizabeth von (née Paget) 88n, 97, 147, 211, 246n, 297
Hofmannsthal, Raimund von 88, 97n, 104, 129, 179, 205, 238n, 246n, 252, 274, 279, 285
Hofmannsthal, Romana von (*see* McEwen) 104n, 238n
Holland-Martin, Christopher 277
Hollis, Christopher 30, 31, 33, 34, 36, 37, 167, 201
Holloway, Thomas 254n
Holy Places, The (Waugh) 150n, 154, 155
Hood, Samuel, 6th Viscount 86, 87
Hore-Belisha, Rt Hon Leslie 194
Horizon 41n, 81n, 91, 99, 100
Horner, Edward 250, 251
Horner, Sir John 31, 251
Horsbrugh, Florence, Baroness 190
Howard, Elizabeth Jane 305n, 313
Hulton, Sir Edward 116n, 117
Hulton, Lady (Nika, née Yourivitch) 164, 272
Hunt, William Holman, 164, 286
Huston, John 198n, 248n, 313
Hutchinson, Jeremy (later Lord Hutchinson of Lullington) 135n
Hutten, Ulrich von 133n
Huxley, Aldous 154, 223n
Huxley, Sir Julian 86, 87, 97
Hylton, Perdita, Baroness (née Asquith) 31, 110, 190, 226, 238n, 265, 291

Hylton, William, 4th Baron 110n, 238n, 265

International Herald Tribune 160n
Ioannovitch, HH Prince Vsevolode 29n
Isaacs, Sir Rufus (later 1st Marquess of Reading) 302
Isherwood, Christopher 87
Island in the Sun (A. Waugh) 44n
Ismay, General Hastings, 1st Baron, ('Pug') 136, 292n
Iveagh, 2nd Earl of 34n

Jacobs, Barbara 44n
Jaipur, Maharajah of ('Jai') 210–11
James, Edward 193, 194, 292
James, Henry 92
James, Robert Rhodes 298n
Janzé, Phyllis de 153
Jarrett, Father Bede 194
Jebb, Eleanor 298n
Jebb, Gladwyn (later 1st Baron Gladwyn) 86, 87, 110, 111
Jebb, Julian ('Belloc's Leprechaun') 298n
Jebb, Reginald 146n, 298n
Jellicoe, George, 2nd Earl 224n
Jellicoe, Patricia, Countess, (née O'Kane) 224
Jenkins, Roy 312
Jessell, Edward, 2nd Baron Jessel 137n
Joad, Dr C.E.M. 87n
John, King of England 257
John XXIII, Pope 251n, 297, 316n, 322n
John of Gaunt, 2nd Duke of Lancaster 77n
Johnston, Edward 272
Jolliffe, Alice (later Chancellor; Windsor-Clive) 238, 243, 257, 258, 259, 260n, 295n
Jolliffe, William *see* Hylton, Baron
Jonathan Swift: a Short Character (Dennis) 320
Jones, Enid Lady, (née Bagnold) 9, 96, 117, 123, 134n, 158, 159, 164, 172, 200, 219, 225, 239, 294n
Jones, Laurian (later Winn) 134, 147
Jones, Sir Roderick 96n, 134n, 231
Jones, Timothy 117n
Jordan, Mrs Dorothea 235
Joseph I, Emperor 316n
Joy, Thomas Musgrave 118n
Julian of Norwich 154n
Jungman, Nico 5, 29n

Jungman, Teresa ('Baby'; the 'Dutch girl' later Mrs. Graham Cuthbertson) 5, 6, 8, 9, 12, 20, 29n, 38, 39–40, 42, 51, 64n, 110, 148n, 171
Jungman, Zita 5, 19, 29n, 171
Justinian, Emperor 110

Kahn, Otto 227n
Keeler, Christine 299n, 302n
Kemsley, Edith, Viscountess 137
Kemsley, 1st Viscount
Kennedy, President John 297n
Kent, Prince George, Duke of 43n
Kent, Princess Marina, Duchess of 43n
Khan, Aga 144, 210
Khan, Prince Aly 45n
Khrushchev, Nikita 480n
Kinloch, Sir David, Bt 14n
Kinross, Patrick Balfour, ('Pauper') 3rd Baron 19, 47, 49, 52, 53, 56, 71n, 172, 238, 249, 280, 289, 313, 318, 321
Kinross, Angela, Baroness (née Culme-Seymour) 71
Kipling, Rudyard 325
Knickerbocker, H.R. ('Cholly') 54n
Knox, Monsignor Ronald 12, 31, 61, 83, 89, 98, 100n, 102, 111, 118, 150, 178, 180, 182, 196, 216, 217, 228, 231, 234, 237, 238, 239, 241, 242, 244–7, 250, 251, 253, 254–5, 257, 260, 261, 265, 267, 268, 269, 272, 273n
Koestler, Arthur 82n, 83
Kommer, Dr Rudolf 13, 15, 29, 66, 297
Korda, Alexander 49n, 62n, 140n, 141
Kreipe, General 136n

Lady Chatterley's Lover (Lawrence) 297n
Lafone, Michael 55
Lambert, Mme de 184
Lambton, Antony, Lord 137
Lambton, Lady Beatrix 293n
Lambton, Belinda, Lady ('Bindy') 137n
Lambton, Edward, Viscount 293n
Lambton, Lady Isabella 293n
Lambton, Lady Lucinda 293n
Lambton, Lady Mary 293n
Lambton, Lady Rose 293n
Landseer, Sir Edwin 254
Lattre de Tassigny, Marshal Jean de 175
Lauritzen, Peter and Lady Rose 249n
Lavery, Lady (Hazel) (née Martyn) 4, 14, 30, 41, 90n, 267

Lavery, Sir John 4, 14n, 199n, 206
Lawrence, D.H. 294n
Lawrence, Gertrude 28n
Laycock, Lady (Angela) 137, 138
Laycock, Major General Sir Robert 12, 17n, 29, 74, 76, 79–80, 148n, 165
Le Fanu, Sheridan 51n
Leclerc, General 175
Leconfield, 2nd Baron 48n
Ledebur, Count Christian ('Boon') von 95n
Ledebur, Count Friedrich von 95, 136n, 198, 248
Lees-Milne, Alvilde (née Molesworth Bridges; formerly Viscountess Chaplin) 136n
Lees-Milne, James 136n
Legacy, A (Bedford) 223
Legge, Diana 32, 35, 37
Lehmann, John 277
Lehmann, Rosamond (later Baroness Milford) 200, 277n
Leigh, Vivien (Lady Olivier) 213
Leo X, Pope 132, 133
Leopold I, Emperor 316n
Letters of Ann Fleming, The (ed. Amory) 210n, 260n, 269n
Leverson, Ada 111
Levita, Bill 325
Lewis, C.S. 219
Lewis, Sir Duncan Orr, 2nd Bt 173n
Lewis, Lady Orr (Phyllis; née Bibby) 173n
Lewis, Rosa 43n, 102n, 307
Life (magazine) 88, 213, 214
Life of Hilaire Belloc (Speaight) 234n
Life of Ronald Knox, The (Waugh) 251n, 256, 260n, 272, 273
Light of Common Day, The (Cooper) 65n, 261, 265n, 266–7, 268–9, 270n
Lincoln, Charles 117n
Lister, Charles 253
Lister, Laura see Lovat
Little Learning, A (Waugh) 276, 303n, 307n, 309, 313
Living Room, The (Greene) 164n, 165n
Lloyd George, Rt Hon. David 169n
Lolita (Nabokov) 218, 250, 269
Long Day's Journey into Night (O'Neill) 259n
Longford, 6th Earl of see Pakenham
Longford, Elizabeth Countess of see Pakenham

Lonsdale, 4th Earl of 48n
Loom of Youth, The (A. Waugh) 44n
Loos, Anita 139n
Lord Derby, King of Lancashire (R. Churchill) 190n
Lord M (Cecil) 199n
Lorenzo the Magnificent 133n
Losch, Otillie (later James; 'Tilly') 7, 193n, 203, 292
Loughborough, Francis, Baron 45n
Loughborough, Sheila Baroness 45
Louise, Princess 250n
Lovat, Laura Baroness (née Lister) 30, 32, 33, 36, 100, 143n
Lovat, Simon Fraser, 14th Baron 32n, 33n, 83n
Love Among the Ruins (Waugh) 157n, 170, 171, 173
Loved One, The (Waugh) 95n, 99n, 100, 102, 103, 123
Lovelies Over London (film) 62n
Lowell, Robert 293n
Lucan, 7th Earl of 4
Lucas, Audrey 20
Luce, Henry 216, 217
Lunn, Sir Arnold 30, 35, 36, 138
Lutyens, Sir Edwin 45n, 61
Lygon, Lady Dorothy ('Coote', 'Poll',) 6, 8, 16, 221
Lygon, Henry 45n
Lygon, Hugh 6
Lygon, Lady Lettice 6
Lygon, lady Mary ('Maimie') 6, 29, 38, 43, 50, 61, 184, 199, 255, 292
Lygon, Richard 6
Lygon, Lady Sibell 6, 13, 14, 43, 197
Lygon, William (Lord Elmley; later 8th Earl Beauchamp) 6, 61n
Lynn, Olga ('Oggie') 40, 116n, 124, 127, 135, 136, 147, 158, 210, 219, 220, 238, 239, 240
Lyttelton, George 180n, 265n, 271n

Macaulay, Rose 242n, 257
MacCarthy, Sir Desmond 15n, 139
MacDougal, Tommy 13
McEwen, Bridget 194, 306
McEwen, Sir John 1st Bt 306n
McEwen, Roderick (Rory) 104n, 238, 257n, 306n
McEwen, Romana 104n, 238n
Mackenzie, Compton 88n, 137

Mackeson, Sir Rupert, 2nd Bt 2, 3, 4
Mackintosh, Alastair 136
Maclean, Fitzroy, 1st Bt 83, 229
Maclise, Daniel 254
Macmillan, Lady Dorothy (née Cavendish) 277n
Macmillan, Harold, 1st Earl of Stockton 196n, 216, 250, 262, 272n, 300n, 301, 314n
Madame de (Vilmorin) 162, 163
Madame de Pompadour (Mitford) 153, 161, 189–90, 192
Magnus-Allcroft, Sir Philip Montefiore and lady 291n
Malinovsky, Bronislaw 102
Mallett, Lady ('Peggy') 58n
Mallett, Victor (later Sir Victor) 58n, 114
Man Between, The (Wapshott) 138n
Man I Knew, The (Haig) 219
Man Who was Greenmantle, The (M. FitzHerbert) 191n
Manuel 'The Happy', King of Portugal 133, 144n
Marcel Proust (Painter) 325n
Marching into April (Charteris) 191n
Margaret, Princess 14n, 151n, 204, 210
Maria Pasqua (Goffin) 222, 224, 228, 229
Marie Louise, Princess 32, 33, 35
Marlborough, Laura, Duchess of (née Charteris) 19, 191n
Marling, Colonel Sir Percival and Lady 34
Marriott, Major General Sir John 277n
Marriott, Lady ('Momo') 277
Mary, Queen 145
Mary Gloster, The (Kipling) 325n
Massigli, Odette 102, 116
Massigli, René 102n
Maugham, Syrie (née Barnardo) 17, 51
Maugham, William Somerset 17n, 97n, 132, 134, 135, 139, 249, 261, 262, 289
Mauriac, François 125
Maurice Baring, A Postscript (Lovat) 100, 143n
Maurois, André 71
Max (Cecil) 312n
Melbourne, William, 2nd Viscount 199n, 220
Melville, Herman 198n
Men at Arms (Waugh) 115n, 124, 132, 141, 164
Mendl, Lady 218
Mendl, Sir Charles 120, 136

Mercury Presides (Fielding) 201n
Messel, Oliver 12, 28n, 41, 273n
Mestrovic, Ivan 34
Meyrick, Mrs 55
Milford, Wogan, 2nd Baron 47n, 200n
Millais, Sir John Everett 164, 254
Milmo, Helenus 237n
Milner, 1st Viscount 157n
Milner, Viscountess 157
Milnes-Gaskell, Charles 53, 56
Minton, John 234
Miracle, The 4, 7–8, 12, 13n, 16, 18, 20, 21, 23, 25, 27, 28, 31, 32, 33, 36, 65, 127, 195n, 267n, 300
Mitford, Deborah ('Debo') *see* Devonshire
Mitford Diana *see* Guinness
Mitord, Nancy (Mrs Peter Rodd) 10, 17, 83, 109, 112, 115, 117n, 121n, 125, 126n, 127n, 128, 129n, 134n, 138, 139, 153n, 161, 163, 183, 189–90, 192, 201n, 202, 209, 216, 218, 221–4, 242, 244, 267n, 290, 294n, 325
Mitford, Unity ('Bobo') 215n
Moffat, Curtis 13n, 17
Moffat, Ivan 13n, 20
Monsell, 1st Viscount 136n
Monsieur Verdoux (film) 95
Montagu, Rt Hon. Edwin 77n, 111n
Montagu, Judy *see* Gendel
Montesi, Wilma 236n
Moore, Sir Thomas 270n
Moorehead, Alan 230, 231, 232
Morgan, Charles Langbridge 199
Morgan, Hilda (née Vaughan) 199n
Morgan, Sir John 258n
Morning Post 57n
Morris, Ivan 314n
Mortimer, Raymond 294
Morton, J.B. ('Beachcomber') 20n, 137, 138n
Mosley, Lady *see* Guinness, Diana
Mosley, Sir Oswald 14n
Moss, William Stanley 136n
Mountbatten of Burma, Edwina, Countess 197
Mountbatten of Burma, Louis, 1st Earl 151, 181
Mowbray, Sheila, Baroness (née Gully) 172
Mowbray, William Stourton, 25th Baron 172n

Moyne, Bryan, 2nd Baron see Guinness
Moyne, Walter, 1st Baron 30
Mr Loveday's Little Outing (Waugh) 61n
Mrs Dale's Diary (radio series) 153
Muggeridge, Malcolm 226, 230, 242
Mussolini, Benito 49, 52n, 59
My Fair Lady (musical) 252
My Father: The True Story (Baldwin) 218
Myers, Eve 37n

Nabakov, Vladimir 218
Nasser, Gamal Abdel 229n
Nelson, Maud 238n
New Statesman 239n, 268
Newby, P.H. 205
News Chronicle 51, 57n
Newton, 3rd Baron 36
Niarchos, Stavros 209n, 228n
Nicholas, Prince of Greece 43n
Nichols, Sir Philip & Lady 226n
Nicholson, Jenny (Mrs Patrick Crosse)
    108, 132n, 188, 205, 219–22, 228, 234,
    235, 239, 244, 245, 249, 253, 260, 262,
    263, 265, 297, 302, 304, 305
Nicolson, Sir Harold 155, 157
Ninety-Two Days (Waugh) 23n, 38, 91n
Niven, David & Hjordis 117n
Noailles, Comtesse de 222n
Noblesse Oblige 209n
Noel-Buxton, 2nd Baron 208n, 223n,
    324
Nollekens, Joseph 67
Norfolk, Lavinia, Duchess of 226, 227
Norfolk, Bernard, 16th Duke of 8
Northcliffe, Alfred, 1st Viscount 294
Norton, Jean 14
Norton, Richard (later 6th Baron
    Grantley) 14n
Norwich, Anne (née Clifford) 9, 119n,
    140n, 156, 251n, 256n, 258, 291, 313
Norwich, John Julius, 2nd Viscount 1, 2,
    7, 9, 27, 43, 45, 46, 52, 74, 77, 84, 90n,
    108, 119, 140, 143, 146, 151, 152, 178,
    200, 235, 236, 252, 256n, 276, 280, 293,
    309–10, 313, 324

O'Connell, Rev Sir John 35
Officers and Gentlemen (Waugh) 190, 200n,
    207, 208n
Old Men Forget (Duff Cooper) 159, 185n
Oldmeadow, Ernest 28n, 44
Olivier, Laurence (later Baron) 49n, 213n

O'Neill, Eugene 259n
O'Neill, Fionn (Mrs Morgan) 258, 260n,
    311
O'Neill, Raymond, 4th Baron 209
O'Neill, Shane, 3rd Baron 124n, 209n, 258n
Onions, Dr Charles Talbut 296n
Onslow, 6th Earl of 285, 289n, 301n
Onslow, Pamela Countess of (née Dillon)
    301, 304
Onslow, Lady Teresa see Waugh
Operation Heartbreak (Duff Cooper) 138n
Ordeal of Gilbert Pinfold, The (Waugh)
    187, 204, 234n, 239, 241–4
Ormsby-Gore, David (later 5th Baron
    Harlech) 90n
Orton, Arthur 240n
Osborn, Franz 135n
Osborn, June (née Capel; later Lady
    Hutchinson) 103n, 134–5, 151, 280,
    286, 287
Osborne, D'Arcy 291, 235
Osborne, Colonel Rex 103n
Oxford and Asquith, Anne Countess of
    96n
Oxford and Asquith, Julian, 2nd Earl of
    ('Trim') 31, 32n, 33, 35, 37, 43, 44, 47,
    96, 98, 110, 143, 146, 245

Paget, Lady Caroline see Duff
Paget, Lady Elizabeth see von
    Hofmannsthal
Paget, Lady Mary 189
Pakenham, Elizabeth (later Countess of
    Longford) 14n, 313
Pakenham, Frank (later 6th Earl of
    Longford) 14, 29, 87, 197, 242n
Palairet, Sir Michael 96n
Palewski, Gaston 109n, 242, 244, 267n,
    277
Palewski, Violette 267n
Palffy, Count Paul 86n
Pall Mall Gazette 6
Parsons, Alan 318, 322
Pascal, Blaise 310
Passionate Heart, The (Crosby) 210n
Patmore, Coventry 177–8
Patten, Susan Mary (née Jay; later Alsop)
    136, 170, 188–9, 190, 223–4, 244, 277,
    283, 284, 297, 306
Patten, William 136, 277n
Pembroke and Montgomery, 16th Earl of
    41n

Pembroke and Montgomery, Countess of 138
Peters, A.D. 28n, 31n, 50, 138n
Phillips, Edward ('Teddy') 103n
Phipps, Lieutenant Alan, RN 83n
Phipps, Sukie 293
Picasso, Pablo 82n, 83, 162, 266, 279
Pickwick Papers (Dickens) 230
Picnic at Sakkara (Newby) 205
Piper, John 298n
Pius IX, Pope 265
Pius XII, Pope (Cardinal Eugenio Pacelli) 235n, 237
Pleydell-Bouverie, Alice (née Astor) 104n, 238n
Pleydell-Bouverie, David 104n
Pol Roger, Odette 224, 232
Ponsonby, Elizabeth 71
Porchester, Lord (later 7th Earl of Carnarvon) 151n
Powell, Anthony 201, 308
Power and the Glory, The (Greene) 191
Prater Violet (Isherwood) 87
Priestley, J.B. 97, 239n
Private Lives (Coward) 29n
Profumo, John 299n, 302n
Proust, Marcel 71n, 101, 325
Pryce-Jones, Alan 151, 199
Publish and be Damned (Cudlipp) 183n
Punch 25, 93, 161, 172, 183, 242
Pursuit of Love, The (Mitford) 83

Queen Anne Press 150n, 154, 155
Quennell, Peter 85, 87, 92, 105, 164, 199, 205, 230, 241, 301

Radziwill, Dolly, Princess 192
Railway Club 49n
Rainbow Comes and Goes, The (Cooper) 220n, 247n, 252–3
Rayleigh, 4th Baron 59n
Rayner, Joan (later Leigh Fermor) 148n, 197n, 198, 219
Read, Sir Herbert 157n, 161
Redesdale, 2nd Baron 17n
Redgrave, Sir Michael 173n
Reed, Sir Carol 138, 139n, 140, 141
Reeve, Mrs (of *Life* magazine) 88
Reinhardt, Max 7, 13
Remote People (Waugh) 5
Return of Hyman Kaplan, The (Rosten) 274
Ribblesdale, 4th Baron 32n, 135n, 253n

Richards, Sir Brooks 200, 211
Richmond, 6th Duke of 234n
Rickett, F.W. 52
Rise and Fall of Anthony Eden, The (R. Churchill) 271n
Ritchie, Sir Charles 219, 240
Robbery Under Law: the Mexican Object Lesson (Waugh) 67n
Rock, The (Eliot) 45n
Rodd, Mrs Peter *see* Mitford, Nancy
Rodd, Peter 109n, 122, 201, 294
Rommel, General Erwin 76
Roncalli, Cardinal *see* John XXIII, Pope
Roots of Heaven, The (Gary) 248n
Roper, Lanning 313
Rosebery (James) 298
Ross, Professor Alan 209n
Rosse, Michael, 6th Earl of 14, 71, 292
Rossetti, Dante Gabriel 66, 150
Rosten, Leo Calvin ('Leonard Q. Ross') 274n
Rota, Anthony 1, 2, 4
Rothenstein, Sir John 114n, 118
Rothermere, Ann, Viscountess *see* Fleming
Rothermere, Esmond, 2nd Viscount 124n, 129n, 130, 160n, 277
Rothermere, Harold, 1st Viscount 50
Rothschild, 2nd Baron 193
Rothschild, Victor, 3rd Baron 313n
Roughead, W.N. 31n
Round, Horace 83
Rowley, Flt-Lt Michael 13n
Russell, Aliki, Lady (née Diplarakos) 114n, 130, 154
Russell, Lord Arthur 46n
Russell, Bertrand 116n
Russell, Conrad 9, 46n, 56, 61, 63, 64, 66, 67, 68, 74, 95, 98, 110, 124, 125, 159, 269, 281, 290, 312
Russell, Sir John 114, 130, 131
Russell, Martin 211
Russell Pasha, Sir Thomas 114n
Rutland, John, 9th Duke of 253n
Rutland, Kathleen ('Kakoo'; née Tennant) Duchess of 253n
Rutland, Violet (née Lindsay), Duchess of 6, 8, 60, 65n, 253n
Rutland, Henry, 8th Duke of 6, 65n, 292

Sackville-West, Edward (later 5th Baron Sackville) 157

Sackville-West, Vita 155n
Sagan, Françoise 250n
St George's Society 167
Salisbury, Marchioness of see Cranborne, Viscountess
Salisbury, Robert, 5th Marquess of see Cranborne, Viscount
Salisbury, Robert, 6th Marquess of see Cecil, Robert
Sand, George 71n
Sanderson, Misses 37
Sartre, Jean-Paul 83
Sassoon, Siegfried 180n
Scoop (Waugh) 50, 62n, 63, 66n, 91, 317
Scott-King's Modern Europe (Waugh) 93n
Searle, Alan 134n, 261, 262
Sebag-Montefiore, Sir Joseph 291n
Sekers, Sir Nicholas 286, 287
Sempill, Lady, (Eileen née Lavery) 199n
Sempill, Elisabeth (later Ewan Forbes-Sempill, then 11th Bt Forbes of Craigievar) 199n
Sempill, William, 19th Baron 199n
Sexual Life of the Savage (Malinovsky) 102
Shaftesbury, 9th Earl of 204n
Shaw, Glen Byam 228, 261
Shaw-Stewart, Patrick, 253
Shawcross, Sir Hartley (later Baron), QC 227, 236–7
Sheppard, Canon H.R.L. 59n
Sherwood, Hugh, 1st Baron, 207, 226
Sicketrt, Walter 157n
Simon, John, 1st Viscount 190
Simpson, Mrs Wallis (later Duchess of Windsor) 61n
Sinister Street (Mackenzie) 88n
Sitwell, Georgia (Mrs Sacheverell, later Lady) 19
Sitwell, Osbert 19n, 71n, 104, 109, 111, 157, 243
Sitwell, Sir Sacheverell, 6th Bt 19, 71n, 104
Skelton, Barbara (later Connolly, then Weidenfeld) 113n, 215n
Slim, General William, 1st Viscount 220
Smith, Lady Eleanor 171
Smith, John Thomas 67n
Smith, Logan Pearsall 116n
Smith, Rev. Sydney 229
Society Racket: A Critical Survey of Modern Life (Balfour) 19n
Some Immortal Hours- (Betjeman) 298n
Sonnets and Verses (Belloc) 320n

Sorensen, Virginia 44n
South Wind (Douglas) 87
Spain, Nancy 208, 223n, 234n, 236n, 237, 241n, 324
Sparrow, John 233, 297
Speaight, Robert 234
Spectator, The 213, 223n, 245n, 268, 278
Spencelayh, Charles, RA 66, 88, 95, 112, 191, 237, 238, 296, 297
Spencer, Sir Stanley 213
Spencer-Churchill, John 37n
Stable, Mr Justice 237n
Staerke, André de 211
Stalin, Joseph 90, 100–101, 151n, 162
Stallings, Lawrence 56n
Stanhope, Lady Hester 252
Stanley of Alderley, 4th Baron 77n
Stanley of Alderley, Edward, 6th Baron 48, 89, 158, 187, 201, 204n
Stanley, Venetia (later Montagu) 31n, 77, 111, 312
Stanley, Victor 249
Stannard, Martin 50, 52n, 53n, 59
Stark, Freya 154
Steer, Wilson 157n
Stein, Gertrude 71n, 82n
Stevens, Alfred (Belgian) 99
Stevens, Alfred (English) 99
Stirling, Colonel David 74
Strand magazine 311
Strauss, Eric Benjamin 284
Strutt family 245n
Sunday Dispatch 241
Sunday Express 43n, 150, 185n, 218
Sunday Telegraph 117n
Sunday Times 81n, 139n, 150n, 201, 220, 221, 224, 225, 232, 247, 261, 265, 267, 269, 280, 291n, 301n, 313n
Surprised by Joy (Lewis) 219
Sutherland, Graham 316
Sutro, John 49, 71
Sutro, Mrs John 102
Swaythling, 3rd Baron 193, 194
Swift, Jonathan 320
Sword of Honour (Waugh) 19n, 66n, 115n, 157n, 325n
Sykes, Christopher 1–4, 50, 69, 83n, 91, 110, 209n, 241n, 276
Sykes, Christopher MP 91n
Sykes, Mark 3
Sykes, Colonel Sir Mark, 6th Bt 137n, 226n
Sykes, Sir Richard, 7th Bt, 12, 14, 15, 292

Tablet, The 28n, 62, 183
Tangiers Story, The (Reed) 138n, 139n, 141n
Thomson, Roy, Baron 301n
Tichborne Claimant The, (Woodruff) 240
Time magazine 226
Time to Keep Silence, A (Fermor) 163
Times, The 18, 47, 53, 59, 66–7, 84, 199n, 243, 254, 255n, 277n, 301n
Times Literary Supplement 151n
Tito, Marshal 89n, 151, 157, 160, 161, 162, 299n
Torlonia, Prince Alessandro 32n
Tourist in Africa, A (Waugh) 278, 280, 281
Townsend, Group Captain Peter 210n
Trafford, Sir Humphrey de, 3rd Bt 14n
Trafford, Raymond de 14, 60
Tree, Lady Anne (née Cavendish) 149, 278n, 279, 325
Tree, Felicity (Mrs Cory Wright) 28n
Tree, Sir Herbert Beerbohm 13n
Tree, Iris (later Moffat; Ledebur) 9, 13, 17, 95, 102n, 108, 198, 200, 219, 244, 248, 260, 265, 297, 300, 319, 322–5
Tree, Michael 149n, 279, 325
Trefusis, Violet 139
Trevor, Major Keith 48n
Trevor-Roper, Lady Alexandra (née Howard-Johnston) 105n
Trevor-Roper, Hugh (Baron Dacre) 105, 220
Trumpets from the Steep (Cooper) 279n, 281

Umberto II, King of Italy 109n
Uncle Silas (Le Fanu) 51
Unconditional Surrender (Waugh) 272n, 276, 284, 289n
Undset, Sigrid 154
Unquiet Grave, The (Connolly) 81
Urquhart, F.F. ('Sligger') 301n
Uttley, Thomas 235

Vane-Tempest-Stewart, Lady Helen (Baroness Jessel) 137n
Vassall, John 302
Verdura, Fulco, Duke of 321
Vesci, Lady de 62n
Vesey, Hon. Mary *see* Herbert, Mary
Vice Versa (Anstey) 79n, 179n
Vickers, Hugo 12
Victoria, Queen 32n

Victoria R.I. (Longford) 313
Vile Bodies (Waugh) 4, 42, 71n
Vilmorin, Louise de (later Palffy) 86n, 96, 101n, 109, 120, 122, 162n, 271
Vinci, Count 52n, 53
Viollet-le-Duc, Eugène 162n
Visit to Morin, A (Greene) 282n
Vittorio Emanuele III, King of Italy 109n
Vivian, 4th Baron 102n

Wade, Kate 23, 77, 225
Waiting for Godot (Beckett) 218
Wakefield, Anthony 228n
Wakefield, Daphne (née Marler) 228, 322
Wallace, Mrs Euan (Barbara, née Lutyens) 45
Wallace, Edgar 151n
Wallace, Rt Hon. Euan 45n
Walpole, Horace 155n
Walpole, Sir Hugh 97, 155n
Walsh, Leonard 143, 144
Walston, Catherine (née Macdonald) 142
Walston, Henry, later 1st Baron Walston 142n
Ward, Aileen 304n
Watkin, Dom Aelred 222n, 224n, 229
Watson, Peter 41
Watts, George Frederic 163
Waugh, Alec (EW's brother) 44n, 234n, 263n
Waugh, Andrew (EW's nephew) 263n
Waugh, Arthur St John (EW's father) 202n
Waugh, Auberon (EW's son; 'Bron') 69, 82n, 87, 140, 227, 229, 230, 231, 237, 243, 245, 250, 254, 255, 256, 259, 261, 262, 266, 278, 282, 285, 289, 292, 301n
Waugh, Catherine (née Raban; EW's mother) 202n
Waugh, Harriet (EW's daughter; later Dorment; 'Hatty') 159n, 215, 230, 245, 246, 256, 257, 270, 287, 288, 291, 292, 311, 316
Waugh, James (EW's son) 3, 82n, 92n, 227
Waugh, Laura (née Herbert; EW's wife) 9, 30, 31, 50, 51n, 54, 59–63, 63, 65, 66, 69, 70, 74, 76, 82, 87, 88, 90, 91, 108, 110, 115, 116, 118, 123, 124, 142, 145, 165–6, 171, 176, 183, 195, 197, 207, 217, 221, 222, 224, 226, 227, 230,

Waugh, Laura – *cont'd.*
237, 240, 255–8, 262, 282, 295, 304,
307, 311, 312, 320, 322, 326
Waugh, Margaret (later FitzHerbert;
EW's daughter; 'Meg') 48n, 82n, 168,
171, 173, 180, 191n, 192, 198, 201, 210,
212, 211–4, 227–31, 233, 240, 242, 243,
246, 247, 249–52, 255, 256, 259, 262,
266, 270, 277, 278, 279, 282, 284–8,
291–6, 298, 303–6, 311, 312, 313, 317,
318, 320, 326
Waugh, Mary (EW's daughter) 82n
Waugh, Septimus (EW's son) 82n, 105n,
240, 258
Waugh, Lady Teresa (née Onslow) 285,
289
Waugh, Teresa (EW's daughter) 65n, 66,
68, 82n, 214, 218, 219, 220, 225, 227,
234, 243n, 246, 250–51, 256, 282, 283,
285
Waugh in Abyssinia (Waugh) 51n, 59
Waverley, Ava, Viscountess 172, 225
Waverley, 1st Viscount, 172n
Webb, Norman 5
Weidenfeld, George 113n, 215n
Weil, Simone 126
Weiller, Paul Louis 119n, 128, 153, 172,
179, 211, 217n, 225, 226, 228, 308, 325
Welbey-Gregory, Emmeline 308n
Welch, Denton 157, 158, 159, 164
Welles, Orson 136
Wemyss, Mary, Countess of (née
Wyndham) 298
Wemyss, 11th Earl of 277n
Wescott, Glenway 111n
Westmacott, Richard 67
Westminster, Bendor, 2nd Duke of 6, 43
Westmorland, 14th Earl of 135n
Westmorland, Diana, Countess of (née
Lister) 135
What I Said About the Press (R. Churchill)
183n
What Price Glory? (Stallings and
Anderson) 56
When the Going was Good (Waugh) 90n
Where the Rainbow Ends (Mills and
Ramsay) 96n
Whistler, Rex 41, 269n, 273, 281
White, Sam 232
Who's Afraid of Virginia Woolf? (Albee) 318
Wigram, Canon William Ainger 34, 35,
36

Wilde, Oscar 111n, 180n
William IV, King 235
William-Powlett, Vice-Admiral Sir
Peveril Barton Reibey Wallop 263
Williams, Mona Harrison 12
Wilson, A.N. 193n
Wilson, Harold 197n, 314
Wilson, John 2
Wilson, John C. ('Jack') 41
Wilson, Sir Martin, 5th Bt 313
Wimborne, Ivor, 1st Viscount 144n, 193,
194
Wind, Professor Edgar 266
Windlesham, 2nd Baron 243n
Windsor, Duke of *see* Edward VIII, King
Windsor, Duchess of, *see* Simpson
Windsor-Clive, Richard 238n
Winn, Elizabeth 151n
Winn, Godfrey 185
Winn, Rowland (later 4th Baron St
Oswald) 134n, 147
Wise Man from the West, The (Cronin)
230n
Wodehouse, P.G. 105, 285, 308
Wolfe, Elsie de 120n
Wolfe, Humbert 67
Wolseley, Sir Garnet (later Field Marshall
1st Viscount) 51n
Woodruff, Douglas 240, 242n
Woolf, Virginia 81n, 157n
Work Suspended (Waugh) 69, 71
World of the Shining Prince, The (Morris)
314n
Wyborg, Hoytie 306
Wyndham, Mrs George (Violet) 156n

Yogi and the Commissar, The (Koestler)
82
Yorke, Henry (Henry Green) 16, 48n,
127, 128, 129
Yorke, Mrs Vincent (Maud née
Wyndham) 48
Yorke, Vincent 48n
Young, Rev Canon Andrew 282n
Young, Kenneth 298n
Young England (play) 48
Young Melbourne, The (Cecil) 199n
Young Men in Love (Arlen) 39
Young Men in the Arctic (Glen) 45n

Zannuck, Darryl F. 248
Ziegler, Philip 144n

Darling Bo. I am delighted with your book, rejoice in being part dedicatee. It reveals well my part I was giggling over this last night. Waugh much in Vogue at the Embassy — Decline & Fall has been grabbed from John Julius' hand by many other hands Introduction of Mrs Stitch was read aloud, a consider a "frappant" likeness. Thank you very much dear Mr Wu. You write a great deal better than Mr Connelly — a phrase in Horizon (from his pen) struck me just now. he writes on the subject of an artist requiring £5 a day." if" he says" he is prepared to die young of syphilis for the sake of an adjective he can make d on under '(Sic) c'a tombe très mal. Incidentally if the man of letters, fond of the bottle & leisure starts with £1600 a year his output will be meagre — Ld Byron disproved this supposition — & may be the meagrer the better. Take Vox meum. Cyril's an ass

Diana to Evelyn, December 1946 (page 91).